MEDIEVAL
MONEY

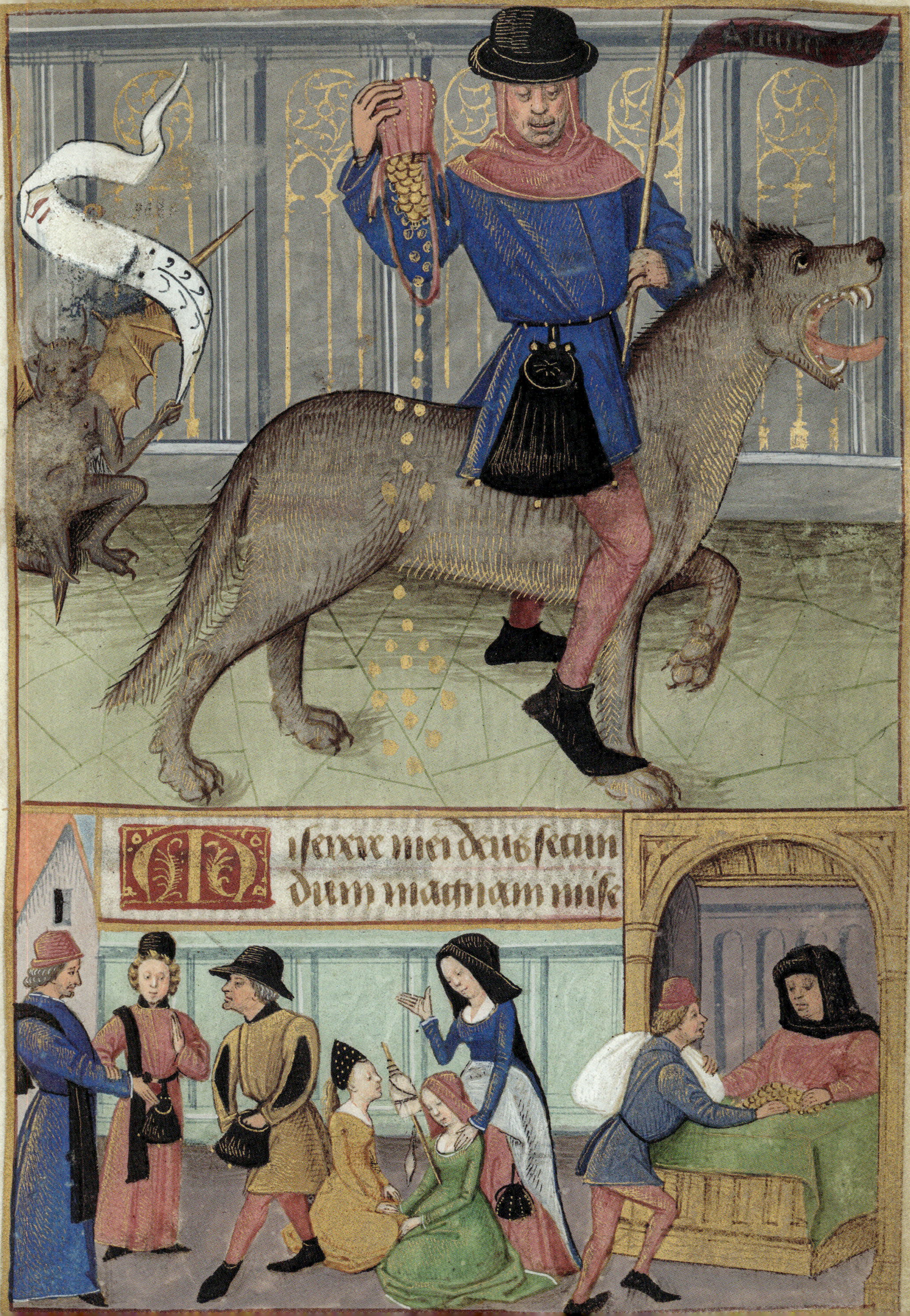
Miserere mei deus secun
dum magnam mise

MEDIEVAL MONEY MERCHANTS *and* MORALITY

DIANE WOLFTHAL

with contributions by

STEVEN A. EPSTEIN and DAVID YOON

and introduction by

DEIRDRE JACKSON

THE MORGAN LIBRARY & MUSEUM, NEW YORK

in association with D GILES LIMITED

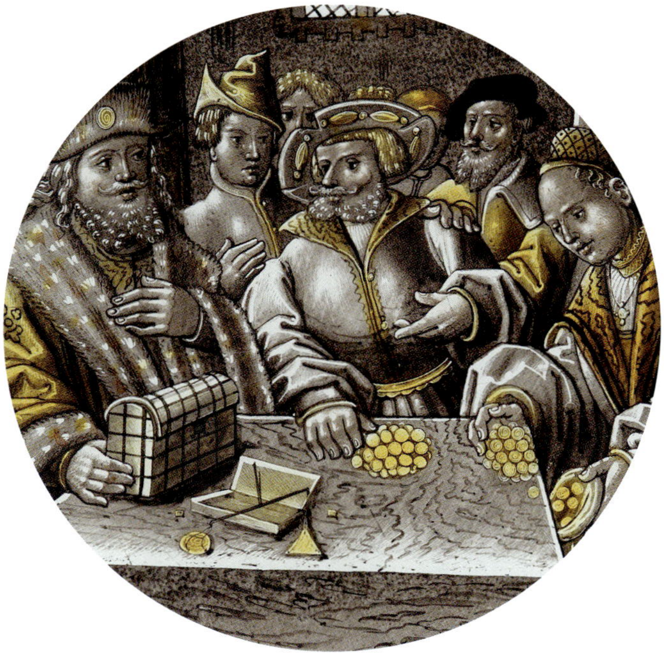

Published to accompany an exhibition at the Morgan Library & Museum, November 10, 2023, to March 10, 2024
Made possible by the Lucy Ricciardi Family Exhibition Fund, an anonymous donor, and the Andrew W. Mellon Fund for Research and Publications, with support from the Achelis & Bodman Foundation, the Samuel H. Kress Foundation, the David L. Klein Jr. Foundation, Marguerite Steed Hoffman, Virginia Schirrmeister and Anne Goldrach, and the Themis Anastasia Brown Fund. Assistance was provided by Elizabeth A. R. and Ralph S. Brown, Jr., Caroline Sharfman Bacon, Gregory T. Clark, and an anonymous donor.

First published in 2023 by
GILES
An imprint of D Giles Limited
66 High Street, Lewes, BN7 1XG, UK
gilesltd.com
and
The Morgan Library & Museum
225 Madison Avenue, New York, NY 10016
themorgan.org

ISBN: 978-1-913875-37-4

The Morgan Library & Museum

Library of Congress Cataloging-in-Publication Data
Names: Wolfthal, Diane, author. | Epstein, Steven, 1952- author. | Yoon, David, author.
Title: Medieval money, merchants, and morality / Diane Wolfthal with contributions by Steven A Epstein and David Yoon and introduction by Deirdre Jackson.
Identifiers: LCCN 2023004315 | ISBN 9781913875374 (hardcover)
Subjects: LCSH: Money--Europe--History--To 1500. | Coinage--Europe--History--To 1500. | Money--Moral and ethical aspects. | Merchants--Europe--History--To 1500. | Europe--Social conditions.
Classification: LCC HG243.W65 2023 | DDC 332.4902--dc23/eng/20230228
LC record available at https://lccn.loc.gov/2023004315

Project Staff for The Morgan Library & Museum:

Publications
Karen Banks, Publications Manager
Ryan Newbanks, Editor
Yuri Chong, Assistant Editor

Medieval and Renaissance Manuscripts
Deirdre Jackson, Assistant Curator
Roger S. Wieck, Melvin R. Seiden Curator and Department Head
Juliana Amorim Goskes, Belle da Costa Greene Curatorial Fellow

Imaging and Rights
Marilyn Palmeri, Director
Eva Soos, Manager
Janny Chiu, Photographer
Min Tian, Special Project Assistant
Nickoline Djonovich, Intern

For D Giles Limited:
Produced by GILES, an imprint of D Giles Limited
Copy-edited and proofread by Sarah Kane
Designed by Helen Swansbourne
Printed and bound in Europe

Front cover: Nicolò di Giacomo di Nascimbene, called Nicolò da Bologna, *Goldbeating*, headpiece from a register of creditors of a Bolognese lending society, Italy, Bologna, 1394–95. The Morgan Library & Museum, New York, MS M.1056v. Detail of Fig. 6.10b.

Back cover: Master of Catherine of Cleves, *St. Gregory the Great* and *Coins*, from the Hours of Catherine of Cleves, The Netherlands, Utrecht, ca. 1440. The Morgan Library & Museum, New York, MS M.917/945, p. 240. Detail of Fig. 6.29.

Spine: Adriaen Isenbrant, *Man Weighing a Gold Coin*, oil on panel, Netherlandish, ca. 1515–20. The Metropolitan Museum of Art, New York, 32.100.36. Detail of Fig. 6.5.

Frontispiece: Robinet Testard, *Avarice*, from a book of hours, France, Poitiers, ca. 1475. The Morgan Library & Museum, New York, MS M.1001, fol. 91r. Detail of Fig. 4.2.

Above: *The Prodigal Receives His Share*, from a series of eight scenes from the parable of the Prodigal Son, colorless glass, vitreous paint, and silver stain, Germany, 1532. The Metropolitan Museum of Art, The Cloisters Collection, New York, 41.190.442. Detail of Fig. 6.35.

MIX
Paper | Supporting responsible forestry
FSC® C118234

Contents

Director's Foreword

COLIN B. BAILEY

Medieval Money, Merchants, and Morality charts the economic revolution that took place in the late Middle Ages and early Renaissance. The major themes of this ambitious exhibition at the Morgan Library & Museum and its accompanying publication offer insights into how the era grappled with this major economic and cultural shift. Resulting monetary growth transformed every aspect of European society, including its values and culture. As people today reflect on fluctuating markets, disparities in wealth, personal values, and morality, the subjects addressed here are as relevant as ever.

The exhibition explores the fate of the avaricious, attitudes towards the poor, contentious lending practices, and money management. A range of objects—including a money chest, a brass alms box, a hoard of coins—help tell the story of the material culture of money, a subject by no means limited to numismatics, although coinage—which proliferated from the thirteenth century onwards—was indispensable to medieval life.

Readers may be surprised to learn that commercial activities still in place today—including bank transfers, extending of credit, and exchange of foreign currency—were routinely carried out by medieval bankers and merchants. Stunning portraits of individuals engaged in these professions are featured in the following pages. In the twenty-first century, when financial volatility remains a concern, and cryptocurrencies rise and fall, it is fascinating to reflect on the origins of banking in Europe, and methods then employed to regulate transactions. *Medieval Money* opens with chapters by economic historian Steven A. Epstein and numismatist David Yoon that provide information on the financial innovations and the dynamic markets of western Europe centuries ago.

As revealed by Diane Wolfthal, principal author and curator of the exhibition, medieval attitudes to money are reflected in numerous artworks, many by the most outstanding artists of the day. Hieronymus Bosch's *Death and the Miser*, for example, speaks to ethical and theological issues that emerged from the widespread role of money in daily life. Wolfthal's exploration of the ambivalence evoked by money sheds new light on some of the Morgan's most acclaimed illuminated manuscripts, among them the Hours of Catherine of Cleves, the Hours of Henry VIII, and the Prayer Book of Queen Claude de France. These are discussed alongside lesser-known treasures, including a sixteenth-century Italian account book in its original binding and an oath of office for coiners and minters illuminated in Avignon around 1411. Opening with images of the Virgin and Child and the Crucifixion, this manuscript reflects the strong link between religion and commerce that prevailed throughout the period.

It is, of course, appropriate that an exhibition devoted to commerce was inspired by the breadth, depth, and diversity of the collection founded by J. Pierpont Morgan, financier, collector, and cultural benefactor. In addition to Morgan holdings, which form the core of this study, we are grateful for important loans from Boston's Museum of Fine Arts, the Glencairn Museum, the Houghton Library of Harvard University, Houston's Museum of Fine Arts, the American Numismatic Society, the Metropolitan Museum of Art, the New York Public Library, the Free Library of Philadelphia, the Philadelphia Museum of Art, Vassar College, Washington's National Gallery of Art, and a private collector.

Medieval Money was conceived and curated by Diane Wolfthal, David and Caroline Minter Chair Emerita in the Humanities and Professor Emerita of Art History, Rice University. Roger S. Wieck, Melvin R. Seiden Curator and Department Head of Medieval and Renaissance Manuscripts at the Morgan, guided the project from the outset, and Deirdre Jackson, Assistant Curator of Medieval and Renaissance Manuscripts, served as in-house curator of the exhibition. Special thanks are due to the dedicated Morgan conservators who prepared the manuscripts for display: Frank Trujillo, Reba Snyder, Shaoyi Qian, Yungjin Shin, Michael Caines, and Ian Umlauf.

This exhibition was made possible by the Lucy Ricciardi Family Exhibition Fund, an anonymous donor, and the Andrew W. Mellon Fund for Research and Publications, with support from the Achelis & Bodman Foundation, the Samuel H. Kress Foundation, the David L. Klein Jr. Foundation, Marguerite Steed Hoffman, Virginia Schirrmeister and Anne Goldrach, and the Themis Anastasia Brown Fund. Assistance was provided by Elizabeth A. R. and Ralph S. Brown, Jr., Caroline Sharfman Bacon, Gregory T. Clark, and an anonymous donor.

Acknowledgments

I WOULD LIKE TO THANK ROGER S. WIECK, Melvin R. Seiden Curator and Department Head of Medieval and Renaissance Manuscripts at the Morgan Library & Museum, for his generosity and wisdom at every stage of the production of this book and the exhibition it accompanies. Without him, neither would have been possible. I also owe a debt of gratitude to the other members of the department: Deirdre Jackson for co-editing this volume with Roger, and devising and overseeing the exhibition as on-site curator; Joshua O'Driscoll and William M. Voelkle for their advice on organizing the show; and Juliana Amorim Goskes for her editorial assistance. This project builds on a team-taught course and a co-edited collection of essays on the theme of the mercantile economy; to my partner in these endeavors, Juliann Vitullo, I am deeply appreciative. I also thank the contributing authors, Steven A. Epstein and David Yoon, who were ideal collaborators. David, moreover, was instrumental in teaching me about all things numismatic. Specific queries regarding coinage were also addressed by Martin Allen, Senior Curator Medieval Money, The Fitzwilliam Museum, Cambridge; and Joe Cribb, Adjunct Professor of Numismatics, School of History and Culture, Hebei Normal University, and Former Keeper of Coins and Medals at the British Museum. This volume would also not have been possible without the generous assistance of the librarians at the Morgan Library, Maria Isabel Molestina, Polly Cancro, and Sylvie Merian. I also thank Rice University for its generous research funds and research leaves, which made this project possible.

I thank Anne Derbes and Juliann Vitullo for carefully reading an earlier draft of this manuscript and for their many astute suggestions, and Maryan Ainsworth for inviting me to speak on this topic at the Metropolitan Museum of Art in New York and for reading and commenting on Chapter 4. I owe a debt of gratitude to Mauro Carboni, Anne Harris, Neil Harris, Sherry Lindquist, Amy Neff, Julia Miller, Laurie Mitchell, Asa Mittman, Debra Pincus, Kyle Sweeney, and Nicholas Terpstra for so many illuminating discussions, and Thelma Fenster and Anne Marie Rasmussen for advice on translations. For their generosity, I thank Dita Amory, Barbara Boehm, Julia Perratore, Allison Rudnick, Leslie Bussis Tait, and especially Christine Brennan of the Metropolitan Museum of Art; Joost Vander Auwera of the Oldmasters Museum, Brussels; Dirk Elbert of the Stadtarchiv in Soest; Ed Gyllenhaal of the Glencairn Museum; Ronald Patkus and Dean Rogers of Special Collections, Vassar College Library; Marietta Cambareri and Abigail Hykin of the Museum of Fine Arts, Boston; and John Thomassen of the American Numismatic Society in New York. Finally, I wish to thank my colleagues and students at Rice University: Elizabeth Narkin, Linda Neagley, Joseph Manca, Layla Seale, Weijiao Wang, and Ruoxin Wang.

This book is dedicated to Roger Wieck in gratitude for his unfailing wisdom and generosity this past half century.

DIANE WOLFTHAL

Master of Catherine of Cleves, *Deathbed*, from the Hours of Catherine of Cleves, The Netherlands, Utrecht, ca. 1440. The Morgan Library & Museum, New York, MS M.917/945, p. 180. (Detail of Fig. 4.8.)

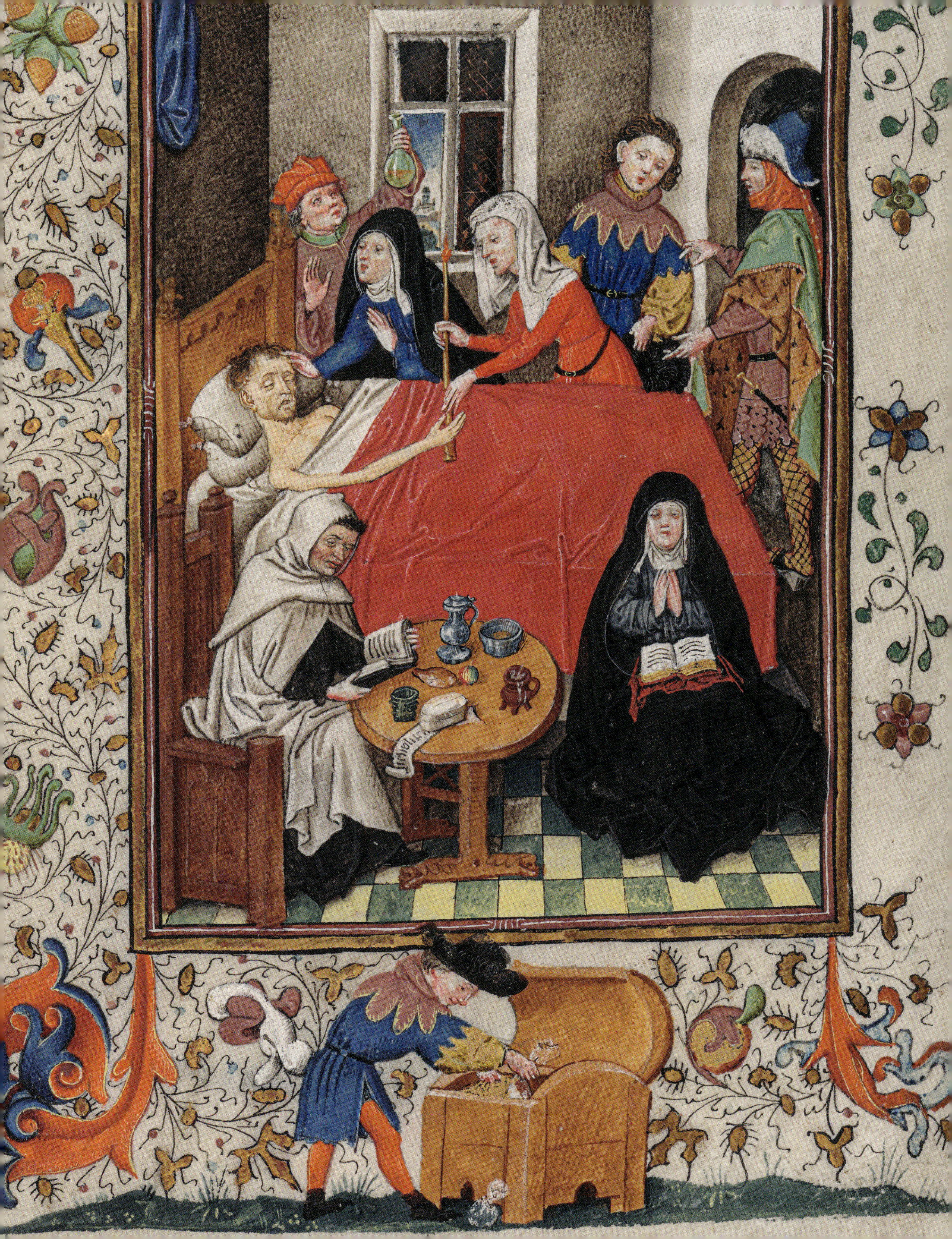

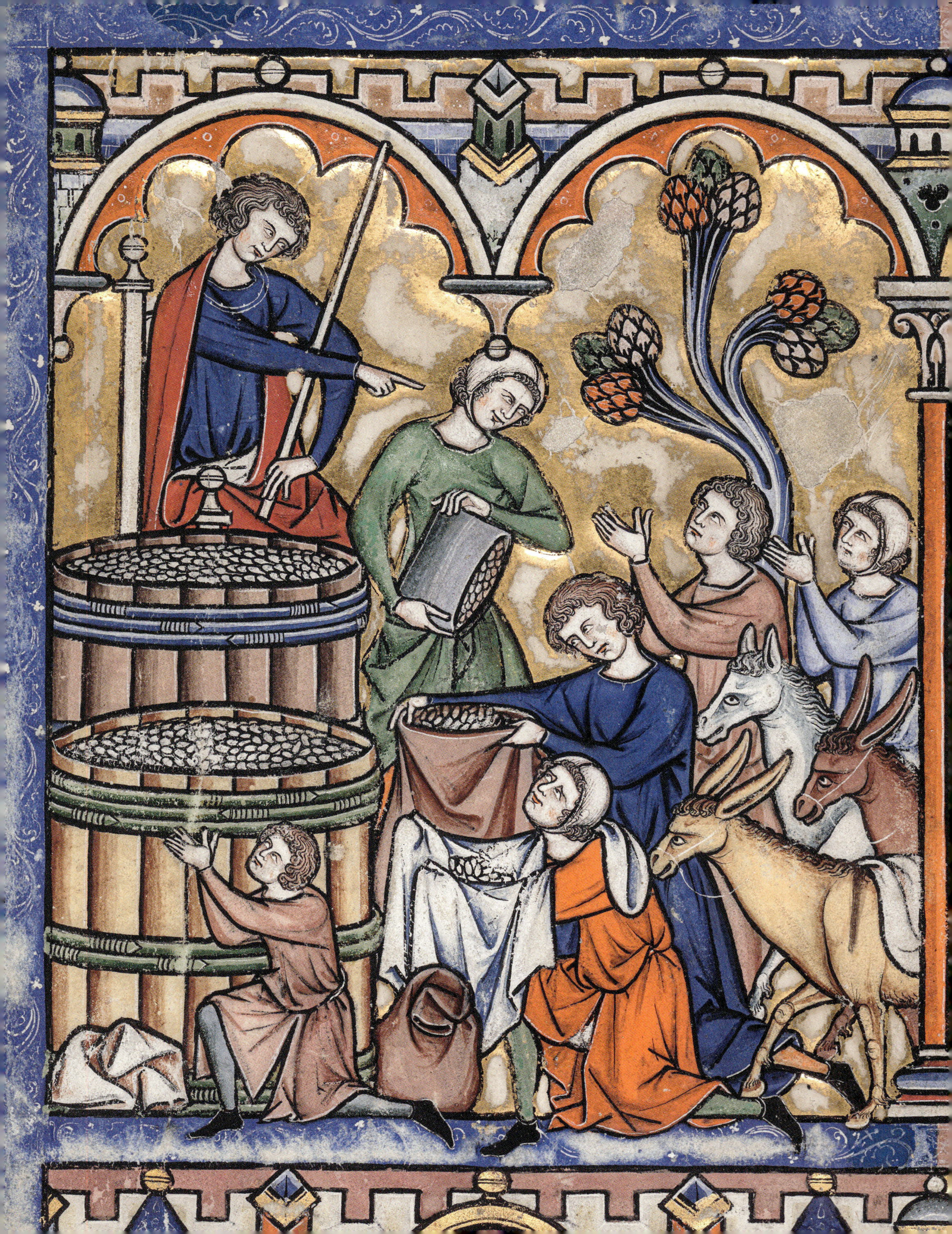

INTRODUCTION

The Origins and Uses of Money

DEIRDRE JACKSON

Joseph, Governor of Egypt, Oversees the Sale and Distribution of Grain, during a Great Famine, **from the Crusader Bible, France, Paris, ca. 1244–54. The Morgan Library & Museum, New York, MS M.638, fol. 6r (det.).**

MONEY IS EMBEDDED IN SO MANY DIFFERENT strands of human life that economic history alone does not explain its significance. As outlined in this book, to fully understand the role played by money, it is essential to consider its political, religious, social, and cultural significance alongside its economic functions. *Medieval Money, Merchants, and Morality* focuses on the commercial revolution that took place in the Middle Ages and early Renaissance in Europe. Beginning in the thirteenth century, trade was conducted on an unprecedented scale, banks were established, and coinage proliferated like never before, making it possible for more people to participate in exchange networks and turn a profit. The growing monetary economy transformed numerous aspects of European society. To appreciate these achievements, however, we first need to consider the origins of money, a complicated, yet captivating story.

FIG. 0.1. **Cowrie money, issued in West Africa. Collected in the Kingdom of Bambara, 1796. The British Museum, London, SSB,155.5.**

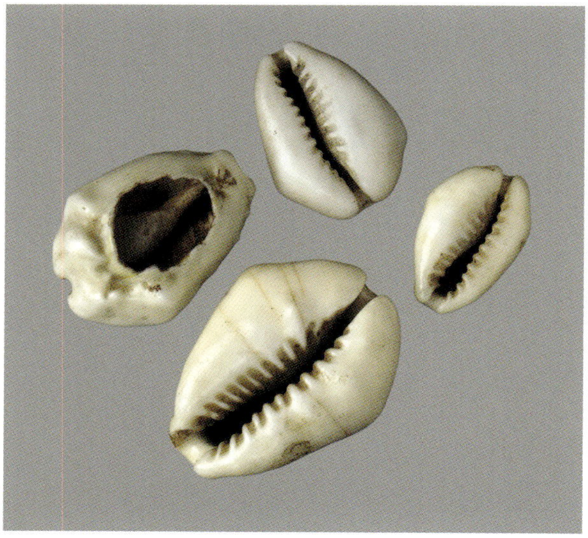

From the Upper Paleolithic period onwards (35,000–8,000 BC), people assigned particular value to a range of different objects and sometimes transferred these items from one group to another. The transfer, and possibly trade, in objects functioned at local levels, but also created links between groups of people separated by considerable distances. Amber discovered at some Neolithic sites in the Iberian Peninsula, for example, is thought to have come from Sicily and the Baltic.[1] The evidence of prehistoric trade in Europe and elsewhere is tantalizing, but in the absence of written records we cannot say whether our remote ancestors perceived some of the items involved as a type of currency.[2]

We are on firmer ground with cows. These animals, along with other livestock, including buffalo, goats, sheep, and camels have, justifiably, been called "man's first working-capital asset."[3] As documented in primary sources, the inherent value of the animals, as well as their by-products (milk, hides, and so forth) led "cattle," an all-encompassing term for useful beasts, to be used for monetary purposes from ancient times onwards, a function they continue to serve in some pastoral societies. Cattle were not, of course, small change, but, as the economic historian Glyn Davies explains, "so many sheep and goats for a cow or camel, so many chickens for a sheep or goat, and so on—can easily supplement the apparent . . . problem of having a heavy accounting unit."[4] English words that reflect the venerable economic function of cattle include "pecuniary" (relating to or consisting of money), from the Latin word for cattle, *pecus*, as well as "capital" and "chattels."[5] Agricultural products also acquired the status of money—grain was the principle form of money in ancient Egypt, for instance.

Among the most ubiquitous items used historically as money was the cowrie shell, which was far less bulky and more portable than cattle (Fig. 0.1). Cowrie shells are not only beautiful, tactile, durable, and easy to count, but also impervious to counterfeiting, which enhanced their utility as money. The shell of the mollusk, a type of sea snail native to the Indian and Pacific oceans, and particularly abundant in the Maldives, was used as a store of value, a primary medium of exchange, and means of payment for people in various parts of India, Africa, and Asia into the modern era.[6] The resilience of this shell currency is demonstrated by the fact that in Uganda it was still possible to pay taxes in cowries until the beginning of the twentieth century.[7]

Beads made from the clam *Venus mercenaria* and other shells were assigned particular value and served as adornment for indigenous peoples in North America. Known as wampum, strings of beads and belts made from the shells were used for ceremonial purposes,

FIG. 0.2. Wampum belt, Eastern Woodlands Iroquois, 17th century. The British Museum, London, Am1949,22.119.

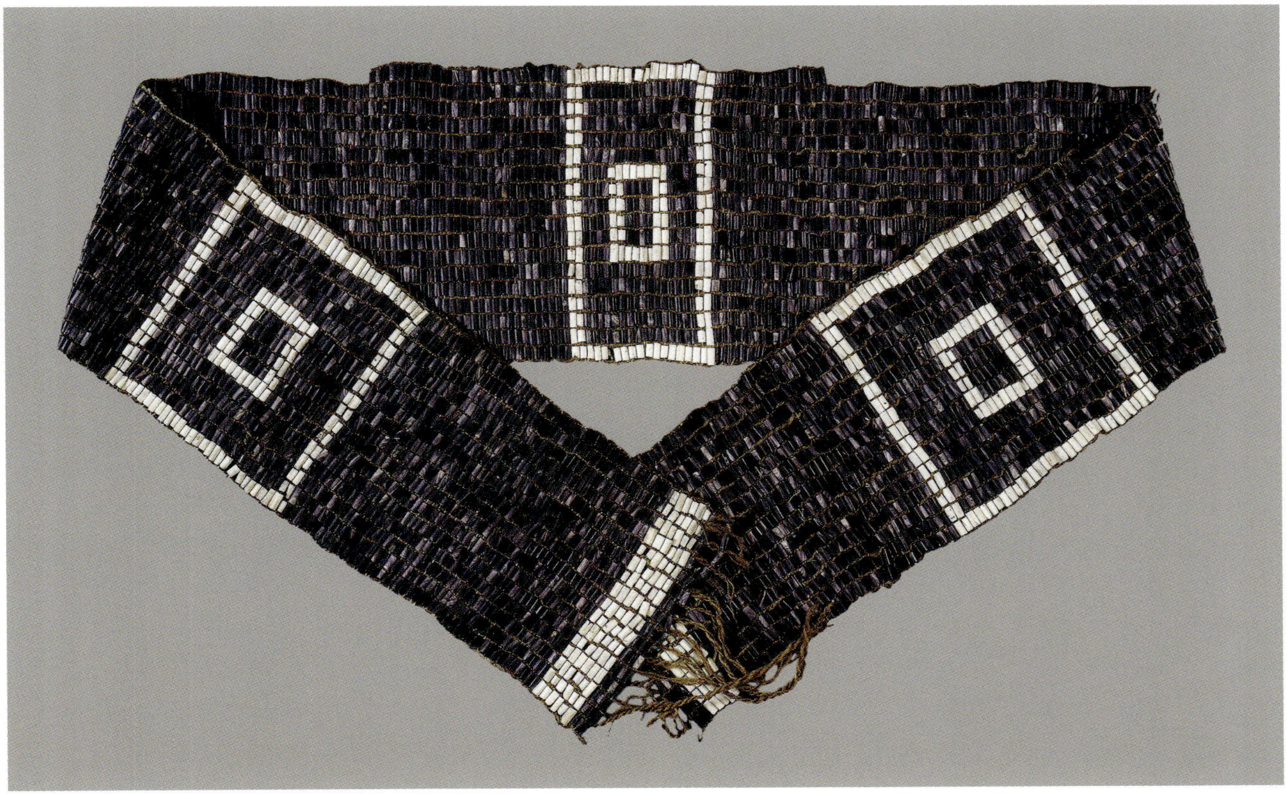

as objects of tribute, and as records of alliances, the making and breaking of treaties, and other key events (Fig. 0.2). Wampum was also used for gift giving, reinforcing the social status of those involved.[8] In the early seventeenth century, however, in addition to these purposes, wampum came to function as the primary currency between Native Americans and Europeans. In fact, the phrase "shelling out" comes from the practice of paying in wampum. Despite the Europeans' dependence on coinage, a story told in this book, they recognized the commercial efficacy of wampum and made it legal tender in several colonies.

Historians often use the term "primitive money" to refer to "all money that is not coin or, like modern paper money, a derivative of coin," but this designation can be misleading to non-specialists.[9] As cowries and wampum demonstrate, such items are capable of fulfilling the functions of money as we know it and, over the course of history, so-called "primitive" and "advanced" currencies generally coexisted. The metallic coinage of medieval Europe did not abolish other forms of money, but was used alongside so-called "primitive money" and payments in kind.[10] Different currencies—including leather, furs, linen, pepper, fish, grain, and butter—were used for different types of payments and transactions.[11]

A key lesson to be learned from wampum is that its significance and function changed over time; it evolved from an indigenous store of value and marker of religious and cultural beliefs to a currency as a result of the outside forces of colonial expansion. The political and historical context is vital to understanding how the economic value of wampum, in the eyes of Europeans, took precedence over all other values originally assigned to the beads. Social forces are thought by some scholars to underlie the adoption and use of money in certain societies. In some cultures, the need for men to make payments to a woman's father in order to marry her (bride-money) or to compensate for killing someone (blood-money) may have heralded the rise of currency in various forms. Vestiges of these practices are found in the English lexicon; the Latin word *pacare* ("to pacify, appease or make peace with") is the root of the English word "pay."[12]

The custom of paying bride-money, which reflects the subordinate status of women since it treats them like commodities, has a very long global history. A prenuptial contract inscribed on a cuneiform tablet from the Kingdom of Hana, dating from between 1,750 BC and 1,600 BC, appears to reference bride-money, and stipulates economic penalties on both parties if they dissolve the marriage (Fig. 0.3).[13] In some cultures, including medieval and Renaissance Europe, as discussed by Diane Wolfthal in Chapter 5, in order for a woman to marry, her family had to make a payment of money, goods, or property to her prospective husband.[14] Transfers of wealth of this type, called dowries, were beyond the means of many poor women, who were consequently prevented from marrying. Again, we are reminded that the history of money is not simply an account of technological innovations and paradigm shifts, but of complex interactions between individuals.

Base and precious metals, from which coins continue to be made, first attracted the attention of humans in the Stone Age. Over time, copper, bronze, silver, and gold, whose scarcity added to their perceived value, were adopted as currency in various forms, including lumps of metal and ingots, as well as rods and coils, which could be weighed to determine their worth. The earliest evidence of money comprises silver ingots, rings, and scraps from ancient Mesopotamia, and clay tablets and stone inscriptions describing payments with such things.[15] Metal ornaments worn on the body, and thereby safeguarded, also served as early forms of money, as did miniature replicas of weapons and tools made of copper, bronze, and iron, including cauldrons, cooking spits, nails, and knife blades.

In 2021, archaeologists excavating the remains of the ancient city of Guanzhuang in the central plains of China, in Henan province, published an outstanding find: the world's earliest known mint for producing standardized metallic currency.[16] Not only did they discover the remains of a bronze foundry established around 2,800 years ago (ca. 780 BC), in which the mint was situated, but they also found two fragments of coins in the form of miniature spades (*kongshoubu*). One of the spades, believed to have been created between 640 and 550 BC, is among the earliest known metallic coins in the world (Fig. 0.4).

Earlier excavations uncovered metallic coins of a roughly similar date minted in Lydia, in present-day Turkey. These were made of electrum, an alloy of gold

FIG. 0.3. A prenuptial contract between Kikkinu, the groom, and Bitti-Dagan, the bride. Kingdom of Hana, between 1,750 and 1,600 BC. The Morgan Library & Museum, New York, MLC 613.

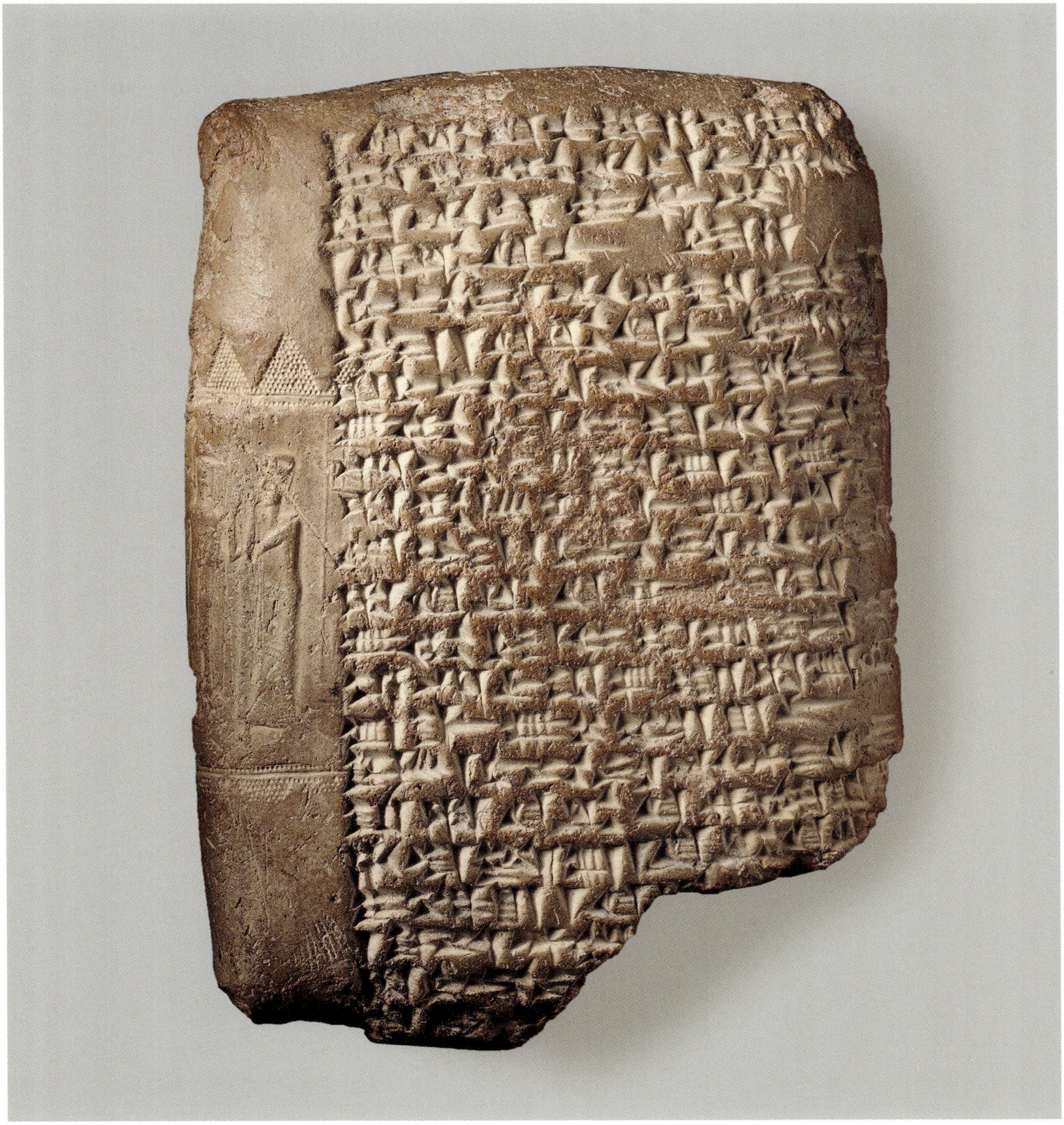

FIG. 0.4. **Bronze spade coin (right), its reconstruction (left), and part of a clay mold used to cast coins of this type (bottom left). China, Guanzhuang, 640–550 BC.**

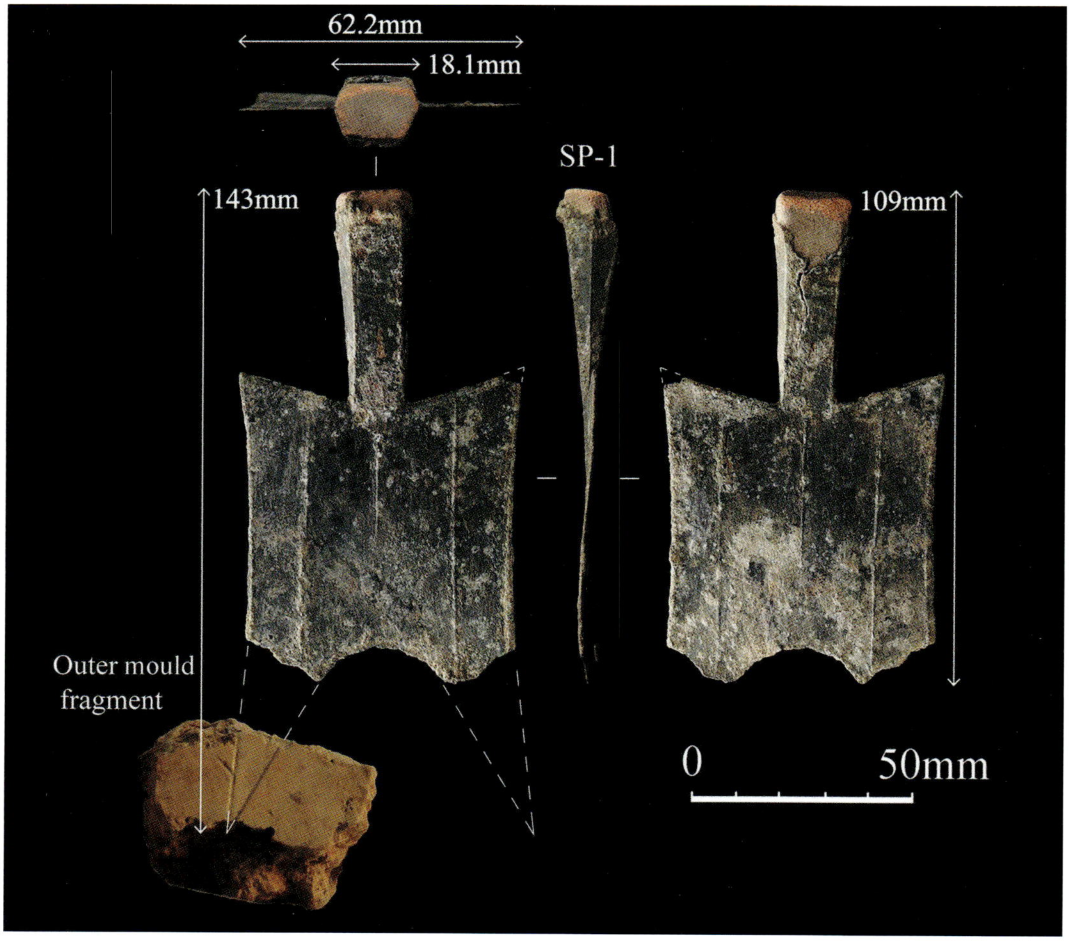

and silver. Although electrum occurs naturally, it can also be created by adding refined silver to the natural alloy, or by mixing refined gold with refined silver. The electrum used by the Lydians to mint their first coins is now thought to have been manufactured.[17] Alongside precious objects, 108 Lydian coins were discovered in the ruins of the Greek temple of Artemis at Ephesus.[18] The earliest were struck between 650 and 625 BC and deposited in the sanctuary as a foundation offering. Coins bearing lion motifs were among these outstanding finds, and other Lydian lion coins of a comparable date have been uncovered elsewhere (Fig. 0.5).[19] The lion was a venerable symbol of royal power, but whether the Lydian coins were minted by the reigning Mermnad dynasty is unknown, and numerous coins bear different designs.[20]

For decades, scholars have been asking: why were these coins made? We cannot assume that the Lydian coins, the oldest found outside China, were invented to enable commercial transactions, and, in fact, a plausible argument against that idea has been advanced: perhaps these coins were used by "secular or religious authorities to establish fixed norms for taxes, fines, or temple offerings."[21] As explained by Joe Cribb, the Lydian coins "might have been invented, like those in China, to manage a tribute system, rather than to facilitate the monetary system, but as in China, the advantages brought by these new units of money ensured their assimilation into current monetary practice."[22] In brief, generating revenue, rather than encouraging trade, may have served as the catalyst for coinage.

Culturally, Lydia was influenced by the Greek city-states of Asia Minor, but it led the way in monetary matters. Inspired by the Lydians, administrators of Greek city-states began minting their own coins, and, within a relatively short period, they raised the striking of coins to an exquisite art form. Following the lead of the Greek city-states, metallic coinage was adopted in Persia, India, and beyond, and later employed by the Romans.[23] Greek and Roman coinage exerted a major influence on the development of European money, and can be said to be the foundation of the western European coinage described in this book.[24]

Features of ancient coins are apparent in medieval examples. Both ancient and medieval coins often bear images or symbols referring to the political authorities responsible for their manufacture. As noted by David Yoon in Chapter 2, coins were also embellished with rulers' portraits (first schematic and later individualized), a practice that continues to this day. Inspired by Roman examples, medieval European coins were frequently stamped with crosses or other Christian symbols, underscoring the bond between temporal and spiritual realms, a chief subject of this book. Images and inscriptions on coins could send out political messages, but they also served as a form of guarantee of value, "a pledge that the ruler would honor—and possibly compel others to honor—the piece of metal at a given value."[25]

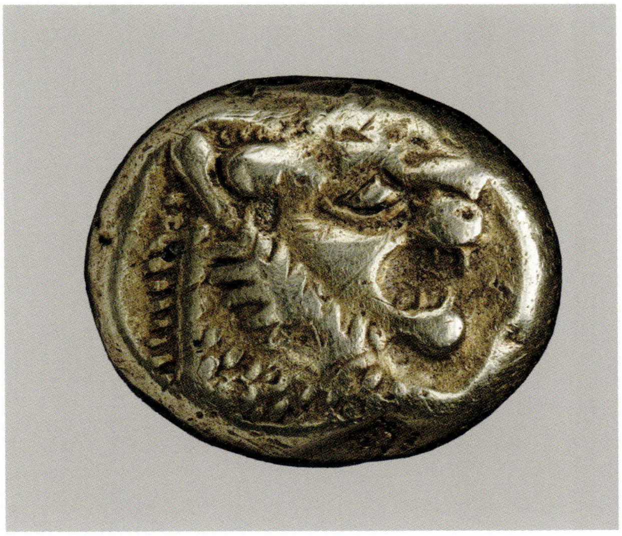

FIG. 0.5. Electrum stater, Kingdom of Lydia (modern Turkey), ca. 650–600 BC. The British Museum, London, 1866,1201.3671.

Although some medieval coins were inherently valuable because of their high percentages of gold or silver, others had far lower quantities of precious metals, and some were forged from base metals. In the fourteenth century, for example, the great trading state, Venice, issued the *tornesello*, a coin "denominated as silver," but made of a bronze alloy, to be used exclusively in its Greek colonies (see Fig. 6.26).[26] The value of the *tornesello* was not intrinsic, but depended on its "legal value," the amount that its issuers and users agreed

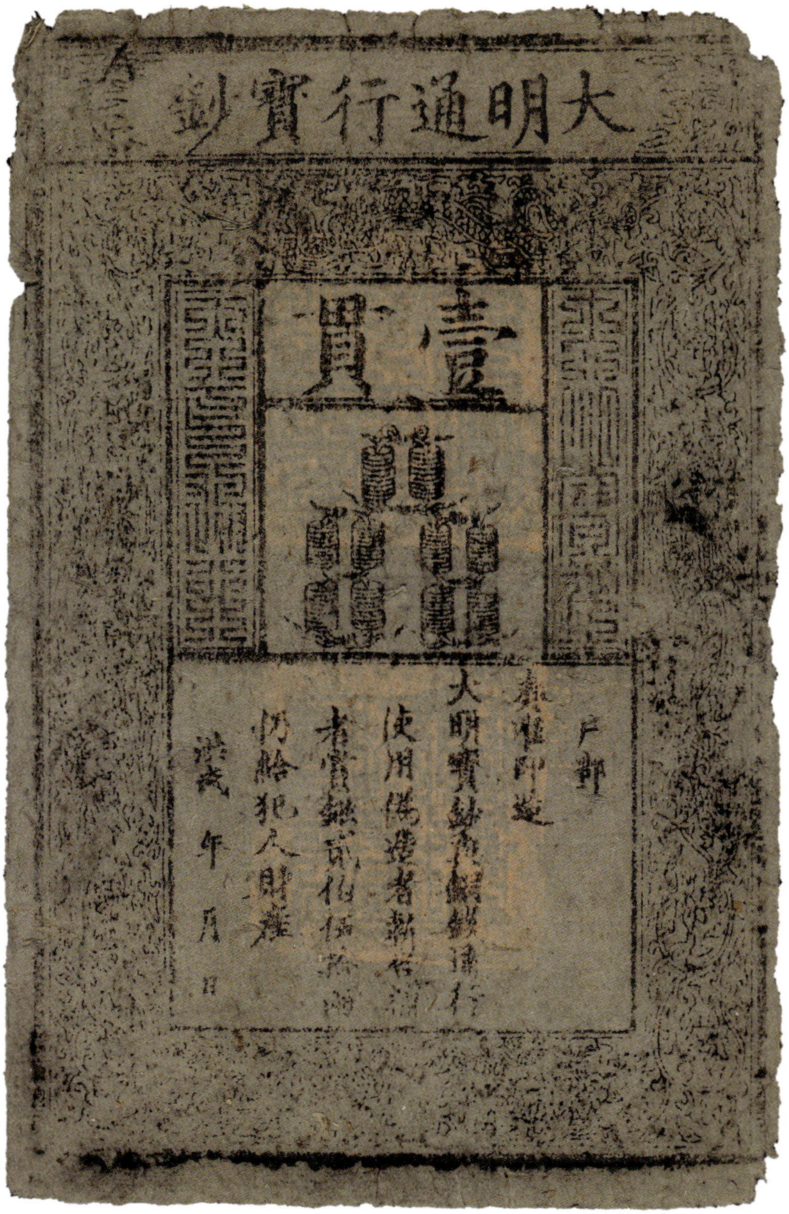

FIG. 0.6. Paper banknote, Ming dynasty, China, 1375. Banknotes were invented in China over 300 years before this one was issued. The British Museum, London, CIB,EA.260.

the coin was worth. Currency of this type, known as fiduciary money, multiplied in the mid-thirteenth century, and achieved the highest circulation of any kind of money, as more people participated in "urban economies whose general growth created a higher demand for money than the available stock of metal could fulfil."[27]

A logical outgrowth of coins was the banknote, another type of medieval money whose worth was dependent on assigned, rather than intrinsic value (Fig. 0.6). To overcome the problem of transporting large amounts of coin over vast distances, Chinese merchants, as early as ca. 900 CE, began to use a system of trading receipts that served as a form of paper money. The advantages of this system were not lost on the state, and, in the 1120s, the Song government, taking control of affairs, created the first government-issued banknotes.[28] Paper money was among the marvels described by Marco Polo in his account of his travels to Asia in 1271:

> With these pieces of paper, made as I have described, he [Kublai Khan] causes all payments on his own account to be made; and he makes them to pass current universally over all his kingdoms and provinces and territories, and whithersoever his power and sovereignty extends. And nobody, however important he may think himself, dares to refuse them on pain of death. And indeed everybody takes them readily, for wheresoever a person may go throughout the Great Kaan's dominions he shall find these pieces of paper current, and shall be able to transact all sales and purchases of goods by means of them just as well as if they were coins of pure gold. And all the while they are so light that ten bezants' worth does not weigh one golden bezant.[29]

Despite Marco Polo's endorsement, banknotes were not issued in Europe until 1661, although European bankers, with northern Italians in the lead, developed a type of paper money known as the bill of exchange, which facilitated cashless payments, as discussed by Steven Epstein and David Yoon in the initial chapters of this book. Not surprisingly, as emphasized by all contributors to this volume, bankers, moneylenders, entrepreneurs, and merchants played key roles in monetary innovations.

Cashless payments relied on mutual trust, as did long-distance trading networks. Acceptance and trust also characterized financial transactions large and small, from the payment of wages, rents, and taxes, and the granting of loans, to the buying and selling of goods in the growing urban markets of medieval Europe. As today, how people perceived and used money was not only governed by their access to cash and need to make a living, but also by tradition, deeply held beliefs, social customs, and political factors that make the story of money central to human enterprise.

NOTES

1. Murillo-Barroso and Martinón-Torres 2012.
2. Cribb 2004. I thank Joe Cribb, Adjunct Professor of Numismatics, School of History and Culture, Hebei Normal University, and Former Keeper of Coins and Medals at the British Museum, for his perceptive critique and valuable suggestions. I am also grateful to David Yoon for his guidance, especially on Lydian coinage.
3. Davies 2005, 42–43.
4. Ibid., 43.
5. Ibid., 44.
6. Cribb 1986, 16, 27; Einzig 1966: see "Cowrie," Subject Index, 552; Yang 2019.
7. Davies 2005, 36.
8. "Wampum" in Johansen and Mann 2000, 325–37; Muller 2007; Kelsey 2019.
9. Grierson 1977, 14.
10. Einzig 1966, 250–77.
11. Einzig 1966: see multiple references in Subject Index; Cipolla 1956, 3–12.
12. Davies 2005, 25.
13. Johns 1907.
14. For more on medieval women, see Jackson 2015.
15. "The documents used to identify them as money are contracts, business accounts and legal codes written in cuneiform characters on baked clay tablets or stone monuments"; Cribb 2004, 85–86. See also Powell 1996.
16. Zhao et al. 2021.
17. Cahill et al. 2020.
18. Kerschner and Konuk 2020.
19. Fifty-six coins found at the Temple of Artemis at Ephesus were stamped with lion motifs; Kerschner and Konuk 2020, 91–111.
20. For lion symbolism, see Jackson 2010.
21. Cribb and Williams 1997, 20.
22. Cribb 2005, 433.
23. Cribb and Williams 1997, 20.
24. Howgego 1995, 10; Schaps 2004.
25. Naismith 2018a, 6.
26. Kuroda 2020, 75.
27. Feliu 2018, 31.
28. Ebrey, Schirokauer, and Hansen 2022.
29. Polo 1875, 410: "Book Second, Part I, Chapter XXIV: How the Great Kaan Causeth the Bark of Trees, Made into Something Like Paper, to Pass for Money over All His Country."

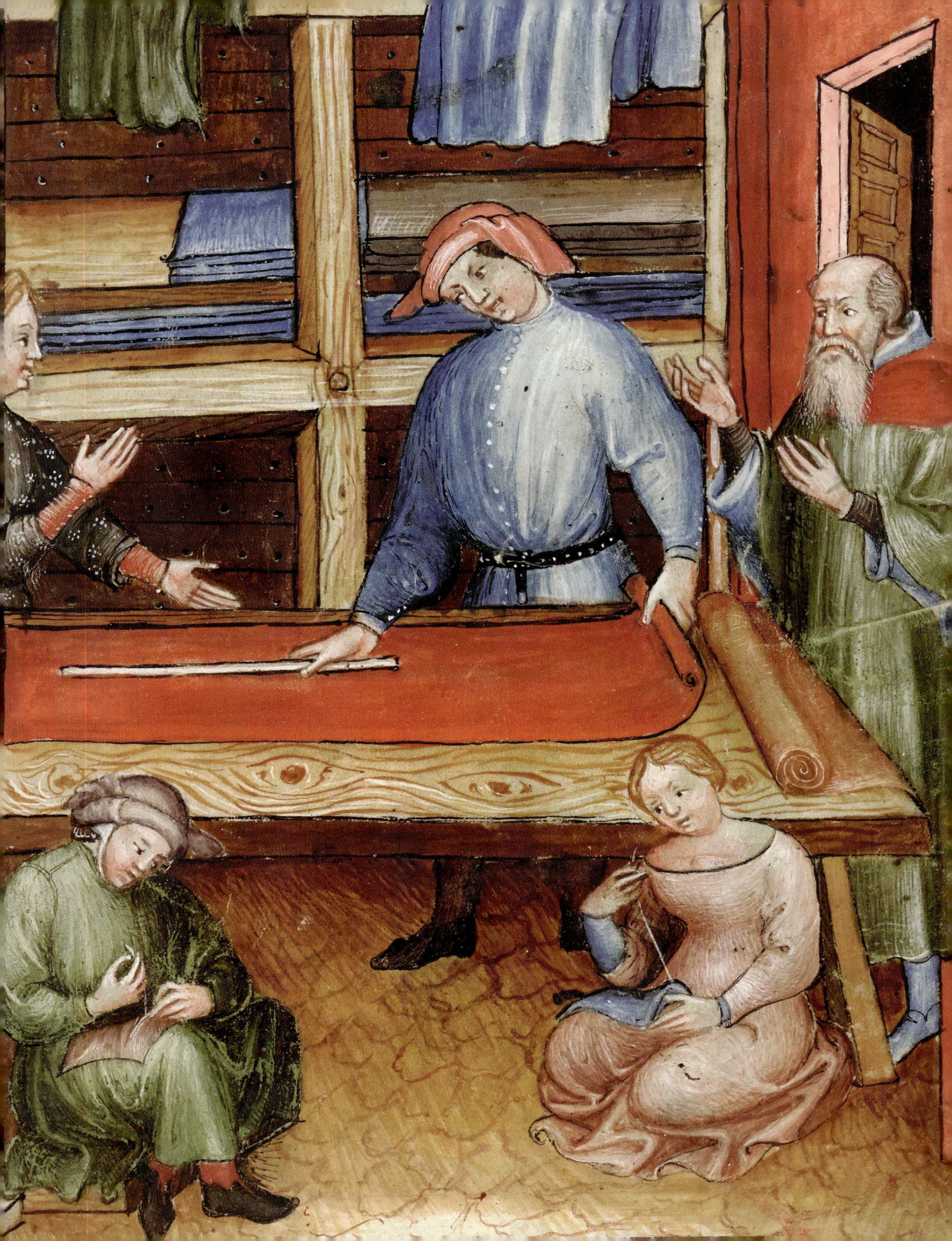

1

The European Economy 1200–1500

STEVEN A. EPSTEIN

Workshop of Giovannino de Grassi, *Wool Seller*, from *Tacuinum sanitatis* (Handbook on Health), Italy, Pavia or Milan, 1380–1400. Bibliothèque nationale de France, Paris, MS nouv. acq. lat. 1673, fol. 94r. (Detail of Fig. 1.12.)

Contexts

"Europe" is a geographical term defining no coherent sphere of late medieval economic and social history.[1] Europe, or even better West Asia, is a place with natural advantages and disadvantages, and our current sense of ecology and environmental history suggests that these perspectives are vital even if medieval Europeans did not know these terms.[2] Recently, nature has been increasingly valued as a protagonist in history, as a factor with its own history and role to play in shaping the opportunities of all creatures living within it. Europe was, and is, in general terms, a relatively placid part of the planet, not afflicted by frequent great natural disasters like massive earthquakes, tropical storms, and volcanoes. Europe's place in global weather patterns frees it from great deserts and supplies moderate climates in places farther north than in other parts of the world. Complicated geography,

FIG. 1.1. Simon Bening, *Hay Mowers with Windmill*, from the Da Costa Hours, Belgium, Ghent, ca. 1515. The Morgan Library & Museum, New York, MS M.399, fol. 8v.

mountain ranges, river systems, and climate divide Europe into regions and microregions. Two important economic facts derive from these considerations. First, catastrophic storms or earthquakes do not destroy the accumulated wealth of European economies. (Wars are another matter, discussed below.) Second, the sheer variety of regions means that Europe is well positioned to minimize risks as changing environmental factors like sea rise or temperature affect some places more than others. Europe's environmental diversity was, and remains, an advantage.[3] Although the Arno occasionally flooded and the Dutch have been fighting the North Sea for centuries, in this period more Europeans than ever before enjoyed prosperity and accumulated material possessions. It is worth remembering that the images reproduced in this volume have survived the ravages of time and nature. Many documents reveal societies devising new ways, like maritime insurance, to manage risk. Perhaps these developments were only possible in a region where geography produced such wide variety in climate and soils fostered diversity, an antidote to risk.

Natural resources and energy supplies seem to be advantages helping to explain the chances for having a developing economy.[4] These factors have been put forward to explain the Industrial Revolution and the modern economy, with places rich in coal and iron ore deposits sparking economic growth, and places poor in such resources left behind. By contrast, late medieval Europe did not exploit its massive coal resources, probably because transportation costs were prohibitive. Forging iron, or even better steel, was a new and developing technology with modest outputs and niche producers in Sweden and England, among other places. Instead, the economy was by contemporary standards remarkably "green." Solar power and gravity provided all the energy available, from the calories fueling human and animal muscle power to windmills (Fig. 1.1), from wood and peat to burn and falling water to turn millstones or increasingly complicated machines. Medieval people lacked the ability to destroy their environment; even the small dents made in Europe's great forests hardly mattered, and the periodic widespread fires of the Mediterranean coasts were part of a natural system of clearance and renewal.

Two final facts about climate and the biosphere help round out a view of Europe's basic state from 1200 to 1500. Climatologists have discovered a period known as the medieval warm period, or climatic optimum, a climatic anomaly that affected Eurasia from some time in the tenth to the thirteenth century; by 1300 temperatures cooled during a period of slow transition to about 1450, when the Little Ice Age commenced, lasting to about 1860, when the current warming period began, coinciding with the age of fossil fuels.[5] This medieval warm period, favorable to farming across Europe, led to improved agricultural yields, better diets, increasing population, and the settlement of Iceland and Greenland. The boundaries of this period are vague, as is usually the case in climate matters, and of course there were occasional intervening years of famine and drought. But by 1200 the European economy had reaped many benefits from climate changes of a few degrees of warmer annual temperatures, which almost no contemporaries noticed. By 1315/17, at the peak of Europe's medieval growth and prosperity, much of northern Europe suffered a devastating famine.[6]

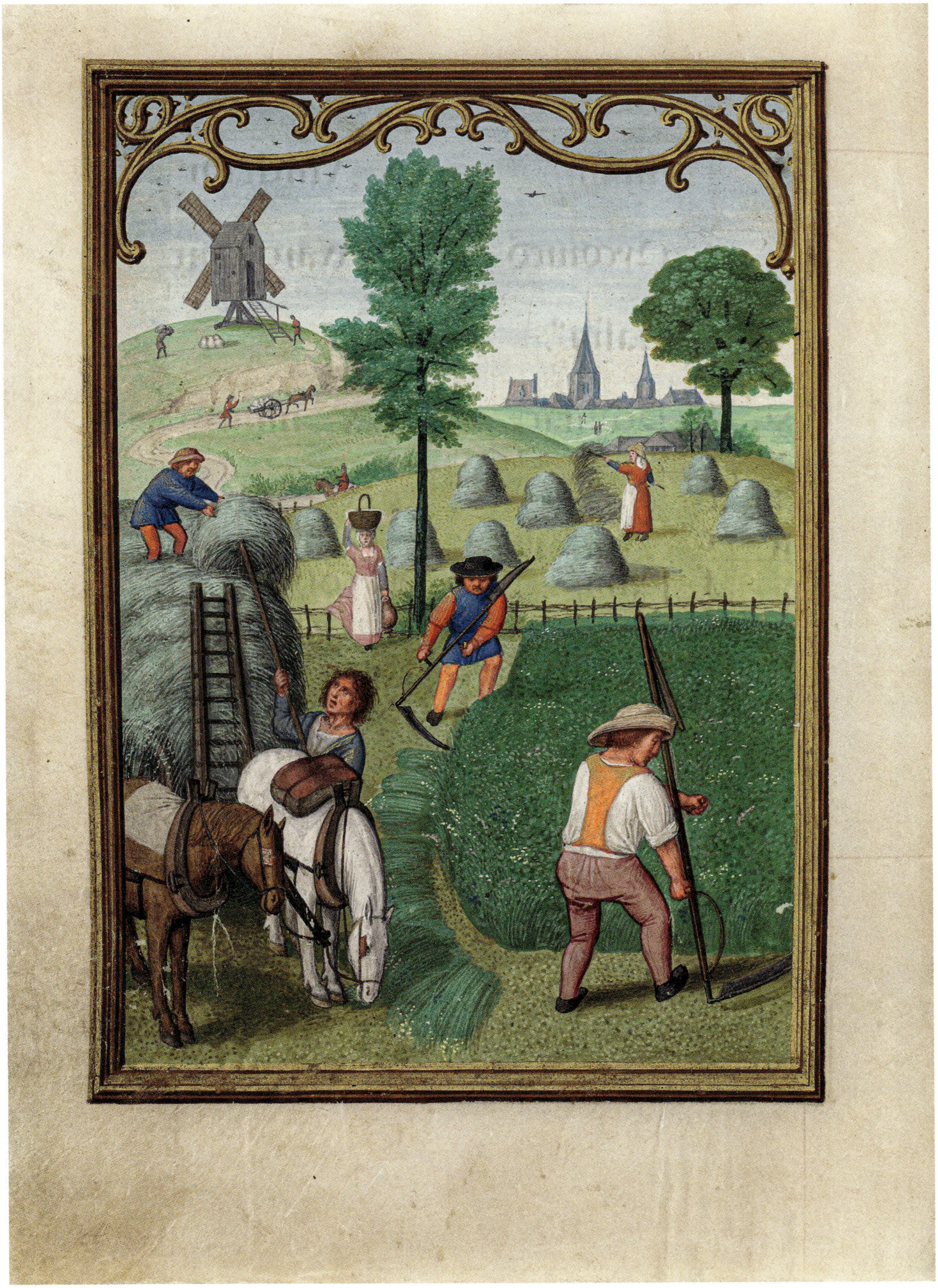

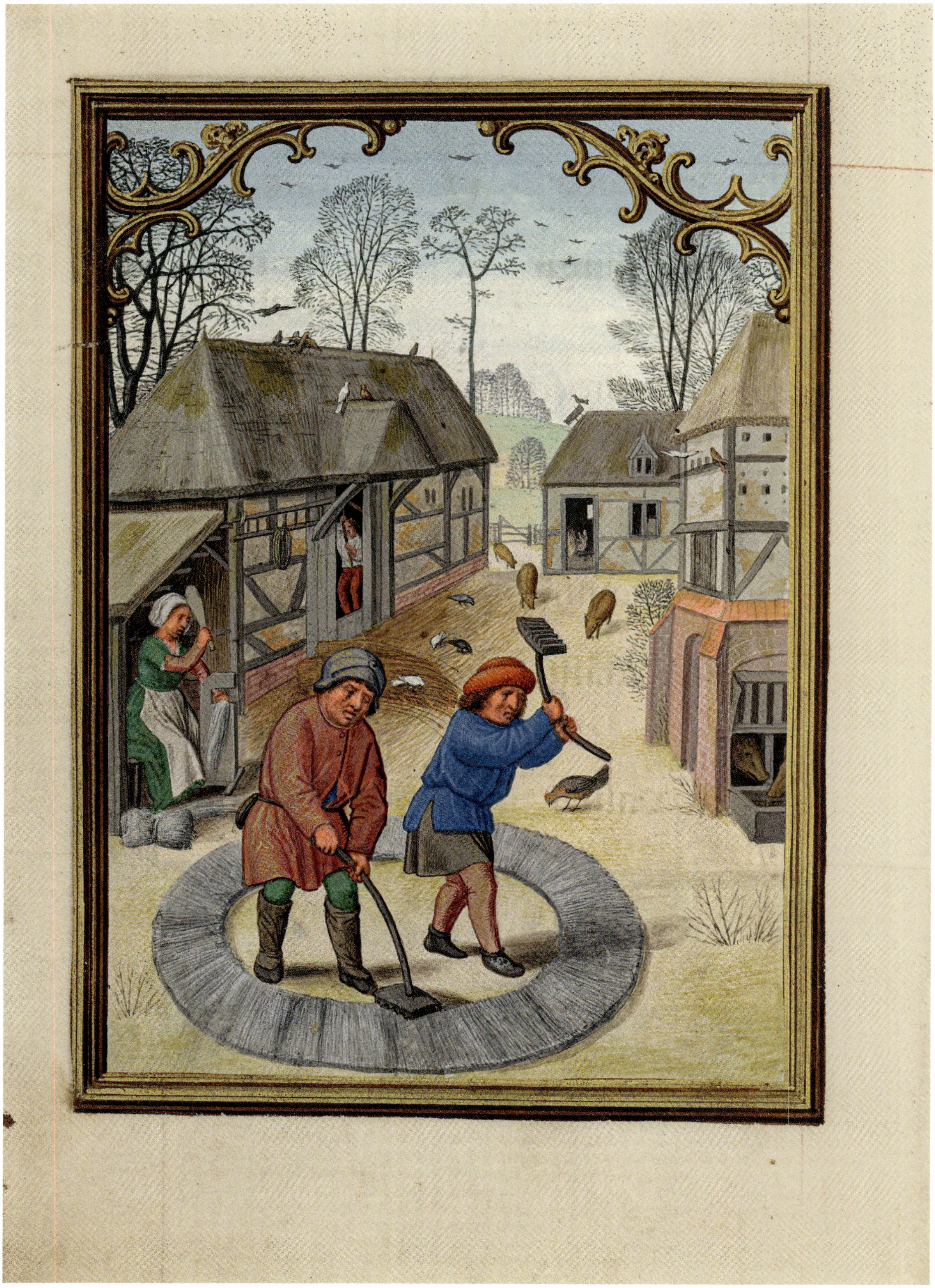

FIG. 1.2. Simon Bening, *Workers Prepare Flax*, from the Da Costa Hours, Belgium, Ghent, ca. 1515. The Morgan Library & Museum, New York, MS M.399, fol. 12v.

The greatest natural resource of Europe (apart from its people) was its soils, and most of its inhabitants were farmers. If activities also related to the food supply like fishing and animal husbandry are included, at least 90 percent of the population was working in agriculture in 1200 and by 1500 at least 80 percent. European agriculture must have been remarkably inefficient to require such a massive commitment in the labor force, four farmers to feed one other person, not like the ratio of 1:166 in the United States today. Some people, including wealthy estate holders, might have preferred rural life, and many peasants were compelled into it, but eventually large numbers of people moved into towns and cities to engage in artisan and servant work, and this coincided with increased prosperity. By about 1300, at its medieval height, Florence, one of Europe's great cities, contained perhaps 120,000 people, and Paris surpassed all the others at over 200,000, but all these people depended on the rural economy to produce the food they ate and many of the products they needed for manufacturing, like wool, flax (Fig. 1.2), wood, and leather. An unknown but significant part of Europe's capital derived from the profits of landowners plowed into consumption, trade, or investment. It is easy to start with capital and forget where it came from. Medieval consumers knew better.

While the thirteenth century witnessed population growth that had started before 1000, numbers increased slowly, just like productivity. A virtuous cycle of increased population, prosperity, and investment made it possible for a growing but still small percentage of the population to engage full-time in crafts and commerce. Mainly in cities, craftspeople ranging from humble cobblers and candle-makers to tapestry weavers and goldsmiths banded together and formed guilds to control competition and foster their trades. Many guilds also attended to the spiritual needs of their members, and sometimes employed artists to decorate their chapels and halls. These guilds—a characteristic feature of the urban medieval economy—were not trade unions; they excluded ordinary workers and apprentices from membership. Strong in some places, weak or nonexistent in others, the medieval guild, with origins in the early Middle Ages and, in some regions like Germany, lasting into modern times, established an apprenticeship system and provided vocational education overseen by masters. Rules about quality helped sustain the artisan trades but raised entry barriers. Individual masters had the chance to excel and pass on what they learned to their own children and others placed with them to train. Merchant guilds stimulated local and international commerce by making trade a more routine and collective endeavor, yet they also manipulated tariff rates and city governments to their own benefit.

Guilds often conspired against consumers and their own employees, stifling efficiency, technological development, and simply guaranteeing the interests of those employers within the privileged circle of membership.[7] Guild rules usually institutionalized patriarchy and ratified a gender division of labor—in some cases, absolutely prohibiting women from learning or practicing certain trades, usually the most lucrative such as smithing and lawyering. Guilds also universally denied Jews and Muslims membership. From these perspectives, the best thing medieval or early modern governments could have done to foster free markets and prosperity would have been to abolish the guilds. Nevertheless, guilds were strong in the cities

FIG. 1.3. Gutenberg Bible (*Biblia latina*), with printed text and painted decoration, Germany, Mainz: Johann Gutenberg and Johann Fust, ca. 1455. The Morgan Library & Museum, New York, PML 12, vol. 1, fols. 303v–304r.

of northern Italy and the Low Countries, precisely the most economically vibrant parts of Europe, and, in the great capital cities like Paris and the much smaller London, they provided a convenient way for monarchs to regulate trades. Standards of production of material objects, including paintings, looms, clothing, urban buildings, and weapons, and other sundry goods, seem higher in 1500 than they were in earlier centuries. These improvements were not in the main happening in the cottage industries scattered across the countryside. Instead, what had changed most were the skill levels of the urban masters, journeymen and journeywomen, and apprentices, the essential workforce of Europe—along with farmers. Ordinary boys and some girls in the cities found in the apprenticeship system the best and only method to learn skills intended to produce masterpieces, at best surpassing the goals and methods of their predecessors. Their teachers may not have wanted to compete based on quality or wages, but their customers and workers could tell the difference between quality merchandise and junk. Vocational education, like wage labor practiced outside guild regulations, did not yet depend on literacy but instead on hands-on training over years. The market rewarded the acquisition of specialized skills and promoted pride in a job well done. Wage labor was more efficient than serfdom and slavery and fostered a "culture of improvement."[8]

Plague

A shock, originating outside Europe's biosphere, began in 1347 and continued to 1352 in the calamity of the Black Death, a bubonic plague coming from Asia and devastating every corner of Europe with losses ranging from a third to perhaps half of the continent's population.[9] Florence, a good indicator of urban losses, collapsed to perhaps 40,000 people from 120,000, and after repeated severe outbreaks had barely surpassed 50,000 by 1500. Some areas of rural Europe were completely depopulated, and villages were deserted as survivors left in search of better soils in which to plant their crops. Extant documents and artworks created before this disaster reflect an economy and society coping with "ordinary" Malthusian pressures of births and deaths in relation to the food supply. By contrast, post-plague evidence reflects sudden shocking levels of mortality and efforts to recover. Not forgetting localized episodes of hysteria and massacres (explored below), most students of this ongoing crisis are impressed by the capacity of Europeans to endure and survive this shock. Even during years of crisis, people continued to work, make art, write documents, and produce children. No society in Europe collapsed; even social rebellions that may be tied to the plague in most instances took a while to occur, and all failed. Survivors, perhaps experiencing post-traumatic stress disorder, collective depression or guilt, or even a fatalistic joy, adjusted to an economy where labor was in short supply, land prices and rents plummeted, and prices fluctuated as some basics declined while some luxuries grew costlier. The so-called "Golden Age of Labor" perhaps lasted for a century and may have improved the economic circumstances of women whose work was by necessity now more valuable, as every person was needed to keep wages from increasing even more. The gender division of labor changed, but any gains and opportunities available to women did not

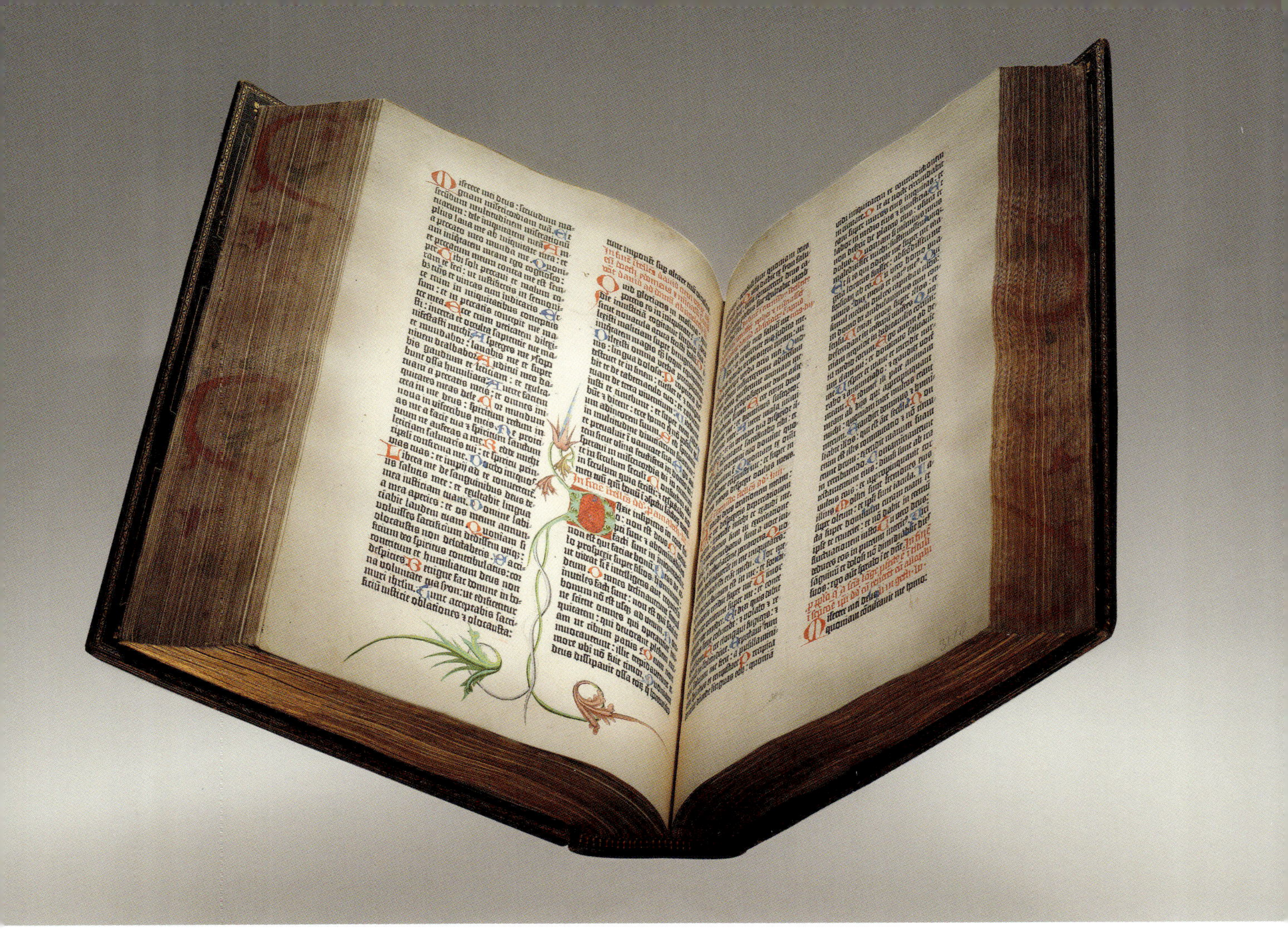

prove to be permanent. Employers did not simply let the market set wages but, in many places, mobilized the powers of government to fix or even roll back wages. More likely to succeed were strategies economists call factor substitution, where the owners deployed capital in the form of labor-saving technologies rather than pay higher wages. The clearest example of this phenomenon may be the invention of movable type for printing books, which gradually replaced so many copyists working by hand (Fig. 1.3). This innovation appeared in Mainz, however, about a century after the first outbreak of plague, showing that the basis for sustained technological development in machines did not yet exist in Europe. Technology could solve some resource issues; for example, better pumps made underground mining more efficient, gunpowder on the battlefield saved some manpower, and bringing more silver ore to the surface in the fifteenth century could even increase the money supply. But these advances, resting on a culture of improvement and industriousness, usually depended on tinkering and incremental changes in workshops, and resulted in mainly anonymous discoveries, like eyeglasses in late thirteenth-century Italy. Without the benefits of a Scientific Revolution, medieval universities contributed nothing to the prospects of a boom in technologies.

Bubonic plague destroyed people but left their wealth basically intact. Hence there was also a great age of inheritance in which the per capita wealth of the survivors grimly increased. These events occurred

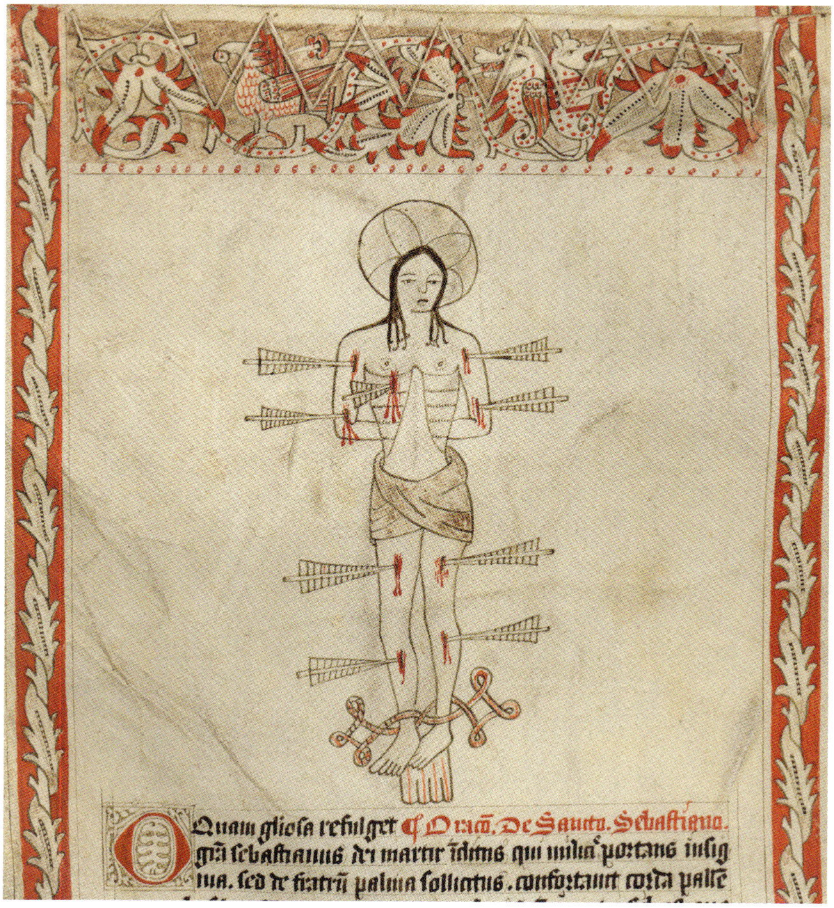

FIG. 1.4. ***St. Sebastian of Rome Illustrating a Prayer for Deliverance from the Plague*, from a prayer roll, England, Yorkshire, ca. 1500. The Morgan Library & Museum, New York, MS G.39, section 6.**

between 1350 and 1500, in the middle of the period covered by this study. Sometimes, as in the case of the increasing popularity of pictures of St. Sebastian, the connection with the collective trauma is obvious. During his martyrdom, the saint's body had been used as a target by Roman archers whose projectiles seemed to presage the plague's random arrows (Fig. 1.4). Since piety, melancholy, and death dominated art during the plague decades, the context of such images makes sense. If long-term investments and strategy seemed less attractive in an age of sudden death, then a certain narrowing of economic entrepreneurialism explains itself. If there was indeed an economic depression in the late Middle Ages and early Renaissance, then the paradox of increased investment in art during a time of economic contraction occurred, not for the last time. In fact, the fifteenth century witnessed the rise of a market for art, especially in the richest cities like Ghent and Florence.[10] Surely the social opinions of the survivors shaped what they wanted to see on their walls and in their churches, what they wanted to eat and drink, what contracts they made and how they reassessed ideas about risk and profit.

Jews

The bubonic plague of 1348 and its sequels serve as a midpoint for exploring the processes of change within the period 1200–1500. After the briefest pause, warfare resumed in medieval Europe, causing widespread devastation, notably across large parts of France during the Hundred Years' War (Fig. 1.5). Jews of medieval Europe, in particular, experienced high mortality rates due to prejudice and propaganda. In many places, Jews, having been blamed for what some contemporaries called the "Big Death," were massacred and their property confiscated or destroyed (Fig. 1.6). By 1348 Jews had already been expelled from parts of Europe, including England in 1290 and northern France in 1306, so they were killed where they were most numerous: in northeastern Spain, southern France, and parts of Germany. Though severe outbreaks of plague continued after 1348, never again were Jews burned or driven out because of it. Evidence of the role played by medieval Jews in the European economy comes mainly from Christian sources, artworks, and

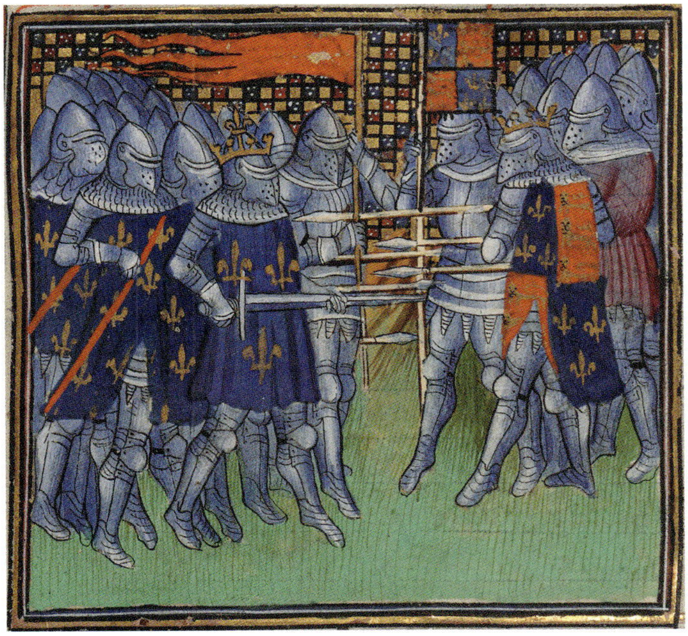

FIG. 1.5. *Battle of the Hundred Years' War: French Soldiers Led by Philip VI of France Advance toward English Soldiers Led by Edward the Black Prince*, from *Chroniques* (Chronicles), France, Troyes (?) or, more probably, Paris, ca. 1412–15. The Morgan Library & Museum, New York, MS M.804, fol. 128r (det.).

FIG. 1.6. *Burning Jews Alive during the Black Death Epidemic in 1349*, from Gilles li Muisis, *Liber secundus Chronicarum* (Chronicles: Second Book), Belgium, Tournai, 1349–52. Bibliothèque royale de Belgique, Brussels, MSS 13076–77, fol. 12v (det.).

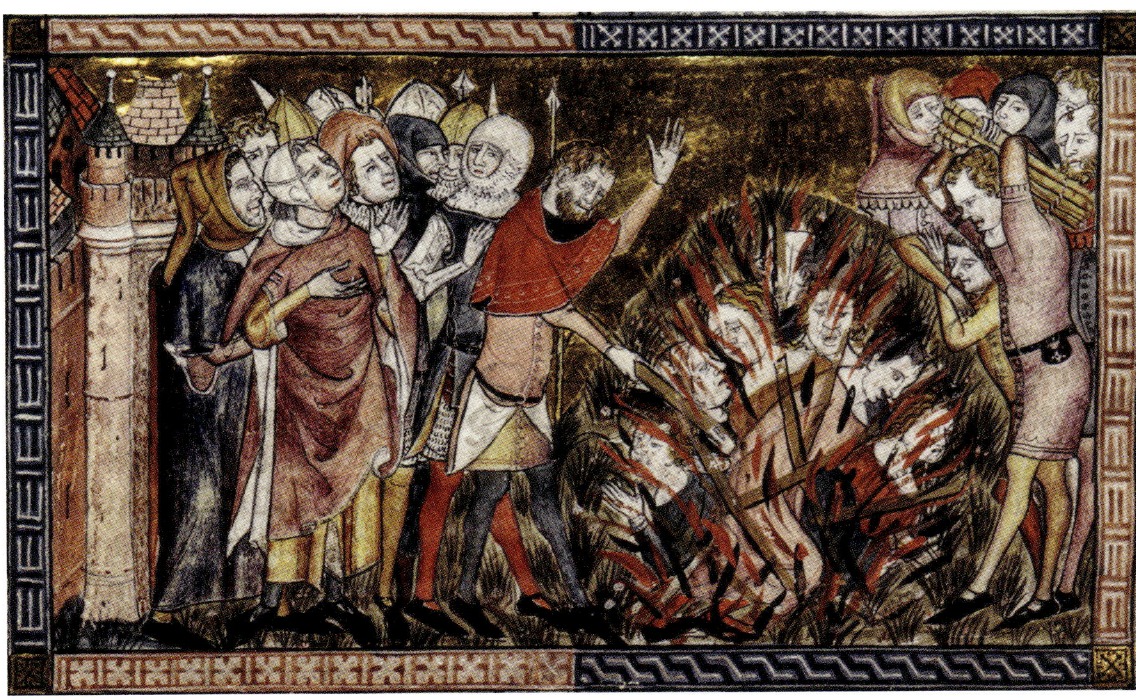

artifacts. Why this tiny minority, non-existent in many places and nowhere outside parts of Spain more than a percent or two of the population, loomed so large in Christian thinking, not only on religion, but also on the economy and society, is hard to understand.

By 1200 most Jews of Europe fell into two distinctive groups, the Sephardim living in Iberia, many still under Muslim rule, and the Ashkenazi Jews of northern Europe.[11] In some places approaching 5 percent of the population, the Sephardim were

FIG. 1.7. Hebrew Bible made for Vidal Astruc de Carcassonne, Arles, and containing his heraldic arms. The scribe, Simon ben Rabbi Samuel (Astruc Samiel d'Ascola), known to be active in Avignon, signed and dated the manuscript. This bible attests to a thriving and prosperous Sephardi Jewish community in the Mediterranean in the fifteenth century. France, Provence, Avignon (?), December 1422. The Morgan Library & Museum, New York, MS G.48, fols. 17v–18r.

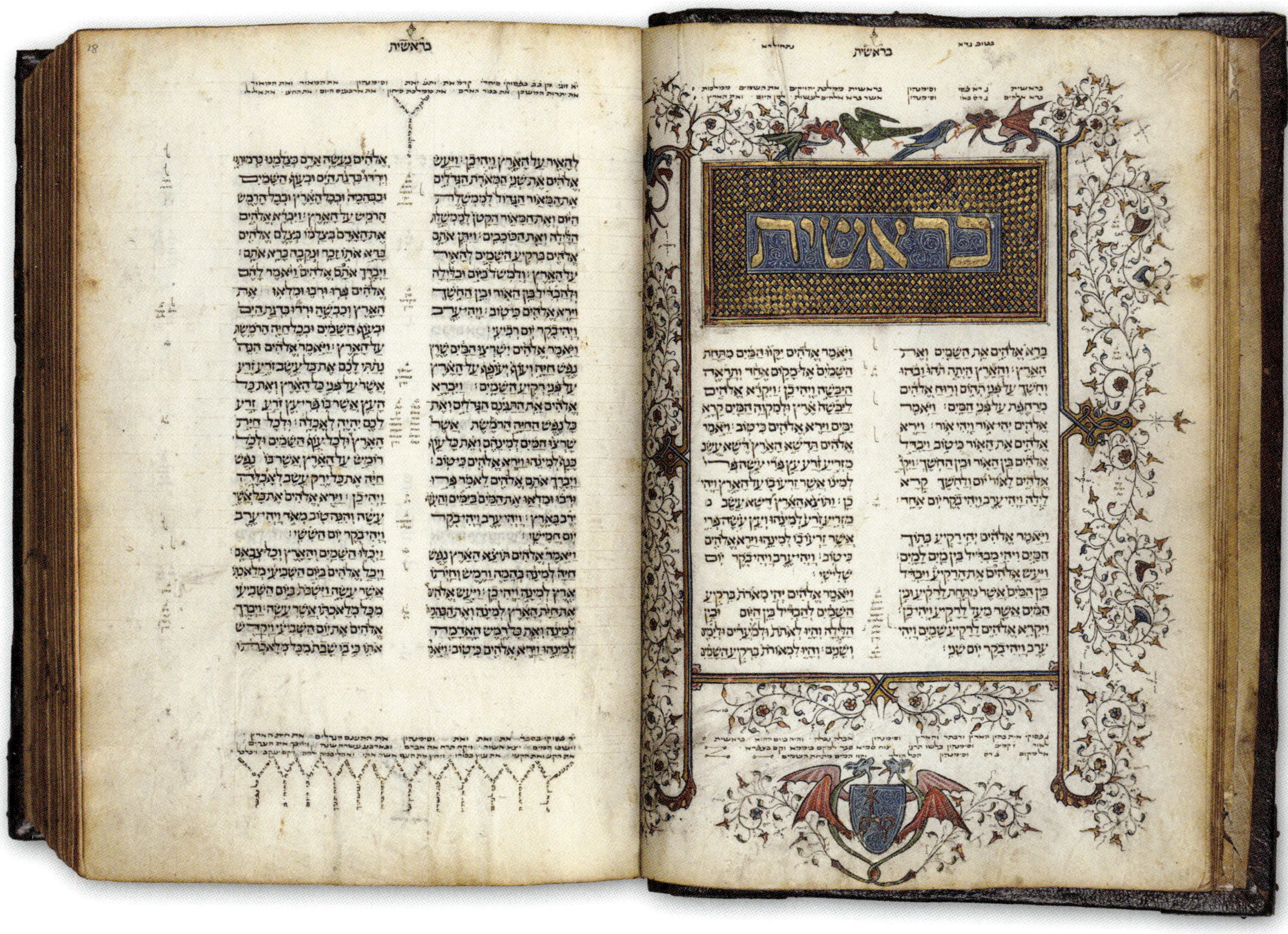

engaged in a wide variety of occupations (Fig. 1.7). The Ashkenazi, by contrast, were a tiny minority largely isolated economically and socially from their Christian neighbors, excluded from agriculture because they were not allowed to own farmland, and pushed or pulled into the business of pawnbroking and moneylending since the Church, at least in theory, forbade Christians from lending money at interest. Some Ashkenazi chose emigration and found a cautious welcome in parts of eastern Europe like Poland. Of course, Jewish communities, almost all urban, contained artisans catering to the needs of the group, but a typical interaction with the Christian majority community involved Jews extending credit to the great and small. An enduring mystery is the source of the capital required to be in the business of

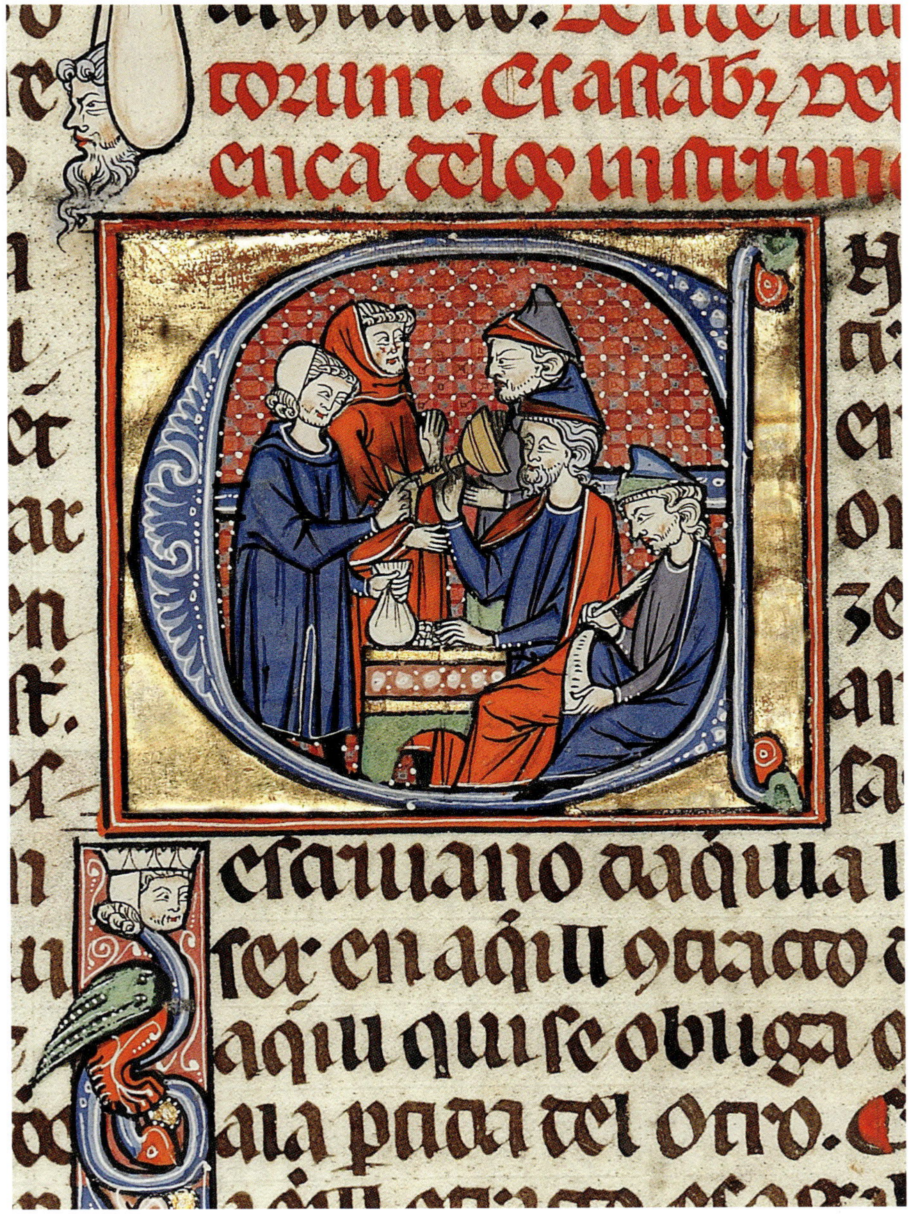

FIG. 1.8. ***Jews and Christians Conduct a Business Transaction,*** **from *In excelsis Dei thesaurus,* known as the "Vidal Mayor," a book on the feudal customs of Aragon compiled between 1247 and 1252 by Vidal de Canellas for King James the Conqueror of Aragon, northeastern Spain, 1290–1310. The J. Paul Getty Museum, Los Angeles, MS Ludwig XIV 6 (83.MQ.165), fol. 114r (det.).**

lending—centuries of saving, tapping into sources of credit outside Europe? In some places like England, which had no Jews before the Norman Conquest of 1066, the main function of the Ashkenazi immigrants was to serve in the morally dubious and unpopular act of lending money at interest.

Jews, Muslims, and Christians all believed that usury, which they initially defined as lending money for interest, was a sin, but only if it concerned co-religionists. Thus Jews lending Christians money at interest, and vice versa, committed no sin (Fig. 1.8). During the thirteenth century, theologians, especially Thomas Aquinas and Peter Olivi, analyzed the sin of usury and found ways to justify profits on loans in some circumstances where the lender was entitled to a risk premium for his money.[12] In other words, if the borrower by misfortune or crime did not repay the amount owing, a person providing credit was on good moral grounds to self-insure against this outcome by collecting a premium, in the form of reasonable interest on all loans. Thus, usury began its long redefinition from any interest at all to permissible interest rates. Later Christian theologians found the subtle right for the lender to recover what are now called opportunity costs, the profitable things he might have done with his own money instead of lending it out to someone else.

Economic development in Europe required credit and investment. Profits from buying and selling seemed moral enough except when they derived from deceptive practices like using false weights and measures. Christian merchants across Europe, and especially in its most prosperous parts, devised institutions and contracts, described below, to create the credit necessary for any economic system more sophisticated than bartering to flourish. Some individuals, tormented by guilty consciences, worried that they had crossed the line and engaged in usury. It was not unusual for people to atone for their financial misdemeanors by compensating victims or leaving money to the Church, which expressed some qualms about accepting this "filthy lucre." Credit is a vital part of the economic history of later medieval Europe. Judging from the percentage of loans on offer, Jews hardly mattered to the overall credit markets, especially in international trade with more prosperous neighbors. This statement requires some immediate qualifications. In the special circumstances of state finances in relative economic backwaters like England for much of the thirteenth century, a small Jewish community might provide timely credit, especially to the powerful dependent on sluggish and irregular incomes from land and taxes. The fate of these Jews was to be inserted into this process to attract all the blame, squeezed for their profits by the monarch, and then eventually expelled when their usefulness came to an end. In the south of Europe, trading giants like Venice and Genoa managed their affairs with hardly any economic role for Jews. Pawnbroking, especially at the low end of the business involving small loans to the desperate on the security of clothing or pots, remained permitted to Jews where they could live. There is a long history of minorities, already unpopular or soon to be so, occupying this small niche in the economy. Even here, antisemitism prompted the rise of savings and loans institutions like the *monti di pietà* in fifteenth-century Italy to provide credit to poor people as a Christian non-profit charity and to dissuade people from borrowing from Jewish moneylenders. Yet Jews often remained more popular with their customers because they charged a lower rate of interest and would take objects in pawn that the *monti* scorned. Wherever Christian moneylenders feared Jewish competition, they speedily removed it.

Despite their overall economic and social insignificance, Jews often featured— and prominently—in portrayals of sins and money (Figs. 4.6, 4.15–16, for example). Avarice and riches often had a Christian face, but stereotypes had especially bad consequences for Jews, who were scapegoated and blamed for changes in fortune and economic problems. No Christians credited Jews for the economic prosperity of Europe, but not for good reasons. There were many old social prejudices and religious opinions going back to the New Testament sustaining anti-Judaism, but antisemites objected to the nature of Jews as people, something they could not change by becoming Christians. Concerns about wealth, the fate of the soul, the pursuit of riches, and lust for money troubled many Christian consciences. One option was to reject gain of any kind and join virtuosi like St. Francis of Assisi in a life of voluntary poverty (see Fig. 5.11). Few chose this path, and the majority therefore needed a means to escape their anxieties. The Church, enormously wealthy in its own right, did its part by setting out a path of repentance and propagating a message that immoderate love of riches was the real sin. It was not so much a question of "your money or your soul," but how to "use money well." Why did Christian uneasiness about wealth so frequently implicate Jews? Scapegoating and projection have always loomed large in explanations, from the Middle Ages to the present. Better to attach economic sins to a despised minority than to examine one's own conscience and faith, or to identify the genuine authors of exploitation.

Entrepreneurs and Institutions

Documents and images about the medieval economy illuminate the institutional and legal advances underpinning it. As the economy and society developed between 1200 and 1500, it increasingly rewarded ambitious risk-takers who rose on the basis of hard work and self-defined merit rather than birth. The remarkable journeys of the Polos to China in the late thirteenth century are testament to this spirit. After the plague, an appetite for long-term risks may have abated, but with the first signs of renewed growth in the mid-fifteenth century entrepreneurs reemerged across Europe.[13] Among the skills an entrepreneur needed were a rational mind, some gift for numbers, and the ability to plan. Many of the most able, especially in trade and banking, also knew vernacular languages, or some business Latin, or at least where to find good interpreters—a growing profession rewarding the multilingual. Throughout the Muslim world Arabic served as a lingua franca, as did Old French in much of the Christian Mediterranean and beyond. Minorities, for example Jews and enslaved people from outside the West, needed the languages of the majority, be they oppressors or owners, to survive. Literacy was another advantage in any business activity where keeping records and reading them mattered, as surviving account books and merchants' handbooks attest (see Figs. 2.9, 6.19). Specialists in redacting contracts and records, notaries thrived in this economy.

Entrepreneurs who were ambitious enough to envision a world beyond gift, pillage, piracy, and beach combing needed institutions that made markets safe and predictable. The current consensus defines an institution as a set of rules, beliefs, and norms affecting the proper scope of any activity, in this case in the economic world of producing, buying, and selling for a market with the hope for legitimate gain or profit. Rules might be a formal legal system enabling commercial disputes to be settled without violence. Beliefs included those derived from religious faith, such as the ability to rely on the good faith of a party to a contract. Norms encompassed all those values not codified by statutes or biblical commandments, for example the qualities of a good personal reputation or a sense of fairness in prices and wages. Modern conceptions of an institution often include the impressive buildings housing them or the bureaucracies needed to make them function correctly. Medieval societies had a few impressive buildings like cathedrals or city halls testifying to the organizational power behind them. Other institutions, like a guild or a business partnership, might exist largely on paper, at least before guildhalls and bank offices became common fixtures of late medieval urban life. Access to these institutions determined the extent of one's personal freedom. A downtrodden peasant who appeared in court only to be fined or whipped, or an enslaved person who had little recourse beyond an owner's whim, knew institutions as mechanisms fixing their lack of freedom. Minority groups like Muslims and Jews, ordinarily denied most of the benefits of official institutions, required their own insider rules, beliefs, and norms, often resting on religious courts as well as informal mechanisms like ethnic or religious loyalties, reputation and family ties, to regulate their economic and social interactions.[14]

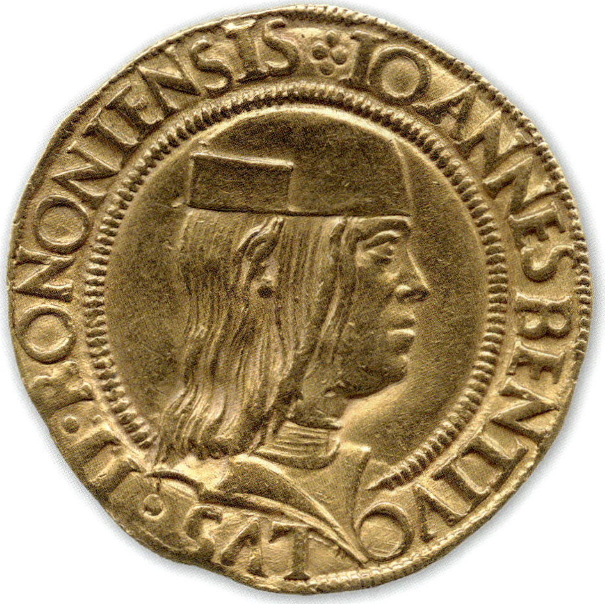

FIG. 1.9. Gold *doppio ducato*, Italian, Bologna, Giovanni II Bentivoglio, 1495. Museo Civico Archeologico, Bologna, Palagi Collection, 59930.

Money

Around 1200, cash in the form of silver coins virtually monopolized the money supply of Europe.[15] Some gold circulated, usually in Byzantine or Muslim coins or simply by the ounce. (David Yoon considers coinage in his contribution to this volume.) An institution guaranteed the value and reliability of the money supply by controlling the right to mint coins of a fixed fineness and weight (Fig. 1.9). The official seal of approval—the head of the king on an English penny, or John the Baptist, patron saint of Florence, on the florin minted there—provided a reliable currency necessary to smoothly functioning markets (Fig. 1.10). In 1252, Florence, precocious in its institutions of trade and finance, first began to mint its famous gold florin, which quickly found imitators and became an internationally recognized means of exchange, much to the benefit of the Florentine economy.[16] A bimetallic currency system required governments to understand and maintain a more or less fixed and "natural" (market) ratio between the value of gold and silver. But these values depended on the vagaries of supply; Europe had silver mines to exploit but did not produce enough gold to meet its needs. Another important factor was whether cash was leaving or entering Europe because of trade balances, especially with initially more sophisticated economies like the Muslim world and sources of gold in North African markets. Silver also flowed from mines in England, Spain, Germany, Austria, and

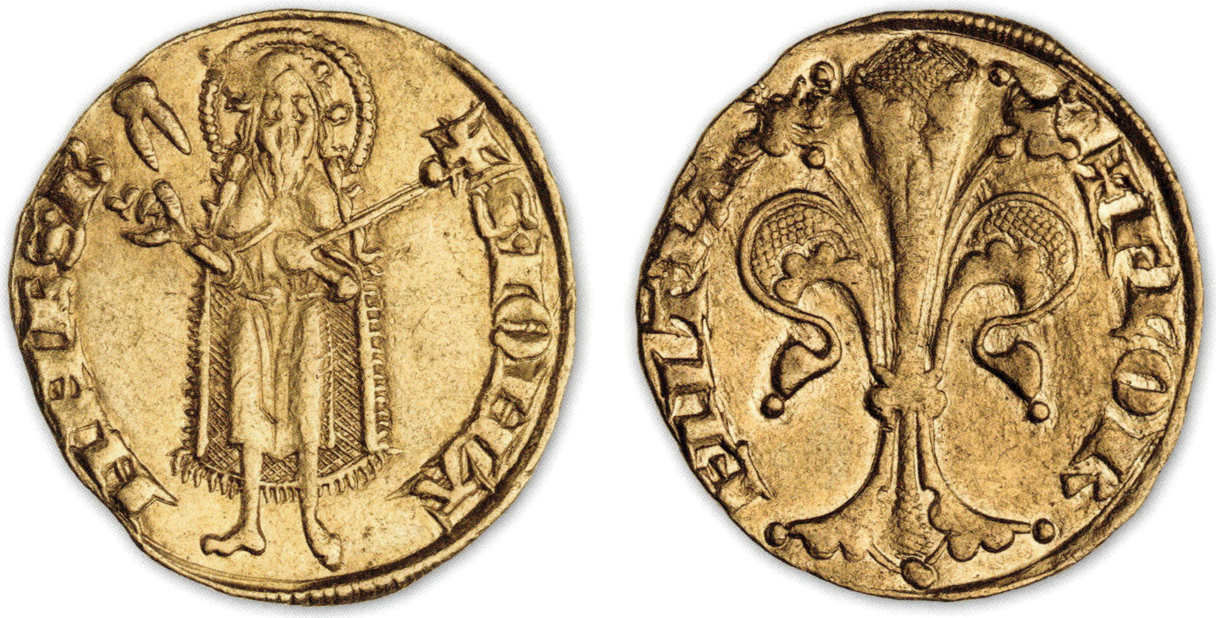

FIG. 1.10. Gold florin, Italy (Florence mint), 1252–1303. American Numismatic Society, New York, 1954.237.214.

Bohemia. If European merchants were cash customers in international markets, bullion would flow outward and cause inflation and other economic problems. People and states tended to measure prosperity by the amount of cash flowing into their economies. Ready money, and the purses and strongboxes in which it was stored, became tangible symbols of wealth—for some hoarders a fetish and an occasion for sin, as noted by Diane Wolfthal in this volume. Some "conspicuous consumers" spent money on luxury display objects such as those produced by goldsmiths and tapestry weavers, which fostered those trades.[17] Any economy or business relying on cash as the principal form of money suffered from the bullion famines and trade balances determining the money supply. Any system depending on trade, investment, and credit was crying out for new ways to increase the money supply beyond its metallic base, as well as safe ways to move cash from place to place. Innovative economic institutions worked to minimize risk, facilitate monetary transactions, and provide the nascent states with the money necessary to fight wars—hence the invention of banking and public debt. Just after 1200, the first evidence for the existence of banks appears in Italy. At the beginning, these were often family-based businesses, not established for a short time like temporary partnerships, but companies intended to last beyond the lifetimes of the original founders (Fig. 1.11). Before banks there were money changers whose job was to provide one type of coin for another, for a fee. The main purpose of a bank was to extend credit to merchants derived from the capital contributions of the original partners, who soon accepted deposits from wealthy investors. Even if clever minds devised fees and other strategies to conceal interest payments, banking always suffered from the taint of usury—though, by 1200, even religious institutions paid and accepted interest without demur. The great temptation of banking was to extend credit well

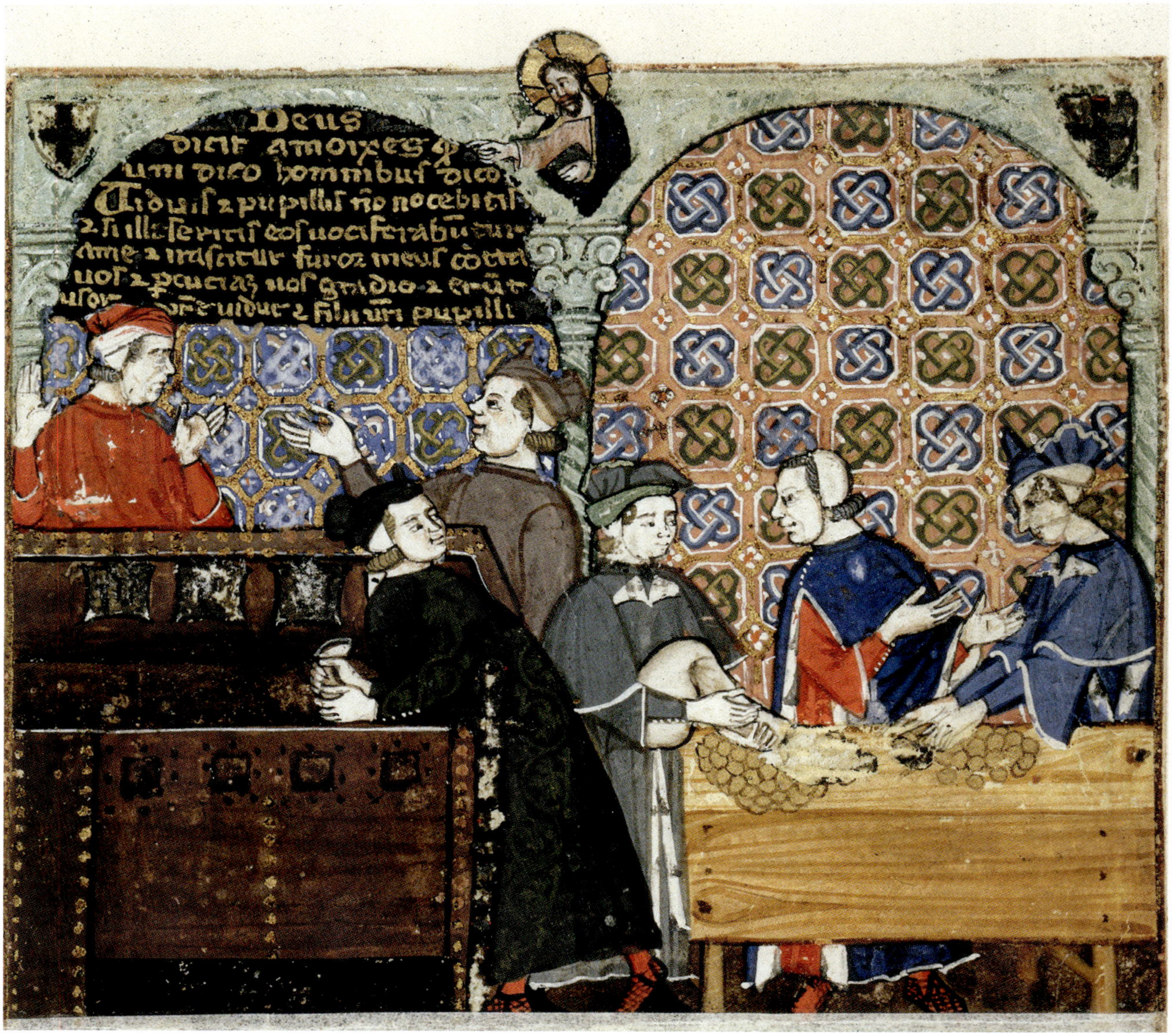

FIG. 1.11. *Italian Banking House*, from *Tractatus de septem vitiis* (Treatise on the Seven Vices), Italy, Genoa (?), late 14th century. The British Library, London, Add. MS 27695, fol. 8r (det.).

beyond its capital. Just as some borrowers defaulted, banks repeatedly failed, and few survived more than three generations. The original partners, generally prudent, were careful to limit their liabilities to the bank's capital and not their entire personal fortunes. Some banks retained a feature of commerce and investment; the partners agreed in advance to dissolve the banks after a fixed term and divide the profits. Joint-stock companies, in which the original partners sought investors who then owned shares in the business, did not appear until the seventeenth century. Most businesses, including even some banks, remained family enterprises with some silent outside partners.

A division of labor in the credit business placed in Christian hands the banks and most loans and public credit, while Jews, not allowed in any guild of bankers and money changers, were confined to being lenders of last resort to the riskiest clients. International bankers of the thirteenth and fourteenth centuries opened branch offices and made it possible to fund trade and warfare by supplying, for example, Florentine merchants in England and Spain with the local currency necessary to buy wool for export home for the manufacturing of cloth (Fig. 1.12). Local money changers could not handle the volume required, so gold florins needed to appear in distant places. Merchants were not likely to carry sacks of cash across Europe, though the first adventurers had to do just that. One of the goals of institutions was to make routine and safe what was at first unique and perilous. In short, bankers experimented with contracts resembling letters of credit, which eventually became bills of exchange, perhaps invented in northern Italy but quickly adopted elsewhere, especially in the Low Countries. A bill of exchange was a piece of paper guaranteeing payment to the bearer in another place, at a different time, in another currency. Ideally a partner deposited florins in Florence, receiving a bill sent to an agent in London, promising a sum of sterling in two or three months. The bank had the use of the florins at home, and, by paying in pounds overseas, where they were just a bit cheaper, took advantage of the differences in exchange rates to make a profit. The bearers of the bill saved themselves trouble and were generally happy to take advantage of this arrangement. Some risks remained at every stage, enough to justify the taking of profits and interest from the transactions. By 1500 it was possible to endorse bills to a third party, and they could become as good as cash, increasing the supply of money beyond the coinage and hence the supply of credit.

One final financial innovation in this period merits notice not simply for its contemporary effect but also because of its future impact. Over the course of the fourteenth century it became possible in some Mediterranean ports, probably at first Genoa, for shipowners and merchants to buy maritime insurance against shipwreck and loss of ships and cargoes, including enslaved people, ironically the first lives incidentally insured (life insurance for free people was centuries in the future). Insurance, unknown in the ancient world or the earlier Middle Ages, was an ideal way to share risk. For this business to be profitable for insurers, there had to be some way of estimating, or simply gambling, on the probabilities of disaster at sea. From the first the contract excluded warfare and acts of God like storms. The real problem was piracy or structural failure in the wooden ships. No insurance companies existed, and no one for centuries

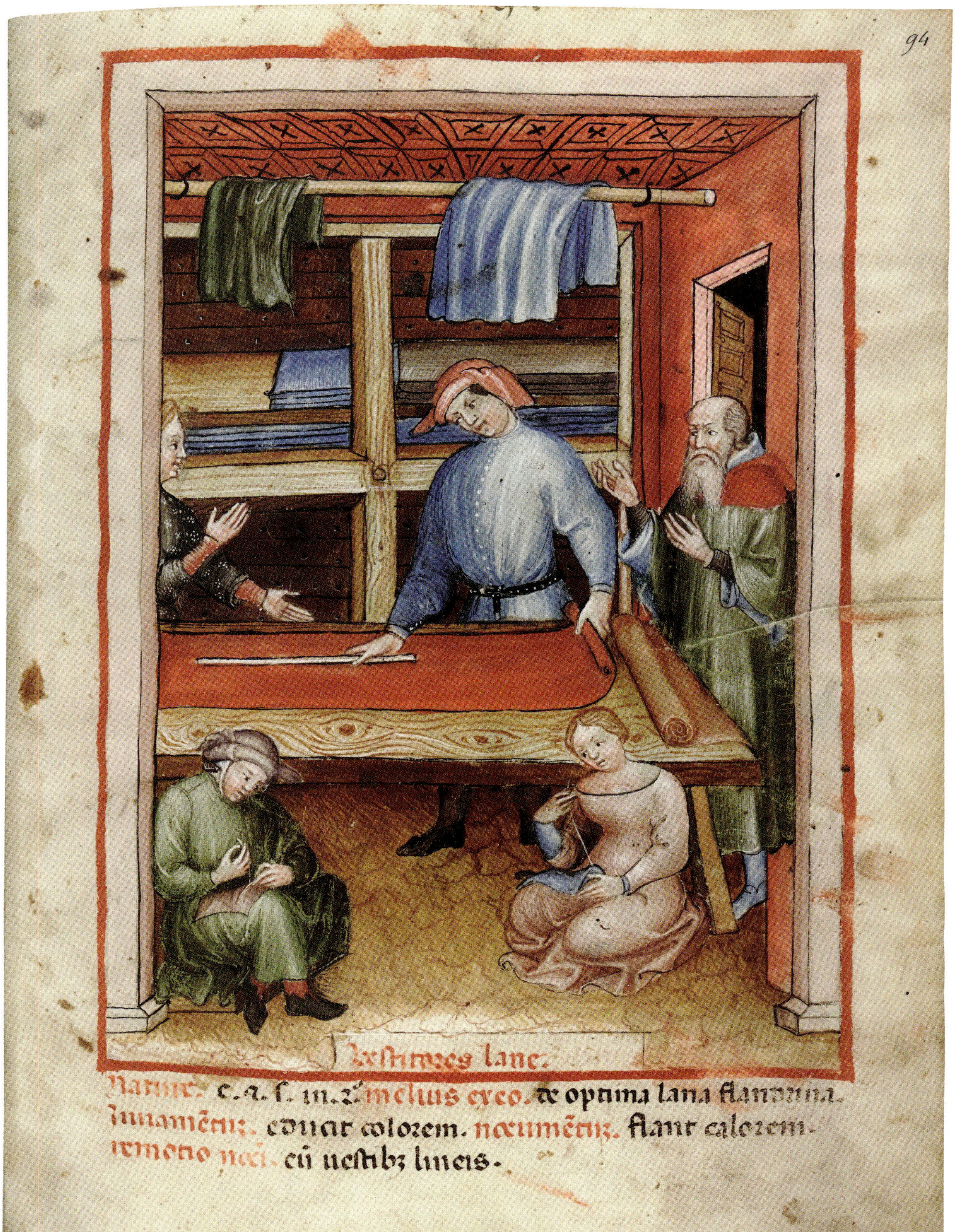
94
lane.
melius ex eo. de optima lana
educit colorem.
cum vestibus lineis.

FIG. 1.12. Workshop of Giovannino de Grassi, *Wool Seller*, from *Tacuinum sanitatis* (Handbook on Health), Italy, Pavia or Milan, 1380–1400. Bibliothèque nationale de France, Paris, MS nouv. acq. lat. 1673, fol. 94r.

was willing to insure against other perils like fire or death. Individual insurers limited their own risk by almost never assuming the entire value of the contract. It was the job of the client to find, say, ten insurers each willing to take 10 percent of the risk, for a small fee: a profitable sideline for many merchants. Early insurance was an amalgam of morally dubious gambling and rational calculations, skillfully blended to escape moral condemnation.

If capitalism is producing for a market with the hope of profit, then many features of the western European economy in 1500 appear more capitalistic than they were in 1200. Since an industrial revolution had not yet occurred, many scholars describe the most advanced parts of the late medieval economy as "mercantile capitalism," privileging trade and its increasingly sophisticated techniques like double-entry bookkeeping, bills of exchange, and insurance. Subsistence farmers hardly participated in this new economy, but all the landlords great and small selling their crops and animals into a futures market certainly did. As warfare became more capital-intensive, money was more clearly the sinews of power, and those governments able to raise money in taxes and credit markets had an advantage over those who could not.[18] Those living mainly from wages, in the countryside as well as the cities, depended on employers to provide a market for their skills. Their bargaining power was slight, even in periods of labor shortages. Some moralists continued to insist on just wages and prices, and some governments assumed responsibility for responding to famines and taking care of widows and orphans, but the major share of this work fell to religious institutions and voluntary charity. Many did not thrive in this economy or were excluded from it. Self-reliance and an afterlife free from work and poverty consoled some, but in this world social and economic realities favored those seeking God and profit at the same time.

NOTES

1. This rapid survey relies on the details and references supplied in Epstein 2009. For another approach, see Persson 2010. The classic studies remain Pirenne 1936 and Cipolla 1994.
2. Hoffmann 2014, especially strong on nature, climate, and energy issues.
3. Jones 1987, emphasizing the roles of disasters and risks.
4. Lopez 1976; Smil 2017.
5. The most recent attempt to integrate the history of climate change and disease into medieval social and economic history is Campbell 2016.
6. Jordan 1996.
7. See Ogilvie 2011 and 2019; and for medieval background Epstein 1991.
8. For this phrase, Friedel 2007.
9. Cohn 2002 and 2018.
10. Meiss 1951 inaugurated a vast literature on this theme.
11. For more on the circumstances of medieval Jews, before and after this period, see Botticini and Eckstein 2012.
12. For the standard work on medieval economic thought, see Wood 2002.
13. This is the thesis of Kedar 1976.
14. Greif 2006; for a critique, Goldberg 2012.
15. Spufford 1988.
16. Goldthwaite 2009.
17. Stuard 2006.
18. Caferro 2018.

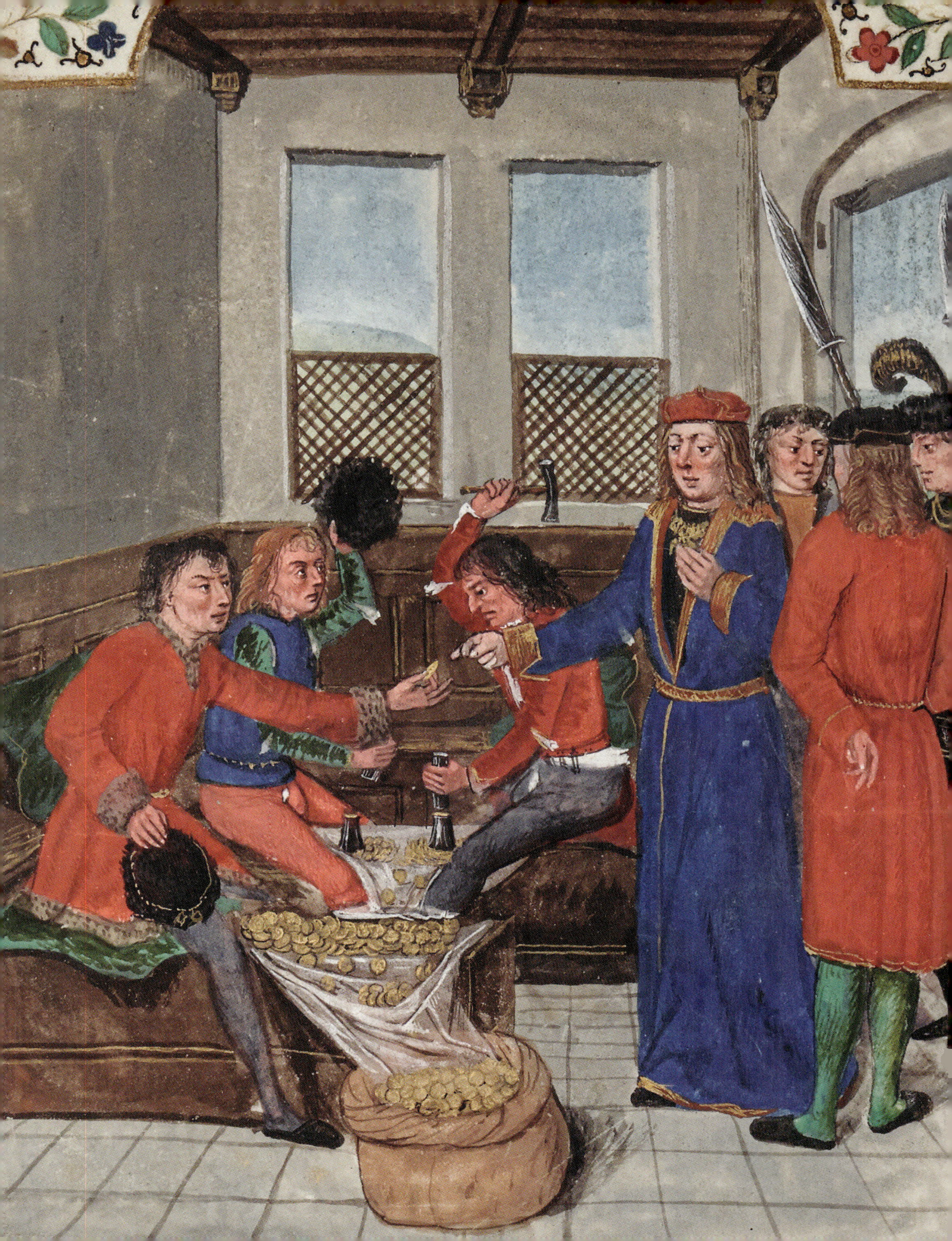

2

Coinage and Medieval Monetary Systems

DAVID YOON

A Different Experience

MONEY WAS WIDELY RECOGNIZED AS PROBLEMATIC within medieval culture. Like sex and food, money was potentially troubling not only because of its association with sin, but also because it was ubiquitous in everyday life. As in modern society, money was essential for making the economy of medieval Europe function. In addition, as today, it was an important means by which social relationships of dependence, hierarchy, obligation, and privilege could be expressed.[1] So for a large proportion of people, regardless of Church teachings reproving material wealth, money was too much a part of life to be shunned.

Bruges Master of 1482, *Mint Workers Striking Coins*, from Nicholas Oresme, *Traité de la première invention des monnaies* (Treatise on the Origins of Coinage), Belgium, Bruges, ca. 1480. Bibliothèque nationale de France, Paris, MS fr. 23927, fol. 5r. (Detail of Fig. 2.2.)

The everyday experience of money for medieval Europeans was in many ways quite different from our own, however. This becomes apparent if we consider the physical appearance of coins. An English penny of King Henry VI (1422–1461) illustrates many typical

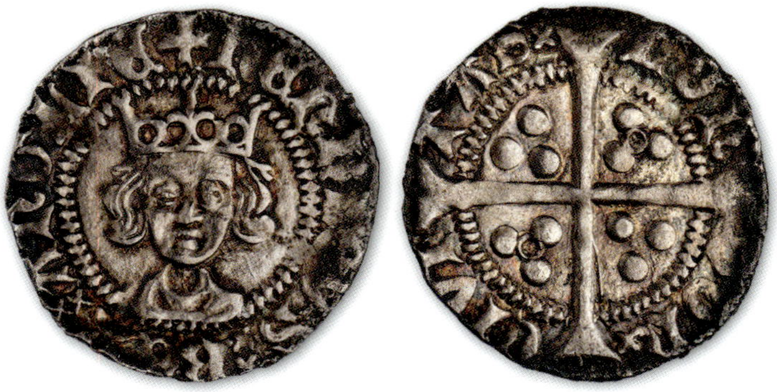

FIG. 2.1. Silver penny, England (London mint), Henry VI, 1422–30. American Numismatic Society, New York, 1943.102.21.

FIG. 2.2. Bruges Master of 1482, *Mint Workers Striking Coins*, from Nicholas Oresme, *Traité de la première invention des monnaies* (Treatise on the Origins of Coinage), Belgium, Bruges, ca. 1480. Bibliothèque nationale de France, Paris, MS fr. 23927, fol. 5r.

features (Fig. 2.1). It is a thin metal disk with designs and words stamped on both sides, much like modern coins. Various features nonetheless point to important distinctions between medieval and modern money. This essay explores those differences.

Making Medieval Coins

The most noticeable feature of the medieval coin to the modern eye is its irregularity. It is approximately circular, but only approximately; the edges are noticeably uneven. The letters and other marks are unevenly spaced; the designs are fairly simple and abstract. These and other features show clearly that the coin was made by hand, before modern machinery facilitated greater precision.[2]

Medieval coins were made by placing a metal blank between two coining dies, and then hitting the upper die with a hammer.[3] This compresses the blank, forcing the metal into the designs carved into the surfaces of the dies. With this technique, coins could be mass-produced by medieval standards: a worker could produce over a thousand coins per day, and a major mint could produce millions per year.[4] A miniature from a manuscript of Nicholas Oresme's *Traité de la première invention des monnaies* (Treatise on the Origins of Coinage) shows three mint workers (Fig. 2.2). One strikes a coin between two dies with his hammer, another holds an upper die while doffing his cap, while a third offers an example of the coins to a dignitary who is accompanied by an armed retinue. Other essential procedures, not shown in this image, included preparation of the dies, refining and alloying the metal for coins, hammering it out into strips or sheets (see Fig. 6.10b), and then cutting it into round blanks with shears.

The technology was simple enough that a small mint needed only a few workers and easily available facilities (mostly a furnace for metalworking) to produce coins. However, a ruler could not appoint just anyone to operate a mint. The skills of making coin dies—by punching and engraving designs into soft iron and then hardening the iron to withstand the process of striking coins—and of refining and alloying precious metals required special expertise.[5]

In contrast to the modern world, where national governments usually have only one major mint (if any), operated by government employees, any moderately large medieval state usually had many different mints, which were often privately managed by contractors.[6] For example, in Castile, Spain, between the mid-thirteenth and mid-fifteenth centuries, there were generally around five to ten royal mints, located in major towns of different regions of the kingdom; their operation was leased out to entrepreneurs with the financial resources and technical knowledge to hire the necessary skilled workers.[7]

Such a system presupposes that the entrepreneur can make a profit by operating a mint. The normal

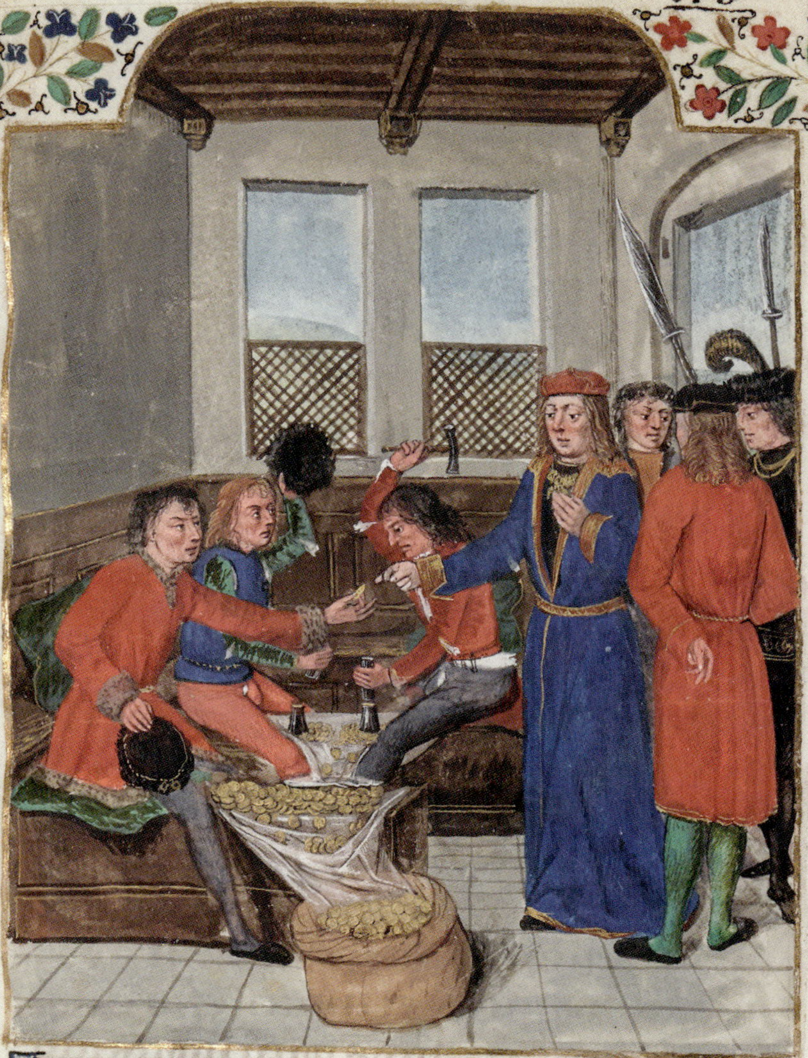

Veritate manifestata cedat oppinio veritati. qui est a dire en francois. que quant verite est manifeste et aperte: toute oppinion doit cesser et lui donner lieu.

practice in medieval Europe was that mints charged a small fee for the coins they made, which was meant not only to cover the costs of production but also to provide a profit for the mintmaster and the government.[8] This small but mostly predictable monetary profit was an important economic resource for entrepreneurs and for rulers who were perennially short of hard cash.

Rulers made use of this profitable aspect of minting economically, as a source of revenue, but they also used it politically. A ruler who wished to give a valuable favor to a useful vassal could grant the right to mint coins. The most centralized medieval monarchies refrained from giving any subordinates the sovereign right to have their own coinage, but many kingdoms did not resist the temptation. In France, the Low Countries, Germany, and northern Italy, many feudal lords, ecclesiastical prelates, and city-states acquired the profitable right to mint their own separate coinages—see, for example, the coins of the count of Holland and Flanders, the duke of Gelderland, and the bishop of Utrecht (Figs. 6.30–6.33), all of whom were subordinate rulers within the Holy Roman Empire.[9]

As a result of this dispersion of minting rights as well as the tendency for large realms to establish many regional mints, most regions of Europe had access to a mint, even under medieval conditions of travel and transport. Whether they had access to an adequate supply of coins is a different question, depending on the amount of production at these mints.

Although major mints could, as mentioned above, produce millions of coins per year, smaller mints might operate very irregularly, producing an issue of coins only now and then when needed. And even major mints varied considerably in their output, according to the supply of precious metals available for use. Depending on trade patterns and mining productivity, supplies of silver and gold could vary widely. Thus, in some times and places there were chronic shortages of coins, especially smaller coins for everyday use.[10]

The fees collected by mints for making coins were usually paid not per coin produced, but rather per amount of silver (or gold) made into coins. Small, low-value coins containing only a little silver took about as much work to produce as larger coins with more silver, so mints tended to put more of their effort into making the larger coins.[11] And in any case, the limitations of pre-industrial technology meant that rates of production were low by modern standards.

In order to produce enough coins at a sensible cost, important innovations to increase efficiency were developed to streamline the minting of coins.[12] Since the precious-metal content represented most of the cost of production, and laws usually required specific standards in that regard, mints tended to seek savings of time and labor with other aspects including the appearance of the coins.

Images and Authority

The designs on the penny of Henry VI are fairly typical of medieval coins (see Fig. 2.1). On one side there is a crowned bust representing the king; on the other, a cross ornamented with clusters of dots. Representations of rulers, religious symbolism, and heraldic emblems (such as coats of arms) are all commonly found on medieval coins. These designs are usually composed of simple elements that are repeated. The design of a penny

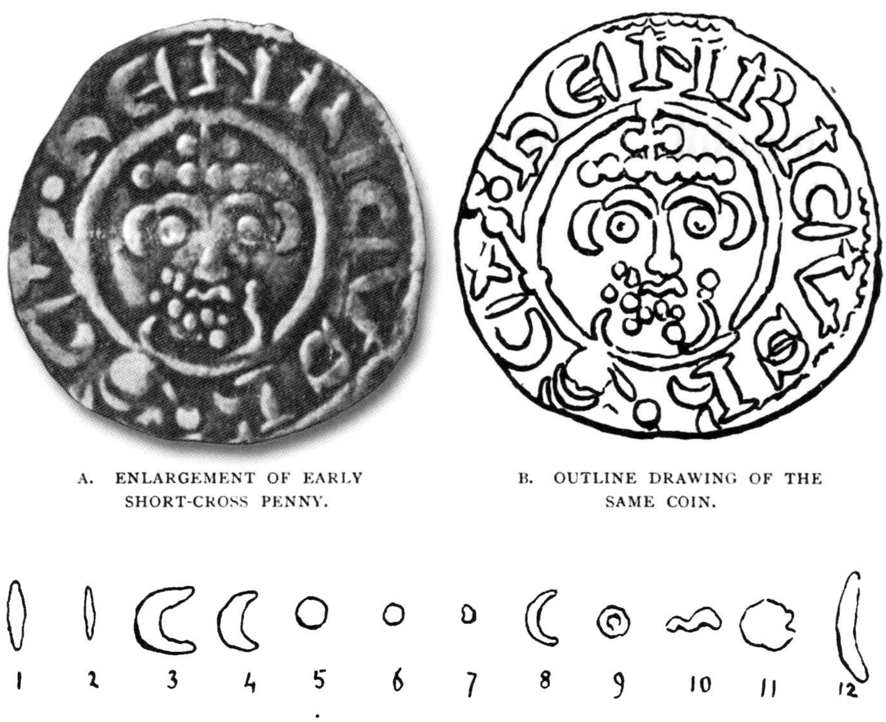

FIG. 2.3. A penny of Henry II of England and a line drawing of the basic shapes that were punched into the die to create the design. From Fox 1909, 192–93.

of Henry II of England or his successors was formed from twelve basic shapes (Fig. 2.3). Each of these shapes was carved on a small steel punch. The punches were then struck with a hammer to create depressions in the working surface of the coining die, corresponding to the raised areas on the coins made from it.

Designs composed of multiple small punches like these were generally simple and abstract in appearance. The royal image on the penny of Henry VI is not an individualized portrait; it is a simplified drawing that offers an abstract representation of kingship. When one king died and another acceded to the throne, the same image could be reused. Fifteenth-century artists were capable of engraving more realistic, individualized depictions if they chose to do so. However, unlike early Renaissance painters and medalists in Italy,[13] the issuers of medieval coins were generally not interested in individualized portraiture until the final decades of the fifteenth century or later.

Instead, issuers of coins aimed to convey different kinds of statements. Money was one of the ways that a government could speak to the general public and literally put its messages into people's hands, as is still true today. The images chosen (or not chosen) for official forms of money thus say something about the messages a government wished to emphasize. Sometimes the message was overt propaganda, but sometimes it was more subtle. For example, old coin designs were sometimes retained for long periods of time to convey an impression of stability.[14]

Medieval governments were never as powerful or as stable as modern nation-states, and the messages on coins were frequently intended to counter tenuous and turbulent political realities. Henry VI of England, for example, was twice overthrown by shifting coalitions of the landed aristocracy in the factional strife known as the Wars of the Roses, and many other medieval monarchs faced similar challenges within their realms.[15] When royal power was contested by feudal lords or the Church—or, for that matter, when a feudal lord was attempting to assert more power in opposition to his suzerain—an abstract, idealized image of rulership or power might be more useful than a realistic depiction of the actual ruler with all his or her

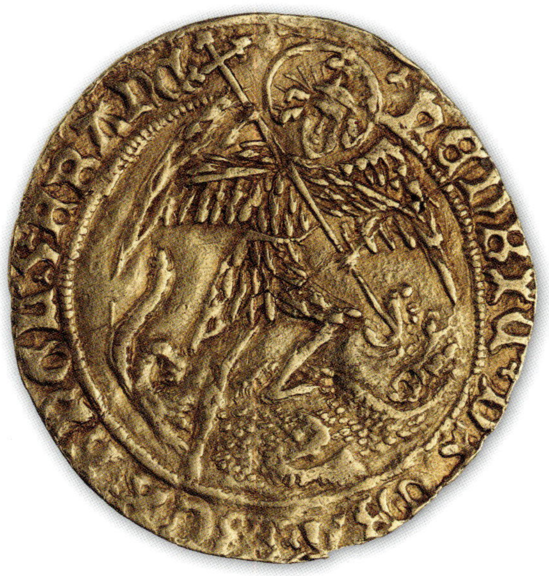

FIG. 2.4. Gold angel, England (London mint), Henry VI, 1470–71. American Numismatic Society, New York, 1954.237.19.

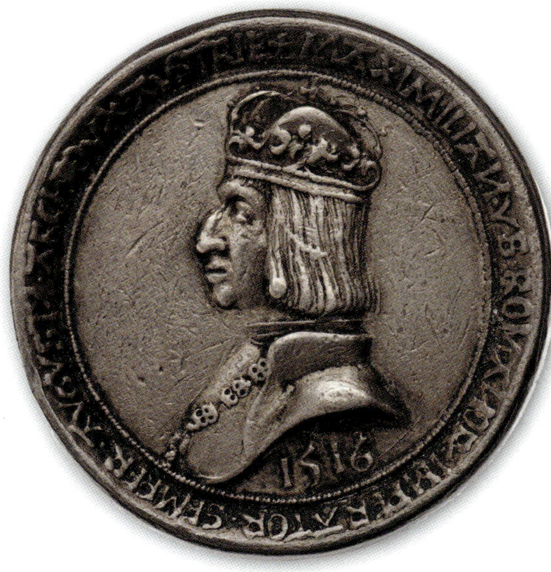

FIG. 2.5. Silver double *guldengroschen*, Tyrol, Maximilian I, 1516. American Numismatic Society, New York, 1960.111.426.

weaknesses. For kings, royal authority could be invoked visually by an image of a generic crowned head, or even just an image of a crown on its own, as with the penning of Eric VII of Pomerania (see Fig. 6.34). Alternatively, symbolic displays of distinguished ancestry in the form of heraldic arms could serve similar purposes. The coins of Philip the Good from the counties of Flanders and Holland (see Figs. 6.31 and 6.32) are prime examples. One side displays his coat of arms as both the local count and the duke of Burgundy (a higher-ranking title), while the other side is embellished with fleurs-de-lis, the heraldic emblem of the French royal family from which he was descended.

In a cultural environment pervaded by religion, symbolic appeal to an even higher authority—the deity—was natural. Crosses are ubiquitous in medieval coinage, and many coins are marked by depictions of a local patron saint, such as the florin of Rudolf of Diepholz, bishop of Utrecht, depicting St. Martin, to whom the cathedral of Utrecht was, and still is, dedicated (see Fig. 6.30). Even more dramatic is the English gold angel of Henry VI (Fig. 2.4). On one side it shows the archangel Michael spearing a dragon; on the other it has a coat of arms representing the Plantagenet dynasty of England and the Capetian line of France, the two kingdoms that Henry VI claimed. First issued during the Wars of the Roses, this coin bearing imagery of a warrior saint conquering evil was a powerful political message framed in terms of the language of religion familiar to the medieval English public.

Inspired by finds of ancient Roman coins with realistic portraits of emperors, fifteenth-century Italian artists began to make medals with portraits of their own rulers and patrons.[16] This marked an important shift in the approach to coin imagery. The techniques involved in manufacturing these types of medals were applied to coins as well, and, by the late fifteenth and early sixteenth centuries, rulers increasingly demanded that their coins bear individualized portraits of themselves. An example of this new style of coinage is the double *guldengroschen* of the Holy Roman emperor Maximilian I, dated 1516 (Fig. 2.5). This coin has a high-relief portrait of Maximilian, not only showing him as an individual but also as middle-aged, distinguishable from earlier portraits of him as a young man. The other side has a battle scene depicting a knight riding over a defeated enemy, along with coats of arms corresponding to some of Maximilian's most important titles.

Thus, despite the change from abstract, generic depictions to more realistic, individualized portraits, many of the same themes and ideas continued to be expressed. Rather than symbols of nationhood, found on most forms of modern money, the focus was on the institutional, military, and dynastic claims of the ruler, but with an increasing emphasis on the ruler as an individual.

Value and Metal Content

To return to the penny of Henry VI, another important feature worth noting is that it is made of silver, containing almost 0.9 grams of pure silver alloyed with a bit of copper to make sterling silver (92.5 percent silver; see Fig. 2.1). Within living memory, it was common for modern coins used in daily transactions to be made of precious metals like silver and even gold,[17] but in recent decades coins for ordinary use have been made of cheaper materials, representing value not because of their metal content but because a stable government guarantees their acceptance at a specified monetary value.[18]

Significantly, nowhere on the Henrician penny is there a written statement of its monetary value. The writing on the coin specifies, in Latin, the ruling authority behind its issue (*Henricus rex Anglie*, Henry king of England) and the place where it was minted (*civitas London*, city of London), but nothing else. Medieval people—the majority of whom were unable to read—relied on size, weight, and design to identify their coins.

Given the political instability and multiple competing types of authority in the Middle Ages, medieval people assumed that the value of the coin came not from the government's authorization but from its precious metal content. Even so, the question of value was more complicated than we might think, because the coins that people used did not always have the simple relationship to monetary values that we expect today. The use of precious metals as money creates many problems for monetary systems, and medieval responses to these problems were pragmatic but not tidy or simple.

As mentioned above, medieval mintmasters and rulers expected to make a profit from producing coins. Because the coins were made of precious metal, though, the profit margin was generally narrow, and at times the only way to make a profit was to skimp a bit on the metal content of new coins. Moreover, rulers sometimes needed more coins than their supplies of silver or gold would allow, so they issued new coins on a lower standard.[19] Occasional attempts were made to restore higher standards, but in general most types of medieval coins gradually declined in precious metal content over time—by being made lighter, by alloying the silver or gold with cheaper metal, or both. English pennies, like those of Henry VI, are among the rare exceptions—their weight and their silver content declined only slightly during the Middle Ages.

More typical is the physical alteration over time of the *denier tournois*. This coin was first issued by the abbey of Saint-Martin in Tours, western France, and, after 1204, adopted as one of the main types of

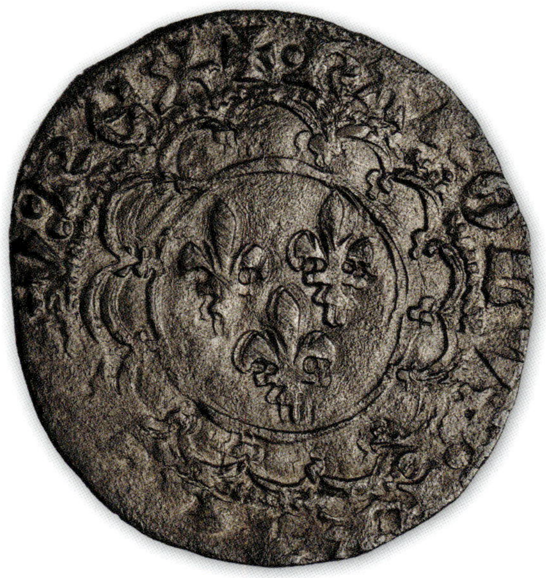

FIG. 2.6. Billon *double tournois*, France (Poitiers mint), Charles VII, ca. 1431. American Numismatic Society, New York, 1942.23.413.

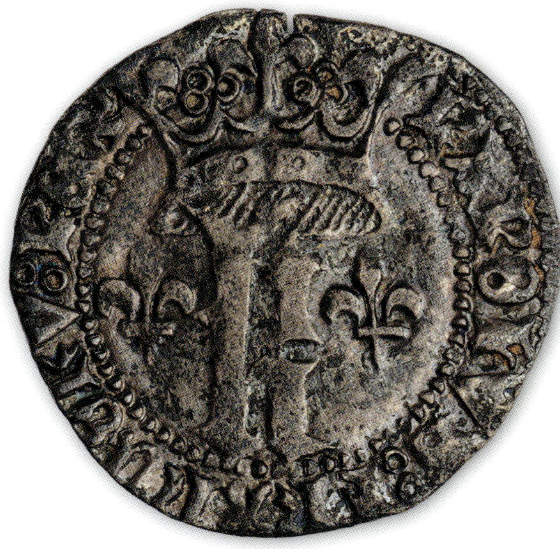

FIG. 2.7. Billon *blanc au K*, France (Beauvais mint), Charles VII, ca. 1431–35. American Numismatic Society, New York, 1942.23.371.

royal French coinage. It derived from early medieval silver coins that, in the ninth century, contained about 1.7 grams of silver, more than early English pennies. However, through a process of slight reductions in weight and fineness, repeated many times over the centuries, the composition of the *denier tournois* changed dramatically. By the mid-fifteenth century, it was made of billon—an alloy of copper and silver—and the typical *denier tournois* contained slightly over 0.1 grams of silver alloyed with around 0.7 to 0.8 grams of copper.[20]

Because the value of coinage in the Middle Ages was assumed to be determined by the precious metal content, it was significant that a *denier tournois* in the 1430s contained less than one eighth as much silver as an English penny. Comparing purchasing power is more difficult due to variations in supply and demand, but, to give a rough idea, in the mid-1430s a building laborer earned about four pennies a day in southern England, compared to about thirty *deniers tournois* in Paris.[21] The amount of wheat needed to make one kilogram (2.2 pounds) of bread, enough to feed an adult for a day, cost about a quarter of a penny (a farthing) in southern England, and about two and a quarter *deniers tournois* in Paris.[22]

Because the purchasing power of the *denier tournois* had sunk to the level of small change, it had ceased to be a useful monetary unit for large transactions. Even for fairly small transactions, it was mostly replaced by the *double tournois* (Fig. 2.6), a coin nominally worth two *deniers tournois* (but containing only about 75 percent more silver than a *denier tournois*). However, this was also less than a quarter of an English penny; for larger transactions, higher-value coins were needed.

To that end, French mints also produced a type of coin with a higher silver content—called a *blanc*, after the white color of silver—that was valued at ten *deniers tournois* (Fig. 2.7).[23] This provided a monetary unit similar to the English penny sterling, though in the form of a larger coin made of billon with a moderate silver content (39.9 percent). Colloquially, low-silver billon coins like the *denier* and *double tournois* were often called "black money" because the copper-heavy alloy quickly turned a dull, dark brown color; higher-silver

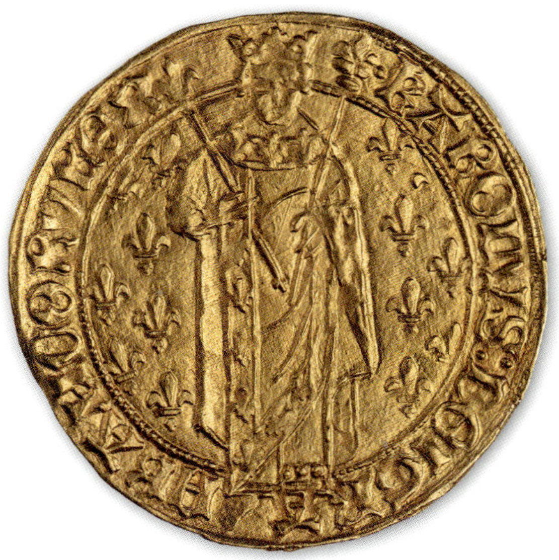

FIG. 2.8. Gold *royal d'or*, France (Tours mint), Charles VII, ca. 1429–31. American Numismatic Society, New York, 1967.182.78.

billon coins like the *blanc* were called "white money" because they retained a silvery appearance longer.

White money and silver were the mainstay of many ordinary transactions, such as wages, rents, and many household purchases like clothing or bulk foodstuffs. Black money was useful for small transactions such as a loaf of bread or a haircut. In countries like France that had both black money and white money, the former was probably used more by urban dwellers than by the rural population.[24] However, neither coinage was suitable for the very large transactions of governments and international commerce.

Gold coins provided a third level of money, more suited to high-value payments. The *royal d'or*, minted under King Charles VII around 1430, was a gold coin worth 300 *deniers tournois* (Fig. 2.8).[25] Such a coin represented so much value that most people would rarely handle one—a peasant family might include a few gold coins in a wedding dowry, but they would not use them for ordinary transactions. However, gold was very useful for paying companies of mercenary soldiers or making wholesale purchases of imported silks and spices, so for rulers and merchants they were the most important type of coins. Thus, different kinds of coins corresponded to different uses and even different demographics.

From Coins to Monetary Systems

Continual changes in coinage caused major changes in monetary systems during the millennium or so that we call the "Middle Ages." Multiple levels of coinage developed gradually. The Roman Empire had a complex monetary system of gold, silver, and bronze coins, but, in the early Middle Ages, western European coinage became simplified, resulting in a system based on a single denomination, the denarius (a silver penny).[26] In the eighth and ninth centuries, Charlemagne made this the dominant monetary system in most of Europe, except where Byzantine or Islamic traditions prevailed, such as Sicily and Spain. The Carolingian denarius was ancestor to the English penny, the French *denier*, the Italian *denaro*, and many other basic monetary units of later medieval Europe, most of which were reduced to small "black money" coins in the centuries after the break-up of Charlemagne's empire. In the Italian states, the reduction of monetary standards was particularly notable; the Venetian *tornesello* (see Fig. 6.26), made by Venice for use in its Greek colonies, contained less silver than the *denier tournois* but was worth three Venetian *denari*.[27] As the silver content of most regions' coins declined and as the economy grew, a single-denomination coinage system no longer sufficed.

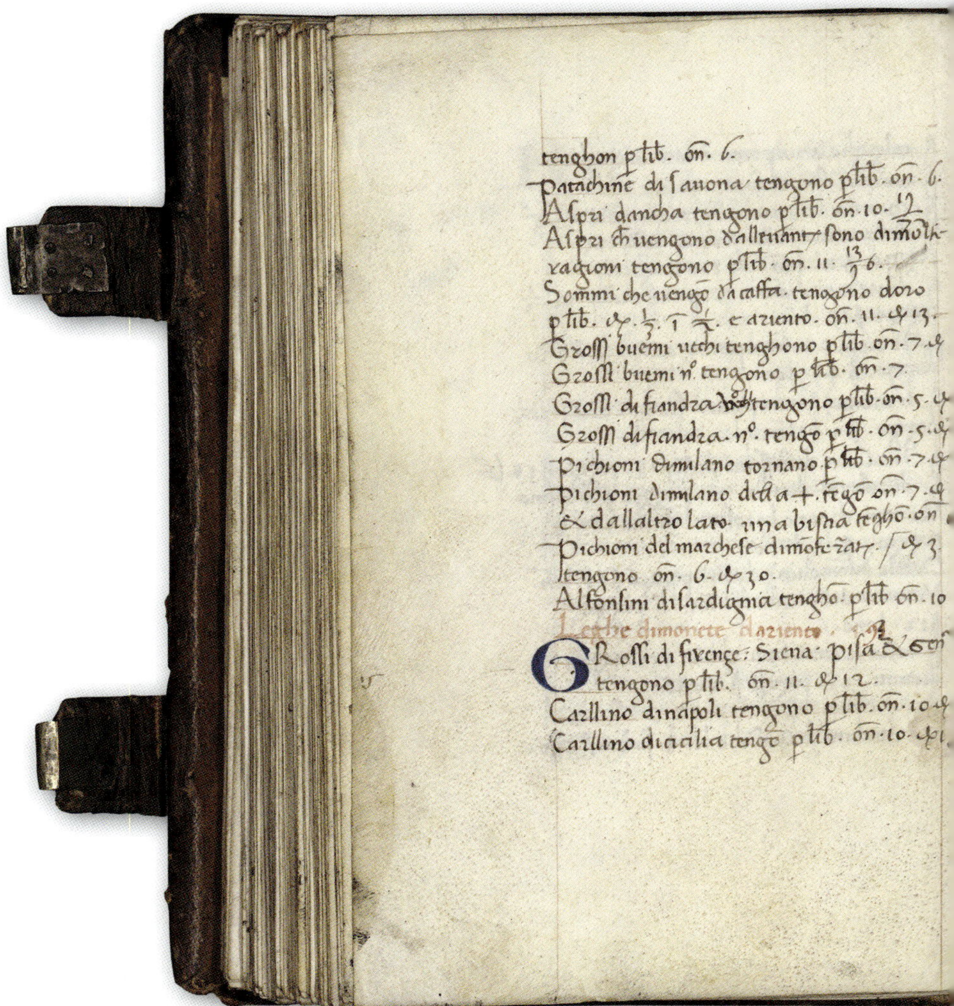

FIG. 2.9. Pages listing fineness of silver and billon coins, from Ludovico Bertini's copy of *Libro che tracta di marcantie et usanze di paesi* (Book Concerning the Trade and Customs of Various Places), Italy, Florence (?), ca. 1481. Temple University Libraries, Philadelphia, MSS BH 007 COCH, fols. 98v–99r.

England was an exception in many ways, because the penny there remained a silver coin throughout the Middle Ages, and black money (in the form of copper rather than billon coins) was not introduced until the seventeenth century. In France, the Italian states, and many other countries, silver coins worth ten, twelve, or more *deniers/denari* were introduced in the twelfth and thirteenth centuries to provide a more convenient coinage for ordinary payments. The papal *carlino* is an example of such a coin, containing about twice as much silver as an English penny (see Fig. 6.12). Many of these types of coins were also debased over time, resulting in "white" billon coins such as the French *blanc* (Fig. 2.7) and the *gros* of the Low Countries (see Figs. 6.31–6.32). And to provide a coinage suitable for large payments, gold coins were introduced in the thirteenth and fourteenth centuries.

Because Italian bankers dominated the financial system of western Europe at the time, Italian gold coins such as the Florentine florin (see Fig. 1.10) and the Venetian ducat were the most important standards for international commerce and were widely imitated throughout Europe. However, although the actual Florentine florins and Venetian ducats maintained a high standard throughout the late Middle Ages, many of the imitations experienced the same deterioration of weight or fineness seen in silver coins. The florins of the bishopric of Utrecht in the Low Countries, for

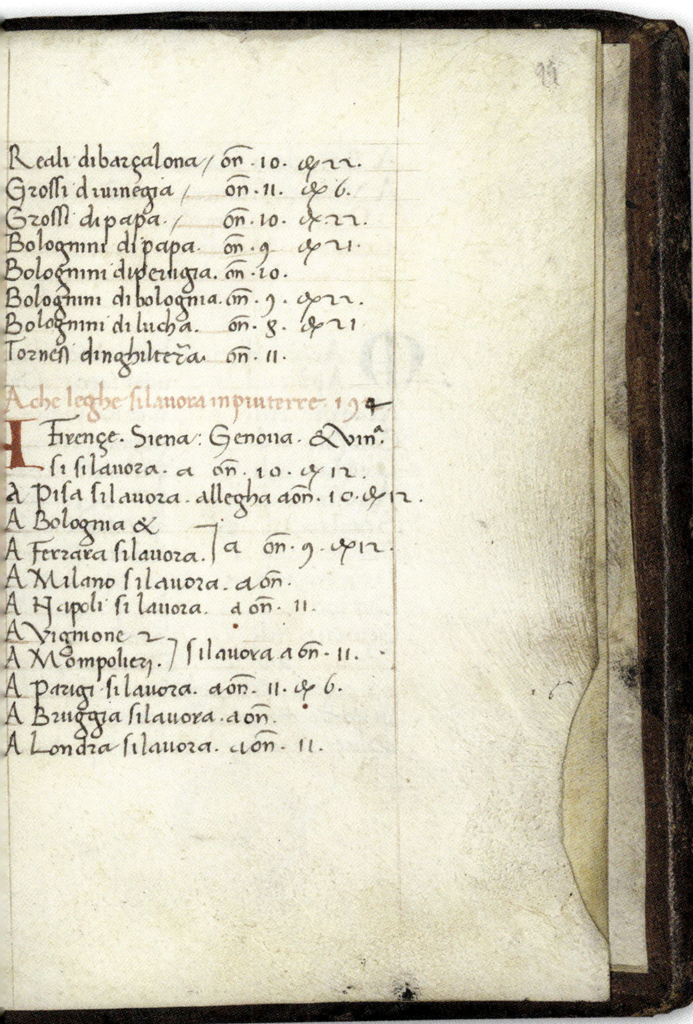

example, declined during the fifteenth century to around 50 percent gold (see Fig. 6.30).[28]

Despite the variation in standards, the silver and gold in the coins gave them value anywhere, so coins regularly circulated beyond the borders of the particular ruler who issued them. In the Low Countries, for example, gold tended to travel farther than billon, not surprisingly, and most finds of coins contain many pieces—sometimes a majority—that had been issued in a different country.[29]

In addition to the changing standards of fineness and weight, another complication was variation in the relative supply of silver and gold. If one of these became more abundant (for example, due to the opening of a productive new mine), it would decrease in value compared to the other. Thus, a gold coin worth 300 *deniers* might be revalued at 270 if the price of gold fell. However, when one type of coin was debased, other types of coins from the same government might very well remain unchanged, so a silver coin that was worth twelve *deniers* at one point in time might be worth sixteen *deniers* after a debasement of the black billon. Therefore, even if the standard for a particular coin was unchanged, its value relative to other coins might change unpredictably.

With so many different kinds of authorities producing coins, and with so many alterations in the standards of weight and fineness, using coins was far more complicated than it is with modern national currencies. A shopkeeper or artisan in a town like Utrecht or Cologne might encounter dozens of different kinds of coins issued in surrounding regions, with the precious-metal standards and relative values of coins in each region changing from time to time. Merchants, money changers, and tax collectors needed to have detailed knowledge of the relative values of many different kinds of coins, and surviving examples of merchants' handbooks are filled with information on different types of coins.

In the absence of any fixed standard for comparison, a merchant handbook, *Libro che tracta di marcantie et usanze di paesi* (Book Concerning the Trade and Customs of Various Places), known in multiple copies including one from around 1481, lists different coins and the fineness of the silver alloy in each (Fig. 2.9). In some cases, the anonymous author distinguishes between older and more recent issues, for example stating that old Bohemian groschen contained seven ounces plus six

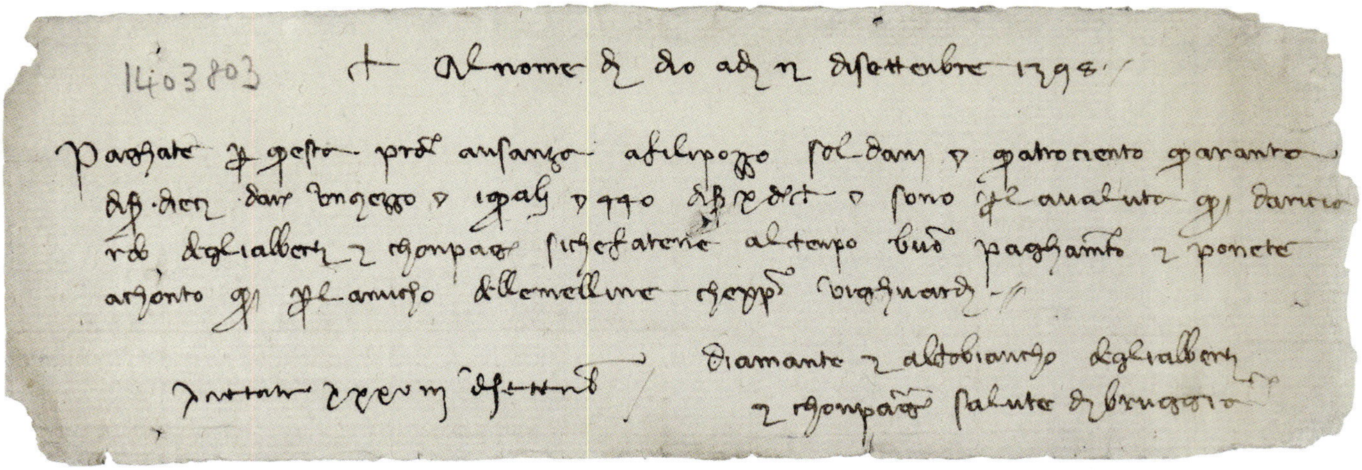

FIG. 2.10. Bill of exchange dated 2 September 1398, ordering payment of 4,620 *sous* of Barcelona for 440 *écus* of Flanders. Archivio di Stato di Prato, Prato, Datini b. 1145 / 1403803.

pennyweights of silver in each twelve ounces, whereas new Bohemian groschen contained only seven ounces of silver in each twelve ounces. Armed with this information, a merchant or money changer could weigh a batch of coins of the same type and then calculate their value in silver. Calculations for currency exchange were among the most common problems taught in medieval arithmetic textbooks.[30] This method, requiring literacy and mathematical skills, was invaluable for large-scale business transactions, but a shopkeeper dealing with black money more likely used a mental rule-of-thumb conversion for familiar types of coins, and perhaps rejected any that were beyond his or her practical experience.

People adapted creatively to the challenges posed by this complex, chaotic monetary environment. In periods when coins were scarce, rents and taxes were often paid in goods or labor. When coins were too low in value, large payments could be made with silver ingots, and, when low-value coins were scarce, credit could be used to aggregate small payments into larger sums. The development of banking and credit systems helped solve both these problems as well as the complexities of having so many local coinages changing frequently in value. By separating the storage and transmission of money from physical coins, the practical difficulties caused by reliance on silver and gold could be avoided. This not only solved problems, it also created new opportunities.

One of the more important financial inventions of the Middle Ages was a simple piece of paper, the bill of exchange. This was, at root, a note written by one banker or merchant to another, specifying that a certain amount of money had been received from someone, and that a corresponding amount in another currency should be paid out to another person in another location at a certain date.[31] In a bill of exchange from 1398, two Italian bankers in Bruges, who received 440 *écus* in money of Flanders, direct other Italian bankers in Barcelona to pay the recipient at a rate of ten and a half *sous* in money of Barcelona for each *écu*, meaning 4,620 *sous* in all (Fig. 2.10).[32] The actual coins to be used are unspecified, but the quantities are large enough that gold was most likely involved.

This device allowed large sums of money to be converted from one currency to another, and to be moved from one place to another, without the risk and inconvenience of moving the coins long distances. Transporting precious metal currency from Bruges to Barcelona would have taken longer and required the added expense of armed guards. The bill of exchange solved those problems, but it depended on the existence of a network of connected banks, a regular flow of information about exchange rates, and confidence that future obligations would be paid.

This system had further ramifications beyond its original purpose. By exchanging pieces of paper, merchants could settle transactions much larger than would have been feasible with pieces of metal, in effect expanding the money supply. At the same time, by moving money beyond the range of things that people could see and handle, complex new financial manipulations became feasible, such as arbitrage of exchange rates, enabling bankers to make money simply by transferring pieces of paper.[33] The bill of exchange, an adaptation to the extreme complexities of medieval coinage systems, was one of the harbingers of a new system of banks, credit, paper currency, and virtual money that exists only as numbers in accounts, the monetary characteristics of the modern era.

NOTES

1. Zelizer 1994.
2. Naismith 2018a, 4–5.
3. Grierson 1975, 100–11.
4. Allen 2012, 306–8; Stahl 2000, 369–406.
5. Allen 2012, 88–130.
6. There are some modern exceptions, such as the United States (two major mints), Russia (also two), and Germany (five). In Germany this is a survival from the time before 1871 when there were many separate German countries; the mints in the United States and Russia serve very large areas comparable to all of medieval Latin Europe.
7. Crusafont, Balaguer, and Grierson 2013, 296–400; Rössner 2018, 160.
8. Spufford 1988, 187, 193.
9. Spufford 1970, 74–76; cf. Yoon 2019.
10. Sargent and Velde 2002, 131–38.
11. Ibid., 52–53.
12. Yoon 2015.
13. Mann and Syson 1998.
14. For example, the retention of Henry II's name on the English coins of his sons, Richard I and John. See Kent 1978, 27.
15. Pollard 2001.
16. Scher 2000.
17. Galbraith 1975.
18. Sargent and Velde 2002, 5.
19. Spufford 1988, 243, 289.
20. Lafaurie 1951, 106, 112.
21. Phelps Brown and Hopkins 1955, 205; Baulant 1971, 482.
22. Rogers 1882, 33; Baulant 1968, 537. The loaf of bread would cost somewhat more, after the miller and baker each contributed labor and use of facilities to the product.
23. Duplessy 1988, 221.
24. Spufford 1988, 323–35.
25. Duplessy 1988, 212–13.
26. Spufford 1988, 40–56, 400. To be strictly accurate, there could be two denominations, because a half denarius was sometimes produced in small quantities along with the denarius, but this did not greatly increase the range of transactions to which coinage was suited.
27. Stahl 2000, 61.
28. Spufford 1970, 117–19.
29. Ibid., 58–63.
30. Van Egmond 2011.
31. de Roover 1944.
32. de Roover 1948, 56–57. The *écu* of Flanders and the *sou* of Barcelona were both money of account rather than physical coins, meaning that they were units in a system for keeping track of monetary value that was tied to a particular type of coin (the *gros* of Flanders and the *diner* of Barcelona, respectively) but allowed other coins to vary in value.
33. Ibid., 64–67.

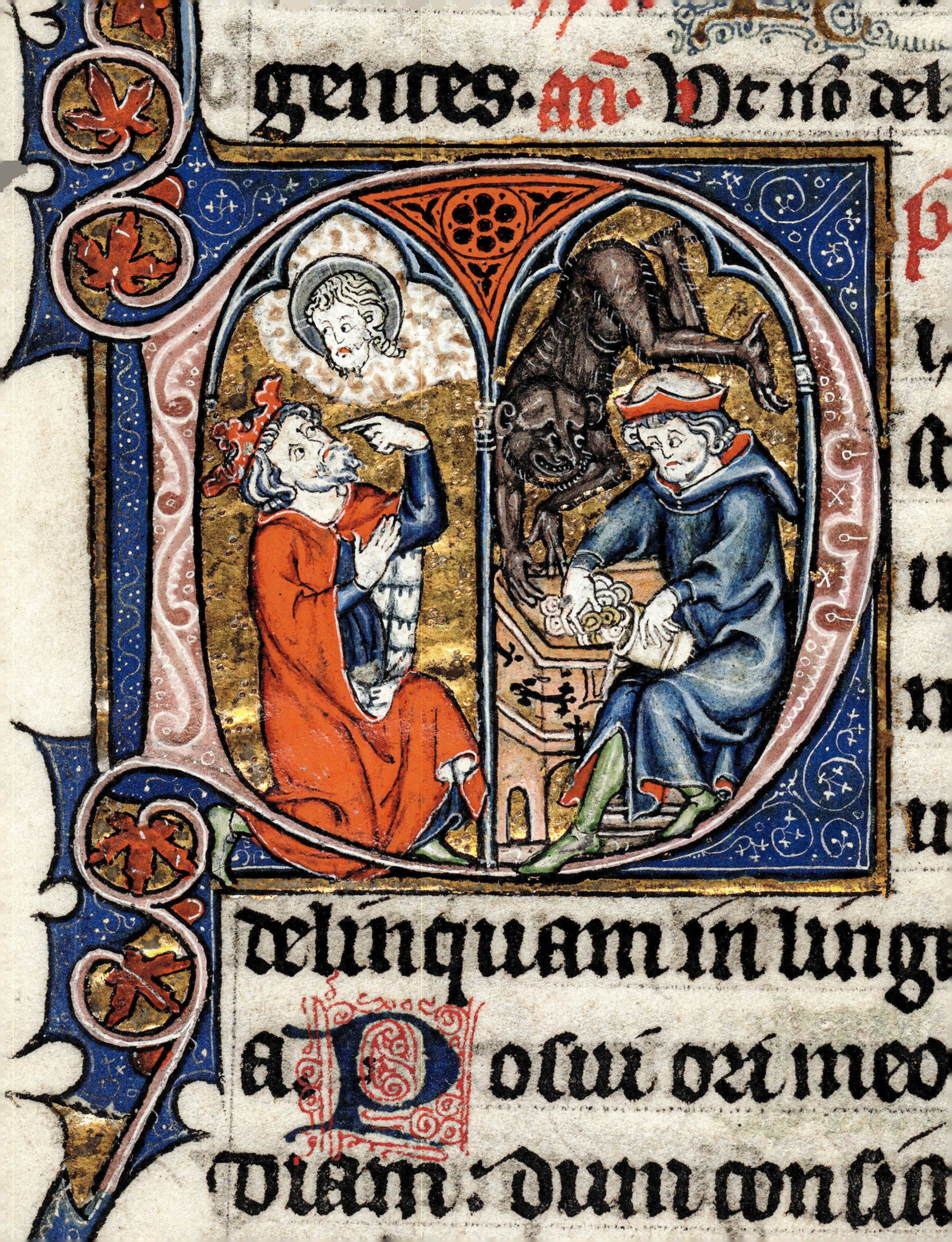
gentes. an̄. Ut nō del
delinquam in lingu
a. Posui ori meo
diam: dum consi

3

Your Money or Your Eternal Life?

DIANE WOLFTHAL

A Changed World

David and an Avaricious Man, in an initial *D* from a breviary, France, Paris, 1285–97. The Morgan Library & Museum, New York, MS M.1042, fol. 29v. (Detail of Fig. 3.6.)

THE RISE OF THE MONETARY ECONOMY transformed every aspect of European society, including its values and culture.[1] From the late thirteenth to the early sixteenth century, western Europe, especially its major urban centers, was dramatically altered by the widespread use of money. A new mercantile class emerged that included bankers, money changers, pawnbrokers, and international traders. New financial practices developed, such as double-entry bookkeeping, insurance on shipping cargo, and the use of letters of credit and bills of exchange (see Fig. 2.10).[2] Nicholas Oresme's *De moneta* (On Money), dated 1356–60, inaugurated a new but increasingly popular genre, the monetary treatise.[3] The needs of the growing merchant class also transformed urban spaces. Financial centers were established, such as the Beurse in Bruges, where Italian merchants lived and traded.[4] New commercial networks developed that operated across vast areas, both within Europe (the Medici banks and the Hanseatic League) and beyond. As feudalism gave way to capitalism, vernacular writers like Geoffrey Chaucer, Giovanni Boccaccio, and François Villon revealed the richness and complexity of thinking about the monetary economy.[5] The sound of money even shaped musical pieces. In fourteenth-century Florence, a madrigal by Lorenzo Masini made money audible by imitating the sound of clinking coins, and by suggesting the accumulation of wealth through the rapidity of its notes.[6] Money flooded Europe, and, although some wished to separate the sacred from the profane, by the fourteenth and fifteenth centuries huge numbers of souvenirs were sold at pilgrimage sites and church fairs became major marketplaces.[7] Money even crossed the boundary between this world and the next when it was buried in tombs.[8]

But it was not simply money and its material culture that permeated medieval society: mercantile metaphors did, too. The merchant banker Cosimo de' Medici (d. 1464) expressed religious concepts in economic terms when he complained that he could never spend as much to honor God as he found himself in God's accounting books as a debtor.[9] A French song about the Last Judgment, composed around 1500, ends each stanza with the phrase "to give an account and settle the balance," meaning to confess one's sins and repent.[10] Similarly, the Breton Franciscan preacher Olivier Maillard (ca. 1430–1502) employed commercial concepts to make his theological ideas more accessible. He warned, for example, "The inheritance we purchase is paradise; the seller, that is God the Creator, places on us conditions, which are his commandments: if we leave out one, the contract is nul."[11] The language of economic transactions became so ubiquitous that it even colored the letters of the sixteenth-century Venetian courtesan Veronica Franco. In response to accusations of "cupidity," she responded, "I plan to repay with my loyalty the debt of affection I owe you, exactly as if I were to return to you a sum of gold which you had lent me, by giving you an equal sum of silver or some other kind of money."[12]

Poverty was widespread in the Middle Ages, but a minority accumulated significant wealth. Among the most prosperous were the nobility, wealthy merchants, and the Church. But most people, even the poor, unless living in very remote areas, were directly involved in the monetary economy, and they learned of the debates about the value of money by hearing the sermons of mendicant friars and seeing the images in churches that condemned greed. The rise of the monetary economy sparked complex ethical discussions, which were rooted in the apparent contradiction between the Christian ideals of poverty and charity, on the one hand, and the pervasive role of money and the desire to accumulate wealth, on the other.[13] Intense debates raged about the proper ways to earn and spend money. The thirteenth-century philosopher and theologian St. Thomas Aquinas expressed the dominant view when he wrote that trade "is justly deserving of blame, because, considered in itself, it satisfies the greed for gain, which knows no limit and tends to infinity."[14] As late as the early sixteenth century, Martin Luther agreed, arguing that "trade can be nothing but robbing and stealing the property of others."[15]

Although the Church recognized the positive good that wealth could contribute to society, and gradually accommodated its teachings to capitalism, fourteenth- and fifteenth-century merchant bankers were plagued by anxiety about some of their business practices. Tommaso Portinari (1428–1501), a Medici banker based in Bruges, voiced his discomfort with the profits that he made on bills of exchange, which permitted merchants to send money long distances where it was converted to local currency. Bankers charged a fee, presumably for the transfer and exchange of the currency, but in reality as interest on a loan. Since many considered bills of exchange to be usurious, Portinari downplayed his dealings in this questionable practice when he wrote, "The foundation of our business is in merchandise which absorbs most of our capital so that there is little left for dealings in exchange. . . . And dealing in commodities is certainly more honorable than dealing in bills of exchange."[16]

Medieval thinkers invited merchants to examine the fairness and communal benefit of even small everyday transactions. Following St. Paul (1 Timothy 6:10), Aquinas argued that greed was the root of all evil. He reasoned, "by riches man acquires the means of committing any sin whatever."[17] So common was this belief that it should not surprise us that of the approximately twenty punishments that Dante explored in his early fourteenth-century vision of hell, ten concern an excessive desire for riches.[18] Medieval Christians understood the appeal of money, but also feared its dangers: material goods could enslave you, and avarice could lead to an empty, sterile life in this world and eternal damnation in the next.

The medieval Church condemned usury, which was initially defined as charging any interest on a loan.[19] The Third Lateran Council of 1179 reminded Christians that the Bible outlawed usury, and proclaimed that "notorious usurers" should be denied both the Eucharist (the ritual consumption of the sacred host at Mass in commemoration of Christ's death) and a church burial until they had returned the interest that they had charged their borrowers. It even forbade churches from accepting donations from usurers. Slowly, however, the Church accommodated capitalism, while still condemning excessive rates on loans. Artists and patrons grappled with issues of money and morality, and late medieval images reflected these economic debates. At least in part to expiate for the sin of usury, Enrico Scrovegni commissioned Padua's Arena Chapel with frescoes by Giotto, Cosimo de' Medici funded frescoes in San Marco in Florence, and Tommaso Portinari (the Medici banker mentioned above) donated Hugo van der Goes's Portinari Altarpiece to the church hospital of Florence's Santa Maria Nuova.[20] Medieval Christians took seriously the biblical assertion that "You cannot serve God and mammon" (Matthew 6:24). This chapter examines the choice that many Christians faced, including members of the burgeoning middle class: should they accumulate wealth or save their souls?

Hieronymus Bosch's *Death and the Miser* presents a clear choice between heavenly salvation and eternal damnation (Fig. 3.1).[21] As Death, a ghastly, shrouded skeleton, enters a bedchamber, a dying man must decide whether to accept the sack of money offered by a demon or to follow the counsel of the angel who urges him to fix his gaze on a crucifix that appears in the window. At the foot of the bed, a man, perhaps the same one in happier days, fingers a rosary while tossing coins into a pot held by a rat-faced demon. Two more demons slither under the chest, while a third, in the foreground,

FIG. 3.1. Hieronymus Bosch, *Death and the Miser*, The Netherlands, 's-Hertogenbosch, ca. 1485–90. National Gallery of Art, Washington, DC, 1952.5.33.

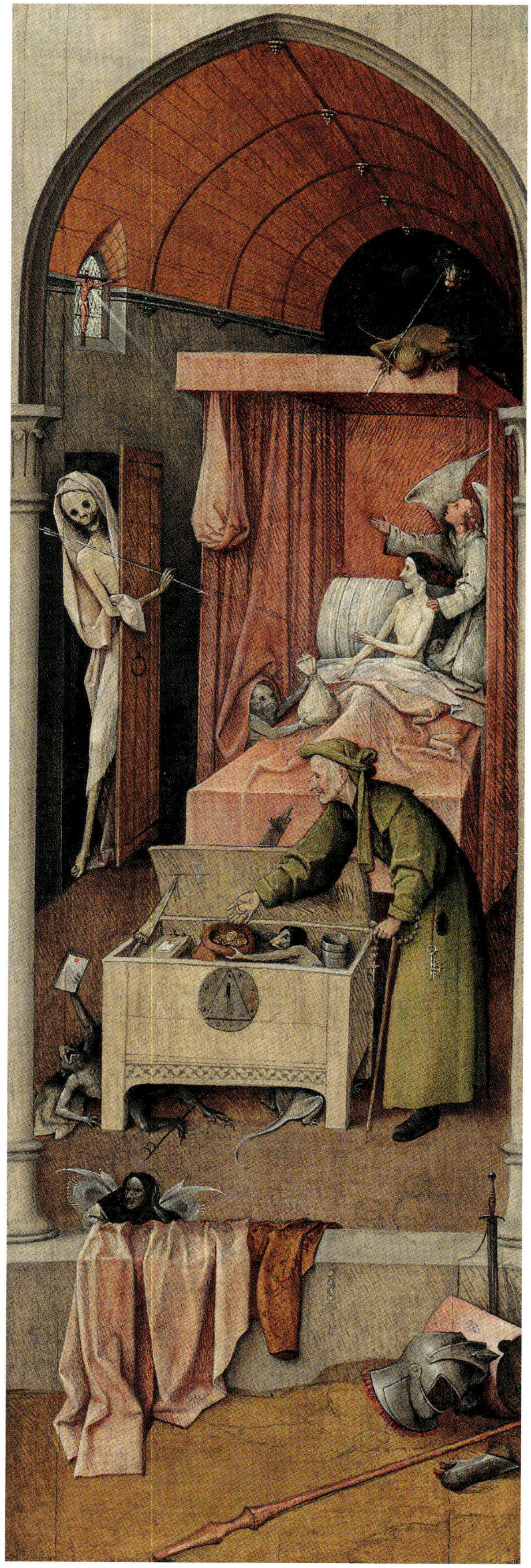

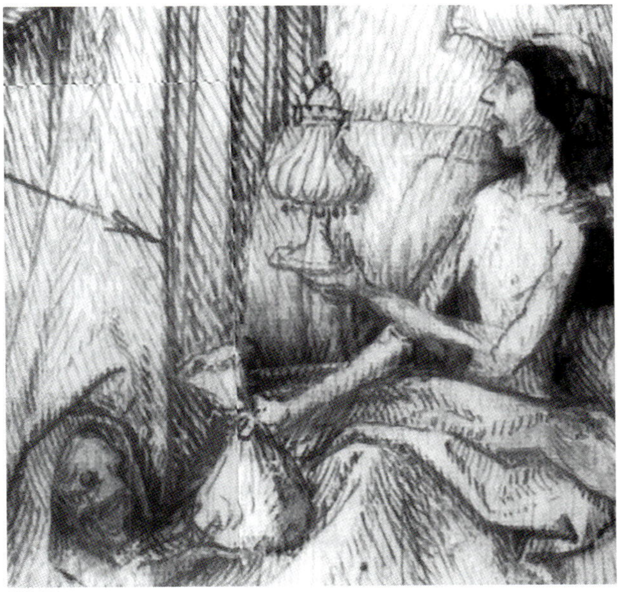

FIG. 3.2. Detail of Fig. 3.1: infrared reflectogram.

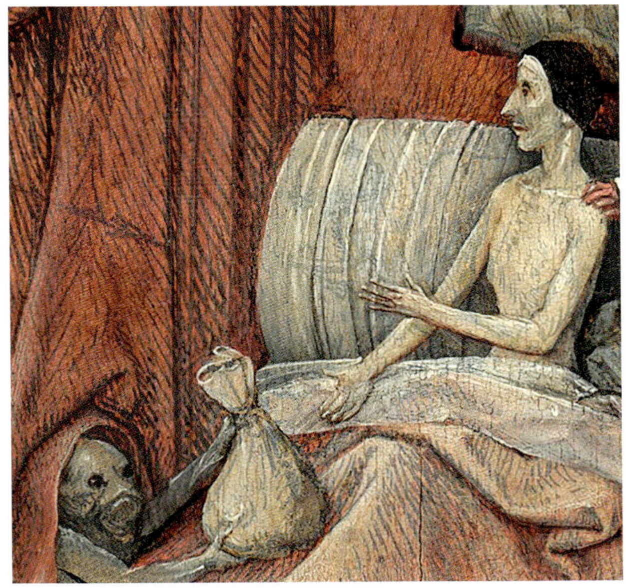

FIG. 3.3. Detail of Fig. 3.1.

squatting near items that have been cast aside, seems to imply that armor, clothing, and weapons are ultimately worthless. Will the dying man choose money and condemn his soul to hell or will he embrace Christ so that his soul ascends to heaven? Bosch keeps us in suspense. The original composition, revealed by the underdrawing (Fig. 3.2), shows the dying man accepting the moneybag from the devil while holding a costly vessel. Evidently, Bosch reconsidered this approach and instead depicted a moment of indecision, perhaps in order to prompt viewers to think about the choices they make in their own lives.

Bosch's panel is suffused with money and its paraphernalia. The demon at the deathbed offers the man a closed sack (Fig. 3.3). Its contents, however, are revealed through an artistic convention: coins press against the bulging bag, creating circular outlines.[22] At the foot of the miser's bed is a strongbox with a large lock. Lurking inside, a demon holds a pot of gold coins, into which a man tosses a couple more. A document sealed by red wax is stored inside the chest and another is held aloft by a nearby demon. These documents—perhaps mortgages, promissory notes, letters of credit, or bills of exchange—no doubt concern monetary matters.

Bosch's painting draws on the text and imagery of the *Ars moriendi* (Art of Dying), which was probably written by a Dominican mendicant in the mid-fifteenth century. This extremely popular book survives in at least 300 manuscripts and well over 100 printed editions dating before 1500.[23] Composed in Latin and translated into numerous vernacular languages, the *Ars moriendi* advises Christians how to resist temptation on their deathbeds so that their souls may enter heaven. As demons tempt a dying man to sin and angels inspire him to virtue, readers learn the path they must choose in order to attain salvation.

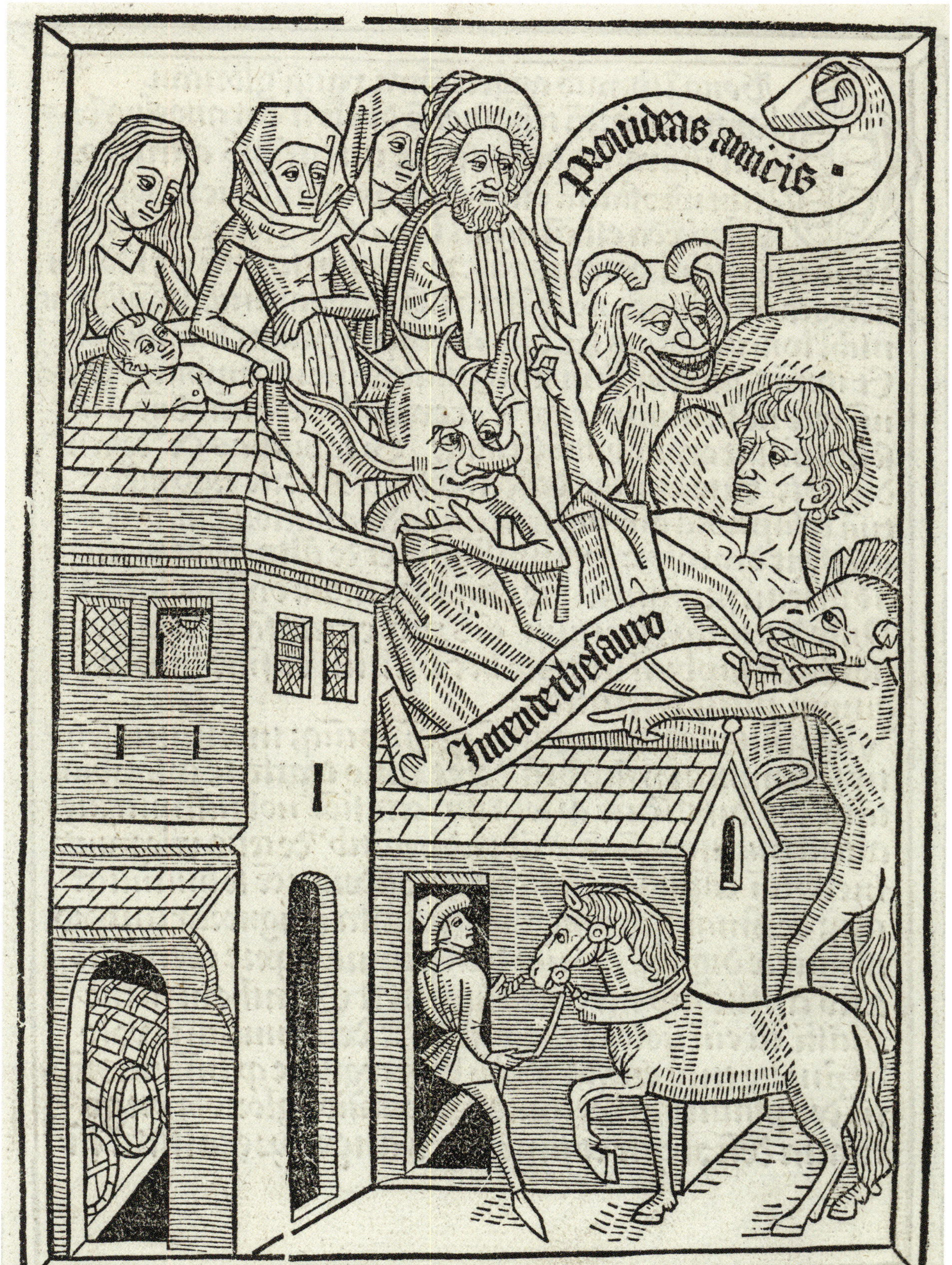
prouideas amicis
Intende thesauro

FIG. 3.4. *Temptation to Avarice*, from *Ars moriendi* (Art of Dying), Germany, Augsburg (?), ca. 1470. The Morgan Library & Museum, New York, PML 273, fol. 10v (det.).

One edition of the text, a block book printed probably in Augsburg around 1470, includes five temptations: lack of faith, despair, impatience, pride, and avarice. A woodcut on the theme of avarice shows hideous demons tempting the dying man in order to distract him from thoughts of heaven (Fig. 3.4). One demon, whose speech scroll, inscribed in Latin, states, "Pay attention to your treasure" (*Intende thesauro*), points emphatically to the man's fine house, the garment displayed in its window, the well-stocked wine cellar, and the elegant groom and steed. Two other demons, whose speech scroll reads, "Provide for your loved ones" (*Provideas amicis*), gesture towards a group of figures, who gaze tenderly at the deceased. The accompanying text advises:

> . . . now you will leave behind all the temporal goods which you accumulated through the greatest efforts and labors; you will leave behind also your wife, children, relatives, dearest friends, and all desirable things of this world . . . be extremely careful lest friends, wife, children, wealth, and other temporal things are remembered by anyone dying. . .[24]

The influential contemporary Franciscan preacher Bernardino of Siena concurred, characterizing as sinful a dying man's attachment to his family.[25] But this idea goes back to Luke 14:26, "If any man come to me, and hate not his father, and mother, and wife, and children, and brethren, and sisters, and his own life also, he cannot be my disciple." In short, being tied to earthly things, even to friends and family, could be deemed avaricious and a danger to one's soul.

The mid-thirteenth-century Dominican William Peraldus of Lyon cautioned that demons, approaching the dying, would play on feelings of parental love, and, even when the dying were no longer interested in riches for themselves, they might want to retain them for their children. Usurers who left their profits to their heirs instead of making restitution to their borrowers risked damnation.[26] Indeed, in the following woodcut, which shows the antidote to avarice, that is, detachment from worldly things, an angel shields the loved ones from the dying man's gaze. The *Ars moriendi* presents a choice: embrace things of this earth (your possessions and your loved ones) or the salvation of your soul.

A similar alternative appears in Ludolf of Saxony's extremely influential *Vita Christi* (Life of Christ), which consists of a biography of Christ interwoven with commentary from Church Fathers (revered theologians), excerpts from ancient Roman authors, moral teachings, meditations, and prayers. Written in 1374 and translated from Latin into numerous vernacular languages, most versions lack images.[27] A French translation by the Franciscan Guillaume le Menand, however, is profusely illustrated.[28] Illuminated in Bruges by the Master of Edward IV and an assistant around 1487, it was made for Count Johann II of Oettingen, a Burgundian courtier and bibliophile.[29]

The manuscript includes a parable related in Matthew 19:16–24. Christ advises a wealthy young man who wants to enter heaven to sell his possessions to aid the poor. When he declines, Jesus famously observes, "It is easier for a camel to pass through the eye of a needle than for a rich man to enter the kingdom of heaven." The accompanying illumination shows Christ and the apostles standing at the left beside the sumptuously dressed youth whose purse is prominently displayed (Fig. 3.5). Unsure whether to save his money or his soul,

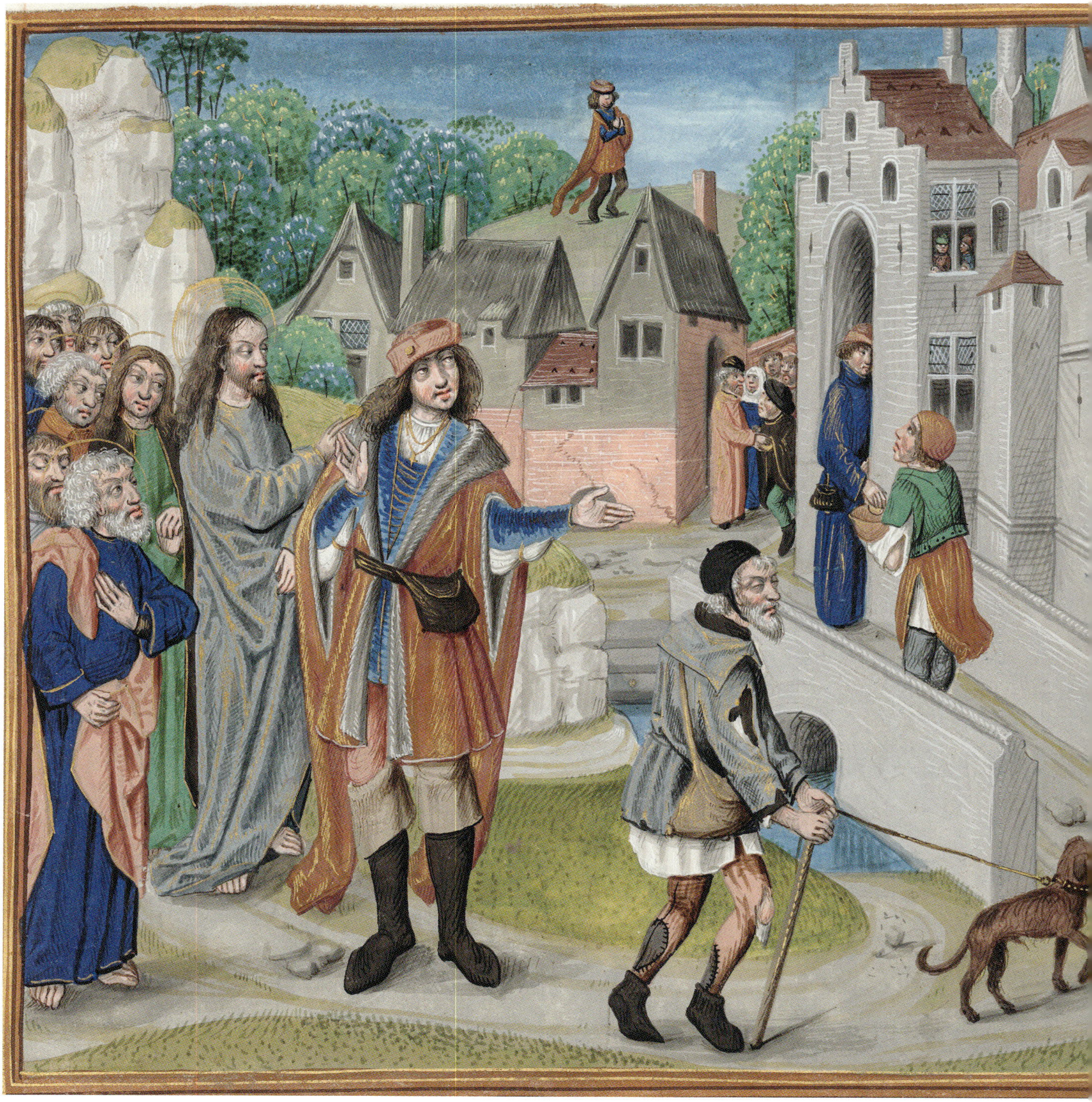

FIG. 3.5. Master of Edward IV and assistant, *Christ and the Parable of the Rich Young Man*, from Ludolf of Saxony, *Vita Christi* (Life of Christ), trans. Guillaume le Menand, Belgium, Bruges, ca. 1487–90. The Morgan Library & Museum, New York, MS M.894, fol. 69v (det.).

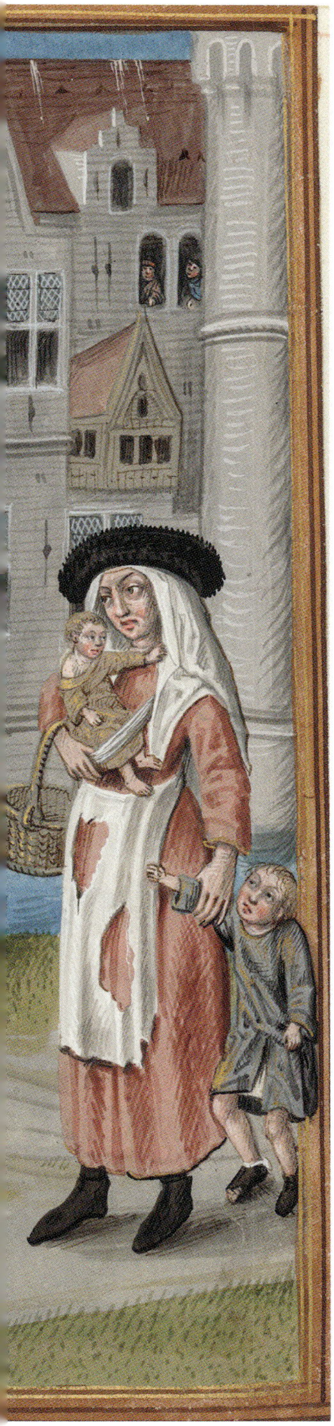

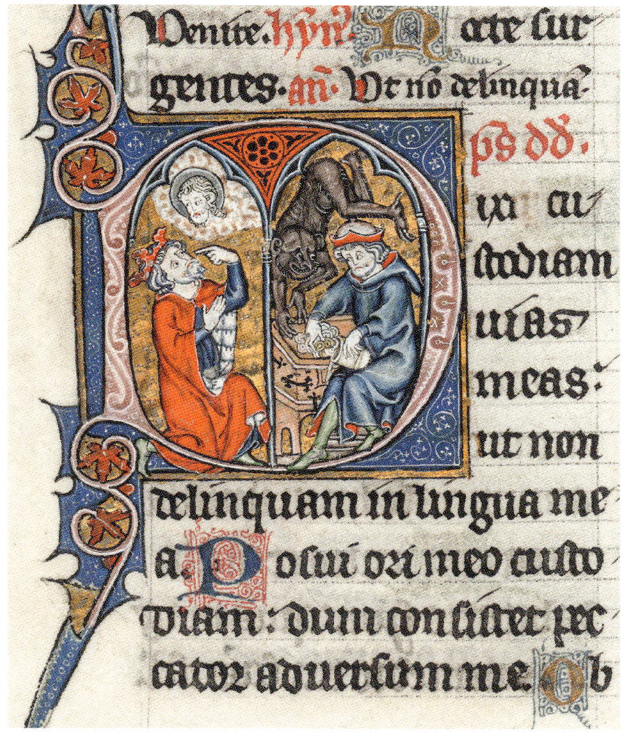

FIG. 3.6. ***David and an Avaricious Man*, in an initial *D* from a breviary, France, Paris, 1285–97. The Morgan Library & Museum, New York, MS M.1042, fol. 29v (det.).**

the young man gestures towards those poor who traditionally elicited the most sympathy: a blind man in torn and patched clothes who is guided by a cane and dog, and a mother in a ragged apron with a baby and toddler in tow. The outcome is depicted in the background: the youth walks away, unwilling to share his wealth. In the town, however, two men in contemporaneous dress model charitable behavior: standing at their doorways they dispense bread to the needy. The illumination presents a clear choice: practice charity and gain salvation or keep your wealth and risk damnation.

A Parisian breviary from 1285–97 presents a similar choice: follow God or the devil (Fig. 3.6). Breviaries contain the Divine Office—prayers recited by priests and other religious, including all 150 psalms, which were prayed over the course of a week. In this breviary, the letter *D* occurs at the start of Psalm 38, "I said [*Dixi*]: I will take heed to my ways that I sin not with my tongue." Gazing upwards, King David, who was believed to have authored the Psalms, points to his mouth as he kneels before God who looks down from a cloud above. Wearing a crown and fur-lined robe, David

FIG. 3.7. ***Avarice*** **and** ***Creation of Eve*****;** ***Charity*** **and** ***Mowing Hay in June*****, from a book of hours, France, Rouen, ca. 1470. The Morgan Library & Museum, New York, MS M.32, fols. 8v–9r.**

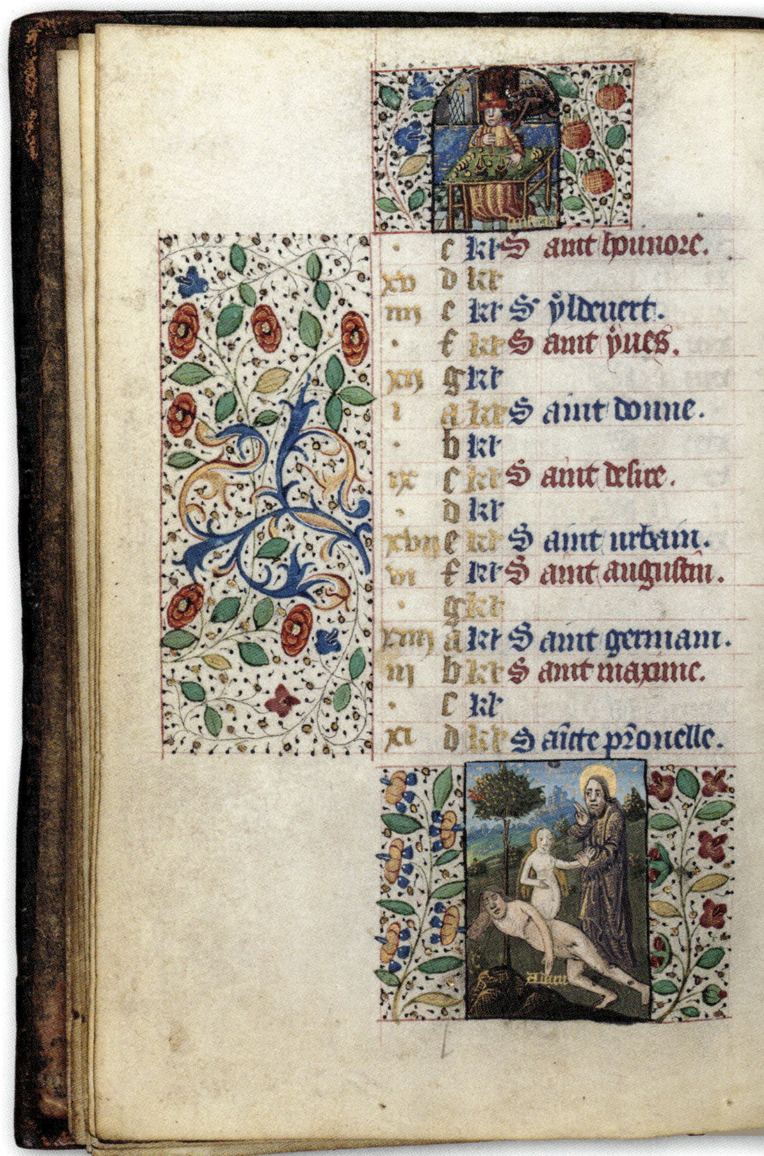

is shown on God's right side, which was traditionally associated with virtue. Facing him, on God's left side, which was often linked to sin (in Latin, the word for left is "sinister"), is an avaricious man who stuffs coins from an open chest into a bag to the delight of a demon who swoops down to grab some.[30] Even in this tiny initial, the artist has differentiated the more valuable gold coins from the silver ones. Phrases within the psalm, such as "all things are vanity" or "he storeth up," almost certainly inspired the idea of the chest full of coins. A slender column separates the virtuous David from the sinful miser, but a luxurious tooled gold ground links them, sparkling in the light and offering visual delight, much like the glittering metal of actual coins.

Facing folios in a book of hours produced in Rouen around 1470 present a similar choice. Books of hours, which grew out of a desire to sanctify lay time, were the most popular type of book produced from the fourteenth through the mid-sixteenth century.[31] They generally begin with a calendar and then a series of prayers—always including those dedicated to the Virgin—that are designed to be recited at the eight canonical hours of the day. At the top of a calendar page, as part of a cycle of virtues and vices not normally found in calendars of this type, "Avarice" (identified by an inscription) is personified as a man using a balance to establish the monetary value of the gold coins scattered on his table (Fig. 3.7). His activity is marked as evil by the bug-eyed, airborne demon who points to the coins. On the facing page, a woman with long blonde hair labeled Charity (*caritesce*) generously pours her coins from a box. Her gesture evokes the words of the twelfth-century theologian Alain de Lille who describes generosity as "the virtue which takes

OVERLEAF:
FIG. 3.8. Master of the First Prayer Book of Maximilian, *Adoration of the Magi*; *Shower of Coins*, from the Hastings Hours, Belgium, Ghent or Bruges, ca. 1475–83. The British Library, London, Add. MS 54782, fols. 42v–43r.

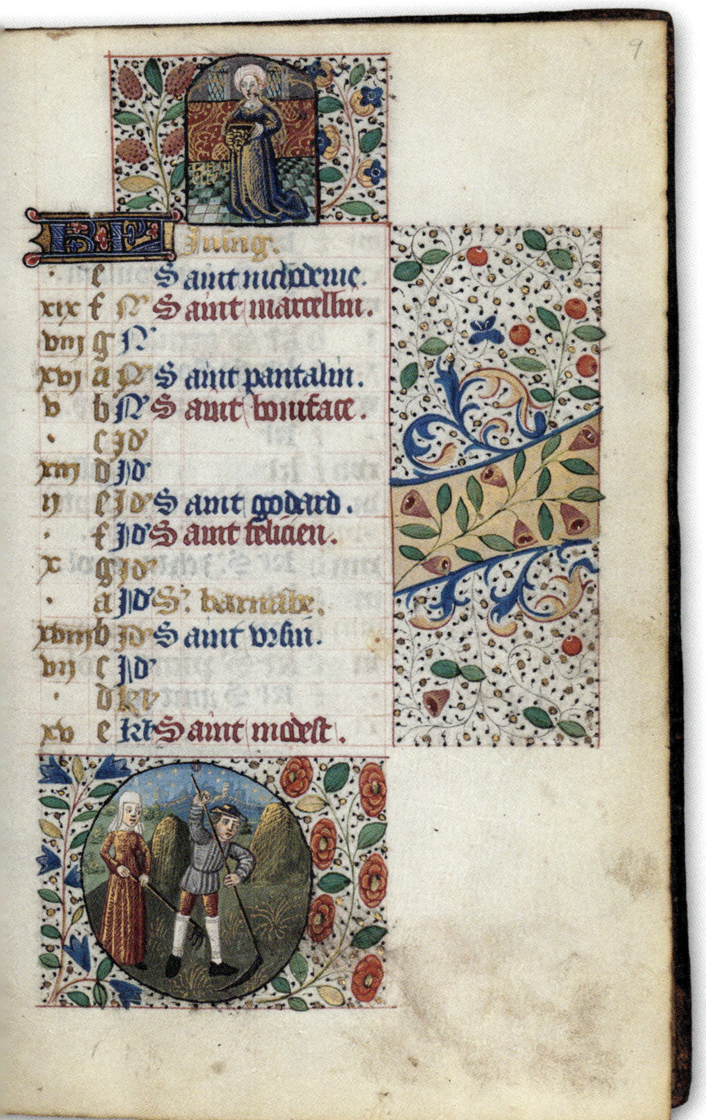

delight in scattering gifts and pouring out wealth and spreading abroad a mass of riches."[32]

Below Avarice is a scene of the Creation of Eve, part of yet another unusual cycle in this calendar. Below Charity are traditional labors for June: mowing and raking hay. The pairing of Avarice and the Creation of Eve is not coincidental. Both Franciscan and Dominican theologians championed the idea, first advanced by the Greek philosopher Aristotle, that money was sterile since it could not reproduce naturally like plants or animals.[33] They condemned usurers and investors who made money multiply "against nature" and then hoarded their earnings rather than recirculating them in the Christian community. In the thirteenth century, Thomas Aquinas and Peter Olivi defined "fruitful" uses of money: meeting the needs of one's family, the poor, and the Christian community.[34] Fourteenth- and fifteenth-century popular mendicant preachers, most notably Bernardino of Siena, translated this tradition into the vernacular, distinguishing for the laity fruitful forms of mercantile activities from sterile ones.[35] Here the image of God creating Eve to provide a partner for Adam indicates that humans will reproduce naturally as opposed to coins. Two other images in the calendar also show money in a negative light. The first depicts Christ driving the money changers from the Temple to separate the sacred and profane (fol. 12r); the other shows Judas, with a purse around his neck, an allusion to his betrayal of Christ (fol. 12v).

Several late fifteenth- and early sixteenth-century illuminations have a four-sided border portraying one or two men tossing coins from on high, while figures below collect them (Figs. 3.8–3.9). The meaning of this marginal composition varies with its context, since

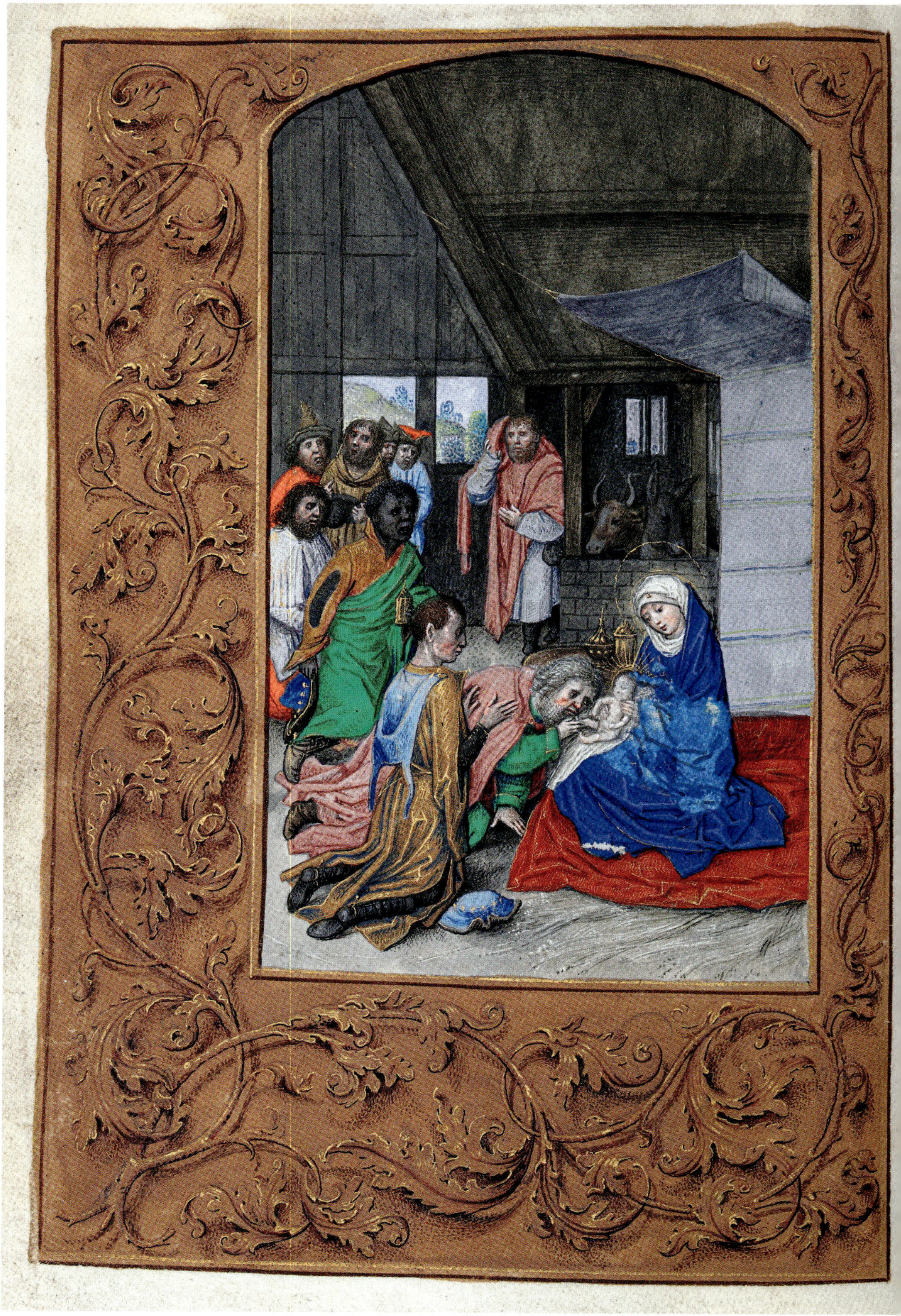

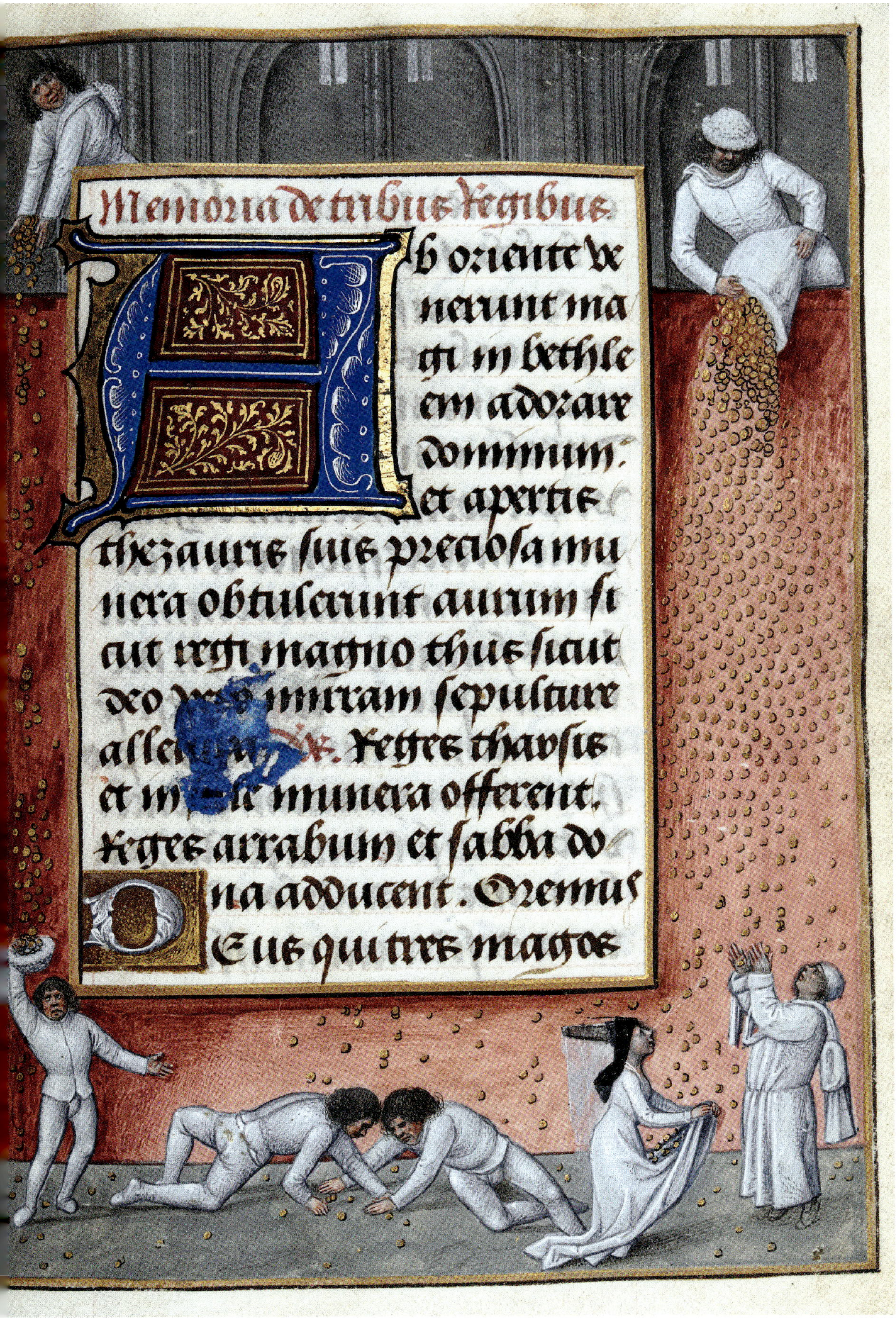
Memoria de tribus Regibus
Ab oriente ve
nerunt ma
gi in bethle
em adorare
dominum.
Et apertis
thezauris suis preciosa mu
nera obtulerunt aurum si
cut regi magno thus sicut
deo mirram sepulture
alle ℣. Reges tharsis
et in e munera offerent.
Reges arrabum et sabba do
na adducent. Oremus
Deus qui tres magos

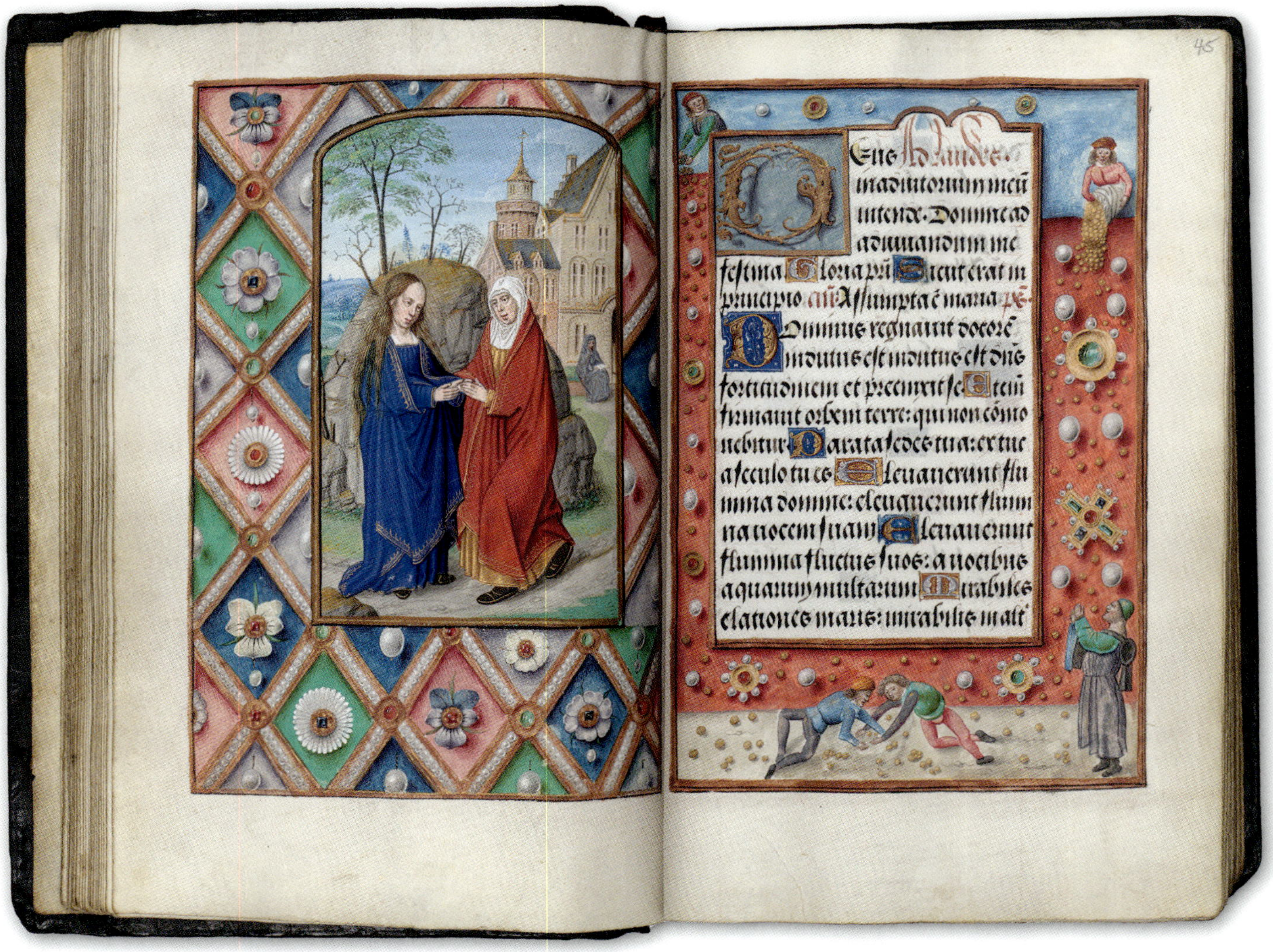

FIG. 3.9. Master of Sir George Talbot, *Visitation*; *Shower of Coins*, from a book of hours, Belgium, Bruges, ca. 1500. The Morgan Library & Museum, New York, MS M.390, fols. 44v–45r.

it was employed to surround a broad range of texts, it faced a variety of pictorial subjects, and its coins were sometimes transformed into jewels, flowers, or manna.[36] The earliest example, produced between 1475 and 1483 in Ghent or Bruges, appears in the Hastings Hours where, set before a cathedral, it surrounds the text of a suffrage (prayer) to the Magi and faces a full-page miniature of the Adoration of the Magi (Fig. 3.8). The text accompanying this marginal illumination relates that the Magi came from the East to worship the Lord and brought precious gifts fit for a king, including gold. The word *aurum* (gold), which appears on the ninth line, may have inspired the depiction of a shower of golden coins in the border. But what is the meaning of this motif? Thomas Kren reminds us that the borders in this manuscript, which also include jousting and wild men, "add a worldly character."[37] Some scholars argue that just as the Magi present the

Christ Child with golden gifts, so the marginal scene represents munificence.[38] According to this theory, the theme of donation links the Adoration of the Magi to the prayer and border on the facing page.[39] Indeed, the inscription "largesse" appears on a similar marginal composition in a later book of hours, illuminated circa 1500 by the Flemish Master of the Prayer Books.[40] Largesse, or generosity, was believed to be one of the most important virtues of a just ruler.[41]

But did the shower of coins in the Hastings Hours refer to largesse? Pamela Tudor-Craig convincingly argues that a closer look reveals that the message of the marginal composition "is not so encouraging."[42] Largesse and its synonym liberality are usually represented either by an allegorical female figure or a ruler who pours coins from a vessel or distributes them by hand.[43] In a mid-twelfth-century manuscript, now destroyed, of the *Hortus deliciarum* (Garden of Delights) by the Alsatian nun Herrad of Landsberg, Liberality, who has seized the wealth amassed by Avarice, dispenses it to the poor, who are visualized as blind, lame, or otherwise needy (Fig. 3.10).[44] Recipients wait their turn, approaching Liberality in an orderly line, with one hand outstretched. Similarly, in an illumination illustrating largesse in a mid-fourteenth-century manual for princes (guide to

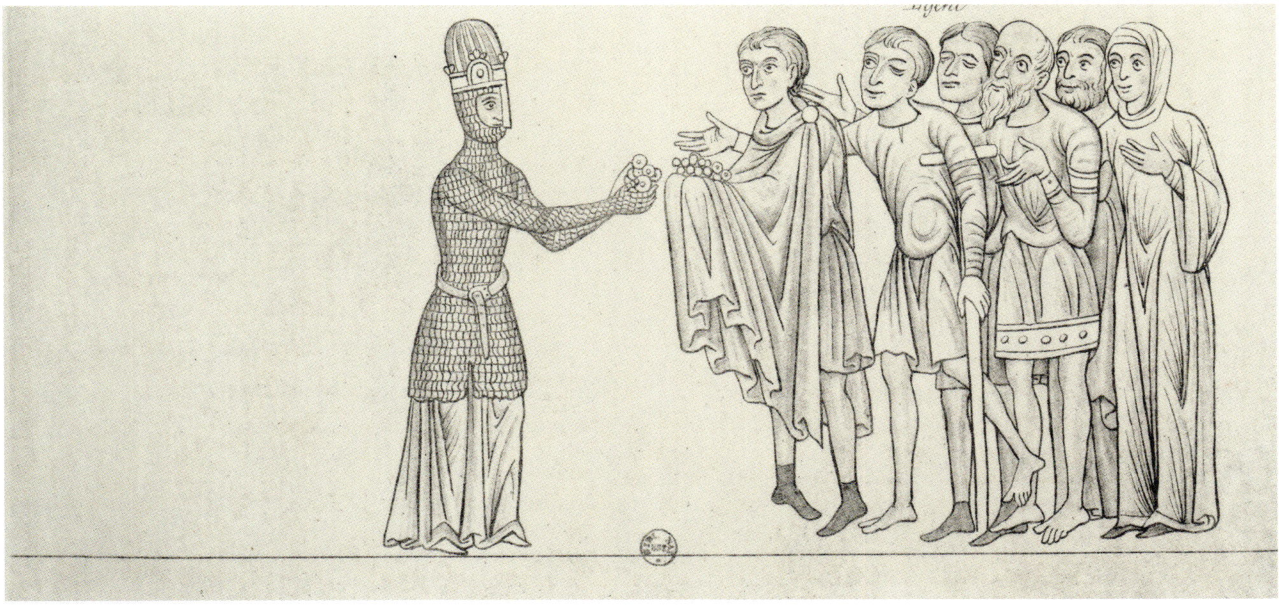

FIG. 3.10. *Liberality Distributes the Booty to the Poor*, based on the *Hortus deliciarum* (Garden of Delights) codex of Abbess Herrad of Landsberg (ca. 1130–95), destroyed by fire in Strasbourg in 1870.

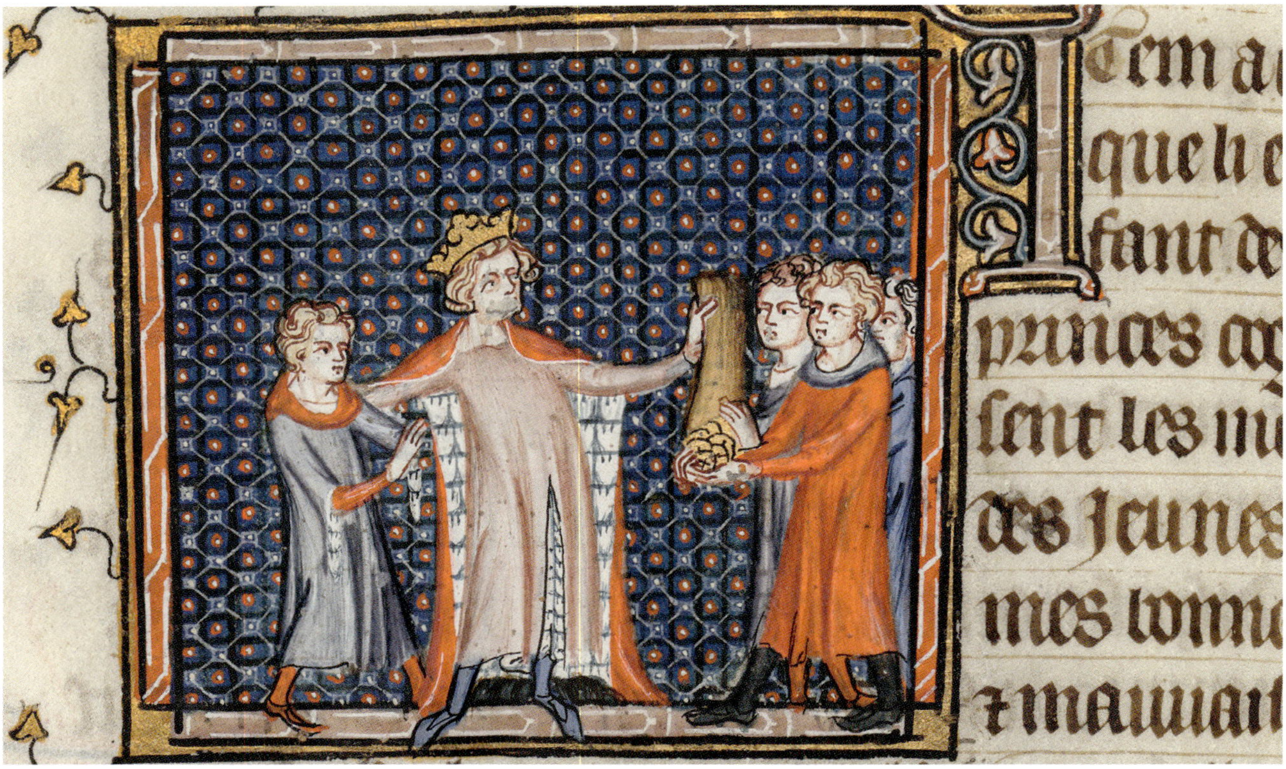

behavior), the *Avis aus roys*, a king pours coins into the hands of his beneficiary (Fig. 3.11). Again, all the poses and gestures are restrained and all the figures decorously dressed.[45]

By contrast, in the Hastings miniature those spilling the coins are neither allegorical figures nor rulers, and their actions have been termed "openhanded to the point of recklessness."[46] In addition, the recipients of the money are neither needy nor restrained in posture and gesture. The unsteady figure on the left of the lower border is tipsy as he holds his hat aloft to maximize his accumulation of coins. The two men on the ground scramble greedily to snatch them up. All three men wear tight-fitting revealing clothes, which suggest their baseness and sexuality.[47] The portly man on the right reaches eagerly for the coins, his head and hands raised as he stands on tiptoes. And a young woman indecorously lifts her skirt to catch the falling money. These figures, elegantly dressed in the latest fashion, are greedy and grasping, willing to sacrifice their dignity in order to gain money.

Furthermore, the illumination forms a striking contrast to the Adoration on the facing folio. Although some contemporary images of Virgins adored by the Magi wear gold-trimmed robes and crowns or are enthroned before a cloth of honor, here a Madonna of Humility sits on a cloth spread on the straw-strewn ground, wearing a simple robe and plain headcloth.[48] This contrasts with the fashionable dress of the marginal figures who collect the coins. Moreover, the quiet, peaceful devotion of the Adoration scene differs radically from the lively worldly activity on the facing folio. Once again, the viewer is presented with a clear choice: to adore the Madonna and Child and enter a world of calm devotion, or to follow the avaricious figures in their frantic accumulation of gold coins.

The juxtaposition of these two images also contrasts the sterility of metal coins with the fertility

FIG. 3.11. ***Liberality*, from *Avis aus roys* (Advice to Kings), France, Paris, ca. 1347–50. The Morgan Library & Museum, New York, MS M.456, fol. 70v (det.).**

of the Virgin.[49] And the shower of golden coins might evoke another idea, common at the time, that shiny metal coins are incredibly seductive. Petrarch, in his popular dialogue *De remediis utriusque fortunae* (Remedies for Fortune Fair and Foul), completed in 1360, describes the attractiveness of glittering coins and links it to the danger that they pose to the soul: "For the shape of money is noxious, its glitter poisonous and destructive. Like a golden serpent it delights with shiny scales, pleases the eye and strikes the soul."[50] These words carried great resonance in late medieval northern Europe.

The opening of the Hastings Hours presents a contrast between the greedy figures grasping golden coins and the quiet sacredness of the humble Virgin. In this way it joins the other images discussed in this chapter, which presented medieval Christians with a clear set of choices: God or the devil, fertile womb or sterile coins, charity or avarice, eternal life in heaven or worldly wealth.

NOTES

1. The title for this chapter is adapted from Le Goff 1988.
2. de Roover 1948; Spufford 2002b; Murray 2005.
3. Oresme 1956.
4. Jacobi 2019.
5. Goddard 2014; Villon 2013, 63; Bertolet and Epstein 2018.
6. Long 2016, 97–102.
7. Hayes 1999, 21–25; Travaini 2015, 218–20.
8. Travaini 2004; Travaini 2015, 210–15.
9. Macfarland 1999, 137; Machiavelli 1988, 283.
10. Loewen 2021, 1104–9.
11. Ibid., 1110.
12. Ray 1997, 307, especially n. 22.
13. Vitullo 2019.
14. Aquinas, *Summa Theologiae* II, ii, q. 77, a. 4.
15. Van Cleve 1991, 132.
16. de Roover 1948, 90; Grunzweig 1931, part 1, 131.
17. Aquinas, *Summa Theologiae* I, ii, q. 84, a. 1.
18. Armour 1994, 14.
19. Nelson 1969, especially pp. 3–4.
20. Derbes and Sandona 2008; Wolfthal 2007; Kent 2000.
21. For this work, see Hand and Wolff 1986, 16–22; Lammertse 2016.
22. For this motif, see Metropolitan Museum of Art, New York, 25.120.54 and 53.137; Hamburger, Suckale, and Suckale-Redlefsen 2018, 70, fig. 1.55; Tomei 2002, 115; and Fig. 4.1 of this volume.
23. Campbell 1995, 1.
24. Ibid., 63–64.
25. Mormando 1999, 112; Bernardino da Siena 1950, 156.
26. Young 2015, 81.
27. Kren and McKendrick 2003, 336–39.
28. Boulton 2014, 139–42.
29. Lemaire 1993; Wijsman 2010, 465–68.
30. Similar scenes appear in contemporary *Somme le Roi* manuscripts: The British Library, London, Add. MS 28162, fol. 9v; and Bibliothèque nationale de France, Paris, MS fr. 938, fol. 105v. Avarice is contrasted with David in Bibliothèque nationale de France, Paris, MS lat. 1023, fol. 21r.
31. For books of hours, see Wieck 1988.
32. Alain de Lille 1973, 185; Alain de Lille 2004, 128, Book 7, lines 378–79.
33. Langholm 1983.
34. Todeschini 2005, 205–6.
35. Bernardino da Siena 1934, 98.
36. Vitullo and Wolfthal 2010b, 195 n. 60; Grebe 2001.
37. Kren 1983, 22.
38. Supporting the theme of largesse are Turner 1983, 132; Kren 1983, 22; Steenbock 1990, 135, 140; and Grebe 2001, 95. Marrow 1984, 549, writes that largesse "may" be the theme.
39. Grebe 2001, 95.
40. Ibid., 95, fig. 2.
41. William, Lord Hastings, master of the English royal mint, was an early owner of the manuscript, but perhaps not its original owner since one of his coats of arms overlap an earlier illumination.
42. Tudor-Craig 1987, 365.
43. For "largece" and "libéralité" as synonyms, see Godefroy 1885, 724. Besides those images discussed here, see also Jean Pichore, *Liberality against Avarice*, in *Rondeau des vertus*, Musée de la Renaissance, Écouen, MS E. cl. 22718c; *The Charitable Prince*, in *Avis aus roys*, Morgan, MS M.456, fol. 39r; Jan van den Hoecke, *Liberality*, Palais des Beaux-Arts, Lille, ca. 1635; and British School, *Liberality*, ca. 1626, Dulwich Picture Gallery, London.
44. See, among others, Herrad of Landsberg 1977, 176–77.
45. See below, Figs. 5.16–5.22, for other illuminations in this manuscript.
46. Tudor-Craig 1987, 365.
47. See, for example, Mellinkoff 1993, *passim*.
48. For more luxurious fifteenth- and sixteenth-century Virgins, see Beer and Woelk 2014, 146–47, 218–19, 222–23, 264–65, 288–89, 314–15.
49. For the association of money with barrenness and sterility, see pp. 110–11 and Vitullo 2019, 13–64.
50. Petrarch 1991, vol. 3, 48; Petrarch 2002, 618; Vitullo and Wolfthal 2010b, 173, 193 n. 51.

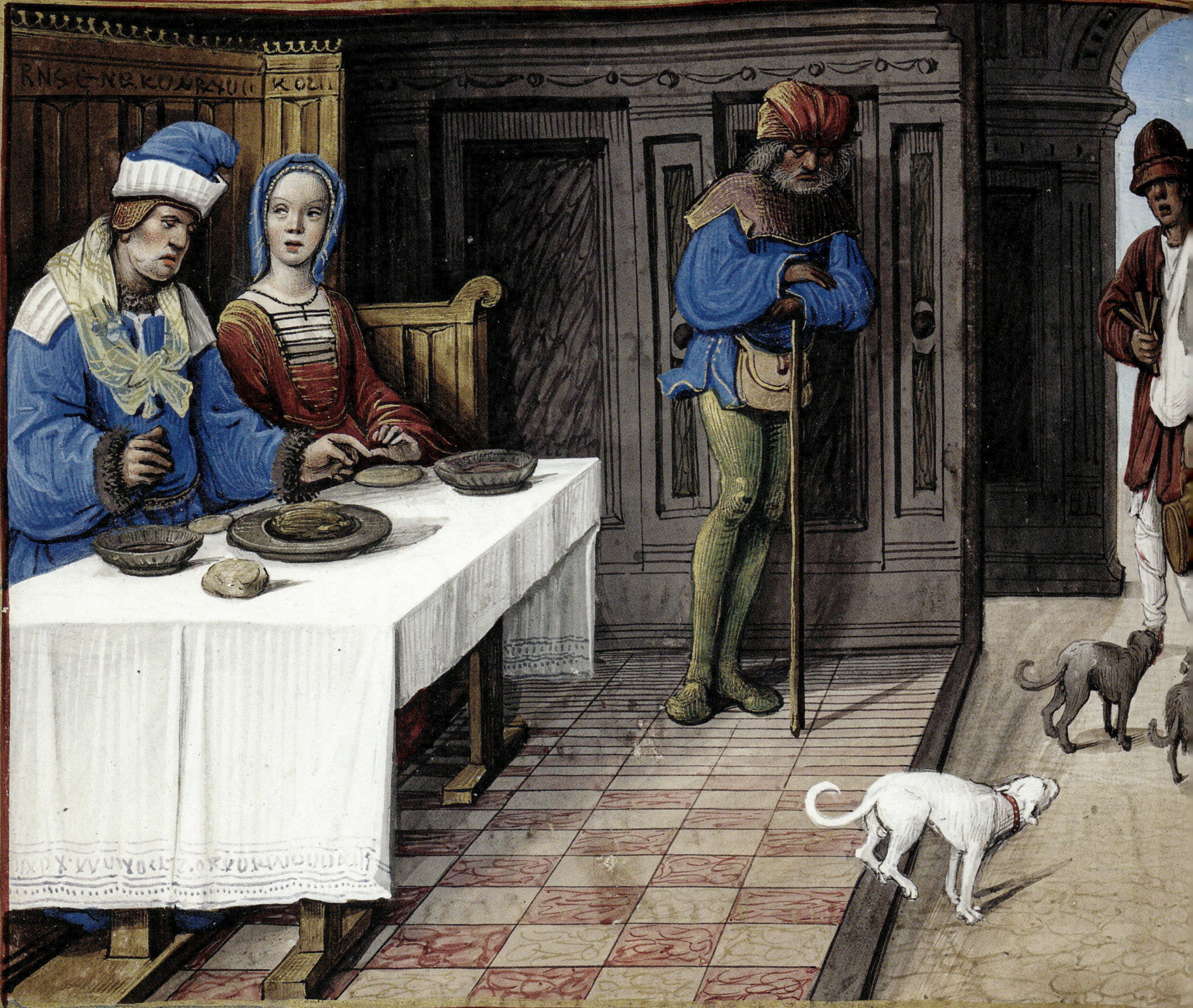

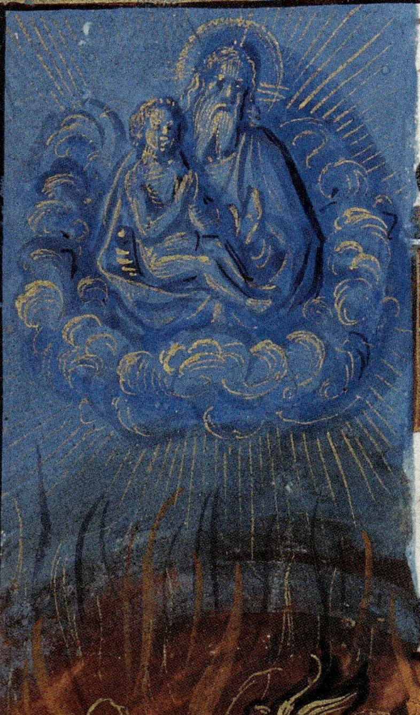

Ad matutinas. Inuit. Regem cui
omnia uiuunt. Venite adoremus.
Venite exultemus ps.
domino iubilemus deo
salutari nostro: preoccupemus faci
em eius in confessione et in psal

4

Will Money Damn Your Soul?

DIANE WOLFTHAL

A Deadly Sin

MEDIEVAL CHRISTIANS AGREED THAT AVARICE was a deadly sin that involved an inordinate longing for worldly things. For some, "worldly things" included family and friends. But with the rise of an economy that increasingly centered on commerce, investment, and banking, many interpreted avarice more narrowly as an uncontrollable lust for money.[1] Theologians acknowledged that greed was harmful to society. In the twelfth century, Alain de Lille, a monk of the Cistercian order known for its privations, lamented, "Avarice weakens friendship, generates hatred, breeds anger, plants wars, nourishes controversies, and ruptures bonds of children to their parents."[2] The thirteenth-century theologian Jacques de Vitry similarly bemoaned the fact that, because of avarice, "the poor are robbed, [and] churches are plunged into misery."[3] But merchant-bankers were also concerned

Jean Poyer, *Lazarus and Dives*, from Hours of Henry VIII, France, Tours, ca. 1500. The Morgan Library & Museum, New York, MS H.8, fol. 134v. (Detail of Fig. 4.21.)

FIG. 4.1. ***Avarice*, limestone relief, France (central or Limousin), 1125–50. Museum of Fine Arts, Boston, 48.255.**

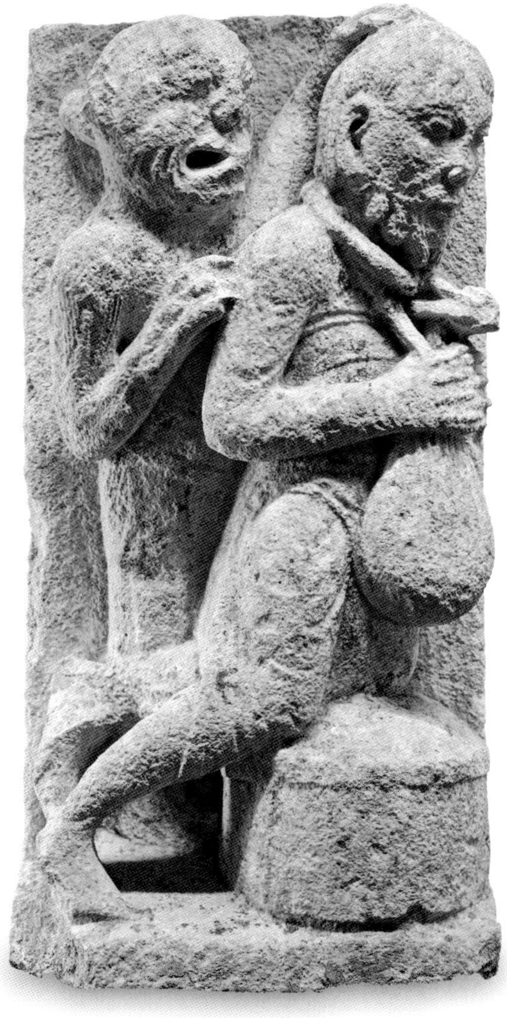

with the danger that avarice posed to their souls. In her book on Cosimo de' Medici, Dale Kent concluded, for example, that in fifteenth-century Italy "normal business activity made merchants morbidly conscious of their sins and the need for expiation."[4]

Personifications of Avarice

Could money damn your soul? A finely carved twelfth-century sculpture strongly suggests that it could (Fig. 4.1). It shows a man who is marked as avaricious by the bulging moneybag that he greedily grasps with both hands, and by the cylindrical strongbox on which he kneels in a parody of pious genuflection.[5]

The sculptor carved flat, circular indentations to represent the coins that fill the bulging sack.[6] But the moneybag also suggests the consequences of avarice. The cord, which is draped around the man's neck, resembles a noose, alluding to hanging—the fate of Judas, the disciple who betrayed Christ for money and was therefore seen as the archetype of greed (see Figs. 4.22–4.23). In medieval depictions of hell, the avaricious are also frequently depicted with nooses around their necks. The sculpted figure may have been intended as a miser, as it is often referred to today, or as a usurer, as medieval inscriptions on similar monuments suggest; these and related subjects often share the same iconography.[7] But it is certainly a personification of Avarice.

Behind him stands a monstrous demon with a low protruding brow, snout-like nose, snarling mouth, clawed hands, curled horns, and furry body. He places one hand on the man's head in a gesture that signifies that he is taking possession of him, and shoves him with the other hand, presumably towards hell.[8] Yet even at the moment of damnation, the greedy man cannot bear to part with his money.

This high relief from Limousin in central France (or a neighboring area) likely adorned part of a church that was accessible to the public. Priscilla Baumann has noted a "moral preoccupation" with avarice in twelfth-century architectural sculpture of this region, which she links to the anxiety caused by the shift from an agrarian to a mercantile economy.[9] The carving, now quite weathered, probably formed part of an ensemble with one or more other relief carvings of the seven deadly sins, as on the porches of Moissac and Beaulieu.[10] Especially in its original polychromed state, the relief would have frightened and horrified viewers. Designed to warn churchgoers that avarice could lead to damnation, the sculpture conforms to the standard way Avarice was represented on French Romanesque churches: as a man clutching a moneybag with both hands while one or more demons seize him.[11] In later centuries, however, artists portrayed Avarice in a multiplicity of imaginative ways.

A miniature in a book of hours illuminated by Robinet Testard in Poitiers around 1475 also makes clear that money can damn your soul.[12] The manuscript includes an unusual cycle of personifications of sins, which illustrate the Penitential Psalms. For Psalm 50, which asks God for mercy, Avarice, labeled on his banner, sits on a ferocious, snarling wolf that bares its teeth and thrusts out its tongue (Fig. 4.2). A large purse hangs from Avarice's belt as he empties a smaller one, filled with shiny gold coins, wastefully on the ground. Crouching on the floor is a horned devil with glittering, golden wings. The inscription on his scroll has been damaged, but the first letter, *M*, remains, identifying the creature as Mammon, the demon of greed. The three vignettes below suggest avaricious behavior, although their precise meaning is unclear. In the two scenes at left and center, purses play a dominant role. At the right, a man carrying a bulging sack approaches a corpulent merchant at his counter. Both finger a large pile of gold coins.[13]

The wolf, Avarice's mount, had long been associated with the vice because it was viewed as a wild and frightening predator and a greedy thief.[14] Herrad of Landsberg envisioned Avarice personified, holding coins while surrounded by animals, including a wolf, which she associated with the rapaciousness of greed.[15] Bestiaries portray wolves cruelly attacking innocent sheep; one bestiary text states that "maddened by greed, wolves kill whatever they find."[16] Indeed they attack men as well as their flocks. Dante's *Inferno*, from 1345–55, describes the terror of encountering a ghastly, ravenous wolf "all hide and bones" (*Inferno* 1:49–54).[17] In the thirteenth century, the Dominican friar Vincent of Beauvais relates that a wolf carried off a son of St. Eustace. In the fifteenth century, the Sienese painter Stefano di Giovanni (known as "il Sassetta") depicted a wolf beside the bones of the inhabitants of Gubbio that it had devoured.[18] Dating from the same century is the saying "to keep the wolf from the gate," meaning "to ward off poverty or hunger."[19]

A more complex conception of greed appears in the most influential book written in medieval French, *Le roman de la rose* (The Romance of the Rose), an allegorical poem about chivalric love.[20] Begun by Guillaume de Lorris around 1230 and completed by Jean de Meun some forty years later, the long text survives in 300 manuscripts.[21] The first section relates the narrator's dream, the Lover's quest for a beautiful rose, which represents his beloved, held captive in the walled garden of Pleasure. Outside this garden are anti-courtly vices, including Covetousness and Avarice. They sit side by side, but the text distinguishes their behavior and appearance so that they present two facets of greed. Covetousness is acquisitive and desires "to heap up

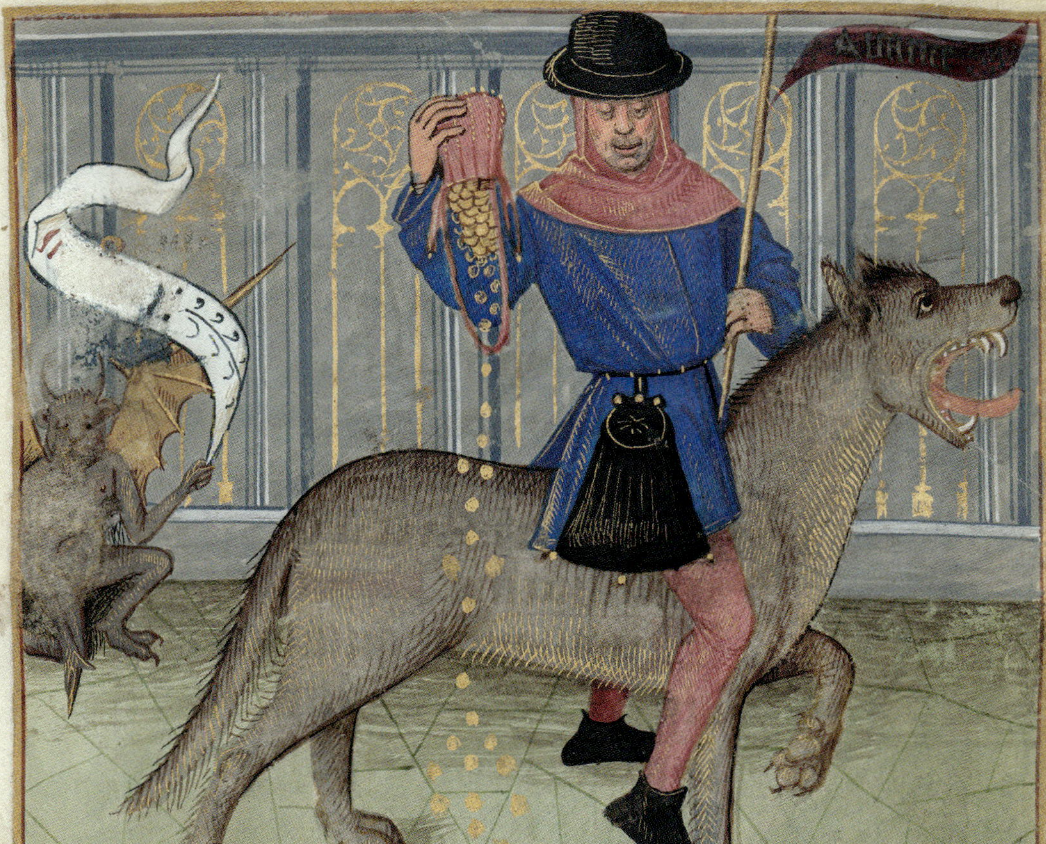
Miserere mei deus secun
dum magnam mise

FIG. 4.2. **Robinet Testard, *Avarice*, from a book of hours, France, Poitiers, ca. 1475. The Morgan Library & Museum, New York, MS M.1001, fol. 91r.**

OVERLEAF:
FIG. 4.3. ***Avarice* and *Covetousness*; *Envy*, from Guillaume de Lorris and Jean de Meun, *Le roman de la rose* (The Romance of the Rose), France, Paris, ca. 1350. The Morgan Library & Museum, New York, MS M.324, fols. 2v–3r.**

great possessions," whereas Avarice is miserly, unable to part with her wealth. The text observes that "Avarice held a purse hidden in her hand, which she tied up so tightly that it would have taken her a very long time to remove anything from it, but she had no interest in doing that; her only desire was to take nothing from the purse."[22] Another distinction is that Covetousness entices people to follow her; they become usurers, swindlers, robbers, embezzlers, tricksters, and harlots. But Avarice has no followers.[23] Although the poem is silent concerning the appearance of Covetousness, Avarice is described in great detail as ugly, sickly, gaunt, and dressed in patched rags because she cannot bear to part with money to buy a new dress.

In a copy of the *Roman de la rose* illuminated in Paris around 1350, the images of Covetousness and Avarice, seated side by side on the page, conform to the text to a great extent (Fig. 4.3). Covetousness has amassed riches; with each hand she extracts a moneybag from a strongbox containing a sparkling gold goblet and silver coins. Additional wealth is suggested by the garments hanging on a rod above. By contrast, the miserliness of Avarice is communicated by her closed moneybag grasped with both hands. Her robe is torn, and the text describes the clothes hanging on her rod as shabby and ten years old (although in the miniature they appear intact).

Perhaps because the poem states that Covetousness "entices men," she is portrayed as young, beautiful, and alluring, with blond, uncovered hair.[24] By contrast, Avarice, who tempts no one, is older and wears a crude headcloth that covers her hair and neck. Forming a stark contrast to both these vices, Envy, who appears on the facing folio, lacks money, golden vessels, additional garments, or any sign of wealth; her hands are empty. Like Covetousness and Avarice, Envy is viewed as an impediment to love.

An intriguing image of Avarice appears in a northern French copy of *Le pèlerinage de la vie humaine* (The Pilgrimage of Human Life), datable between 1325 and 1350 (Fig. 4.4).[25] Written by Guillaume de Deguileville, a Cistercian monk from the abbey of Chaalis, the *Pèlerinage* was inspired by the *Roman de la rose*. It, too, is an allegorical dream-vision written in the vernacular to reach a large audience. Its plot, however, is far from a chivalric romance. It concerns the Pilgrim who, with the help of the Grace of God and Lady Reason, is able to resist deadly sin and reach his spiritual goal, Heavenly Jerusalem. Avarice plays a major role in this poem. As in the *Roman de la rose*, she is described as an old woman dressed in ragged clothes, but in the *Pèlerinage* she has six pairs of hands that threaten the Pilgrim. These signify different aspects of the vice, including mendacity, idolatry, thievery, simony, pillaging, fraud, forgery, and vagrancy. Avarice states that her hands' only function is to grab, not to give, and that the more she has, the more she wants. The theme of the insatiability of avarice is reiterated in many medieval sources. The *Roman de la rose* asserts that merchants are so greedy that they "aspire to drink the whole of the Seine but will never be able do it, because there will always be some left."[26] A fourteenth-century English preachers' manual, the *Fasciculus morum* (Little Bundle of Morality), similarly observes, "when it [avarice] has gained the whole earth, it wants the sea; and after that, it soon craves for what is in the air. And by rising thus it knows no limit."[27]

Like the *Roman de la rose*, the *Pèlerinage* associates Avarice with miserliness and Covetousness

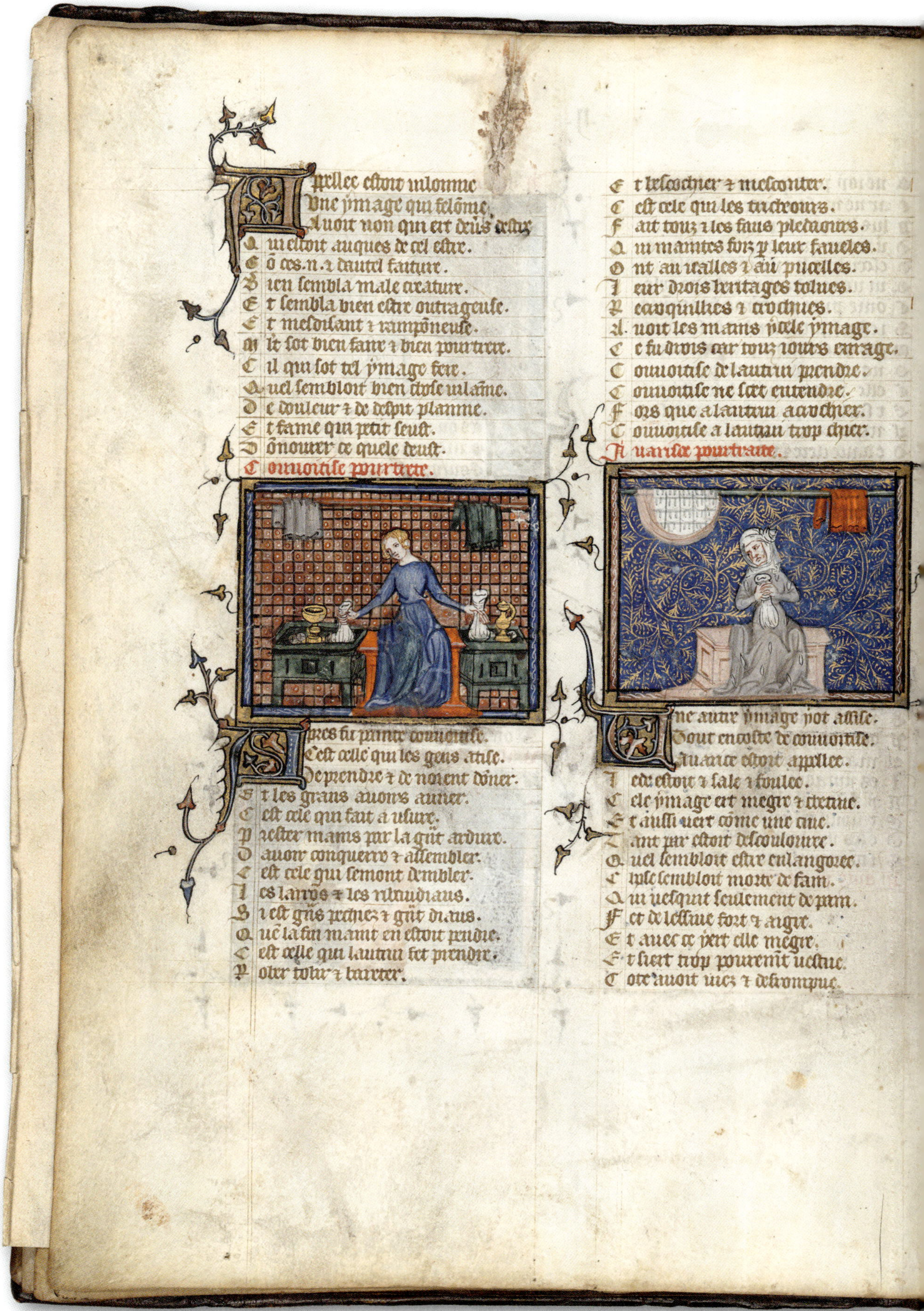

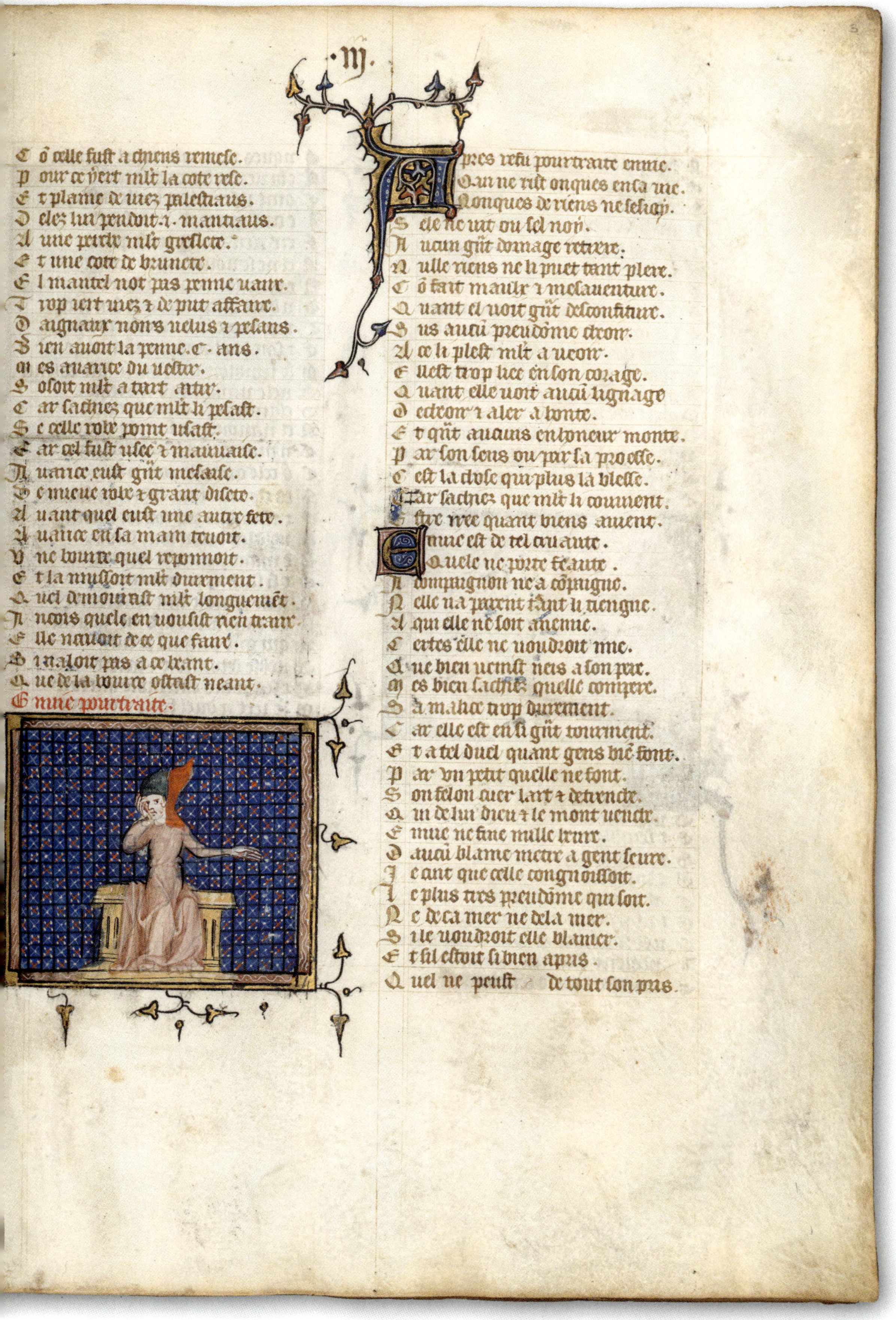

.iij.

Co celle fust a chiens remese.
Pour ce iert mlt la cote rese.
Et plaine de viez palestiaus.
Delez lui pendoit .i. mantiaus.
A une perche mlt greslete.
Et une cote de brunete.
El mantel not pas penne vair.
Trop iert viez et de put affaire.
Aignaux noirs velus et pesans.
Bien avoit la penne .c. ans.
Mes avarice du vestir.
Sosoit mlt a tart atir.
Car sachiez que mlt li pesast.
Se celle robe point usast.
Car cel fust usee et mauvaise.
Avarice eust grāt mesaise.
De nueve robe et grant disete.
Avant quel eust une autre fete.
Avarice en sa main tenoit.
Une bourse quel repunoit.
Et la nuoit mlt durement.
Quel demouroit mlt longuemēt.
Ainçois quele en vousist rien traire.
Elle navoit de ce que faire.
Si naloit pas a ce beant.
Que de la bourse ostast neant.
Envie pourtraite.

Apres refu pourtraite envie.
Qui ne rist onques en sa vie.
Ne onques de riens ne se resjoi.
Se elle ne vit ou sel oï.
Aucun grāt domage retraire.
Nulle riens ne li puet tant plere.
Cō fait maulx et mesaventure.
Quant el voit grāt desconfiture.
Sus aucun preudōme cheoir.
Ce li plest mlt a veoir.
Elle est trop liee en son corage.
Quant elle voit aucū lignage
Decheoir et aler a honte.
Et quāt aucuns en honeur monte.
Par son sens ou par sa proesse.
Cest la chose qui plus la blesse.
Car sachiez que mlt li couvient.
Estre iree quant biens avient.
Envie est de tel cruaute.
Que ele ne porte feaute.
A compaignon ne a cōpaigne.
Ne elle na parent tant li tiengne.
A qui elle ne soit anemie.
Certes elle ne voudroit mie.
Que bien venist neis a son pere.
Mes bien sachiez quelle compere.
Sa malice trop durement.
Car elle est en si grāt tourment.
Et a tel duel quant gens biē font.
Par un petit quelle ne font.
Son felon cuer lart et destrenche.
Qui de lui dieu et le mont venche.
Envie ne fine nulle heure.
Daucū blame metre a gent seure.
Je cuit que celle congnoissoit.
Le plus tres preudōme qui soit.
Ne deça mer ne dela mer.
Si le voudroit elle blamer.
Et sil estoit si bien apris.
Quel ne peust [illegible] de tout son pris.

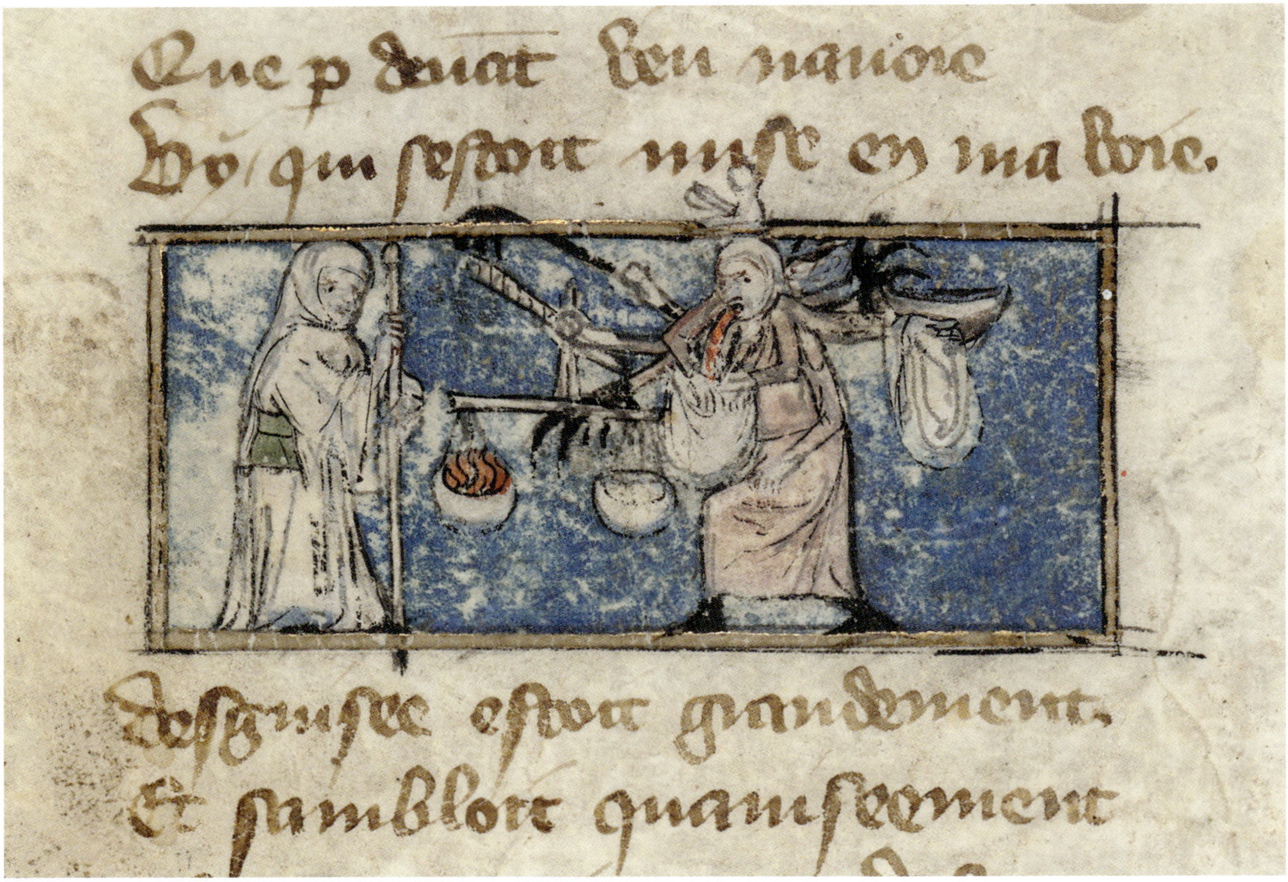

with acquisitiveness. But now they are joined in a single figure who explains, "I am called Covetousness, because I covet the wealth of others, and I am called Avarice, because I guard my own wealth too much."[28] A fascinating passage concerns usury, which the poem entangles with profiteering, noting that Avarice stores grain and waits for it to double in price.[29] Here, as so often, usury is not defined narrowly as charging interest on a loan, but rather more broadly as any practice that produces an unjust profit.

In its discussion of usury, the *Pèlerinage* describes Avarice as holding a balance in whose pans rest the sun and the zodiac. The Pilgrim asks Avarice why she weighs them, and she replies that the Grace of God put the zodiac in the heavens and caused the sun to shine on everyone, but she has seized them and placed them on her scale so that she can charge different amounts of interest depending on the duration of the loan.[30] Guillaume de Deguileville here echoes a common argument against usury: that time belongs to everyone, and so the usurer cannot morally sell it. In the second decade of the thirteenth century, William of Auxerre, a deacon of Beauvais, had asserted this principle, and in 1278 the Dominican scholastic philosopher Giles of Lessines, in his treatise on usury—the first dedicated to this subject—argues that it is clear that the usurer sells time, since his fees vary according to the length of the transaction. Giles then declares that time is not "the proper possession of anyone, but is given by God equally."[31]

In the miniature illustrating the confrontation with Avarice, the Pilgrim, wearing a monk's habit, is identified by his scrip (pilgrim's wallet) and staff (Fig. 4.4). Avarice is immediately recognizable by her multiple sets of arms. As in the text, a bag that hangs round her neck holds the objects that she steals, and she thrusts

FIG. 4.4. ***Pilgrim with Avarice*, from Guillaume de Deguileville, *Le pèlerinage de la vie humaine* (The Pilgrimage of Human Life), France, 1325–50. The Morgan Library & Museum, New York, MS M.1038, fol. 76v (det.).**

her tongue out, much like Testard's wolf (see Fig. 4.2). An older woman, Avarice wears a patched dress that speaks to her miserly character, while her multiple hands, claws, and arms signal her grasping nature. On her head she balances a seated figure holding an object, which is described as Avarice's idol (presumably a coin) made of "gold or silver, and imprinted with the figure of the lord of the land."[32] Avarice has even seized the sun and the planets, as can be seen by the balance held by one of her griffin claws. Bestial and fearsome, she strides broadly towards the Pilgrim. This tiny miniature skillfully suggests hoarding through Avarice's overwhelming number of possessions, including the bag round her neck, her balance, file, hook, idol, beggar's bowl, and bread bag.

Unlike the images in the fifth chapter of this book, which visualized the possibility of a virtuous life, the depictions of Avarice described in this chapter do not contain references to angels, God, or salvation. Instead they are filled with an accumulation of material objects: chests overflowing with coins, golden vessels and moneybags, hands gripping bulging sacks of money, cascades of glittering coins, and money piled high on counters. Although the divine is not present, the devil sometimes is shown, serving as a reminder that wealth can damn your soul. In the secular *Roman de la rose*, however, avarice is not an obstacle to salvation, but to love.

If the *Pèlerinage* visualizes the popular modern belief that time is money, personifications of Avarice collectively highlight one of the differences between today's discourses on money and medieval ones. Whereas saving money is now generally viewed in a positive light, medieval Christians who acquired riches beyond their needs or those of their families were expected to donate the excess money to the poor, to their communities, or to their churches. If they failed to do so, they risked losing both earthly love (as in the *Roman de la rose*) and heavenly salvation.

Immoral Ways to Acquire Money

The ancient Roman philosopher and statesman Marcus Tullius Cicero observed, "It is a duty to make money, but only by honorable means." In his *De officiis* (On Obligations), one of the most widely read treatises on ethical conduct in medieval Europe, he related that when Cato was asked, "'How about money-lending?' he replied, 'How about murder?'"[33] Similarly, medieval Christians deemed some ways of earning money sinful. Prostitution, gambling, and thievery were among those judged immoral, then as now, but some everyday aspects of mercantile life were also viewed as unethical. When Adam ate from the tree of knowledge, God punished his disobedience by expelling him from paradise and ordering him to work (Genesis 3:17–19). Earning money by farming or producing needed commodities was deemed worthy because it conformed to God's commandment. But some medieval thinkers were troubled by those who acquired money through investment, usury, or profiteering without any apparent labor. They also noted that in the Gospels Jesus expelled merchants and money changers from the Temple, and this episode became one of the subjects through which artists explored the morality of the new monetary economy.

FIG. 4.5. *Christ Expelling the Money Changers from the Temple and Its Prefigurations,* **from Ulrich von Lilienfeld,** ***Concordantiae caritatis*** **(Concordances of God's Love), Austria, ca. 1460. The Morgan Library & Museum, New York, MS M.1045, fol. 39v.**

All four Gospels relate that at the Temple in Jerusalem, Christ "cast out all them that sold and bought in the temple, and overthrew the tables of the money changers, and the chairs of them that sold doves: And he saith to them: It is written, My house shall be called the house of prayer; but you have made it a den of thieves" (Matthew 21:12–13). John 2:15 adds that Jesus drove the merchants and money changers out with a whip and scattered their coins, manifesting his disapproval. Merchants had set up shop in the Temple to sell small animals, including doves, which priests then offered as sacrifices. Money changers facilitated those purchases as well as the payment of taxes for the upkeep of the building.

One elaborate example of the Expulsion from the Temple appears in a copy of the *Concordantiae caritatis* (Concordances of God's Love), which the Cistercian abbot Ulrich von Lilienfeld wrote between 1345 and 1351 (Fig. 4.5).[34] Designed as a picture book for laymen with little learning and for parish priests who needed to compose sermons but lacked a well-equipped library, the *Concordantiae caritatis* was designed to cover the entire liturgical year. Ulrich's goal was to convey the available knowledge about God's plan for salvation. His methodology was typological, that is, he interpreted episodes from Jewish scripture as prefigurations or parallels of those in the Gospels. However, unlike similar books, the *Concordantiae* integrates into its typological program incidents from saints' lives and tales about plants and animals. Each of Ulrich's 238 typological groups is explained through a full-page image on the verso and its text on the facing recto. An event from the life of either Christ or a saint, flanked by authors of Hebrew scriptures, is depicted at the top of each image; in the middle are two scenes from Hebrew scriptures illuminating the significance of the Christian scene; and below, two moral lessons from nature.

Only eight of the seventy surviving manuscripts of the *Concordantiae caritatis* are illuminated, and only two are on parchment, a much more expensive support than paper.[35] One of these luxury copies—profusely illuminated (although unfinished), large in size, rich in color, and generous in its use of gold leaf and shell gold (a liquid form of the precious metal, sometimes stored in shells)—was commissioned around 1460 by Leonhard Dietersdorfer, a Salzburg cleric and notary (who may have served as one of its scribes).[36] Its Expulsion from the Temple is at the top, in the central roundel (Fig. 4.5).[37] Jesus stands at the Temple entrance, with his raised whip, threatening two fleeing men.[38] Each shelters his possessions in his garment: doves for the merchant, coins for the money changer. The tragic nature of their separation from Christ is suggested by the money changer, who is the furthest from Jesus and the only figure to step out of the roundel while poignantly turning back to gaze at Christ.

Paradoxically, this image, despite its criticism of greedy merchants and money changers, is enriched with a considerable amount of precious metal. The background of the Expulsion scene is painted with rinceaux (leafy branch motifs) executed in shell gold, and the coins, in silver leaf, sparkle when they catch the light. Some who embraced the virtue of poverty, such as Gerard Groote, a founder of the Devotio Moderna (Modern Devotion), a lay movement emphasizing a personal, mystical relationship with God, preferred unadorned manuscripts. Thomas à Kempis recalled how Groote's breviary "was of no great value since he

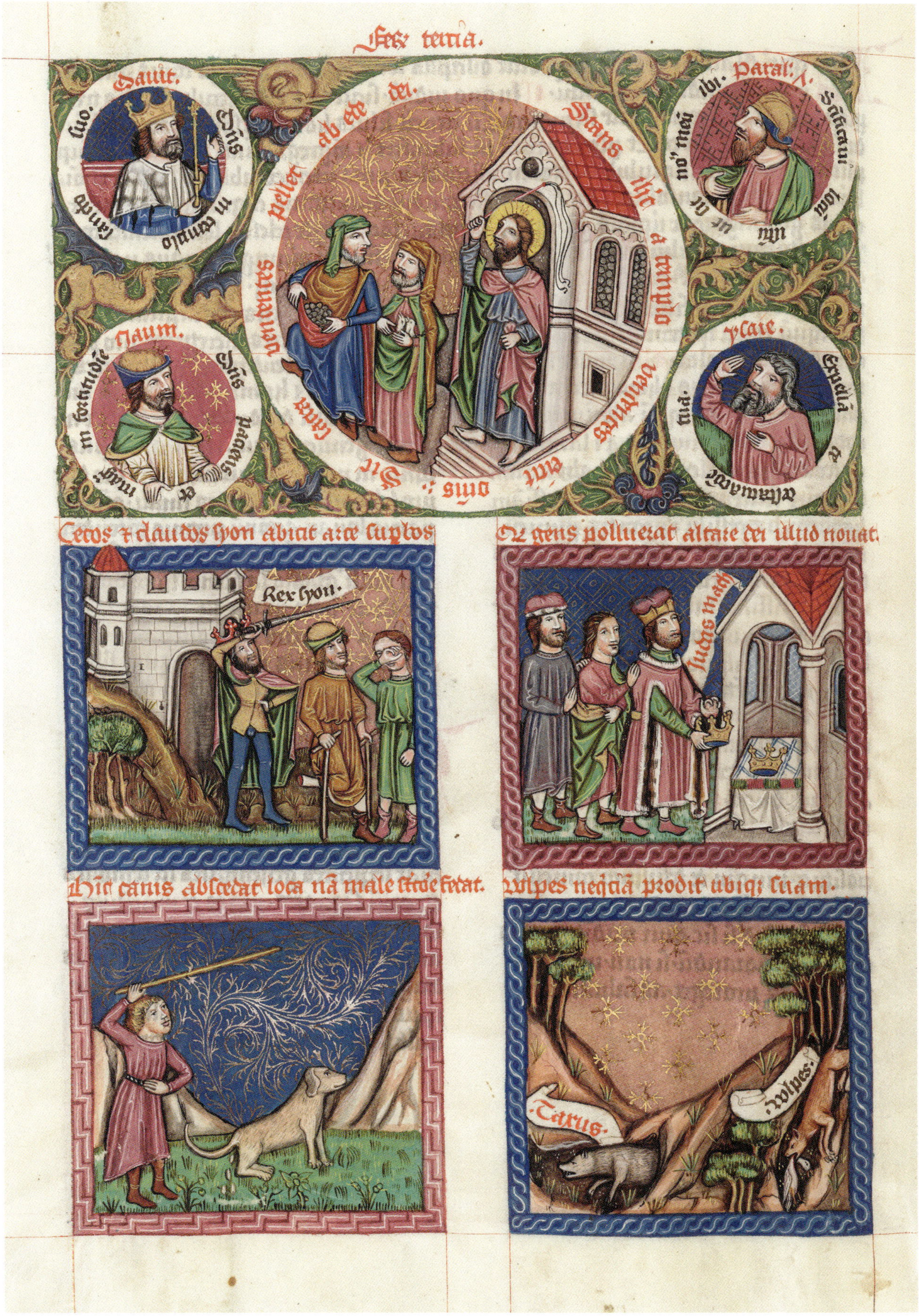
Fer. tercia.
Dauit.
Naum.
Paral.
Ysaie.
Rex syon.
Cecos & claudos syon abiciat arce superbos
Ut gens polluerat altare dei illud nouat.
Hic canis abscedat loca nã male sorde fedat.
Vulpes nequiciã prodit ubiqz suam.
Tarus.
Vulpes.

avoided using anything that was outwardly splendid or that savoured not of simplicity." He warned that "books should serve the interests of their reader's mind, not the nice taste of him who doth look at them."[39] Yet others, like Dietersdorfer, believed that richly decorated books best honored God.

The Expulsion is flanked by small roundels containing prophets who gaze at the central scene: David, Nahum, Isaiah, and the author of the Book of Chronicles, who is sometimes identified as Ezra. A relevant text surrounds each. For example, encircling Isaiah are the words "I will drive you out of office" (Isaiah 22:19).

In the middle level, Christ's expulsion of the money changers is compared, at the left, to an earlier example, that of David's casting the blind and lame out of Sion (2 Kings 5:7). David's raised arm and threatening sword echo Christ's elevated arm and whip. At the right, Christ's expulsion is compared to the Jewish warrior Judah Maccabee's cleansing of the desecrated Temple and adorning of its new altar with gold crowns (1 Maccabees 4:41). Together, these scenes suggest a contrast between the proper and improper uses of precious metal. Golden objects, such as crowns, were sometimes melted down to produce coins. Conversely, molten coins were at times transformed into precious metal objects, both sacred and secular.

In the lowest level, at the left, in an iteration of David's gesture, a man raises a stick to expel a dog that soils a "beautiful and blooming" meadow.[40] These parallel gestures visually equate merchants and money changers with the blind, the lame, and defecating dogs. Finally, at the lower right, a badger, which is unable to tolerate the smell of a fox in his underground burrow, moves to a new home. The accompanying text compares this to evildoers who must, like the money changers, be separated from Christ.

The diagrammatic approach of the illumination and the repeated, threatening gesture of the raised arm would have helped readers understand the typology, despite the obscure biblical tales. The contemporary dress of some of the figures probably encouraged medieval viewers to think about the morality of merchants and money changers in their own time.

In a slightly later proof impression from a *Speculum humanae salvationis* (Mirror of Human Salvation), printed in Basel between 1471 and 1481, the scene is modernized through the contemporaneous garments of the evil merchant and money changer who are depicted as Jews, as their characteristic pointed hats attest (Fig. 4.6). The printmaker illustrates a popular theme that arose with the rise of the monetary economy: the identification of Jews with money, especially ill-gotten gains.[41] Leviticus 23:36–37 unequivocally forbids charging "thy brother" interest on a loan, and medieval Europeans interpreted the word "brother" as "co-religionist." The Church forbade Christians from charging other Christians interest, and Jewish law prohibited Jews from charging other Jews. Yet, from the thirteenth through fifteenth centuries, Christian moneylenders from northern Italy, often termed "Lombards," were active north of the Alps, and native Christians in every land also loaned money at interest.[42] Several forces, however, ensured a higher involvement in moneylending among Jews. A small minority, Jews were freer, according to how Leviticus was interpreted, to lend money to Christians, who were the overwhelming majority. In addition, secular

FIG. 4.6. Master of the Richel Speculum, *Christ Expelling the Money Changers from the Temple*, proof impression, woodcut, from *Speculum humanae salvationis* (Mirror of Human Salvation), Switzerland, Basel: Richel Bernhart, ca. 1476. The Morgan Library & Museum, New York, PML 224, fol. 33 recto (det.).

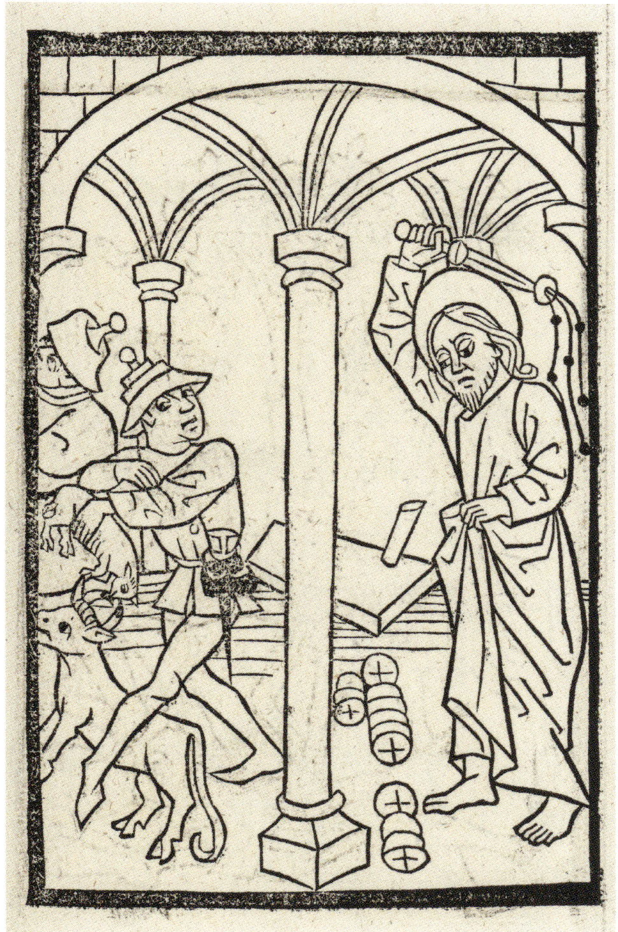

rulers encouraged Jewish moneylending by granting privileges that supported the Jewish credit business. They did this so that they could have ready access to cash, and levy high taxes on Jews. As a result, as Sarah Ifft Decker concludes, "many Jews relied on moneylending for some or all of their income . . . [and] credit formed an important part of Jewish economic life."[43] Jews would not have been tolerated in most European regions if they were not moneylenders. The sad truth is that medieval Jewish communities depended on moneylending for their continued existence.[44] Yet it is false to paint all Jews with the broad brush of usury, as some medieval Christians did. Depending on the time and place, some Jews were poor, worked as artisans or in other trades, or even owned agricultural lands.[45]

The initial motivation for associating Jews with usury was to discourage Christians from such "predatory" practices. But soon Jews were seen as avaricious in part because of a growing anti-Jewish theological polemic (especially encouraged by the Franciscans), and in part because Jews were viewed as outsiders (even though they had lived in Europe for over a thousand years), and thus deemed an acceptable scapegoat for Christians' anxieties about the rise of the monetary economy.[46] This occurred even though Jews often lived in the center of town, sometimes on the same street as Christians, and had innumerable everyday interactions with Christians, some economic, others purely social.[47] When the association between Jews and money turned violent, it was often their Christian neighbors—who knew that not all Jews were moneylenders—who attacked Jews.

Just as Christ raises a whip against his fellow Jews in this and many other images, so medieval Christians assaulted both individual Jews and entire Jewish communities (see Fig. 1.6). Sometimes spontaneous and sometimes planned, such massacres were perpetrated by those who owed Jews money and those who did not, and by every class of Christian society.[48] From the mass murders unleashed by the Crusaders in 1096 through those inspired by libelous charges of ritual murder and the poisoning of wells in the fourteenth and fifteenth centuries, Christians in western Europe repeatedly slaughtered Jews. Nor is the unjust association of Jews with immoral economic practices consigned to the past. The first definition of the verb "Jew" in the online Oxford English Dictionary is "To cheat or overreach, in the way attributed to Jewish traders or usurers," and antisemitic movements today still invoke the false stereotype of the avaricious Jew.[49]

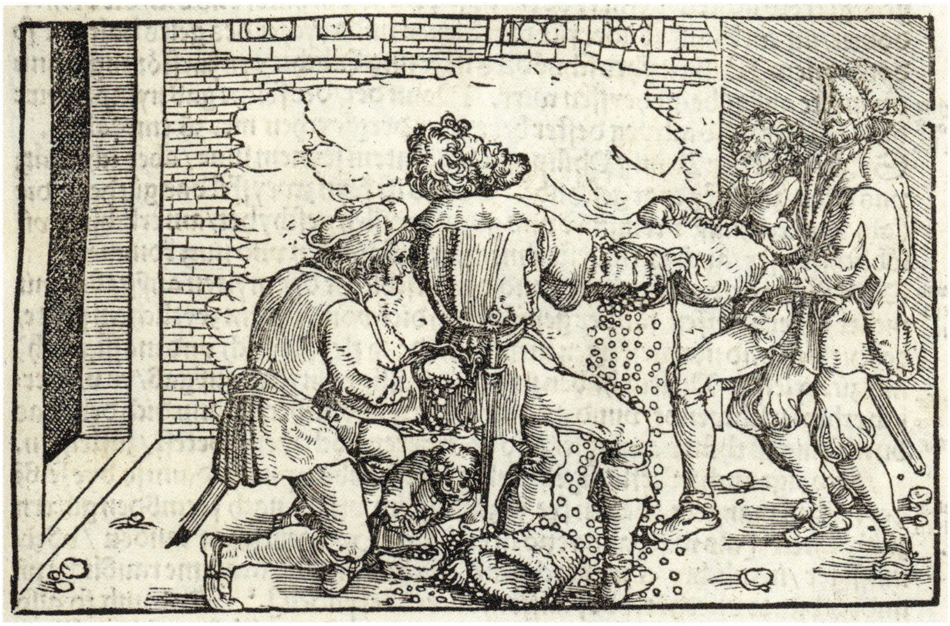

FIG. 4.7. Petrarch Master (Hans Weiditz?), *Robbery*, from Marcus Tullius Cicero, *De officiis* (On Obligations), trans. Johann Freiherr von Schwarzenberg and Johann Neuber, Germany, Augsburg: Heinrich Steyner, 1531. The Morgan Library & Museum, New York, PML 23007, leaf I5 recto (det.).

Besides moneylending, medieval Christians, unsurprisingly, deemed robbery a sinful way to acquire money. The Petrarch Master, a German artist often identified as Hans Weiditz, produced a remarkable scene showing how greed sparks a frenzy of unrestrained thievery (Fig. 4.7). The woodcut shows a pickpocket stealing coins from a man's purse, while two other thieves try to seize the victim's huge sack of money. Although the man struggles to retain his treasure (recoiling so forcefully that his hat falls off his head), coins rain down from his purse and sack. Even a small boy gets caught up in this greedy fever, stooping to fill his cap with fallen coins. The immoral nature of the thieves' actions is underlined by the seedy setting; the theft is staged against a dilapidated, peeling wall.

This print is based on one of the 261 drawings that the Petrarch Master made by 1520 as models for woodcut illustrations for the first German translation of Petrarch's popular Latin dialogue, *De remediis utriusque fortunae* (Remedies for Fortune Fair and Foul) of 1360.[50] Like many visual artists at the time, the Petrarch Master could not read Latin, and since the German translation, *Von der Artzney bayder Glück*, was only finished in 1520 and published in 1532, he based his designs instead on instructions composed by the satirist and famous humanist Sebastian Brant. The printmaker had considerable artistic freedom, and many of his compositions, derived from the Petrarch Master's drawings, are only loosely connected to the text, including the present example.[51]

In the text that accompanies the robbery scene (Book 2, chapter 13, titled "Financial Losses"), Sorrow repeatedly laments, "I have lost money."[52] Reason responds that one's economic wellbeing is always subject to chance and that, moreover, money does not guarantee happiness, nor can it "sustain the body, nor the mind."[53] The chapter mentions thievery only in passing, quoting Psalm 61, which warns people not to desire plunder. Perhaps this reference inspired the print.[54] The woodcut certainly does not represent the moral arguments voiced by Reason. Instead, like so many images in the volume, it vividly expresses the viewpoint of the passions, in this case Sorrow, by showing the emotional pain that results from losing a large amount of money. By juxtaposing two opposing views in the text, only one of which is visualized in the print, *Von der Artzney bayder Glück* forces the reader/viewer to contemplate the value of money.

The publisher Heinrich Steyner of Augsburg used this same woodcut earlier to introduce a chapter on liberality in a German translation of Cicero's *De officiis* (On Obligations), published in 1531.[55] Although a shower of coins could signal generosity (see Fig. 3.7), in this case the coins are being scattered as a result of thievery—a poor match for the contents of the chapter. Publishers often reused printed images in this way to save time and money, despite the potential discord between textual and visual messages.

In addition to money changing and thievery, another improper way to acquire wealth was to seize an inheritance before one's ancestor died. (See Steven Epstein's essay for the importance of inherited wealth.) In an illumination in the richly illustrated Hours of Catherine of Cleves, duchess of Guelders, produced in Utrecht around 1440, a dying man lies in bed surrounded by mourners as they await the priest who will give him the last rites (Fig. 4.8).[56] Without these sacraments, his soul cannot enter heaven, but he may be admitted to the purifying fires of purgatory, depicted on the facing folio. The themes of the deathbed and purgatory are appropriate for the accompanying text, the Monday Hours of the Dead. The lively scene includes a woman offering the dying man a candle (a kind of ersatz last rite), a doctor examining his urine, a Carmelite monk reading a holy book, and a woman praying. On the right, in the background, a fashionably garbed young man in blue and purple, presumably the heir, converses with an older, decadently dressed man who may be encouraging him to seize his inheritance. The heir, identifiable by his clothing, reappears in the lower margin raiding the dying man's coffer; he reaches for a moneybag to add to the one he has already placed on the ground. The text of the *Ars moriendi* (Art of Dying) mentions relatives such as this who feign compassion, but are only interested in earthly things.[57] Like numerous deathbed scenes (see Figs. 3.1, 3.4), this one suggests the futility of hoarding money, while criticizing the heir's greed and thievery. The flames of purgatory on the facing folio await both the dying man and his immoral heir.

The actions of the greedy heir are reminiscent of a story told by Stephen of Bourbon, a thirteenth-century French Dominican. He recounts that, after a wealthy man died, "his sons by his two marriages pulled out their swords, and, completely forgetting their father, fought over his chests [full of money], which they wanted to keep and to lay hold of, caring little for their father's soul or body."[58]

Of all the ways to acquire money improperly, usury was the most often condemned in the Middle Ages. A usurer appears in *Der Wälsche Gast* (The Italian Guest), a popular entertaining and moralizing poem composed by the Italian cleric Thomasin von Zirclaria in 1215–16.[59] Written in the vernacular for an aristocratic audience as a guide to behavior, it synthesizes conventional wisdom. Thomasin discusses table manners, the ideal lord, courtship, gift giving, and courtly love, and dispenses practical advice on how to lead a virtuous life. Several chapters concern economic issues: a wicked man is betrothed to Avarice, a wise man looks to the poor behind him rather than the rich in front of him, and the foolish envy the rich man. *Der Wälsche Gast* also criticizes moneylenders as foolish, wicked, and destined for hell.

In the passage that concerns us, the narrator notes that the usurer feels superior to his debtors, but he is foolishly mistaken. The borrower enjoys the

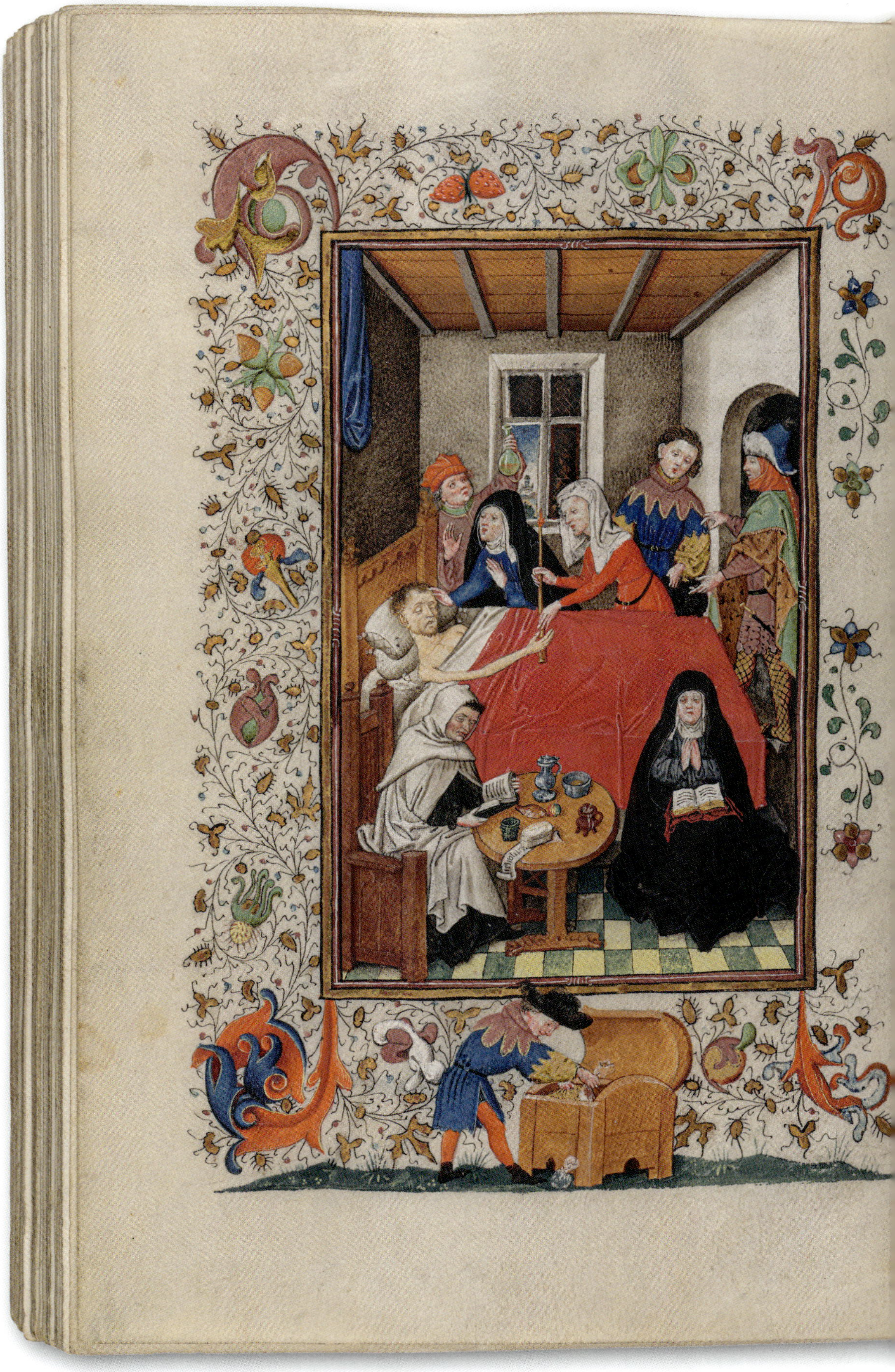

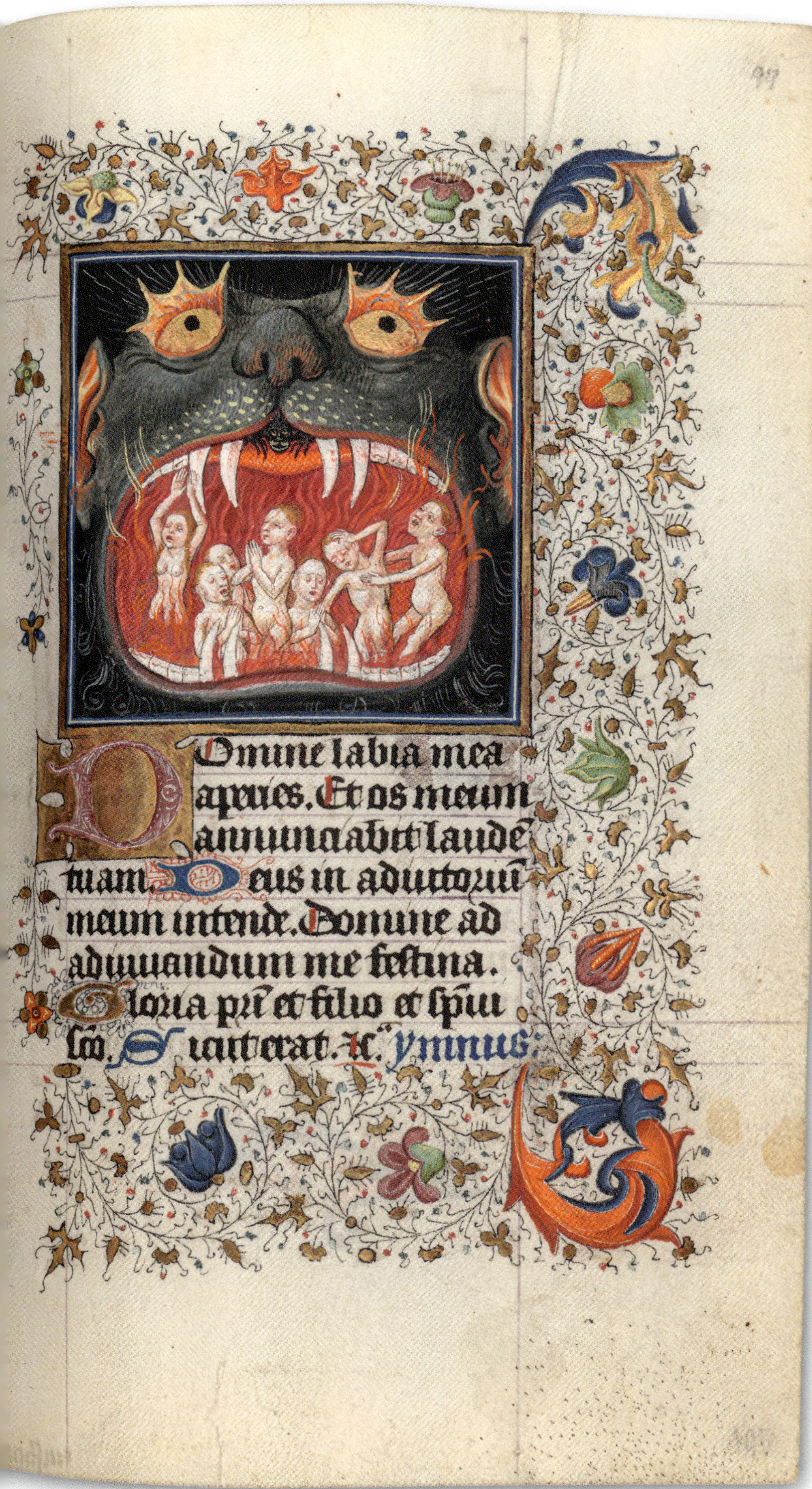

FIG. 4.8. Master of Catherine of Cleves, *Deathbed*; *Purgatory*, from the Hours of Catherine of Cleves, The Netherlands, Utrecht, ca. 1440. The Morgan Library & Museum, New York, MS M.917/945, p. 180–fol. 97r.

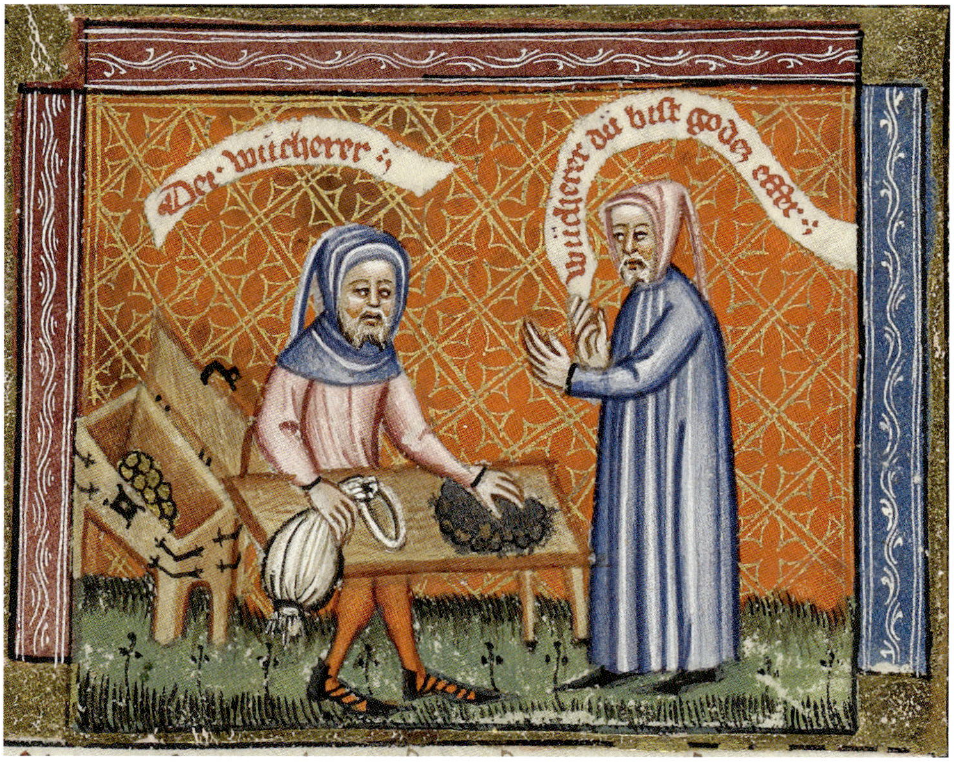

FIG. 4.9. ***Usurer*****, from Thomasin von Zirclaria,** ***Der Wälsche Gast*** **(The Italian Guest), Germany, Trier, ca. 1380. The Morgan Library & Museum, New York, MS G.54, fol. 41v (det.).**

lender's money, which the lender can no longer use. The borrower views the lender as his treasurer, and observes, "I am happy with your wealth, and that way, scoundrel, you are my surety."[60] The text concludes by warning the moneylender, "When you get to the depths of hell you would rather a thousand times over that you had never acquired what has called the wrath of God down upon you."[61] Thomasin's bleak picture of moneylenders echoes papal opinion. Pope Innocent III, who died in 1215, the year *Der Wälsche Gast* was written, sought to curtail usury in part because he wanted funds to support instead either a Crusade or charity for the poor.[62]

Twenty-four manuscripts of *Der Wälsche Gast* survive, the vast majority profusely illustrated. A miniature in the copy produced around 1380 for Kuno II von Falkenstein, archbishop of Trier, depicts a usurer, identified by the label "Der Wücherer" (Fig. 4.9). His fashionable black shoes and red leggings signal his immoral character. Unlike earlier images of this scene, which simply show the usurer, holding a purse and conversing with another figure, in this illumination the moneylender is surrounded by material objects. Seated at his counter, he holds a plump moneybag with one hand and fingers a large pile of dark coins with the other, while behind him gleams an open chest of gold coins. Previous scholars have identified the man standing before the usurer as either the narrator or a borrower.[63] The latter seems more likely, since the narrator does not appear in other illuminations in the manuscript. The long-robed figure mutters the words of resentment inscribed on his scroll, "Usurer, you are God's ape" (that is, the devil).[64]

Medieval Christians also viewed profiteering as an immoral way to acquire riches. The Strasbourg poet and satirist Sebastian Brant (mentioned above) condemns buying low and selling high in *Das Narrenschiff* (The Ship of Fools), published in 1494.[65] This bestseller, translated into numerous languages, includes several chapters that associate avarice with folly, including "Of Greed" (ch. 3), "Of Foolish Plans" (ch. 15), "Of Borrowing Too Much" (ch. 25), and "Of Useless Riches" (ch. 17).[66]

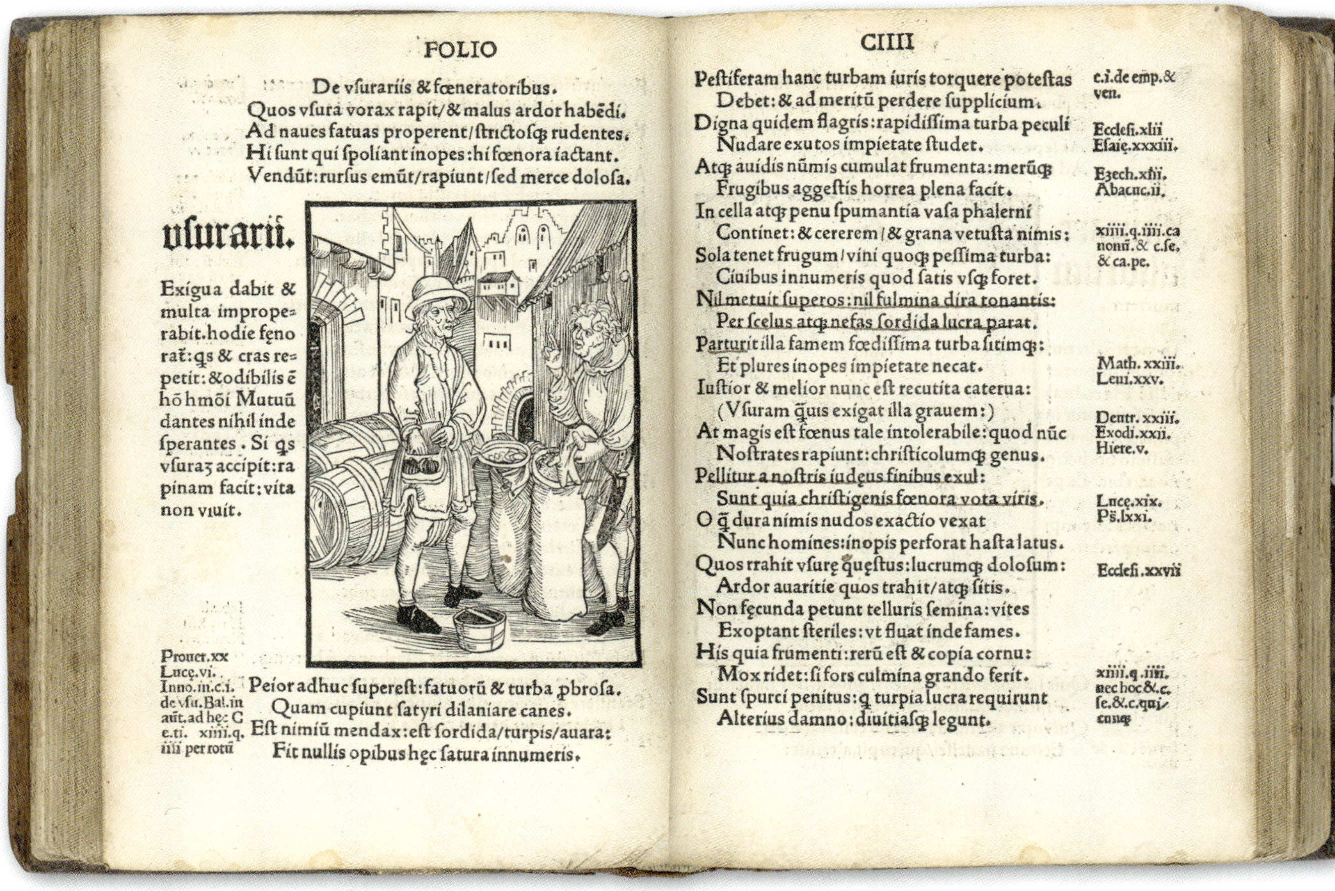
FOLIO

De vsurariis & fœneratoribus.
Quos vsura vorax rapit/& malus ardor habēdi.
Ad naues fatuas properent/strictosqꝫ rudentes.
Hi sunt qui spoliant inopes: hi fœnora iactant.
Vendūt: rursus emūt/rapiunt/sed merce dolosa.

vsurarii.

Exigua dabit & multa improperabit. hodie fęnoratꝰ: qs & cras repetit: & odibilis ē hō hmōi Mutuū dantes nihil inde sperantes. Si qs vsuraꝫ accipit: rapinam facit: vita non viuit.

Prouer.xx
Lucę.vi.
Inno.in.c.i. de vsu.Bal.in aut.ad hęc C e.ti. xiiii.q. iiii per totū

Peior adhuc superest: fatuorū & turba ꝓbrosa.
Quam cupiunt satyri dilaniare canes.
Est nimiū mendax: est sordida/turpis/auara:
Fit nullis opibus hęc satura innumeris.

CIIII

Pestiferam hanc turbam iuris torquere potestas — c.i.de emp.& ven.
Debet: & ad meritū perdere supplicium.
Digna quidem flagris: rapidissima turba peculi — Ecclesi.xlii
Nudare exutos impietate studet. — Esaię.xxxiii.
Atqꝫ auidis nūmis cumulat frumenta: merūqꝫ — Ezech.xlii.
Frugibus aggestis horrea plena facit. — Abacuc.ii.
In cella atqꝫ penu spumantia vasa phalerni
Continet: & cererem/& grana vetusta nimis: — xiiii.q.iiii.ca nonū.& c.se. & ca.pe.
Sola tenet frugum/vini quoqꝫ pessima turba:
Ciuibus innumeris quod satis vsqꝫ foret.
Nil metuit superos: nil fulmina dira tonantis:
Per scelus atqꝫ nefas sordida lucra parat.
Parturit illa famem fœdissima turba sitimqꝫ:
Et plures inopes impietate necat. — Math.xxiii.
Iustior & melior nunc est recutita caterua: — Leui.xxv.
(Vsuram q̄uis exigat illa grauem:)
At magis est fœnus tale intolerabile: quod nūc — Deutr.xxiii. Exodi.xxii.
Nostrates rapiunt: christicolumqꝫ genus. — Hiere.v.
Pellitur a nostris iudęus finibus exul:
Sunt quia christigenis fœnora vota viris. — Lucę.xix.
O q̄ dura nimis nudos exactio vexat — Ps.lxxi.
Nunc homines: inopis perforat hasta latus.
Quos trahit vsurę q̄ęstus: lucrumqꝫ dolosum: — Ecclesi.xxvii
Ardor auaritię quos trahit/atqꝫ sitis.
Non fęcunda petunt telluris semina: vites
Exoptant steriles: vt fluat inde fames.
His quia frumenti: rerū est & copia cornu:
Mox ridet: si fors culmina grando ferit. — xiiii.q.iiii. nec hoc & c. se.&.c.qui/cunqꝫ
Sunt spurci penitus: q̄ turpia lucra requirunt
Alterius damno: diuitiasqꝫ legunt.

FIG. 4.10. ***Profiteering*****, from Sebastian Brant,** ***Das Narrenschiff*** **(The Ship of Fools), in Latin, Switzerland, Basel: Johann Bergmann, 1498. The Morgan Library & Museum, New York, PML 27525.1, leaves N7 verso–N8 recto.**

Perhaps the most biting portrait of a merchant appears in chapter 93, titled "Usury and Profiteering."[67] Brant explains that profiteers buy up essential foods on speculation, which results in galloping prices and massive starvation. He observes that those who hoard grain are delighted by hailstorms, which raise prices on crops, increasing profits. Brant denigrates profiteers by suggesting that they must be picked free of vermin. The accompanying woodcut, in a Latin edition published in Basel in 1498, shows a man purchasing food from a profiteer, standing in a city square amidst the sacks of grain and barrels of wine mentioned in the text (Fig. 4.10). The profiteer is caricatured as a fool, as shown by his cap with its bells and donkey's ears, and his bulging body provides a stinging contrast with the gaunt figure of his customer.

This chapter of Brant's book also condemns pawnbrokers who buy wares cheap and then sell high, and moneylenders who reap huge profits by demanding high interest: "You borrow ten, eleven's due."[68] Brant disparages such businessmen—and Jews—by calling them "Christian Jews."[69] As we have seen, late medieval Christians repeatedly maligned Jews by linking them to the most negative monetary practices. Brant concludes that those who have been financially exploited feel hopeless and hang themselves. This negative view of the economy struck a note with one reader who in 1560 underlined the phrase "filthy lucre" (*sordida lucra*; Fig. 4.10).[70]

Brant devotes his third chapter to greed. Here he writes that only fools save material things that offer them no joy, and notes that "he who spends / To frivolous and wasteful ends" is even more foolish than hoarders.[71] He warns, "The man who wrongful riches wins / Will burn in hell for all his sins."[72] And he denigrates those "who pile up goods" by associating them with "excrement and dung" (*kot und mist*).[73] Brant, however, does not uniformly condemn merchants. Raised in a mercantile family, he understood the uncertainty of a merchant's life. As John Van Cleve notes, Brant valued "hard work, prudent professional practices, and a respectable bottom line."[74] In short, like so many of his contemporaries, Brant was of two minds concerning the rise of the monetary economy, yet he remained convinced that acquiring money in immoral ways was a mortal sin.

Improper Uses of Money

Medieval Christians worried not only about immoral ways to earn money, but also about improper ways to use it, either through hoarding or spending on sinful pursuits. A tiny woodcut addresses the first problem (Fig. 4.11). Part of a series of forty-one prints, brilliantly designed by Hans Holbein in 1523–26 and superbly cut by Hans Lützelburger, this extremely influential series broke the mold for the theme of the Dance of Death.[75] This subject traditionally shows Death summoning people from all walks of life in order to remind viewers of the universality of death and the fragility of life. With its inventive compositions, lively and varied images of death, biting humor, and savage social commentary, Holbein's series surpasses its predecessors and remains immensely popular even today.

Der Rychman depicts a miser. Double metal bars on the window are meant to protect the locked money chests, sacks of cash, and piles of coins that fill the room. The rich man has used his money improperly, hoarding his wealth, rather than donating any excess funds to benefit others. Furthermore, he is oblivious to the hourglass and the extinguished candle on the table, which suggest that his death is imminent. He not only ignores the advice of the *Ars moriendi*—to turn away from earthly things at the moment of death—but he is also, in fact, outraged as Death enthusiastically grabs a large fistful of coins to add to his bowl, already brimming with money. The miser flings up his arms, leans forward, opens his mouth, and puckers his brow in an expression of intense distress at the loss of his money. As Peter Parshall observes, "Death comes to the rich man, neither touching his victim nor conducting him away, but stealing his money, as if to say that to remove wealth from the greedy is tantamount to depriving them of life itself."[76] Latin and French inscriptions added when the prints were republished in 1538 paraphrase Luke 12:20: "You fool! This very night your life will be demanded from you. Then who will get what you have prepared for yourself. This is how it will be with whoever stores up things for themselves but is not rich toward God."

An episode in Thomas Kirchmeyer's play *Mercator seu iudicium* (The Merchant, or Judgment) echoes the miser's reaction. First published in 1540, it traces a

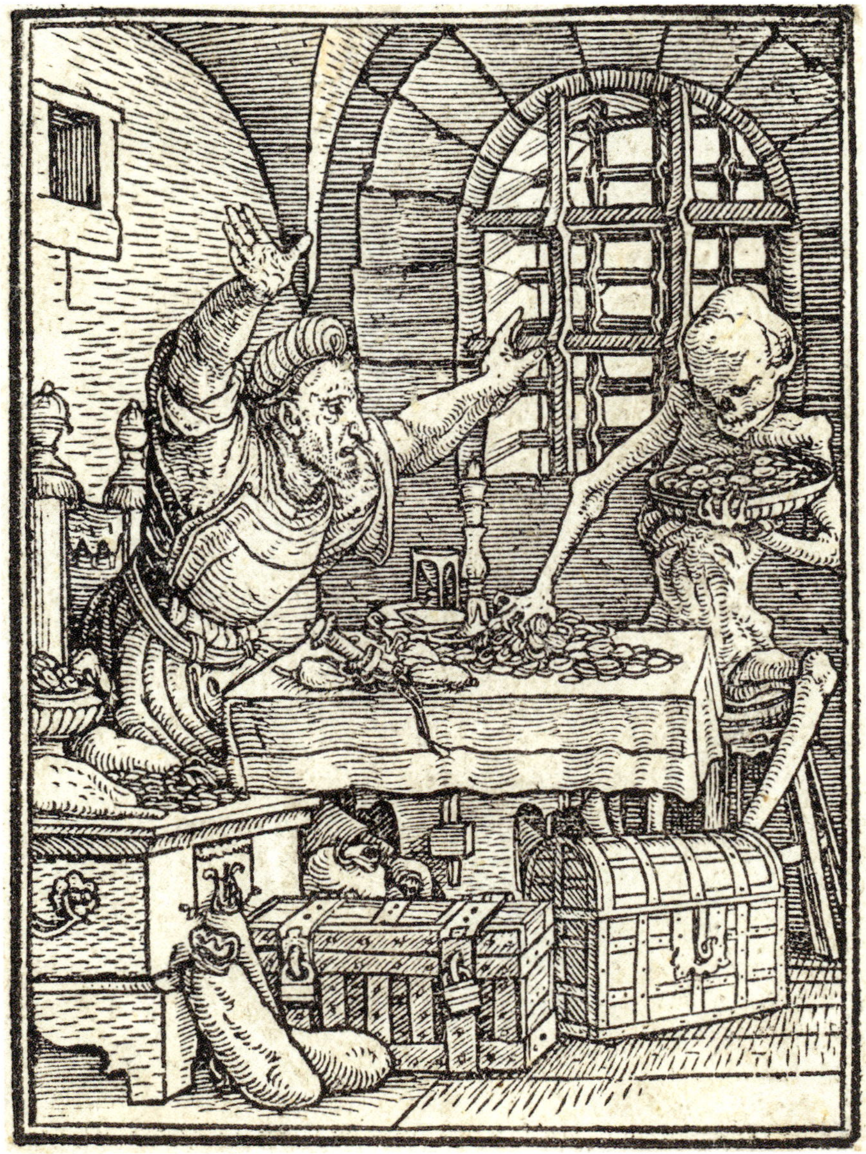

FIG. 4.11. **Hans Holbein the Younger (designer) and Hans Lützelburger (cutter), *Der Rychman*, from the *Dance of Death* series, woodcut, Germany, designed 1523–26, published 1538. National Gallery of Art, Washington, DC, 1948.11.128.**

merchant's gradual realization that he has been living a sinful life. In an early scene he is petrified that he is about to die; he does not fear going to hell, but the loss of business opportunities.[77] But is Holbein's miser, like Kirchmeyer's, a Christian merchant? Holbein denigrates the rich and defames Jews at the same time by depicting this hoarder with a stereotypical Jewish beard, long nose, and a foreign-looking headdress.

Gambling was considered another immoral use of money. The mid-thirteenth-century Dominican William Peraldus of Lyon judged gambling a type of avaricious behavior, and lamented that inveterate gamblers were violent, incurred the wrath of relatives, damaged family harmony, disinherited children, and prostituted their daughters.[78] Supporters of the Dominican preacher Girolamo Savonarola targeted gamblers, seizing their earnings and donating them to the poor.[79] Cheating often accompanied card and dice games, which were frequently played in disreputable brothels or taverns. For all these reasons, moralists, including Desiderius Erasmus and Sebastian Brant, strongly condemned gambling, as did Church and State alike.

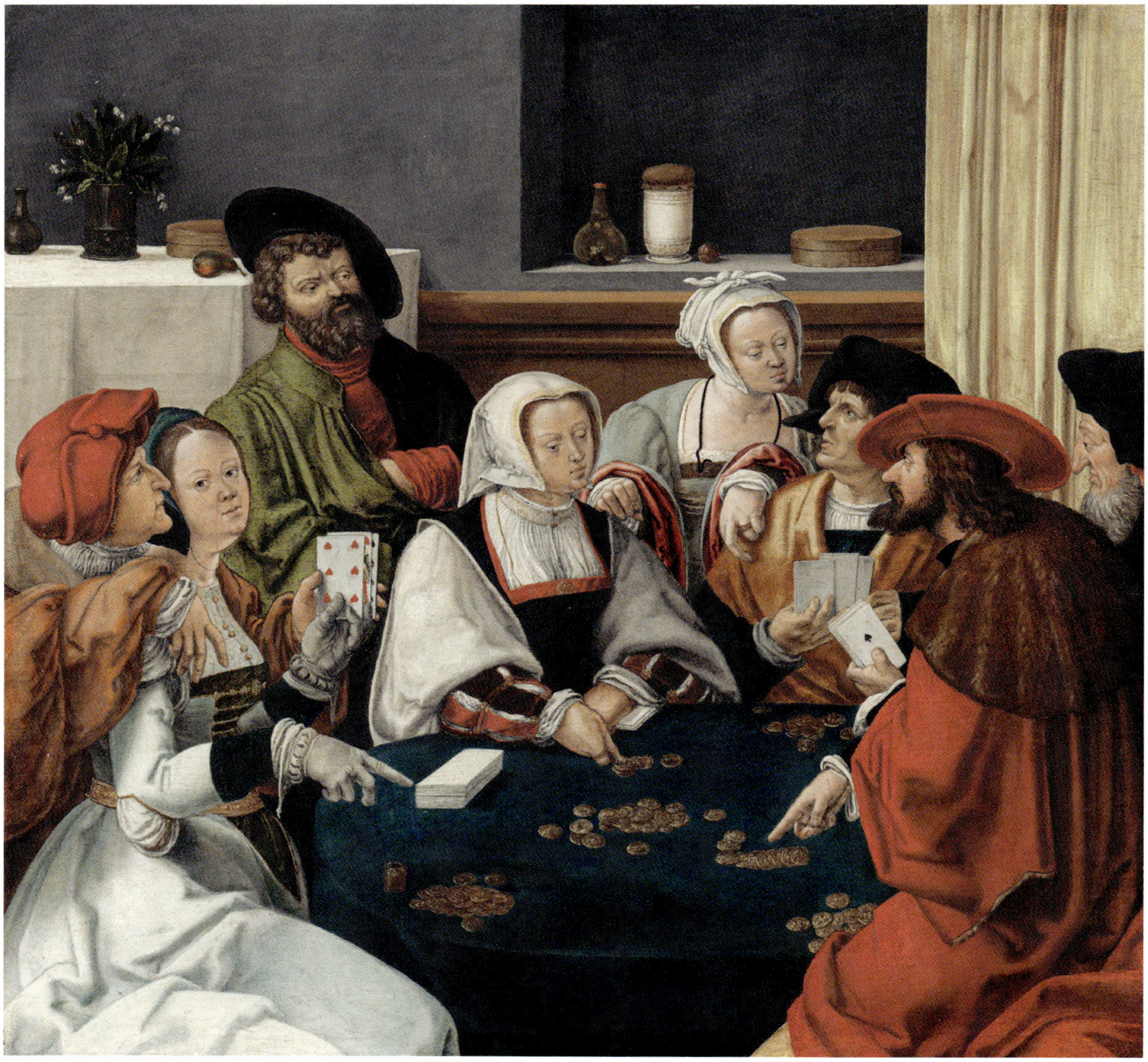

FIG. 4.12. German School, after Lucas van Leyden, *The Card Players*, oil on linden, Germany, ca. 1550–99. National Gallery of Art, Washington, DC, 1961.9.27.

In a painting from the second half of the sixteenth century, likely based on a work by Lucas van Leyden, two expensively dressed men and two women play cards while others observe, leaning familiarly over the players, perhaps to offer advice (Fig. 4.12).[80] Gaming was often associated with lust, and the woman at the left who holds the six of hearts may be hinting at the game of love. (Indeed women gamesters were especially censured.[81]) The man standing beside her hides his hand in his mantle, an artistic convention for a second sin, sloth.[82] The pointing gestures of two players bring our attention to a third sin, avarice, suggested by the piles of money on the table. This may soon be won by the player at the right who holds the ace of spades, often a wild card at the time. Tempted by lust, sloth, and avarice, gamblers risked losing not only their money, but also their souls.

A gambling scene also appears in a silver-stained glass roundel, one of eight that relate the biblical parable of the Prodigal Son (Luke 15:11–32), who wasted his

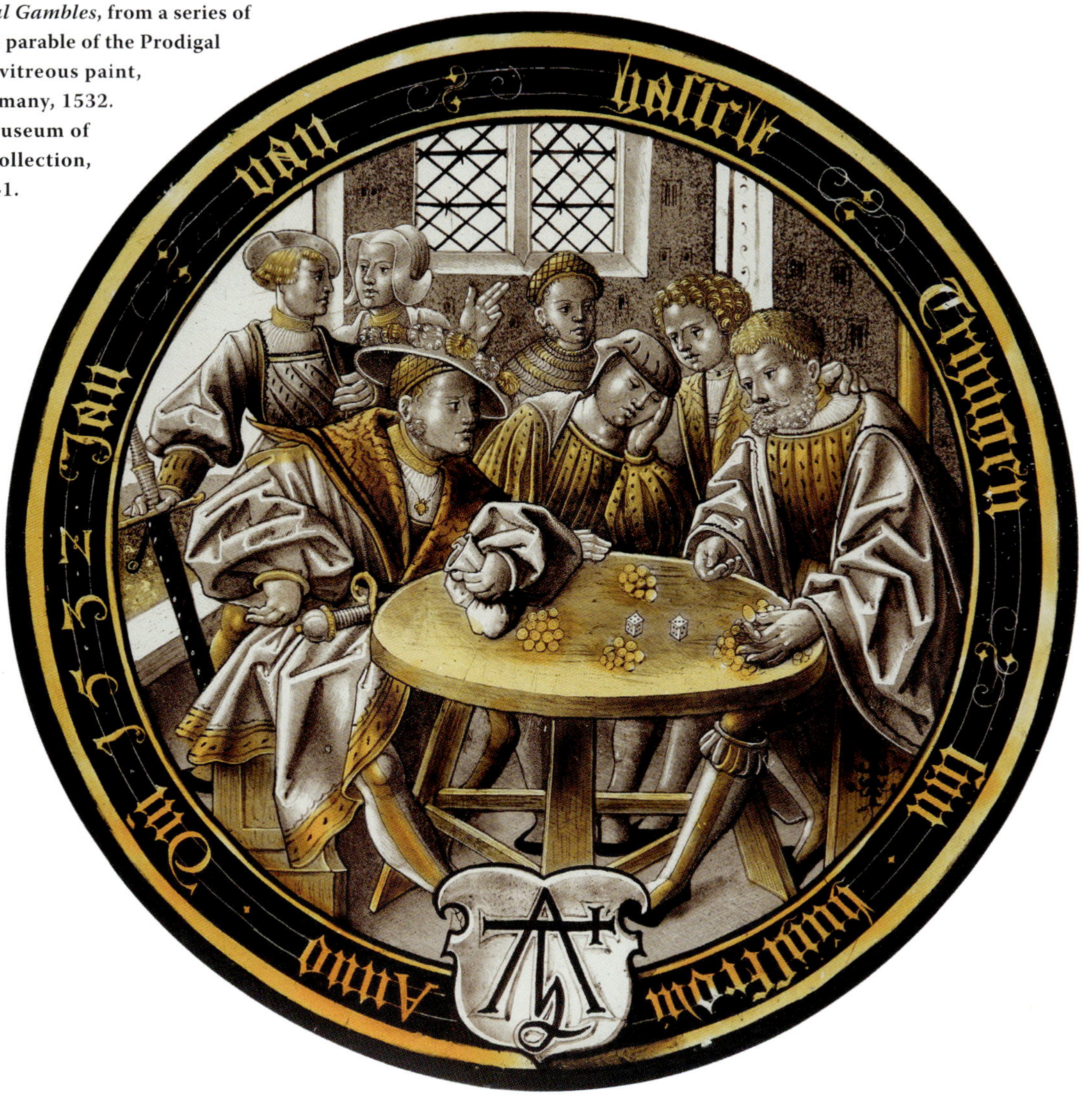

FIG. 4.13. ***The Prodigal Gambles*, from a series of eight scenes from the parable of the Prodigal Son, colorless glass, vitreous paint, and silver stain, Germany, 1532. The Metropolitan Museum of Art, The Cloisters Collection, New York, 41.190.441.**

inheritance on frivolous activities.[83] As the inscription in the black border attests, this series was made in 1532 for Jan van Hasselt Tryngen and his wife, who are otherwise unknown (Figs. 4.13, 6.35).[84] No other colors compete with the luminous, dazzling gold that suffuses the roundel, coloring the coins on the table, the hair, many of the garments, and even the inscription. Seated at the left, the Prodigal Son is the picture of fashion with his feathered hat at a jaunty angle, a tuft of his beard left unshaven, and luxurious garments. Dice and piles of coins make clear that the Prodigal Son is gambling. Conveying the tension of the game, he leans forward expectantly and grasps his moneybag as his opponent, who has apparently just thrown the dice, fingers a coin. As in the painting just discussed, a figure rests his hand on the back of one of the players while watching the game intently, underlining the excitement of the scene.

Other details suggest that gambling is a poor use of money. Once again sloth is signaled, this time by a man sleeping with head in hand. Once again a woman is present, probably one of the prostitutes mentioned in medieval interpretations of the parable. Furthermore, the gambling and mixed company suggest that the setting is disreputable, perhaps a tavern or brothel.

FIG. 4.14. Roberto d'Oderisio or his circle, *Abraham of Edessa in the Brothel*; *Abraham of Edessa Feasting with Mary* from *Vitae patrum* (Lives of the Holy Fathers), Italy, Naples, ca. 1350–75. The Morgan Library & Museum, New York, MS M.626, fols. 94v–95r (dets.).

Brothels were often legal in the Middle Ages, sometimes even run by city governments, but spending money on prostitutes was deemed immoral. Colored pen drawings in the lower borders of a fourteenth-century Neapolitan manuscript offer a rare glimpse of the economic transactions involved in a brothel. These images appear in a compilation of biographies of holy hermits written in the fourth century and known as the *Vitae patrum* (Lives of the Holy Fathers). They depict the story of the hermit Abraham of Edessa and his niece Mary of Egypt, a prostitute who became a saint.[85] The first image in the sequence (fol. 93v) shows Abraham teaching Mary in her monastic cell and then a monk raping her. The next folio (94r) shows a grief-stricken Mary fleeing the monastery while her uncle dreams that she is in danger. On the following folio (94v) Abraham sets out to find Mary, and successfully locates her at a brothel, where he pretends to be a client (Fig. 4.14). In the first of these facing images, the procurer, at the far right, offers him wine. In the facing miniature, at the left, Abraham dines with his niece, who fails to recognize him in his disguise. At the center, he pays the procurer, dropping coins in his hand. At the right, Abraham sits beside Mary on a bed, the only furniture in the room. Revealing his identity, he convinces her to return to a holy life, which she does on the following page. Framed by the rape scene and Mary's return to the monastery, these images emphasize the tragic nature of prostitution, thereby implying that it is an immoral way to spend money.

For medieval Christians, another poor use of money was that chosen by the high priest who paid Judas

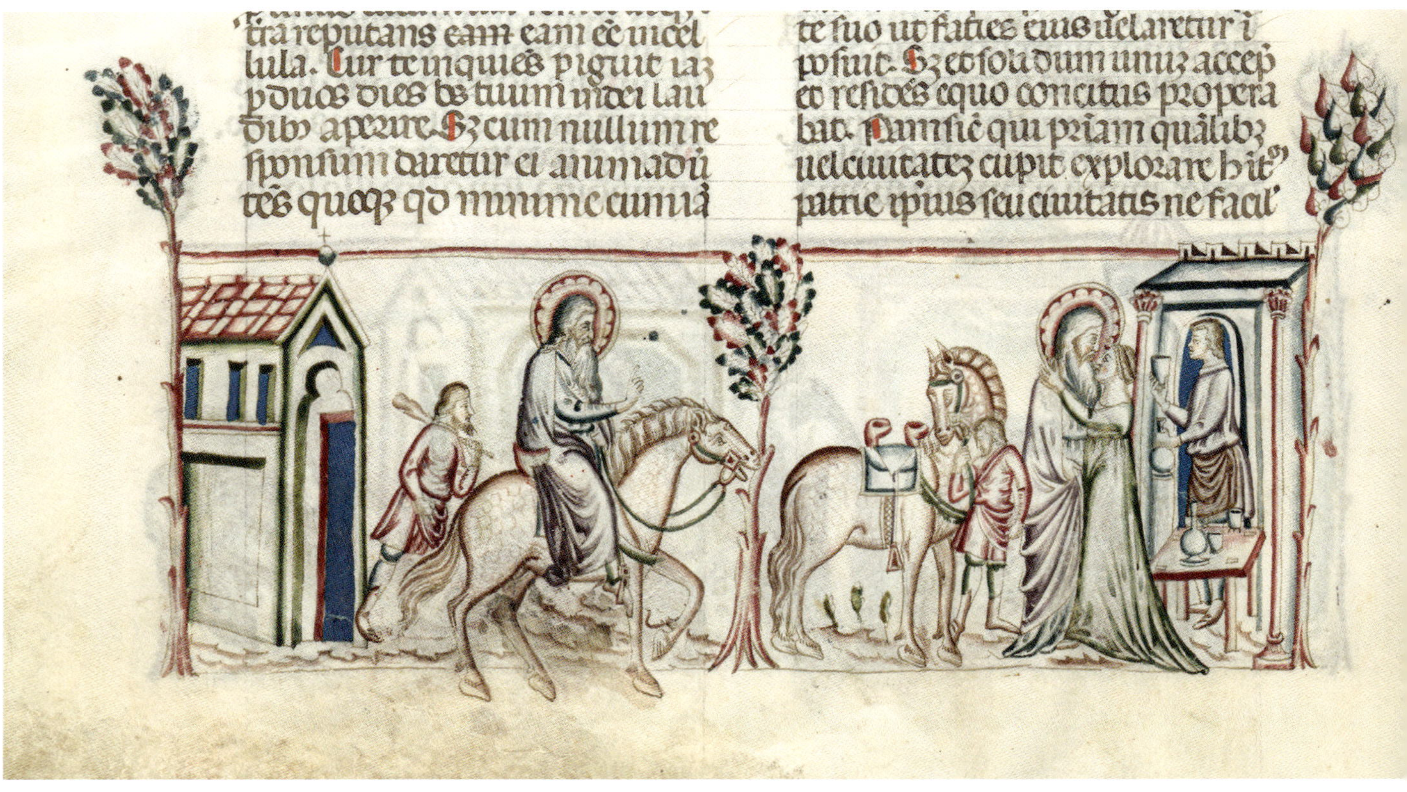

OVERLEAF:
FIG. 4.15. *Judas Receiving Silver, with Prophets and Prefigurations*; *The Betrayal, with Prophets and Prefigurations*, from a *Biblia pauperum* (Bible of the Poor), Austria, perhaps Vienna, or Germany, Regensburg, ca. 1435. The Morgan Library & Museum, New York, MS M.230, fols. 10v–11r.

thirty silver coins to betray Christ. A fascinating image of this episode appears in a *Biblia pauperum* (Bible of the Poor), produced in Regensburg or Vienna around 1435 (Fig. 4.15).[86] Probably composed by a Benedictine monk in mid-thirteenth-century Austria, the *Biblia pauperum* was a popular medieval picture book, which survives in eight manuscripts as well as numerous printed editions.[87] The volume under discussion was never finished; a seventeenth- or eighteenth-century hand added explanatory titles and descriptions to the preliminary pen-and-ink drawings. Much like the *Concordantiae caritatis* (see Fig. 4.5), and the *Speculum humanae salvationis* (see Fig. 4.6), the *Biblia pauperum* shows a complex typological schema. A subject from the Gospels appears at the top center of each folio flanked by four busts of prophets holding scrolls. Below are two comparative scenes from Hebrew scripture. Three consecutive folios relate the tale of Judas's betrayal of Christ.

The most striking image in the series shows the high priest paying Judas, a rarely depicted subject (Fig. 4.15).[88] It had appeared in an earlier German *Biblia pauperum*, dated between 1360 and 1375 (Fig. 4.16), but now the devil is much larger, more frightening, and more sinister. He is not simply bestial with his tail, wings, and drooping dog's ear, but rather predatory. Many of the animal parts that comprise his body are those that are used in acts of aggression: raptor talon feet, grasping clawed hand, long canine teeth, and the single antler that issues from the top of his head. He is also monstrous: part human, part animal, with a second face on his abdomen. On one level, the devil

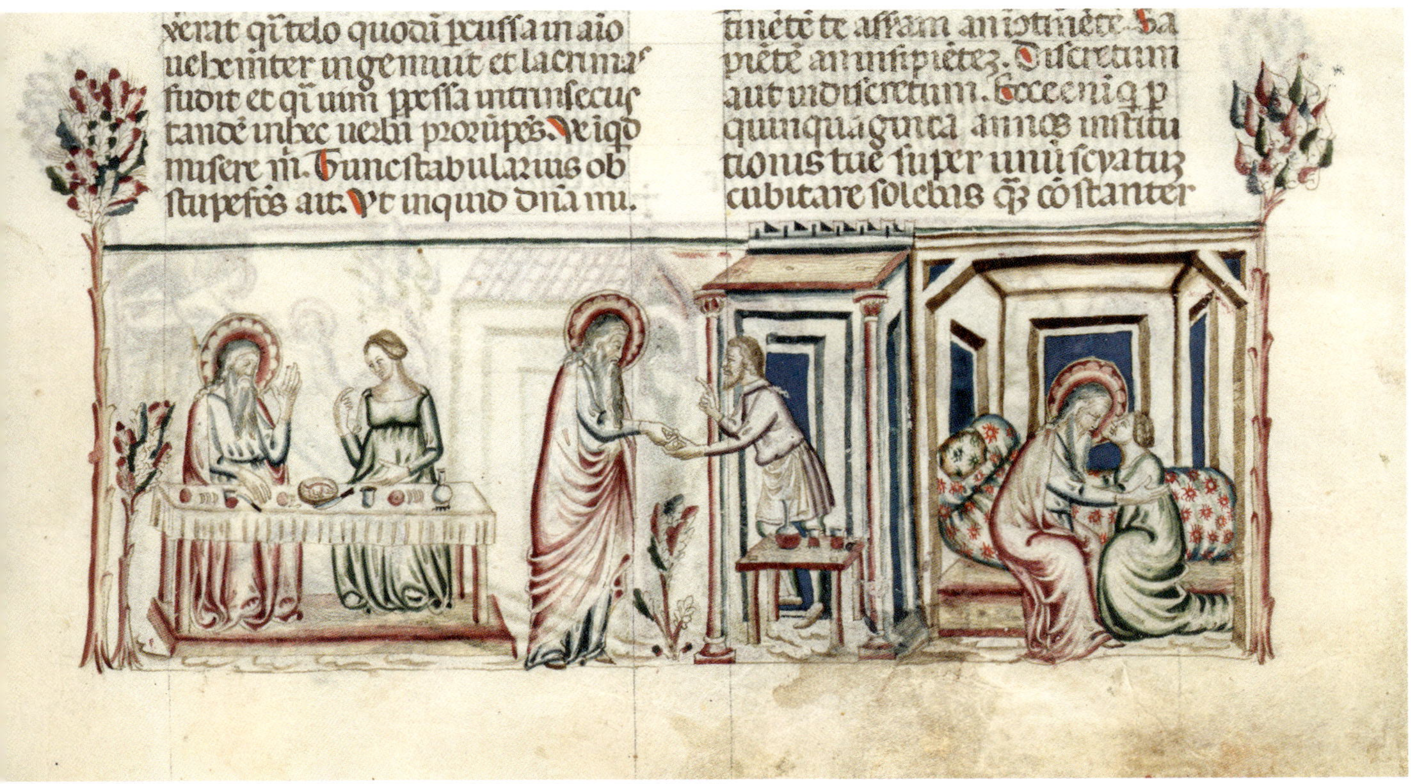

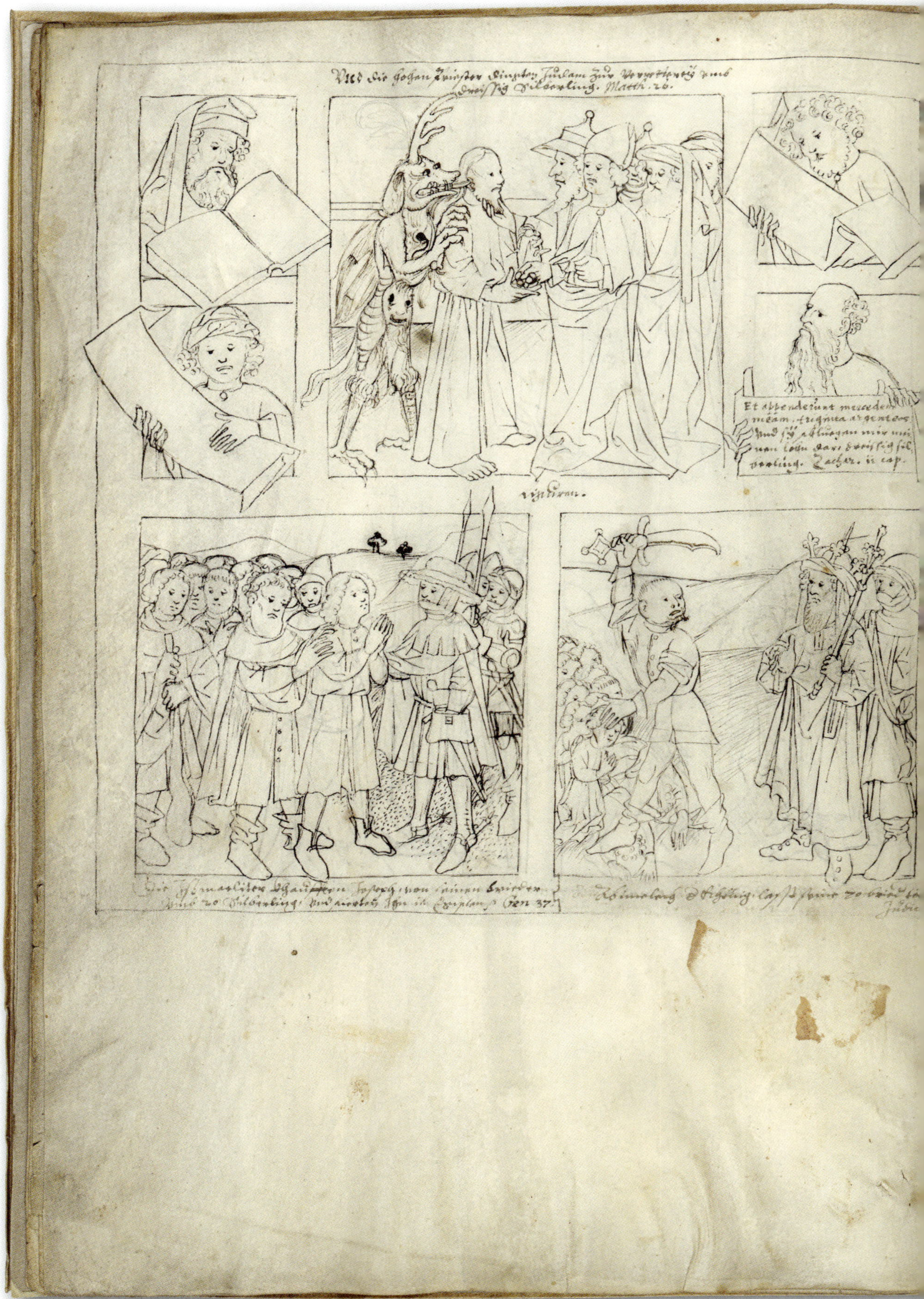
Matth. 26.
Et appenderunt mercedem
meam, triginta argenteos
Zacher. 11 cap.
Gen 37.

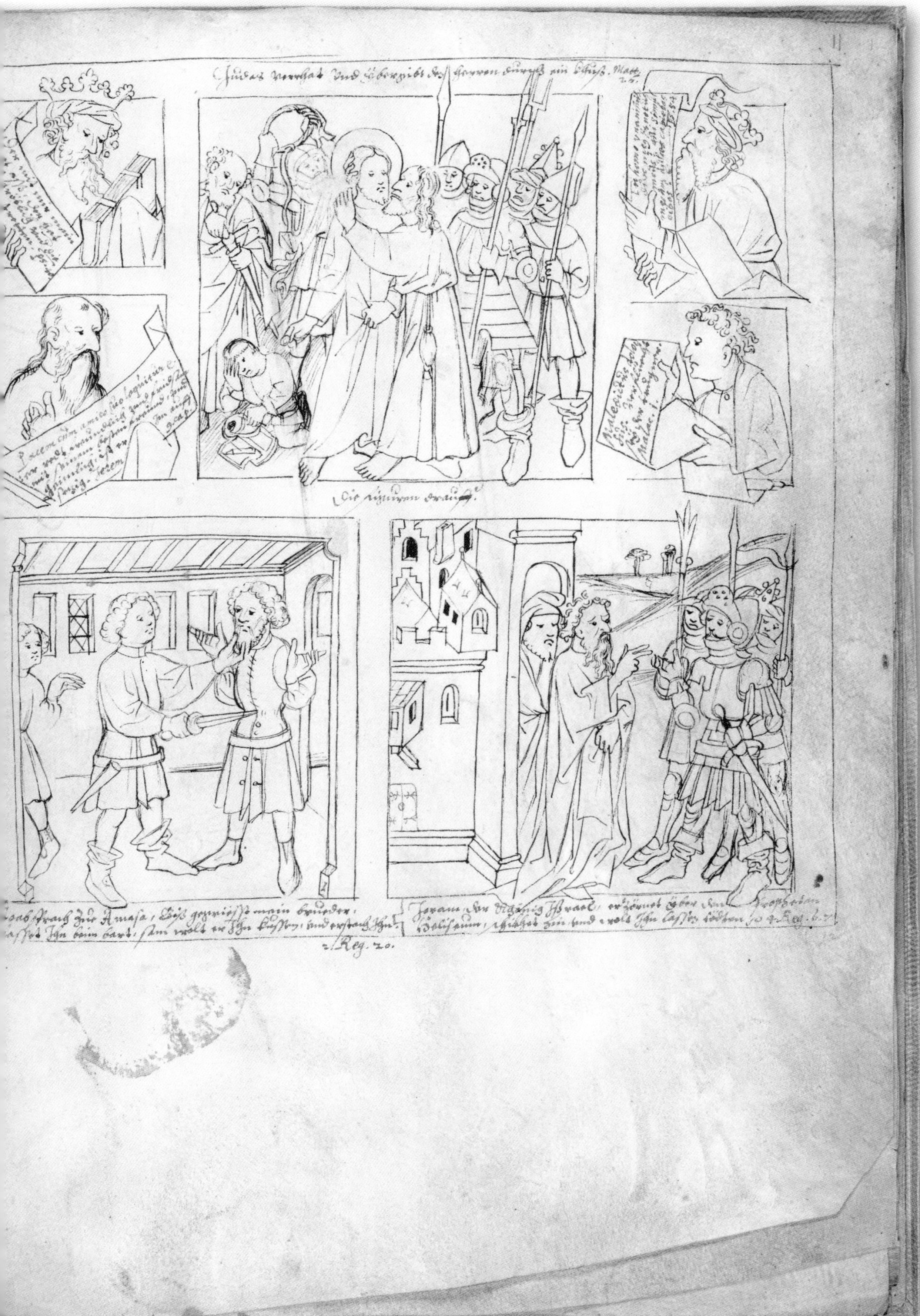
2. Reg. 20.

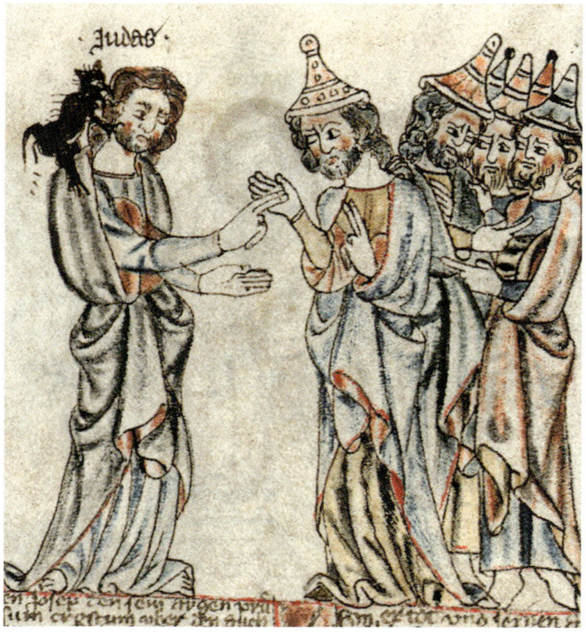

FIG. 4.16. ***Judas Receiving Silver*, from a *Biblia pauperum* (Bible of the Poor), Germany, 1360–75. Staatsbibliothek, Munich, MS Cgm. 20, fol. 10v (det.).**

illustrates Luke 22:3 and John 13:27, who relate that after Judas took the sop (morsel of bread) from Christ at the Last Supper, "Satan entered into Judas." Two fifteenth-century Passion plays, one by the French dramatist and poet Jean Michel, the other by someone deeply influenced by him, have Satan position a little devil on Judas's shoulder at this point in the narrative.[89] (More generally when a devil appears on the shoulders of men it serves to mark them as evildoers: criminals, for example, are shown this way.[90]) But the pose of the devil in the fifteenth-century *Biblia pauperum* also makes clear that he is goading Judas to accept the high priest's payment. The modern scholar, Jean Garnier, has identified a set of features that collectively signify bad counsel: one figure stands behind the other, murmurs in his ear, and places his hand on the other's shoulder.[91] These elements appear in the earlier *Biblia pauperum* (Fig. 4.16; note the devil's open mouth), but the later example shows some unsettling modifications (Fig. 4.15). Not only is the devil as large as Judas and, with his enormous powerful claw, grasps his shoulder, but also, and most disturbingly, he inserts his long tongue into the betrayer's ear. This transformation of the devil into a large, powerful, and repulsive character suggests that Judas, by contrast, is passive, under the devil's control, or at least his influence.

Judas and the devil form a tight unit, standing close together and facing the same way, towards members of the Jewish community, including the high priest, identifiable by his ceremonial headgear, resembling a bishop's miter. The presence of two men in pointed hats (garb associated with medieval Jewry) suggests that Jewish money paid for Judas's treachery. In an unusual gesture, one Jew touches Judas's beard. Is this the chin chuck, which usually connotes love, often of an erotic nature?[92] Is the Jew, in short, showing his affection for Judas? The facing folio offers the key to unlocking the meaning of this gesture: it is repeated at the lower left. The Bible relates that Joab planned to murder his cousin Amasa, who had replaced him as David's military commander. As Joab approached his target, he first greeted him, and then "took Amasa by the chin with his right hand to kiss him" (2 Samuel 20:9). Thus disarmed, Amasa did not notice Joab's sword, and Joab was easily able to kill him. Similarly, Judas, who is not visually identified as a Jew, is shown beguiled by a Jew, leading to his death and damnation. This, too, constructs Judas as passive. Could the artist also be denigrating Judas by constructing him as an object of homoerotic desire? Not only does a Jew stroke Judas's beard in a gesture of love, but the devil also inserts his tongue into the traitor's ear.

Another key difference from the earlier image is that money now occupies the center of the composition and serves to join the two groups (Figs. 4.15–4.16). With his left hand Judas clutches his purse. With his right he accepts the high priest's coins. This affirms Thomas Aquinas's judgment that "Judas fell into the betrayal because he did not restrain his cupidity."[93] The thirteenth-century Franciscan St. Bonaventure agreed that Judas sold his soul because of avarice, and fell "into the snare of the devil."[94]

The series begins (on fol. 10r) with an unusual subject, Judas bargaining with the high priest about the amount of reward he should receive. The next folio (10v; Fig. 4.15), under discussion, shows the payment as the central upper image. At the lower left Joseph's brothers sell him into slavery (Genesis 37), a prefiguration of betrayal and the ill use of money in the Judas scene. One brother places his hands on Joseph's shoulder, echoing the devil's gesture above. The monetary nature of this immoral transaction is underlined by the Ishmaelite's reaching into his purse. At the lower right of this folio is a second tale of betrayal: Abimelech has his seventy brothers slain so that he alone can rule (Judges 9). The final folio of this series illustrates Christ's Betrayal: Judas identifies Jesus to his enemies with a kiss, yet another traitorous sign of affection (Fig. 4.15). Below, Joab betrays Amasa, as discussed above. At the lower right is a scene that is difficult to identify; in some versions of the *Biblia pauperum*, it represents Tryphon's betrayal of Jonathan (Maccabees 19:39–49).

Judas's monetary transaction was taken as proof that he was a poor merchant. Because his payment of thirty silver coins vastly underestimated the value of Christ, he was called *Judas mercator pessimus* (Judas the worst possible merchant). This term would have been well known. It appears in the liturgy of the Passion (in the Divine Office it occurs in a responsory in the second nocturn for Holy Thursday), in Herrad of Landsberg's *Hortus deliciarum*, and in the popular fourteenth-century devotional treatise *Meditationes vitae Christi* (Meditations on the Life of Christ).[95] By assigning a material or monetary value to a spiritual good (Christ), Judas placed a specific price on something of immeasurable value, a poor moral as well as economic judgment.[96]

Consequences of Avarice

Medieval Christians envisioned a range of consequences for avaricious behavior, both in this life and the next. Being enslaved to money was one possible negative outcome. Dialogue 53 of the first book of Petrarch's *De remediis utriusque fortunae* (On the Remedies for Fortune Fair and Foul) models the kind of interior debate that many theologians and moralists hoped would trouble the minds of the monied class. Joy and Reason converse. Joy gleefully exclaims, "I have an abundance of riches," "I possess the great power of riches," "I overflow with wealth," and "My wealth has tremendously increased."[97] These remarks are countered by Reason, who warns that wealth can attract false friends and spark envy, and that many wealthy men were happier before they became rich. In the key passage for the accompanying illustration, Reason counsels:

> Beware, lest you be the one who is being possessed and, in fact, do not hold your riches but are being held by them. . . . Thus your greed and mind bent on profit

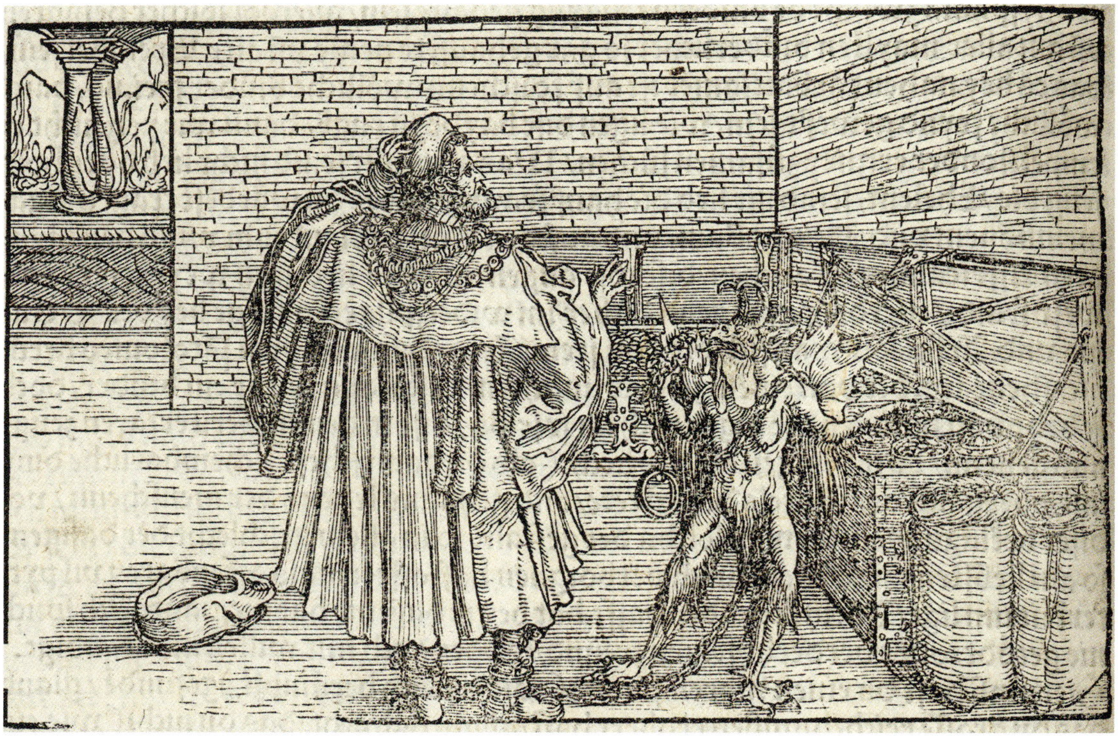

FIG. 4.17. Petrarch Master (Hans Weiditz?), ***Man Chained to His Money,*** **from Francesco Petrarch,** ***Von der Artzney bayder Glück (De remediis utriusque fortunae/ On the Remedies for Fortune Fair and Foul),*** **Germany, Augsburg: Heinrich Steyner, 1532. The Morgan Library & Museum, New York, PML 23220, leaf M3 verso (det.).**

> make servants out of you who should be the masters. Everyone knows that the use of money is to purchase the necessities of life—few in number, simple, and easily to be had. Anything beyond these is burdensome—not so much wealth as shackles and chains.[98]

In or shortly before 1520 the Petrarch Master illustrated this passage for the 1532 edition of *Von der Artzney bayder Glück*.[99] He seized on Reason's idea that wealth becomes "shackles and chains" that weigh down a rich man (Fig. 4.17). His woodcut shows a prosperous man as a prisoner of the devil. His ankles are already chained as a demon offers him even more sacks of money along with another chain. The man's wavering gesture reveals his inner conflict: whether or not to follow his greedy urges. His avaricious behavior, however, has already enslaved his soul in this life and damned it in the next.

Much more common are those images that show hell as a punishment for avarice. A magnificent large limestone capital, carved in Burgundy in the 1150s, probably for the Benedictine abbey of Moutiers-Saint-Jean, makes clear that a lack of charity can lead to damnation (Figs. 4.18–4.20).[100] It portrays the parable of a rich man (traditionally called Dives, after the word for rich man, *dives*, in the Vulgate) who refused the beggar Lazarus's request for crumbs that fell from his dining table (Luke 16:19–31). When Lazarus died, Abraham received him in heaven, but the greedy Dives was condemned to hell.

The capital shows the second part of the story. On the left side, below the blessing hand of God, an angel receives the soul of Lazarus, represented, according to medieval convention, as a small child, while the beggar dies alone outdoors, his hand clutching his bare chest (Fig. 4.18). In a more badly damaged scene on the right side of the capital, demons seize the soul of Dives, who dies comfortably at home in bed surrounded by

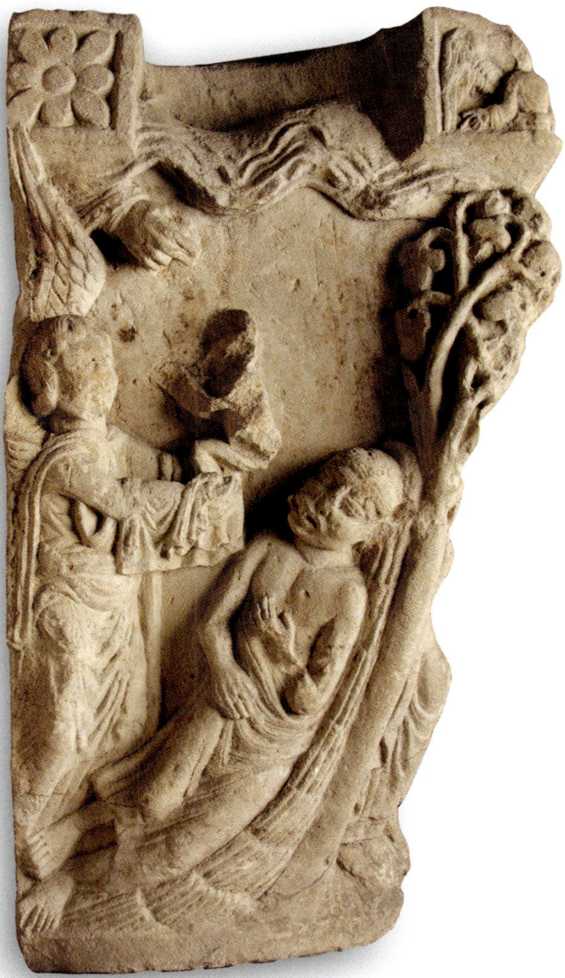

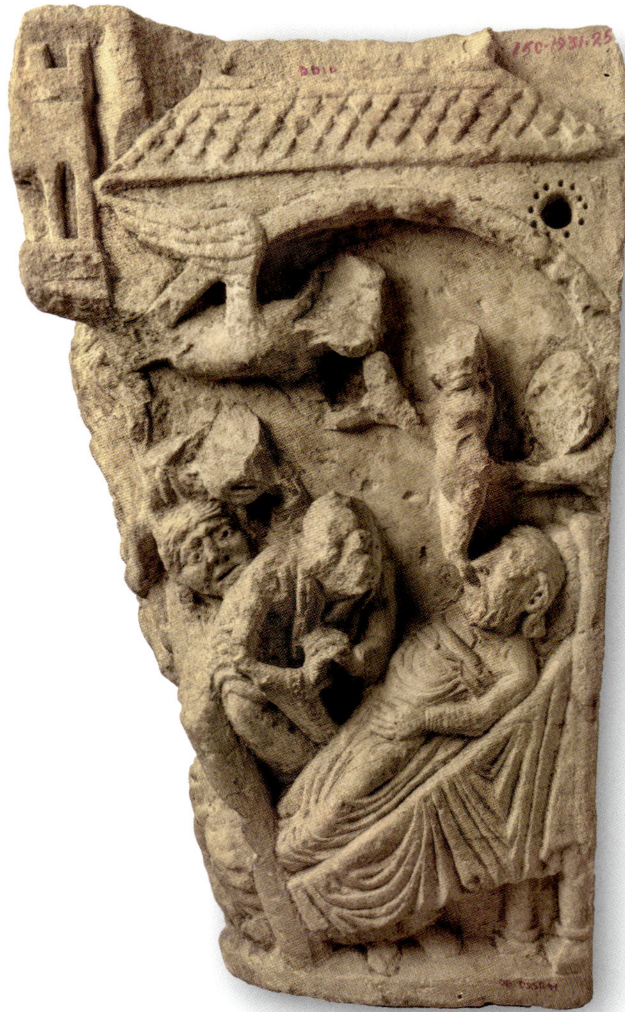

FIG. 4.18. ***Death of Lazarus*, from a capital with the story of Lazarus and Dives, limestone, France, Burgundy, Abbey of Moutiers-Saint-Jean (?), ca. 1150–60. Glencairn Museum, Bryn Athyn, PA, 09.SP.94.**

FIG. 4.19. ***Death of Dives*, from a capital with the story of Lazarus and Dives, limestone, France, Burgundy, Abbey of Moutiers-Saint-Jean (?), ca. 1150–60. Glencairn Museum, Bryn Athyn, PA, 09.SP.94.**

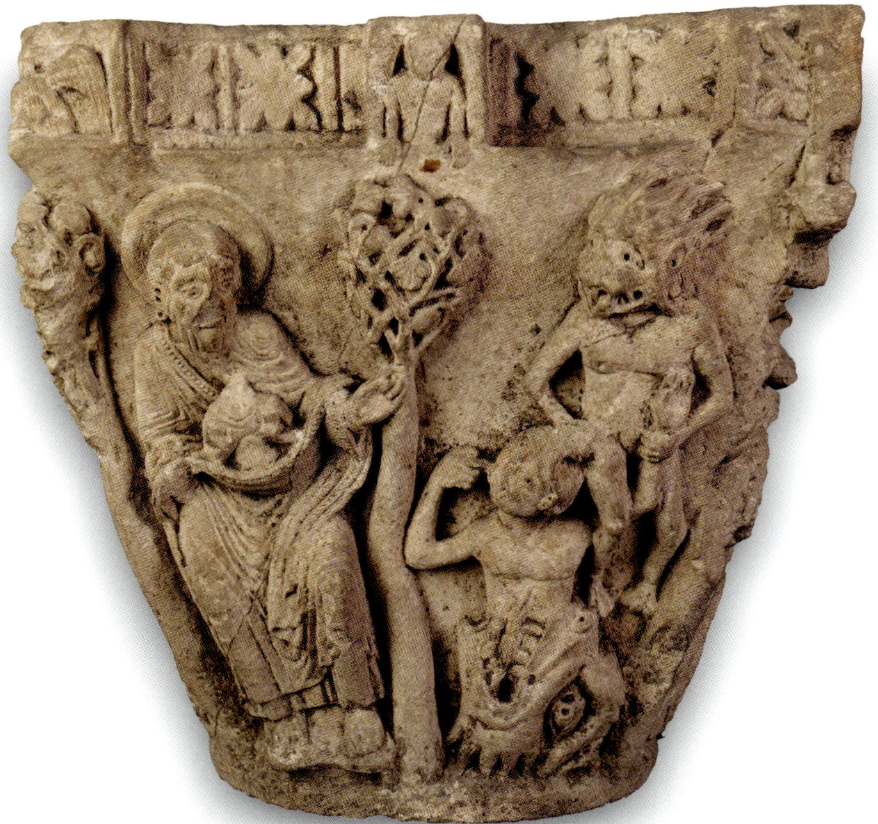

FIG. 4.20. ***Lazarus in the Bosom of Abraham, Dives in Hell,*** **from a capital with the story of Lazarus and Dives, limestone, France, Burgundy, Abbey of Moutiers-Saint-Jean (?), ca. 1150–60. Glencairn Museum, Bryn Athyn, PA, 09.SP.94.**

his family (Fig. 4.19). A woman, presumably his wife, mourns at the foot of the bed, wringing her hands. The central face of the capital presents the most dramatic scene (Fig. 4.20). A tree separates two contrasting but connected episodes. At the left, Lazarus's childlike soul (whose head is lacking) rests in the bosom of Abraham in paradise. The haloed prophet gestures towards the right, where Dives is horrifyingly tormented in hell. A demon yanks the sinner's hair and, pulling his arm between his devilish legs, seizes his wrist, a gesture that signifies taking possession.[101] Unlike Abraham's calm demeanor, the demon's face is frightening, with its bulging eyes and flame-like hair. Dives is further punished by being swallowed by the hellmouth, whose large teeth, extended tongue, and bestial face are meant to terrify viewers. Dives points to his mouth to request a drop of water, which Abraham denies. This sculpture, like the contemporaneous personification of Avarice discussed above (Fig. 4.1), would have been displayed in a church to remind visitors of the horrifying consequences of greed. Its powerful expressive style and deep carving, which creates nightmarish shadows and flickering highlights, would have enhanced the viewer's fear of the dangers of avarice. The subject of Lazarus and Dives was often represented at places where the poor begged for alms.[102] If this capital was produced for the portal of the wealthy monastery of Moutiers-Saint-Jean, it would have served to remind both the monks and the external community to share their riches charitably.

A stunningly beautiful interpretation of Lazarus and Dives appears in a book of hours illuminated in

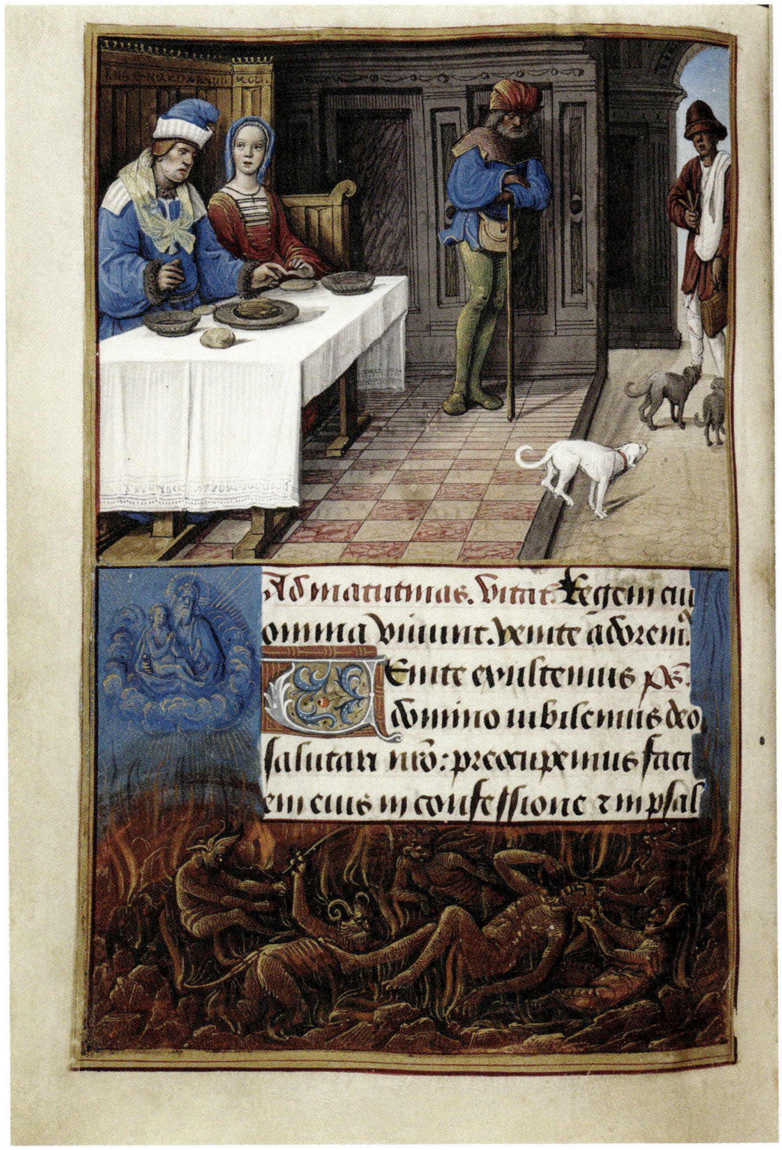

FIG. 4.21. Jean Poyer, *Lazarus and Dives*, from the Hours of Henry VIII, France, Tours, ca. 1500. The Morgan Library & Museum, New York, MS H.8, fol. 134v.

Tours by Jean Poyer around the turn of the sixteenth century.[103] Previously believed to have been owned by King Henry VIII of England, the manuscript's prayers and devotions indicate that its patron must have been someone connected to the French court.[104] Poyer's cool, elegant style appealed to the court, but the manuscript's patron has never been identified. The illumination depicts Dives feasting with an attractive young woman in a room with tiled floor and marble-paneled walls (Fig. 4.21). Seated on an elegantly carved wooden bench, the couple eats poultry and bread at a table covered with a white cloth with crisp folds and a hem with a pseudo-inscription. Luke (16:21–22) describes the beggar Lazarus as having sores, and so he is often portrayed, as here, as a leper. As Dives averts his eyes, Lazarus approaches, a leper's clapper in his hand and blood oozing through his leggings. The three hounds that approach him recall those mentioned in the biblical passage that lick Lazarus's sores.

In the lower margin are two contrasting scenes. Above, painted in gold on heavenly blue, a cruciform-haloed Abraham shelters Lazarus's nude, praying soul.

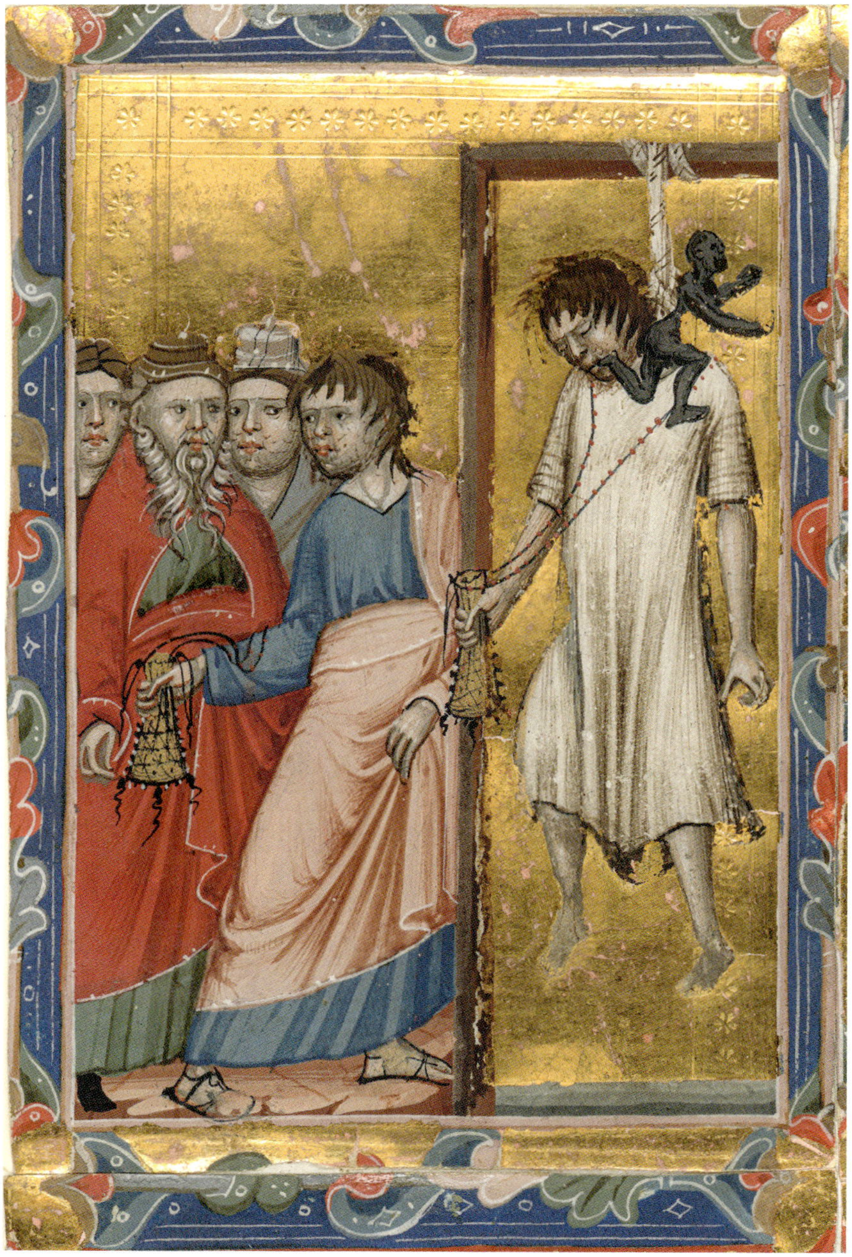

FIG. 4.22. The Hungarian Master and workshop, *Judas Attempts to Return the Silver and Judas Hanged*, from the Hungarian Anjou Legendary, Italy, Bologna (or Hungary), ca. 1325–35. The Morgan Library & Museum, New York, MS M.360.8 (det.).

Below, painted in red to suggest the fires of hell and brown to indicate its rocky barrenness, demons assault Dives, pulling his hair and beating him as flames lick his body. Again Dives asks for water by pointing to his mouth, and again his request is denied. Hell seems to meld with heaven as infernal flames transform into divine rays of light. The accompanying text, the Office of the Dead, would have focused readers' attention on hell and purgatory. The accompanying image would have reminded them that if Dives had acted more charitably towards Lazarus, he might have avoided damnation.

The story of Judas, discussed above, was one of the most popular narratives to illustrate the negative consequences of greed. Not only did his betrayal lead to Christ's Crucifixion, but also to the traitor's own suicide. The latter scene appears on a leaf from a fourteenth-century picture book of the lives of Christ and the saints, made either in Bologna or Hungary for a Hungarian Angevin patron, perhaps Charles of Anjou, king of Hungary, and later disbound and dispersed (Fig. 4.22).[105] First, a remorseful Judas tries to return his payment, stored in an elegant drawstring purse, to the high priest, but is rebuffed. Then, in despair, he takes his own life. His dead body hangs on a gallows, his right hand still grasping his purse. Its cord loops around his neck, drawing our attention to the dark soul that flees from his mouth, its demonic form signaling Judas's damnation. The repetition of the purse visualizes the critical role that avarice played in Judas's fall from grace.

The biblical text states that Judas flung the coins in the Temple, and these spilled coins, like so many other examples of this motif (Figs. 3.8, 3.9, 4.2, 4.7), underline the poor use to which this money was put; these coins are emblematic of Judas's diabolical betrayal of Jesus. Judas's falling coins became a major motif in some images of the Instruments of the Passion. One Dutch sixteenth-century panel shows a bust of Judas, identifiable by the moneybag strung round his neck (Fig. 4.23). This pouch falls freely through the air, turning upside down and opening to release a cascade of coins. This may well have brought to mind not only the sinful use to which this money was put, but also the fear of falling that Janet Robson has demonstrated was associated with Judas: the fear of falling from the noose, from grace, and into hell.[106] Other motifs on the panel include two heads (perhaps Caiaphas and Pilate), nails, dice, the reed, the holy lance, and Pilate's ewer and basin.

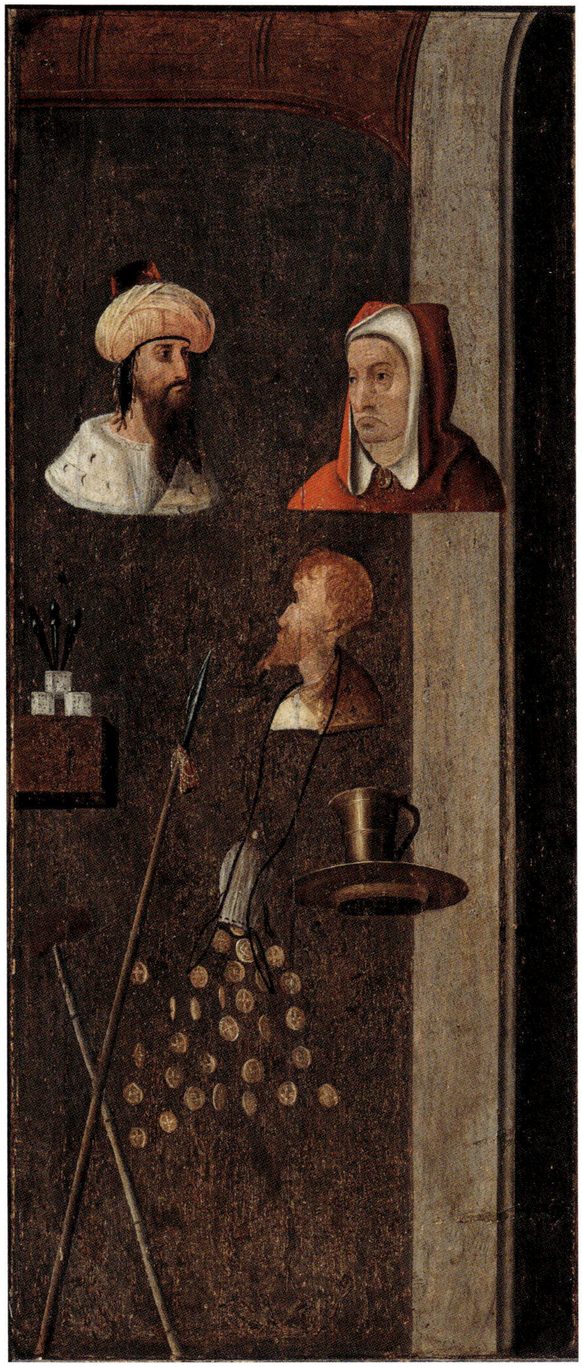

FIG. 4.23. ***Instruments of the Passion*, oil on panel, The Netherlands, 1500–1550. Museum of Fine Arts, Boston, 20.860.**

Images of Judas reflected and reinforced antisemitism. Here he is identified as Jewish by his red hair, yellow shirt, pointed beard, and hooked nose.[107] Images like these collectively construct Judas as the greatest archetype of greed, and strengthen the false association between Jews and ill-gotten gains (see Figs. 4.6, 4.11, 4.15–4.16, 4.22). That Judas betrayed Christ for thirty silver coins reinforced the vicious and profoundly damaging stereotype that Jews love money above all else; the moneybag became an attribute of Jews in medieval art.[108] Images of Judas conflated the Passion narrative with late medieval tensions about the monetary economy, and helped construct Jews as scapegoats for its most devastating aspects.

Christian usurers, however, were also criticized. Five biblical texts forbid charging interest on a loan; Luke (6:34–35), for example, advises that you should even "lend, without expecting to be repaid in full."[109] The medieval Church repeatedly condemned usury, which Gratian's *Decretum*, the influential canon law code compiled in the twelfth century, defined as "[e]verything that is demanded that is beyond the capital."[110] As Jacques Le Goff notes, "Each council—the Second Lateran Council of 1139, the Third Lateran Council of 1179, the Fourth Lateran Council of 1215, the Second Council of Lyon of 1274, and the Council of Vienna of 1311—added a building block to the wall the Church was building to contain the wave of usury."[111]

Medieval Christians developed a set of arguments against usury. Some we have mentioned previously: that the usurer's profits were not due to labor, as God demanded; that he stole time, which belongs to God; and that since money cannot reproduce naturally, it is a sin against nature when it grows through investment or interest. But additional arguments were devised. Usury was condemned as theft. Not only did the usurer take back the money he had loaned, but he also charged interest, which, according to philosophers and moralists, belonged to the borrower, not the lender. Furthermore, the usurer did not use money for the purpose for which it was designed, to buy and sell. Usury was also seen as a sin against justice since it impoverished borrowers and caused social disruption. Yet gradually the Church allowed moneylenders to charge interest under certain circumstances. Nonetheless, many medieval Christians felt anger towards moneylenders—not only on philosophical grounds, but also because borrowers often resent lenders.

One way to gauge this rage is by examining burial practices. The Lateran Church Council of 1179 and the General Church Council of Lyon in 1274 forbade Christian burials for usurers. Such prohibitions continued, albeit sporadically, into the fifteenth century. The Augustinian monk Filippo degli Agazzari of Tuscany, who died in 1422, wrote that usurers' "bodies should be buried in ditches, together with dogs and cattle."[112] In 1487, Piacenza attributed a terrible storm to the recent burial of a usurer in the consecrated ground of a church. The corpse was unearthed, dragged through the streets, insulted by former creditors, and eventually thrown into the Po River.[113]

Artists and writers also expressed anger towards usurers. Florence was a flourishing commercial center, where many, including Dante, condemned those who charged interest on loans as exploiters of the poor.[114] A Florentine manuscript from 1345–55 shows evidence—including candle drippings and readers' marginal and interlineal jottings—that multiple generations used it to

FIG. 4.24. ***Punishment of Usurers,*** **from Dante Alighieri, *Divina commedia* (Divine Comedy), Italy, Florence, 1345–55. The Morgan Library & Museum, New York, MS M.676, fol. 27r (det.).**

study Dante's *Divina Commedia* (Divine Comedy). One illumination depicts Canto 17, which describes Virgil and Dante's visit to the last ring of the seventh circle of hell (Fig. 4.24).[115] The pertinent episode appears at the left, where Dante approaches a group of naked usurers who are punished in a land of burning sands and raining fire, represented by red strokes. One figure raises his hand, as the text relates, to protect himself from the falling flames. Large moneybags, three with coats of arms, hang round the necks of four figures in the front row. Heraldry enables us to identify the families of three of the usurers: the Gianfigliazzi of Florence (yellow with a blue lion), the Ubbriacchi of Florence (red with a white goose), and the Scrovegni of Padua (white with a blue sow). In fact, this last figure must be the well-known Reginaldo degli Scrovegni, whose son Enrico commissioned Giotto's Arena Chapel in part to atone for the family's sin of usury.[116] Dante, and, following him, the illuminator, portray the usurers as sitting perfectly still. Robert Hollander explains that usurers, when alive, "caused money to race from hand to hand, but were themselves stationary, unmoved movers hunched over their desks in the pursuit of gain."[117] Now in hell, they continue to sit without moving.

Above at the left, Virgil speaks to the monstrous beast Geryon, an allegorical figure of Fraud, who rests above the usurers. To the right, Dante joins Virgil to ride the beast and continue their journey. This illumination suggests that more than a hundred years after Dante's death, and at a time when society was beginning to accommodate monetary practices that had traditionally been considered usurious, Florentines still kept alive the poet's characterization of usury as a damnable offense.

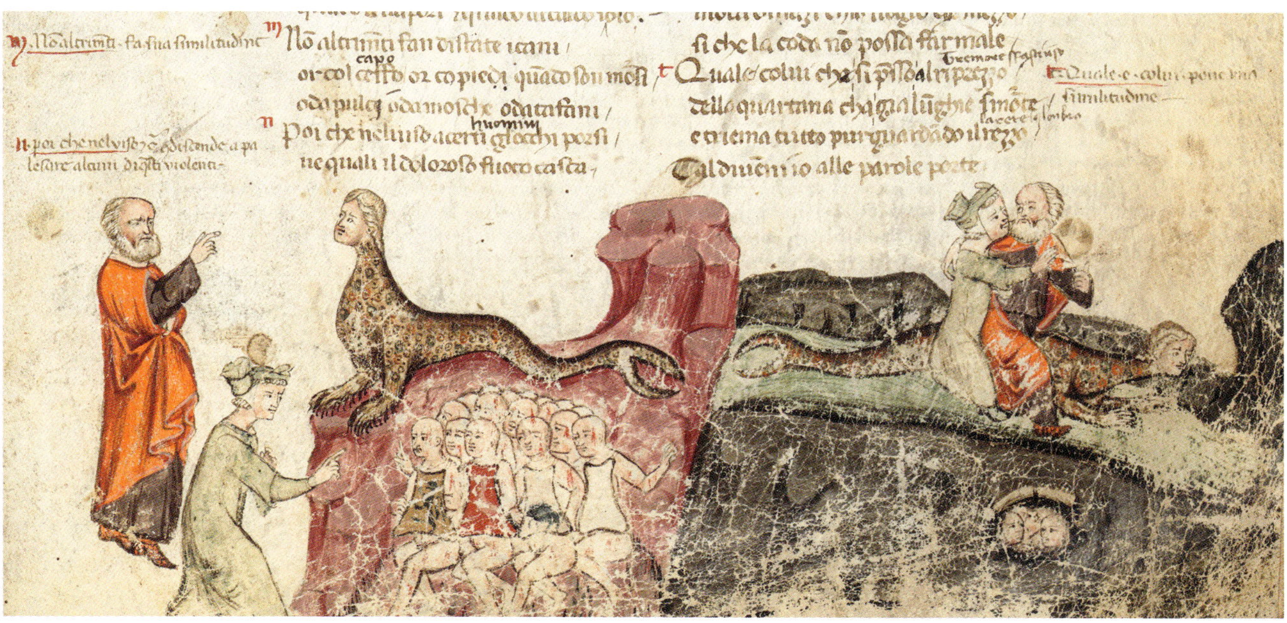

FIG. 4.25. ***Punishments of Sodomites*, from Dante Alighieri, *Divina commedia* (Divine Comedy), Italy, Florence, 1345–55. The Morgan Library & Museum, New York, MS M.676, fol. 25r (det.).**

Dante includes a range of economic sinners, including "hoarders and misers; spendthrifts; profligates; usurers; simoniacs; sellers of public office; thieves; alchemists; counterfeiters."[118] But he demonstrates his particular aversion to usurers by placing them in a deeper part of hell than murderers. In this last ring of the seventh circle of hell, Dante groups together sinners who commit violence against nature. Blasphemers abuse the gift of language, sodomites the gift of sex, and usurers the gift of art, that is, the skills by which we are meant to produce and create. Usury generates nothing worthwhile. Furthermore, by refusing to labor and instead letting money multiply on its own, usurers "scorn nature" (*Inferno* 11:111). Other medieval texts and images also link barren money with sterile sexual acts. Taddeo di Bartolo's fresco of hell in the collegiate church of Santa Maria Assunta in San Gimignano, from 1393–1413, juxtaposes a prone usurer with a prone sodomite. As Robert Mills concludes, monetary imagery is sometimes viewed "as a metaphor for sterile sexual activity."[119] Three illuminations depicting sodomites precede the one of usurers in the Florentine manuscript. The first shows Brunetto Latini, the acclaimed Florentine statesman and intellectual who

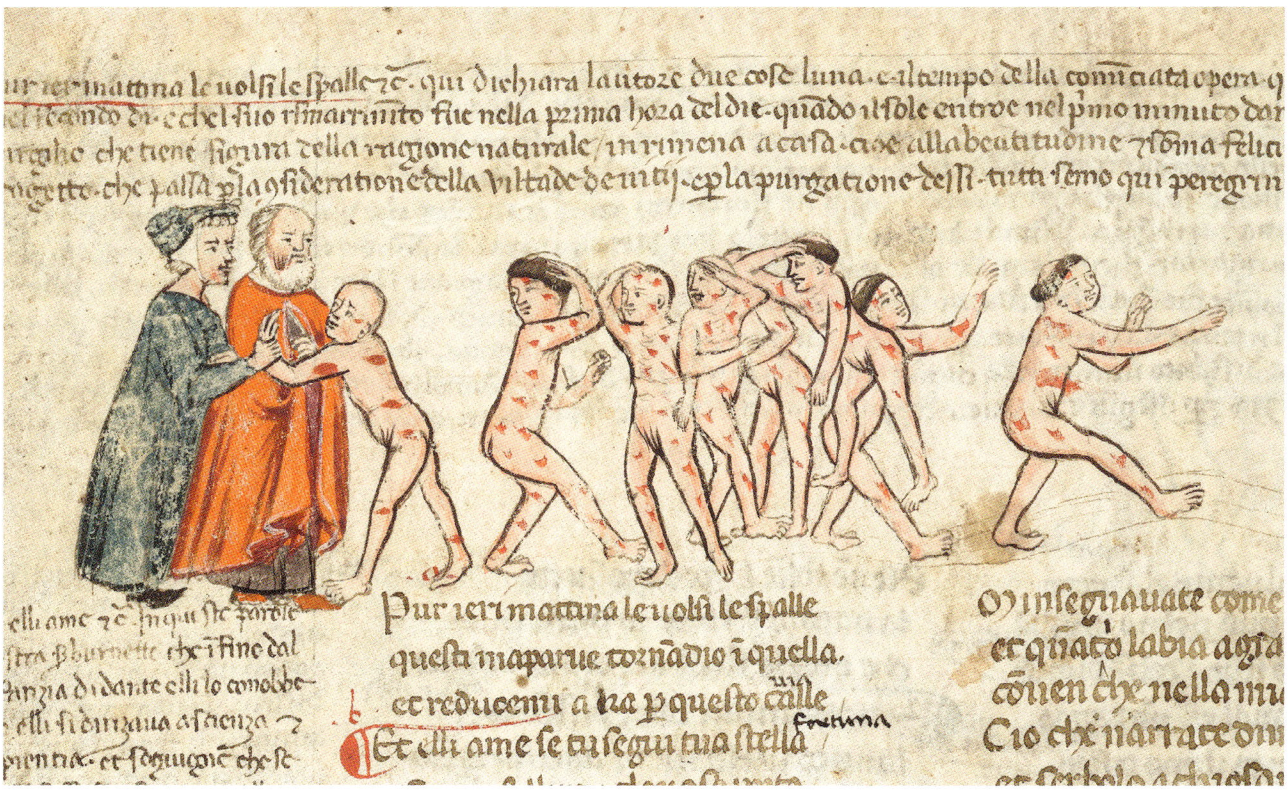

had been Dante's guardian and tutor, stopping to talk briefly to him (Fig. 4.25). If the usurers in the *Inferno* sit still, Latini's fellow sodomites run incessantly, as the illumination suggests. But in other ways the two groups resemble each other. Both are shown as nude men who bear wounds from the falling flames, raise their arms to protect themselves from injury, and share the same barren, burning space in hell.

Sterile Coins, Bleeding Hosts, and Antisemitism

Money performs multiple functions in a fascinating illumination, dating to the 1530s, that depicts an episode from one of the first and most famous host desecration narratives of the Middle Ages (Fig. 4.26).[120] Like other far-fetched and false antisemitic tales, stories of host desecration fostered vicious stereotypes and caused untold damage to Jewish communities across Europe. A Jewish pawnbroker longed for a consecrated host, the holy wafer used in the celebration of the Mass, and believed by medieval Christians to be mystically transformed into the actual body of Christ during the liturgy. During Holy Week, his desire was fulfilled. A poor woman who had pawned to the Jewish broker her only valuable possession, her dress, wanted to wear it for Easter. For this reason, she agreed to give the pawnbroker a consecrated host in exchange for her garment and some money. Once the Jew had taken possession of the host, he stabbed it with a knife to see whether it was the body of Christ, as Christians claimed. The host bled, proving that it was, and the Jew then proceeded to hammer, flagellate, and boil it. After the crime was discovered, the host was miraculously recovered intact, the Jew was burned at the stake, his wife and children were converted to Christianity, his pawnshop was confiscated and razed, and a chapel dedicated to the miracle was erected on the spot. The "miracle" of the desecrated host was said to have taken place in 1290 in Paris, details lending historical veracity to a baseless story.

The illumination shows only a few moments of this complex narrative. Wearing the luxurious, fur-lined dress that she had pawned and holding the coin that the Jew had given her as payment for the host, the Christian woman confronts the pawnbroker in his shop. As she looks on, he stabs the host with a knife, and blood spurts forth.

The image, which has probably been cut down, most likely formed part of a multi-episode souvenir poster that was sold at the Parisian chapel dedicated to the miraculous host, which had become a popular pilgrimage site.[121] The cutting's size and narrow shape suggest that it was one of perhaps eight or ten scenes.[122] Pilgrimage sites, such as Einsiedeln and Dijon, offered souvenirs to fit a range of budgets and functions.[123]

The illumination merges two scenes that were usually separate: the woman receiving money and the Jew stabbing the host. Combining these episodes, the illuminator suggests the pawnbroker's payment via the large coin in the woman's hand. The image also develops an idea found in some earlier depictions of host desecration that juxtapose a host with a pile of coins.[124] The host and the coins are meant to be viewed as similar but opposing motifs, one large white circle contrasted with many smaller, darker ones. The present illumination underscores this opposition of host and

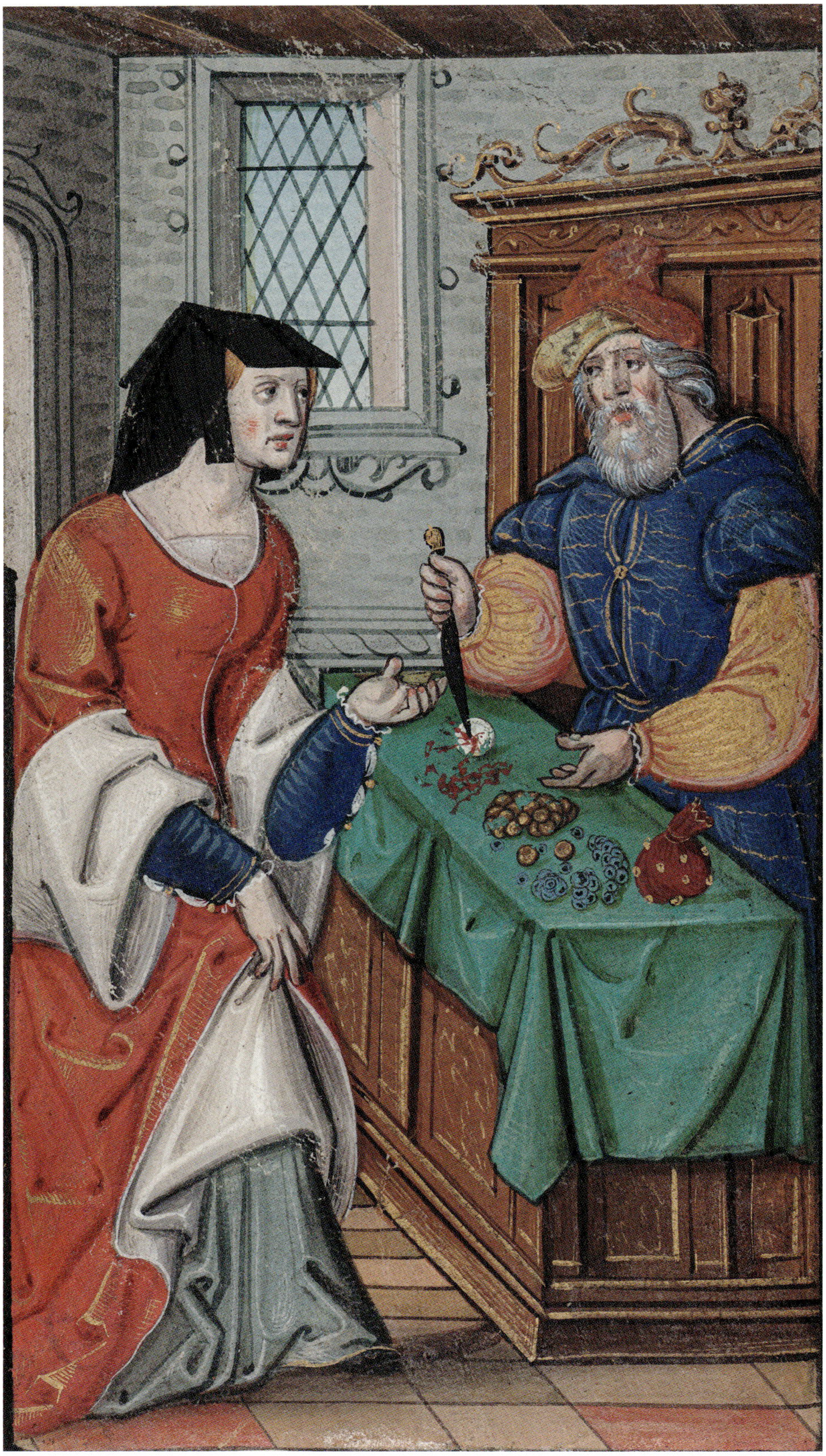

FIG. 4.26. *Parisian Host Desecration of 1290*, cutting, France, Paris, 1530–40. Private collection, New York.

coins, but emphasizes the money even more, including a pile of gold coins, another of blue coins with black highlights (meant to suggest silver currency), a plump and luxurious moneybag, and, finally, the thick gold coin held by the woman. All of this is portrayed on (or near) the counter in the foreground. What is the significance of the large sum of money at the center of a host desecration image?

Host desecration narratives played a critical role in convincing Christians of the doctrine of Transubstantiation, which was codified by the Fourth Lateran Council in 1215 and reinforced by the creation of the Feast of Corpus Christi in 1264. The Church promoted the belief that the host was transformed during Mass into the body of Christ through representations of Masses and episodes of host desecrations; in both the consecrated host is portrayed as alive, sometimes moving on its own, bleeding, or suffering pain. Throughout, however, the host miraculously remains intact. In the present illumination, when the Jew attacks the host because he questions whether it really contains the true presence of Christ, it spurts blood, confirming that it does. Although, as mentioned above, the Jew will go on to hammer, flagellate, and boil the wafer, when it is later recovered, it is miraculously whole.

If doubts about Transubstantiation sparked the thirteenth-century account, the Reformation's resistance to this doctrine contributed to Catholic adherence to it in the sixteenth century. The first Protestant congregation in France was established in 1521 at Meaux, just outside Paris. In 1534, Huguenots posted placards on the walls of major roads in Paris and other French cities; one even found its way to the door of King Francis I's chamber at Amboise. These posters vehemently condemned the doctrine of Transubstantiation, arguing that the body of Christ cannot be present in a wafer or in wine, and that the adoration of the consecrated host and wine was therefore idolatrous.[125]

This intransigence further inflamed Catholics, renewing interest in Eucharistic miracles, such as one that occurred in 1516 at Poitiers.[126] In the 1510s a Parisian publisher printed a booklet that relates the legend of the host desecration of 1290; a second edition followed in Paris between 1530 and 1547.[127] In 1519, Pope Leo X issued a bull of indulgence for visiting the Paris chapel dedicated to the miracle of 1290. Francis I passionately defended Transubstantiation, taking part in a search for a consecrated host that had been stolen. (He also personally witnessed the execution of six Huguenots, and ordered his troops to execute innumerable others.) Numerous stained-glass windows that depict the 1290 host desecration and miracle were commissioned to espouse the doctrine, especially in the Aube district, which had seen an upsurge in numbers of Huguenots.[128] It seems reasonable to conclude, then, that the poster to which this illumination originally belonged was created, in part, to combat Protestants' rejection of Transubstantiation, and that the Jew is a stand-in for the Huguenot.

The image glosses over a difficulty raised by the narrative—that the payment for the host places a monetary value on it. Instead, the illumination contrasts the great value of the consecrated host with the worthlessness of money. Coins resemble Eucharistic hosts; both are round, mechanically produced, and often imprinted with a cross.[129] In art, it is sometimes difficult

FIG. 4.27. Master of François de Rohan, *Avarice*, from Frate Tommaso, *Fiore di virtù* (Flower of Virtue), trans. François de Rohan, France, Paris, ca. 1530. Bibliothèque nationale de France, Paris, MS fr. 1877, fol. 32v.

to know whether a round object should be identified as a coin or host.[130] But to the Church they represented a world of difference. The single large, white, pure, "living" host in the illumination differs strikingly from the piles of smaller, darker, impure, inert coins beside it. And the large number of coins suggests that, unlike the consecrated host, they have reproduced unnaturally. The image, in short, implies that a coin is the diametric opposite of the consecrated host. As a corollary, the picture suggests that the pawnbroker's counter is both similar to and opposite from the church altar where Transubstantiation occurs.[131]

Gold coins were the most expensive currency, generally reserved for aristocrats and royalty (Figs. 2.4, 2.8, 6.3, 6.30, 6.33). Silver currency was also valuable and used, for example, by merchants for major purchases (Figs. 2.1, 2.5, 6.34). For everyday transactions, thinner, smaller, less finely minted coins of base billon were used (see Figs. 6.31, 6.32).[132] It is the valuable gold and silver coins that lie on the pawnbroker's counter. The thickness and wide diameter of the gold coin in the woman's hand mark it as the most valuable coin of all. Although the Parisian text printed in the 1510s states that she was paid only thirty *sous*, this image suggests that she was much more generously rewarded.

The moneybag had different associations. Images meant to criticize those who worked in monetary trades often include moneybags. When the tax collector Matthew follows Christ, he abandons his moneybag (see Fig. 5.13). Usurers, moneylenders, misers, Avarice, Covetousness, and Judas are often associated with moneybags (Figs. 3.1, 3.6, 4.1, 4.3, 4.11, 4.22–4.23). Bearing a remarkably close resemblance to the present illumination is one that shows Avarice behind a counter on which rest piles of gold and silver coins; a large sack of money lies nearby on the floor (Fig. 4.27). In short, unlike the small number of coins that appear discreetly in portraits of merchants, the moneybag was strongly associated with the deadly sin of greed.

The moneybag and large piles of coins in the illumination of the pawnshop, then, speak not only to the Church's doctrine of Transubstantiation, but also to its attitude towards the economic practices that arose at the dawn of capitalism, in particular its condemnation of amassing any amount of money in excess of what was needed for oneself and one's family.

If, in this illumination, money serves as a negative contrast to the host and as a reminder of the sin of avarice, it also functions as an antisemitic attribute of the Jew. The pawnbroker is marked as Jewish by his exotic cap. The motif of the Jew stabbing the host illustrates a core belief of medieval Christians: that Jews were responsible for the violent and painful death of Christ. Since the pawnbroker refuses to accept that the consecrated host is the true body of Christ, the image also confirms the Christian conviction that Jews were blind and stubborn. And the illumination also reinforces the association of Jews with avarice. The Jew is shown as extraordinarily wealthy, not simply through his money, but also through his luxurious garments and furnishings, and his similarity to personifications of Avarice (Fig. 4.27). Furthermore, the booklet printed in the 1510s states that the Jew gave the Christian woman thirty *sous* for her dress, inviting a comparison to the Jewish priest who paid that number of coins to Judas to betray Christ. Jewish pawnbrokers were slandered as economic parasites, and as aggressors who harmed the Christian economy because they devalued

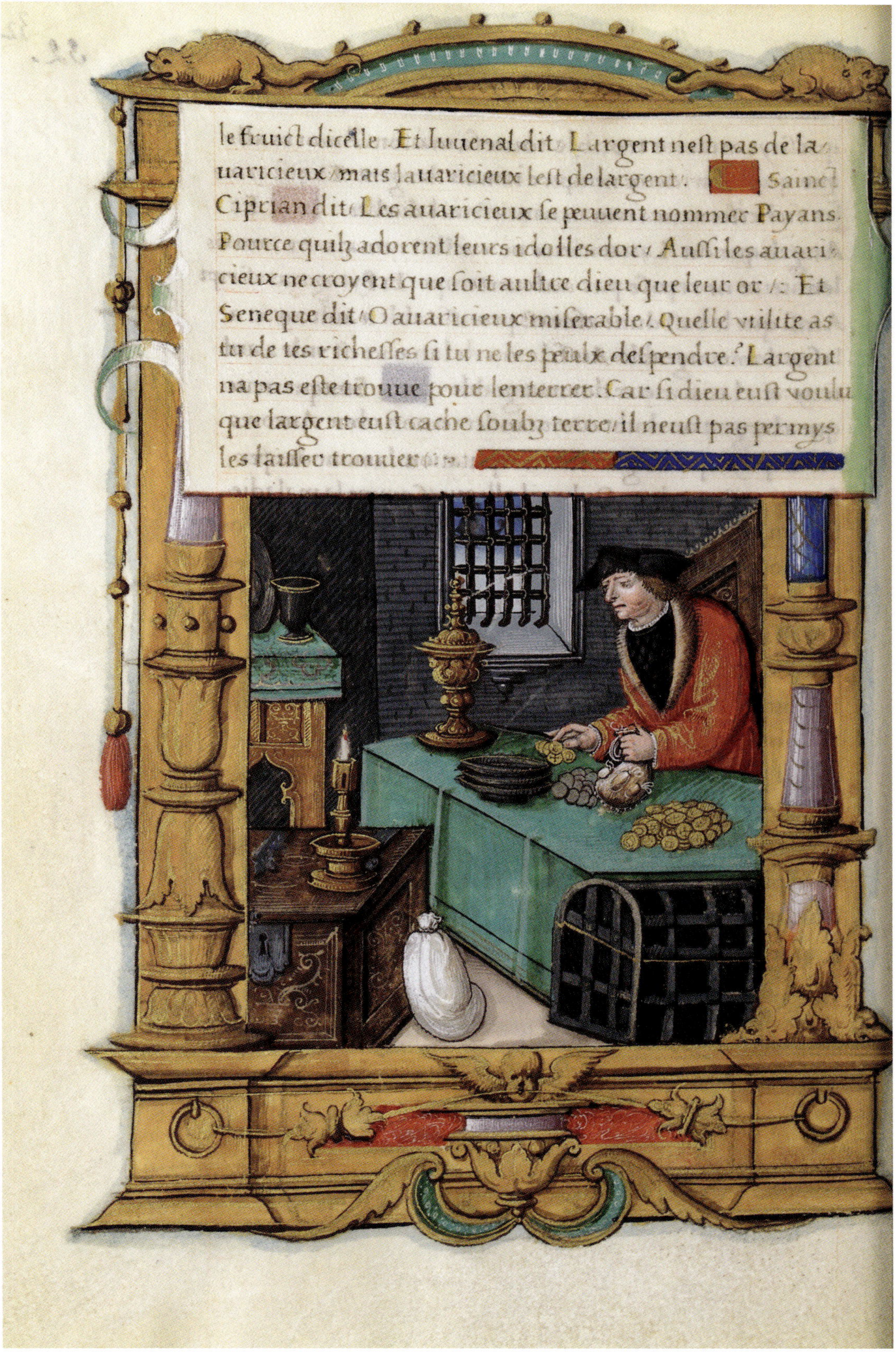
le fruict dicelle Et Iuuenal dit Largent nest pas de la
uaricieux mais lauaricieux lest de largent. Sainct
Ciprian dit Les auaricieux se peuuent nommer Payans.
Pource quilz adorent leurs idolles dor Aussi les auari-
cieux ne croyent que soit aultre dieu que leur or Et
Seneque dit O auaricieux miserable Quelle vtilite as
tu de tes richesses si tu ne les peulx despendre Largent
na pas este trouue pour lenterrer. Car si dieu eust voulu
que largent eust cache soubz terre il neust pas permys
les laisser trouuer

Christian goods and placed a monetary value on the body of Christ, thereby undervaluing its inestimable spiritual worth.[133]

The entanglement in this illumination of sterile coins, a miraculous bleeding host, and antisemitism reveals the complexity of thinking about money in late medieval society while also demonstrating, once again, the belief that money can damn your soul. Avarice was a mortal sin, but, as the images in this chapter have shown, the Church's analysis of money and its teachings on the proper ways to earn and spend money were far more complex than a simple condemnation of greed.

NOTES

1. Little 1971, 20, 23, 25.
2. Little 1978, 36; Migne 1995, col. 465c. For Alain de Lille's economic ideas, see Langholm 2015.
3. Young 2015, 72.
4. Kent 2000, 442 n. 20.
5. See Cahn and Seidel 1979, 105. The moneybag round the neck as a sign of avarice goes back at least to the eleventh century; see Leclercq-Marx 2007, 45. For the iconography of Avarice, see Blöcker 1993, 96–107.
6. For coins that are visible through a moneybag, see Chapter 3, Fig. 3.3, and note 22.
7. Baumann 1996; Leclercq-Marx 2007.
8. Garnier 1982, 190–91, 196; Barasch 1987, 146–51, 166.
9. Baumann 1996, 151.
10. For Beaulieu, see Vescovi 2017, 63.
11. Baumann 1996, 152.
12. For this illuminator and manuscript, see Wieck 1997, 96.
13. The green cloth over the counter suggests that the merchant is a money-lender or money changer. See p. 155.
14. Heck and Cordonnier 2018, 387.
15. Herrad of Landsberg 1977, 178.
16. Morgan, MS M.81, fols. 25r–v.
17. Dante 2000, 5.
18. Wolfthal 2000, xx–xi; Heck and Cordonnier 2018, 386–87.
19. See Simpson and Weiner 1989, 480; Hirsch, Kett, and Trefil 2002, 71.
20. For this poem, see de Lorris and de Meun 1965–75, de Lorris and de Meun 1994, and, for an overview of its imagery, see McMunn 2000 and Ménard 1984.
21. Walters 1989, 33.
22. de Lorris and de Meun 1994, 5, 6; de Lorris and de Meun 1965–75, vol. 1, 6, 8.
23. de Lorris and de Meun 1994, 5.
24. Ibid., 6; de Lorris and de Meun 1965–75, vol. 1, 6; Blamires and Holian 2002, 52.
25. For the *Pèlerinage* and its illuminations, see Tuve 1966, 145–218, and Emmerson 2009. For an English translation, see de Deguileville 1992.
26. de Meun and de Lorris 1994, 78; de Meun and de Lorris 1965–75, vol. 1, 156.
27. Wenzel 1989, 314–15.
28. Stumpf 2010, 82c (Book 3, lines 9365–70; my translation).
29. Ibid., 334–35. For usury as the theft of time, see Le Goff 1988, 39–40.
30. Stumpf 2010, 335–36.
31. Noonan 1957, 43–44, 62–63.
32. Stumpf 2010, 354 (my translation).
33. Cicero 1928, 264–67.
34. For this text and its illuminated manuscripts, see Douteil 2010 and Munscheck 2000. For the Expulsion as a popular subject of sermons, see Kauffmann 1994, 63–64.
35. Boreczky 2017, 8, 11.
36. Frühmorgen-Voss, Ott, and Bodemann 2008, 14; Boreczky 2017, 10–11.
37. Frühmorgen-Voss, Ott, and Bodemann 2008, 16–17; Opll and Roland 2006, 8, 44, 63, 94, 101–2, and especially 95–99.
38. For this opening, see Douteil 2010, vol. 1, 78–79.
39. Thomas à Kempis 1905, 35; Thomas à Kempis 1922, 65.
40. Douteil 2010, vol. 1, 78–79 (my translation).
41. For an early example of an Expulsion scene that features a Jew, see Blumenkranz 1966, 86–87. For a recent publication on the antisemitic association of Jews and money, see Rosenthal and Volovici 2019, especially 27–43.
42. For Christian usurers, see Milton 2011 (Iberia); Heng 2018, 61 (England); and, for Germany, Gilomen 1990 and Gilomen 2010. For their expulsion, see Dorin 2015, 2.
43. Ifft Decker 2020.
44. Dorin 2020.
45. To cite just one primary source for Jewish poverty, the Iberian rabbi Shlomo ibn Adret, known as Rashba (d. 1310), remarked, "The poor of the community are many" (Rashba Responsa III, 380); see Halbertal 2021. Michael Toch writes of a "sizeable . . . quantitatively significant" segment of the Jew population that was "destitute." See Toch 2003, 230. For Jewish artisans, see Lehnertz et al. forthcoming.
46. Mell 2017–18, especially ix–x.
47. This paragraph disagrees with Steven Epstein's discussion above. For everyday interactions between Jews and Christians, see Wenninger 2016, and, among the many publications of Birgit Wiedl on this subject, Wiedl 2015.
48. See, among many other studies, Heng 2018 and Milton 2011. For an image of one such incident, see Wolfthal 2016, 106, fig. 1.

49. "Jew, *v[erb]*." 2019.
50. Petrarch 1991.
51. For the Petrarch Master's illustrations, see Scheidig 1955; Falkenburg 2006.
52. Petrarch 1991, vol. 3, 47; Petrarch 2002, 618.
53. Petrarch 1991, vol. 3, 49; Petrarch 2002, 620.
54. Petrarch 1991, vol. 4, 87.
55. Cicero 1966, 96–97; Scheidig 1955, 207.
56. On this illumination, see Wieck 1999, 434–35. The bibliography on this manuscript is voluminous; see, among others, Gorissen 1973.
57. Gorissen 1973, 423.
58. Le Goff 1988, 59; Stephen of Bourbon 1877, 364–65, no. 419.
59. For this text, see Starkey 2013; Thomasin von Zirclaria 2009; Bismark and Hüpper 2018, 62.
60. Thomasin von Zirclaria 1852, 192; Thomasin von Zirclaria 2009, 138.
61. Thomasin von Zirclaria 1852, 193; Thomasin von Zirclaria 2009, 138.
62. Nelson 1969, 7; Brodman 2009, 19–25.
63. Starkey 2013, 319. For the illustrated versions of *Der Wälsche Gast*, see Wenzel and Lechtermann 2002. For other scenes of this passage, see Welscher Gast Digital 2015, "Motiv 93." See also Thomasin von Zirclaria 2018.
64. The inscription reads, "wücherer dü bist godez effer"; see Clark 1997, 80–93, for the meaning of this phrase.
65. For an English translation and the original woodcuts, see Zeydel 1944.
66. Brant 1872, 10, 30, 35, 56; Zeydel 1944, 66, 94, 100, 118.
67. Brant 1872, 187; Zeydel 1944, 248.
68. Zeydel 1944, 303.
69. Ibid.
70. The phrase occurs in 1 Timothy 3:8, 1 Peter 5:2, and Titus 1:11. The latter reads: "Who must be reproved, who subvert whole houses, teaching things which they ought not, for filthy lucre's sake."
71. Brant 1872, 10; Zeydel 1944, 66.
72. Brant 1872, 11; Zeydel 1944, 67.
73. Brant 1872, 11; Zeydel 1944, 68.
74. Van Cleve 1993, 93.
75. Parshall 2001.
76. Ibid., 86.
77. Skrine 1990, 193.
78. Young 2015, 79.
79. Delcorno 2018, 287.
80. For this painting, see Hand and Wolff 1986, 142–44; Smith 1992, 175–76.
81. Smith 1992, 52.
82. Ibid., 55, 289–90 n. 30. For the gesture of the hand in the coat as a sign of sloth, see Koslow 1975.
83. For this theme, see Renger 1970 and Delcorno 2018.
84. For this stained glass, see Husband and Caviness 1991, 165–66.
85. For the life of St. Mary the Harlot, see Waddell 1936, 289–302.
86. For this manuscript, see Suckale 1987, 106–7; Frühmorgen-Voss, Ott, and Bodemann 1996, 301–5.
87. For the *Biblia pauperum*, see Hamburger 2005.
88. Schiller 1972, 24.
89. Muir 1995, 129.
90. Hinckeldey 1980, 119, 245.
91. Garnier 1982, 107, 109, figs. E, F, I.
92. Fisher 2013; Steinberg 1996, 5–6, 110–18.
93. Aquinas 1951, Mt 26:15, par. 2146; Robson 2004, 40.
94. Bonaventure 1867, 172–74 (chapter 22).
95. Robson 2001, 131, 149.
96. See, among others, Todeschini 2010.
97. Petrarch 1991, vol. 1, 164; Petrarch 2002, 264.
98. Petrarch 1991, vol. 1, 164–65; Petrarch 2002, 264.
99. For this edition, see above, p. 86.
100. For this sculpture, see Cahn et al. 1999, 49–51.
101. Garnier 1982, 199.
102. Mâle 1972, 200.
103. For this manuscript, see Wieck, Voelkle, and Hearne 2000; and Wieck 2015–16.
104. Wieck, Voelkle, and Hearne 2000, 183.
105. For this manuscript, see Tünde 2000, 73–120. For this scene, see Smith 2012, 53–55.
106. Robson 2002.
107. See Mellinkoff 1993.
108. Strickland 2003, 142.
109. Le Goff 1988, 21–23. See also Exodus 22:24, Leviticus 25:35–37, Deuteronomy 23:20–21, and Psalm 15.
110. Le Goff 1988, 26; Gratian, *Decretum* C. 14, q. 3, c. 4.
111. Le Goff 1988, 24.
112. Origo 1957, 148; Parks 2005, 10.
113. Burckhardt 1892, 520.
114. For Dante's views of avarice, see Black 2017.
115. For the iconography of Dante's *Divine Comedy*, see Brieger, Meiss, and Singleton 1969. For Canto 17, see Dante 2000, 284–93.
116. Derbes and Sandona 2008.
117. Dante 2000, 295.
118. Edwards 2018, 273.
119. Mills 2015, 294.
120. For this story, see Lacroix 1890. For this tale and its visual representations, see Rubin 1999; Petryszcze 2020.
121. I thank Roger Wieck for this idea.
122. For a similar multi-episodic host desecration print, produced in Nuremberg around 1495, see Schreckenberg 1996, 264–65. For an early sixteenth-century French poster of nine scenes, depicting the story of 1290, see Schefer 2007, pl. IX; Charron, Gautier, and Girault 2013, no. 58.
123. For Einsiedeln, see Landau and Parshall 1994, 48–50. For Dijon, see Wieck 2007a; Wieck 2007b; Wieck 2014, 74–75, nos. 59, 60; and Wieck 2016, figs. 109–16, 121.
124. For a fourteenth-century Aragonese altarpiece, see Sobré 1989, fig. 136. Some narratives of the tale show the stabbing of the host, as in our image, on the same table as a large quantity of coins. See, for example, Schreckenberg 1996, 272.
125. Baird 1896, 166 (quote); Browning 1840, 46; Mousseaux 1962; Cabanel 2012, 20–30.
126. Cottret 2000, 47.
127. For an analysis of this and other plays about host desecration, see Clark and Sponsler 1999; Reid-Schwartz 1994.
128. Windows at the churches of Saint-Étienne, Bar-sur-Seine (ca. 1542); Saint-Pierre-ès-Liens, Les Riceys-Bas (1549); Saint-Pierre-ès-Liens, Longpré-le-Sec (ca. 1540–45); Saint-Nicolas, Troyes (1563); Saint-Alpin, Châlons-en-Champagne; Saint-Éloi, Rouen (early sixteenth century); and Sainte-Tanche, Lhuître (1525–50).
129. Ellard 1943 and Kumler 2011.
130. Wolfthal 2004, 59 and fig. 70.
131. The white altar cloth contrasts with the pawnbroker's green cloth, for which see p. 155.
132. See David Yoon's essay in the present volume.
133. Todeschini 2018, 346.

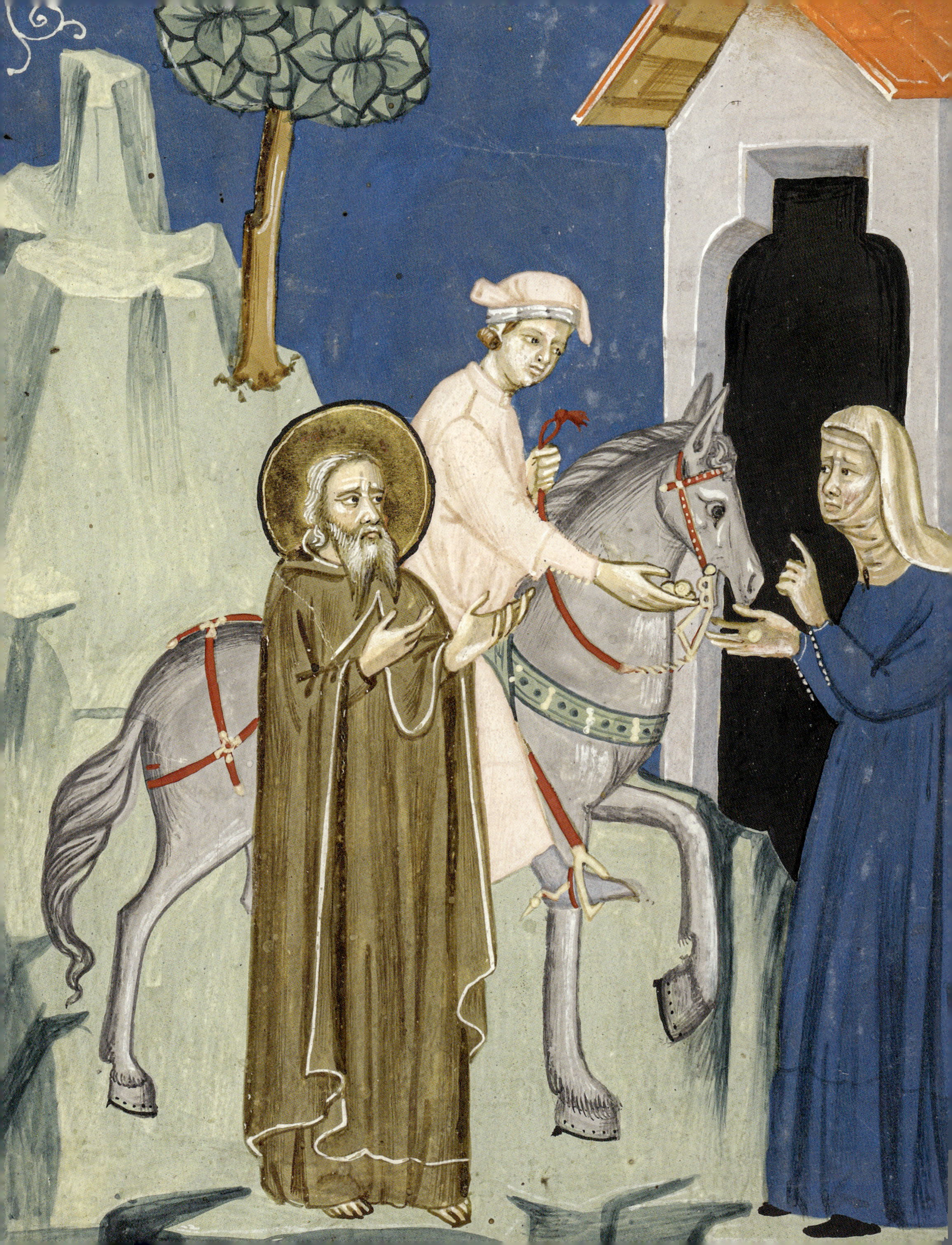

5

Can Money Save Your Soul?

DIANE WOLFTHAL

Charity

Medieval Christians believed that certain monetary practices—charitable giving, embracing poverty, and purchasing indulgences—could save their souls. The Church advanced two main arguments in support of charity.[1] The first was that Christians had a moral obligation to help the poor; it was a matter of justice. Thomas Aquinas asserted that those who have a superabundance of wealth must use it to maintain the poor, "It is the bread of the poor which you are holding back; it is the clothes of the naked which you are hoarding; it is the relief and liberation of the wretched which you are thwarting by burying your money away."[2]

A second argument (which drew on the biblical precepts articulated in Ecclesiasticus 3:33–34, Luke 12:33–34, and Matthew 19:21) held that almsgiving washes away sin, and that the charitable will be

Workshop of Pacino di Bonaguida, *Gerard of Villamagna Soliciting Alms for the Poor*, from a picture book with scenes from the Life of Christ and the Life of the Blessed Gerard of Villamagna, Italy, Florence, ca. 1300–25. The Morgan Library & Museum, New York, MS M.643, fol. 18v. (Detail of Fig. 5.5.)

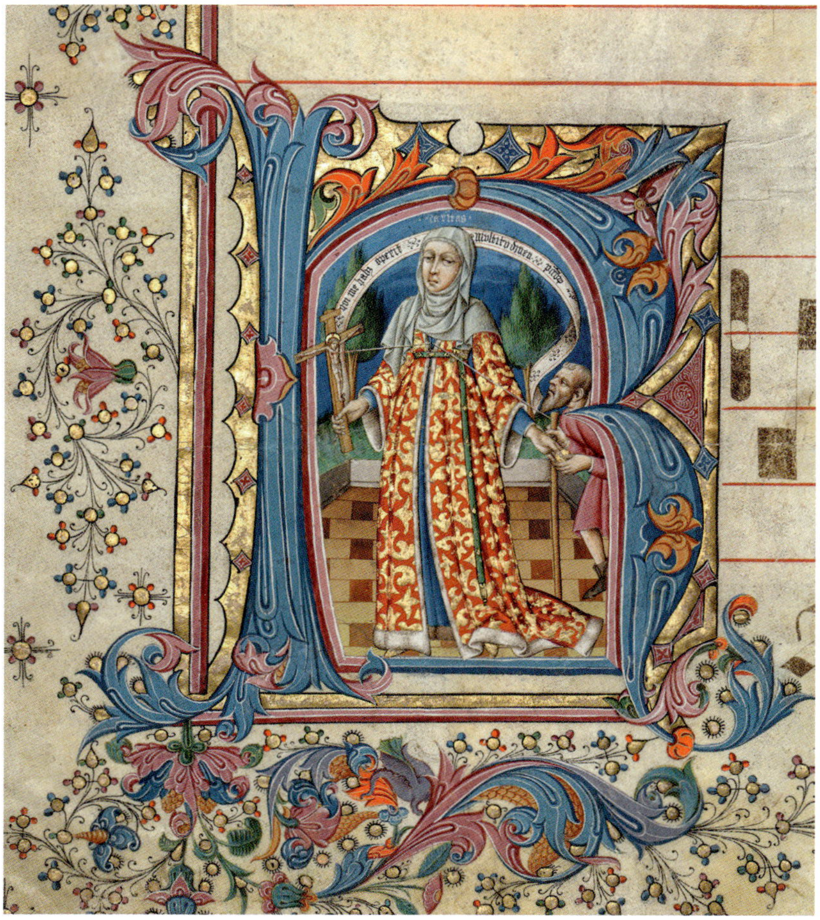

FIG. 5.1. **Master of the Cypresses (Pedro de Toledo?), *Charity*, cutting from a gradual, Spain, Seville, ca. 1430–40. The J. Paul Getty Museum, Los Angeles, MS 15 (85.MS.211).**

rewarded in heaven, an idea repeated in confessors' handbooks.[3] Some theologians went so far as to argue that the poor were put on earth so the rich could redeem their sins and save their souls. In 1304, for example, the Dominican theologian Giordano da Pisa preached, "Why are the poor given their station? So that the rich might earn eternal life through them."[4]

Some medieval Christians, including John Chrysostom, the fifth-century archbishop of Constantinople whose writings maintained their importance for centuries, followed Matthew 5:42 and Luke 6:30, which advised, "Give to him that asketh of thee."[5] But Ambrose (d. 397), another authoritative Church Father, argued that only the deserving poor merit aid, and his contemporary, Augustine (d. 430), similarly maintained that the Church "ought not to provide for a man who is able to work."[6] Medieval laws sometimes forbade aiding the able-bodied.[7] Instead, those deserving of alms were generally defined as those deemed unable to work: the elderly, the lame, the blind, people suffering other infirmities, pilgrims traveling to holy sites, and women with young children. It is the deserving poor who receive alms in medieval art.

An initial *R*, cut from a Spanish gradual (a choir book containing the text and music for Mass) and datable to the 1430s, shows Christ as the ultimate source of charity by drawing a direct line from a crucifix to a personification of Charity and then to a needy pauper (Fig. 5.1).[8] Specifically, the line links the wound in Christ's side to the heart of the woman labeled Charity (*caritas*), and then to the pauper to whom she gives a large gold coin. His bent posture, imploring expression, and cane mark him as one of the deserving poor. This large, lavish initial includes a speech scroll that quotes 1 Peter 4:8, "for

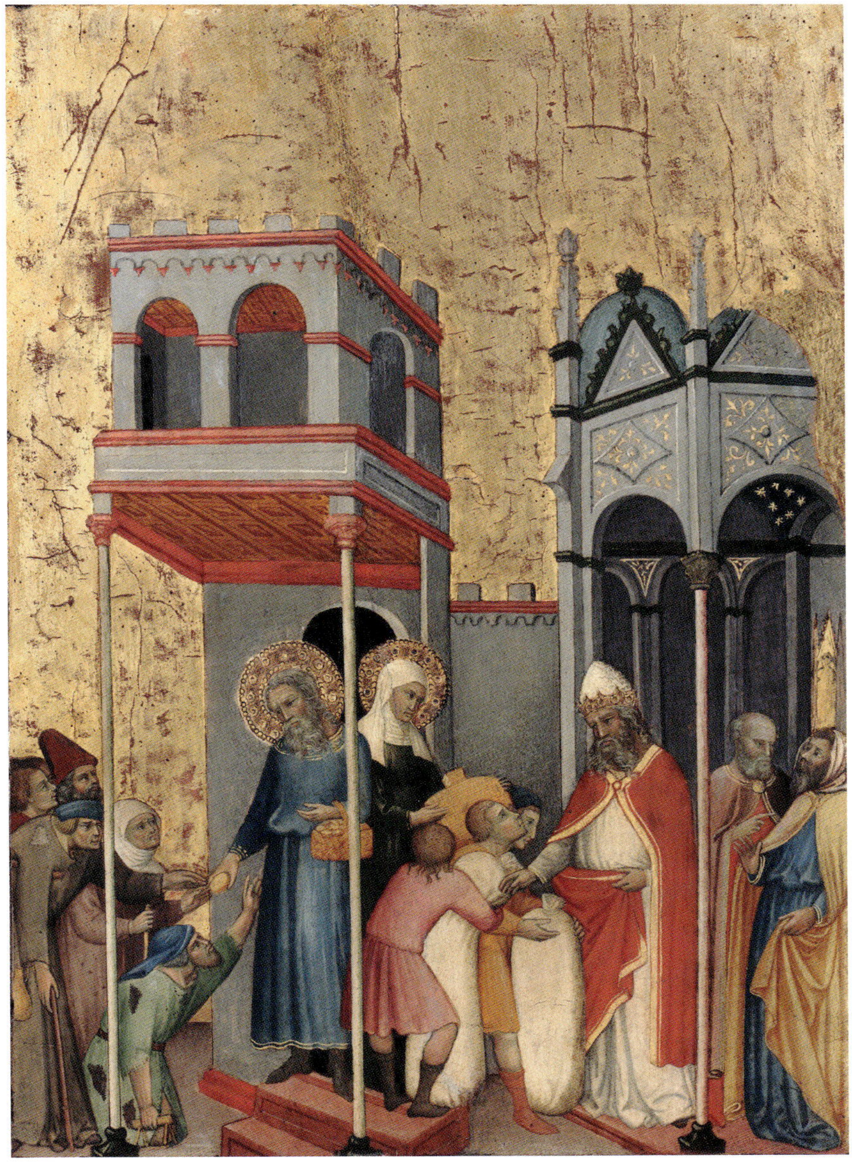

FIG. 5.2. Andrea di Bartolo, *Joachim and Anna Giving Food to the Poor and Offerings to the Temple*, oil on poplar, Italy, Siena, ca. 1400–1405. National Gallery of Art, Washington, DC, 1939.1.43.

charity covereth a multitude of sins."[9] Scenes of almsgiving, generally commissioned by and for the wealthy, usually focus on the benefactor rather than the recipient. Here, Charity is a large frontal figure at center stage; the smaller pauper, shown in profile, is pushed to the side and cut off by the frame. With the rise of the monetary economy, new charitable practices arose. Cash donations became more popular, as depicted in this initial.

If some believed that avarice was the root of all evil, then others, including St. Bonaventure (d. 1274), Thomas Aquinas (d. 1274), and Pope Innocent III (d. 1216), judged charity, by contrast, to be "the mother of all virtues," and believed that all other virtues flowed from it.[10] Images of holy figures served as models of charitable behavior. In Siena, at the turn of the fifteenth century, Andrea di Bartolo painted a multi-winged altarpiece (the panels of which are now dispersed) dedicated to the childhood of the Virgin. One section showed an unusual scene: the Virgin's father, Joachim, donating food to the poor while her mother, Anna, makes offerings to the Temple (Fig. 5.2).[11] Drawing on the second-century Protoevangelium of James, which

FIG. 5.3. Bicci di Lorenzo, *St. Nicholas Providing Dowries*, tempera on panel, Italy, Florence, 1433–35. The Metropolitan Museum of Art, New York, 88.3.89.

became part of the apocryphal Infancy Gospels, the scene depicts, at left, a kindly Joachim distributing bread to the deserving poor, including the elderly and the infirm, the latter shown in patched garments leaning on a cane or crutch. Joachim distributes a plain roll (called *bucella* in Italian), the most common form of public aid to the needy (Figs. 3.5, 7.6).[12] The gnawing hunger of the poor is evoked through their outstretched hands reaching for the food. This panel includes another typical motif in depictions of almsgiving, one that privileges the benefactor: a single donor whose identity is known facing a crowd of anonymous beggars.

Standing beside Joachim, Anna is a model for giving to the Church. Aided by three youths, she presents wine and sacks of grain to the Temple. This panel recalls the couple's extraordinary charitable practices: Joachim and Anna kept only one third of their income, giving another third to the poor and the remainder to the Temple. Although it may seem paradoxical to portray charity through an image with a gold background, gold haloes decorated with ornate punched motifs, gold-trimmed robes, and brilliant colors, such splendor was believed to honor God and inspire the faithful.[13]

Cosimo de' Medici (d. 1464), banker and ruler of Florence, was among those moved to give to the Church in the hopes of expiating his sins. As his biographer Vespasiano da Besticci noted, Cosimo had "accumulated quite a bit on his conscience. . . . [Wishing] God to have mercy on him" he consulted Pope Eugenius IV, who advised him to confer 10,000 florins on San Marco, a suggestion with which he complied.[14]

Charity could take many forms. According to the *Golden Legend*, a vast compendium of saintly biographies, St. Nicholas dropped balls of gold into a home to provide dowries for three sisters whose desperate and destitute father was considering prostituting them because he was unable to support them.[15] Frequently represented in medieval art, this episode, known as the Charity of St. Nicholas, appeared on the predella of the high altarpiece of the Benedictine convent of San Niccolò di Cafaggio in Florence that Bicci di Lorenzo painted in 1433–35 (Fig. 5.3; Bicci must have based his panel on one by Gentile da Fabriano, completed a decade earlier, since the two compositions are quite close). Nicholas steps on a rock to reach the window through which he drops a golden ball. It is evening and the family readies for bed. One daughter removes her head covering, another her dress, and the third her father's leggings thereby exposing his bare flesh. These acts of undressing, coupled with the large, central bed, and the father's inability to effectively lead his daughters either spiritually or physically, mark the family as disreputable and dishonored. This panel would have reminded viewers of two groups of people whose honor could be preserved through charity: young women needing dowries and once wealthy people experiencing financial difficulties.[16] The painter revels in the luxury of the home, its large canopied bed, tasseled pillow, barred window, and verdant garden. But the intended lesson for the viewer is that charity will prevent the daughters' moral and social debasement.[17]

Marriage was a cornerstone of medieval society. Archbishop (later Saint) Antonino Pierozzi of Florence (d. 1459), among others, recommended donating dowries, which allowed poor women to marry, retain their honor, and contribute to the well-being of society.[18] Such charitable giving could also cleanse the soul of the donor. In 1425 the Florentine government established

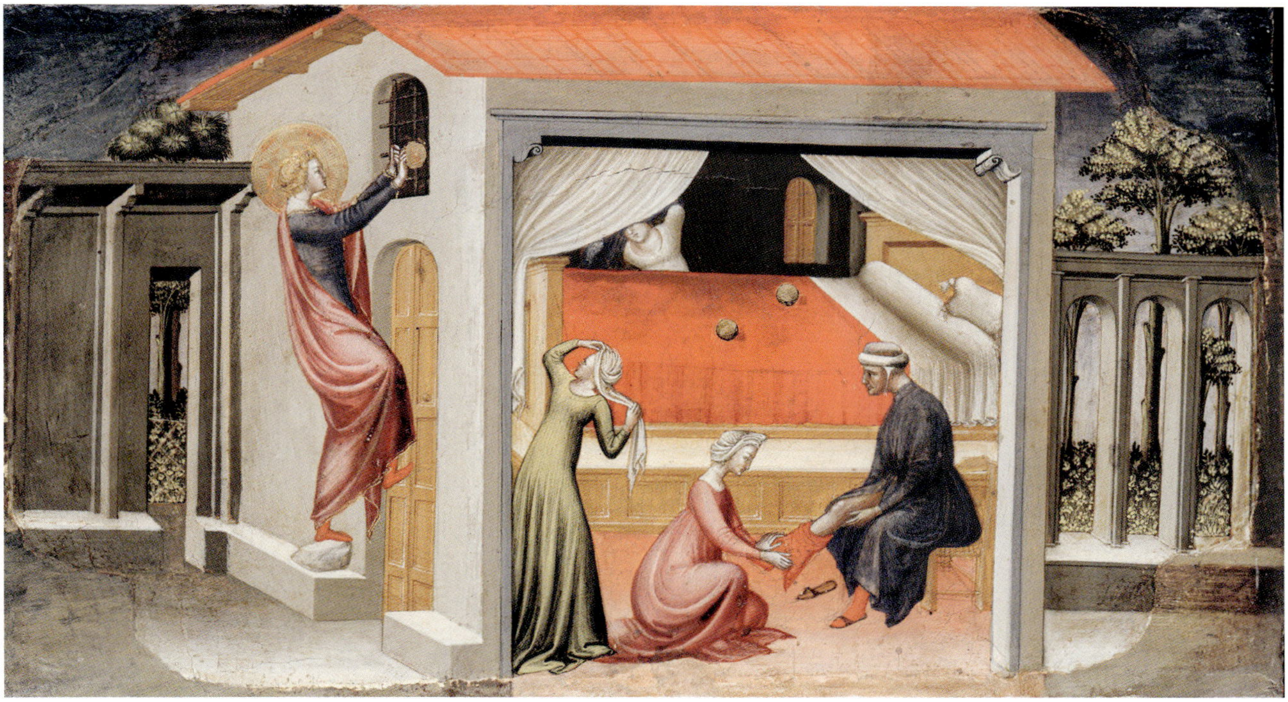

the Monte delle Doti, a fund to provide dowries for the poor. For each of his daughters, a father was encouraged to deposit money that would help ease the public debt and, over time, accrue interest, producing a dowry for the woman at her marriage. The legislation followed a devastating plague that decimated the population of Florence in 1423–24. When few fathers took up the initial offer, the law was revised, first in 1428 and then in 1433, the year the predella was begun. Bicci di Lorenzo's panel, then, can be seen as part of an effort to increase donations to dowry funds for Florentine women.

Why did the nuns of San Niccolò include the "Charity of St. Nicholas" on their altarpiece? Nicholas was their patron saint, so any episode from his life would have been fitting. This scene, however, was the most popular episode in the saint's life in late medieval Tuscan art.[19] Moreover, even nuns, who were the symbolic brides of Christ, needed dowries, which helped support their convents. For example, in the 1420s, Lena di Bartolomeo Barbadori's widowed mother granted her 111 florins to enter the convent of San Niccolò. Furthermore, the dowry scene was especially appropriate for a community of chaste women because Nicholas's gift protected the maidens' virtue.[20] Bicci's tightly closed door, barred exterior window, and shuttered and latched interior window are visual signs of the daughters' virginity, which Nicholas's gift preserved (until their marriages), an aspect of the tale that must have resonated with the nuns.[21]

If Nicholas, at least according to legend, contributed money for dowries, other saints donated to the poor without a specific goal in mind. According to St. Athanasius, when St. Anthony (d. 356) attended church shortly after his parents died, he heard read aloud the words of Matthew 19:21: "If thou wilt be perfect, go sell what thou hast, and give to the poor, and thou shalt have treasure in heaven." Taking the message to heart, Anthony transferred his three-hundred-acre property to the residents of his town, and sold his goods, donating the proceeds to the poor, except for a small portion which he reserved for his sister.[22] In the early 1430s the Sienese Master of the Osservanza portrayed the saint distributing his wealth in a panel that formed part of an altarpiece (Fig. 5.4).[23] In the middle ground,

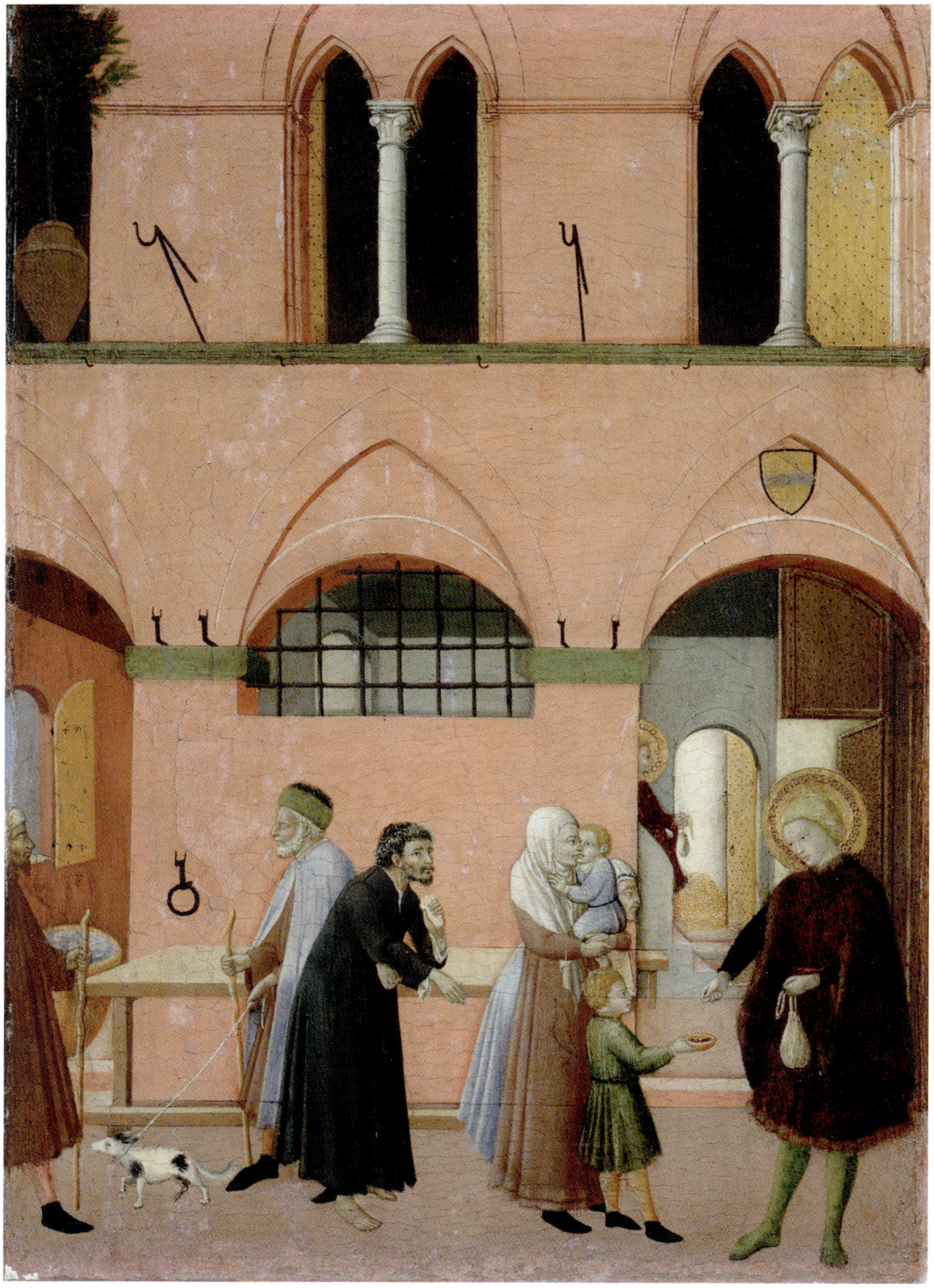

FIG. 5.4. Master of the Osservanza (Sano di Pietro?), *St. Anthony Distributing His Wealth to the Poor*, tempera on poplar, Italy, Siena, ca. 1430–35. National Gallery of Art, Washington, DC, 1952.5.20.

Anthony, carrying a moneybag, descends a staircase. In the foreground, he distributes coins to the deserving poor, including a blind man with a walking stick and guide dog, and a woman with small children. The painter makes clear the saint's wealth. Iron bars on the window protect the ground floor of his palace, and a storage space partially filled with golden grain is visible through an open door. Other saints, such as Roch, are also shown embracing charity by distributing their money to the poor.[24]

In principle, Franciscan friars were not allowed to touch money, but one image depicts a Franciscan

FIG. 5.5. Workshop of Pacino di Bonaguida, *Gerard of Villamagna Soliciting Alms for the Poor*, from a picture book with scenes from the Life of Christ and the Life of the Blessed Gerard of Villamagna, Italy, Florence, ca. 1300–25. The Morgan Library & Museum, New York, MS M.643, fol. 18v.

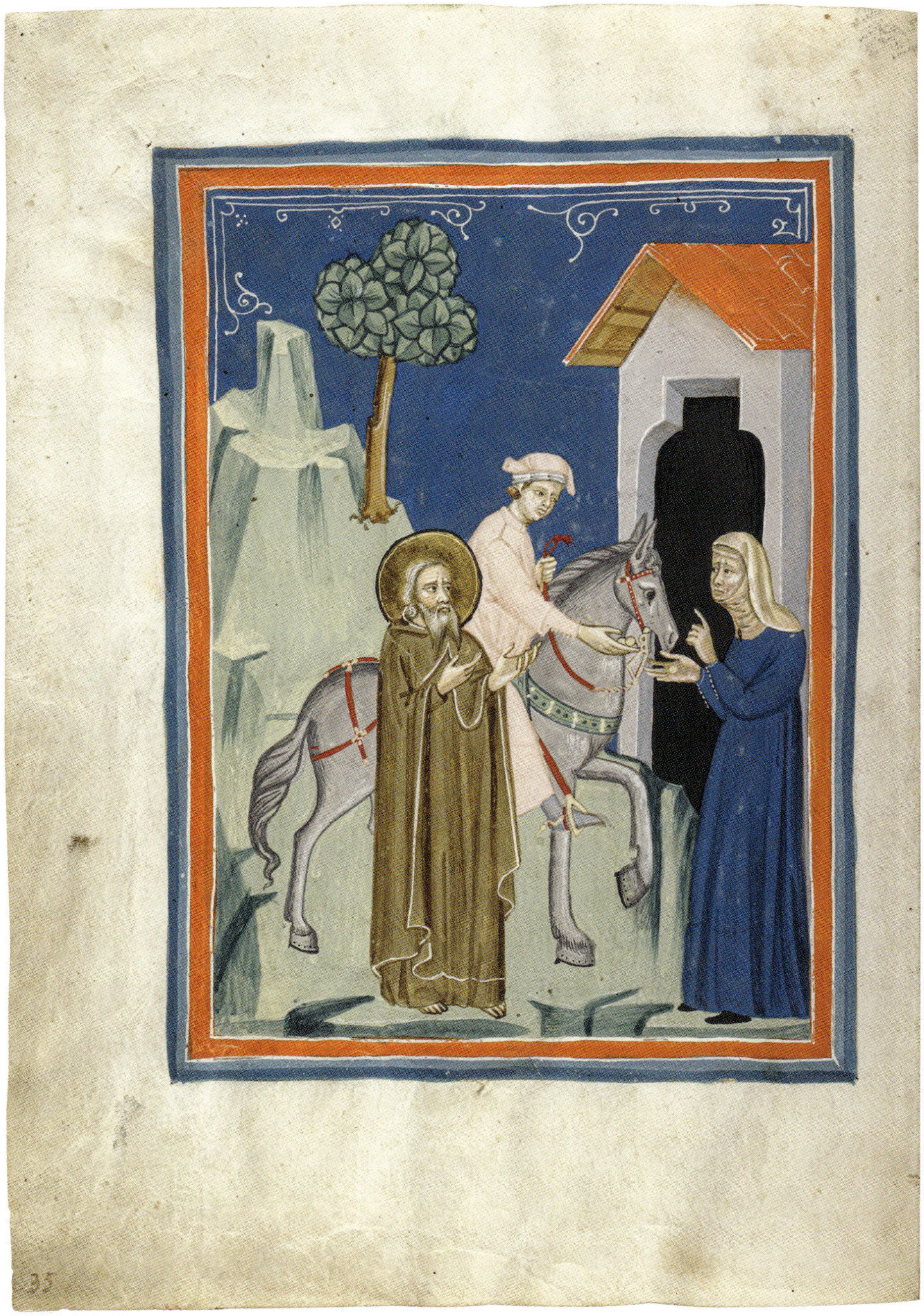

tertiary (a lay follower) encouraging a wealthy man to aid a poor woman. It appears in a Florentine picture book illuminated within the workshop of Pacino di Bonaguida around 1300–1325 with two cycles: the Life of Christ and the Life of the Blessed Gerard of Villamagna.[25] Gerard, who had a strictly local Tuscan cult, was born a peasant, but was adopted by wealthy parents. After he fought in the Crusades in the Holy Land, he returned to the region of Villamagna, where he lived out his life as a holy hermit. The manuscript, the first account of his legend, is suffused with Franciscan ideals. Of the four folios dedicated to Gerard, the first

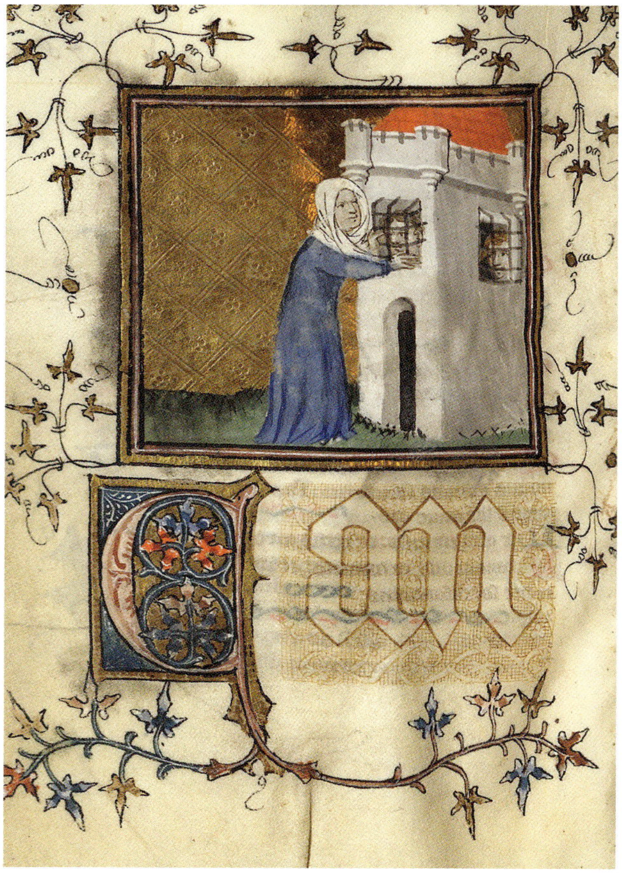

FIG. 5.6. Jean Semont, *A Woman Visits Prisoners*, from a psalter, Belgium, Tournai, 1390s. Archives & Special Collections Library, Vassar College, Poughkeepsie, Mediaeval MS 4, fol. 78v (det.).

shows him distributing bread to the poor, and the next depicts him soliciting alms (Fig. 5.5). Barefoot, haloed, bearded, and wearing Franciscan brown, Gerard raises his hands, entreating a rich young man (foppishly dressed and riding an expensively outfitted horse) to give alms to a poor woman. Leaning forward to drop gold coins into her hand, the rider complies. The scene takes place before the woman's house, which may be set in the countryside because civic authorities often excluded those who were involuntarily destitute.[26] On the facing folio Gerard's piety is further demonstrated through praying and preaching.

In addition to saints and holy men and women, ordinary people are shown dispensing charity in medieval art. An illumination of the biblical parable of the young man unwilling to share his wealth contrasts his greed with the generosity of the townsmen who give bread to the needy (see Fig. 3.5). Indeed, burghers are frequently shown performing the Seven Acts of Mercy, which, as described in Matthew 25:35–40, include giving food, drink, clothing, and shelter to the needy, burying the dead, tending to the sick, and visiting prisoners. The only known example of the Seven Acts of Mercy in a psalter is a series of illuminations by Jean Semont of Tournai from the 1390s (Fig. 5.6).[27] Although one or two of the images in the series have been lost, the others form a coherent group. Each shows a lay woman performing one of the charitable acts. The miniatures bear no relation to the content of the psalms that they introduce. For example, the miniature marking Psalm 97, which begins "Cantate domino canticum novum" (Sing to the Lord a new song), shows a charitable woman, her hair modestly covered, visiting a prison, the scene set against a richly tooled gold ground. Two inmates peer out of the barred windows of the cells that confine them. Getting as close as she can, the woman touches the bars with both hands as she visits one of the prisoners. Below, a colorfully decorated *C* for "Cantate" (Sing) marks the first word of the text. On this and the following page, the large letters of the psalm, outlined in brown ink, are set against an elaborate network of floral, vegetal, and geometric pen-work.

A later polyptych, commissioned in 1504 for the Heilige-Geest-Hofje (Holy Spirit Almshouse) in Alkmaar, in the Netherlands, shows the same subject in its final panel (Fig. 5.7).[28] Burghers not only visit the incarcerated, but also give them money. One opens his purse to donate cash; his neighbor offers a handful of gold coins. Christ is included among those offering comfort. Other panels depict Christ receiving food, drink, clothing, and shelter, a motif inspired by Matthew 25:35–40:

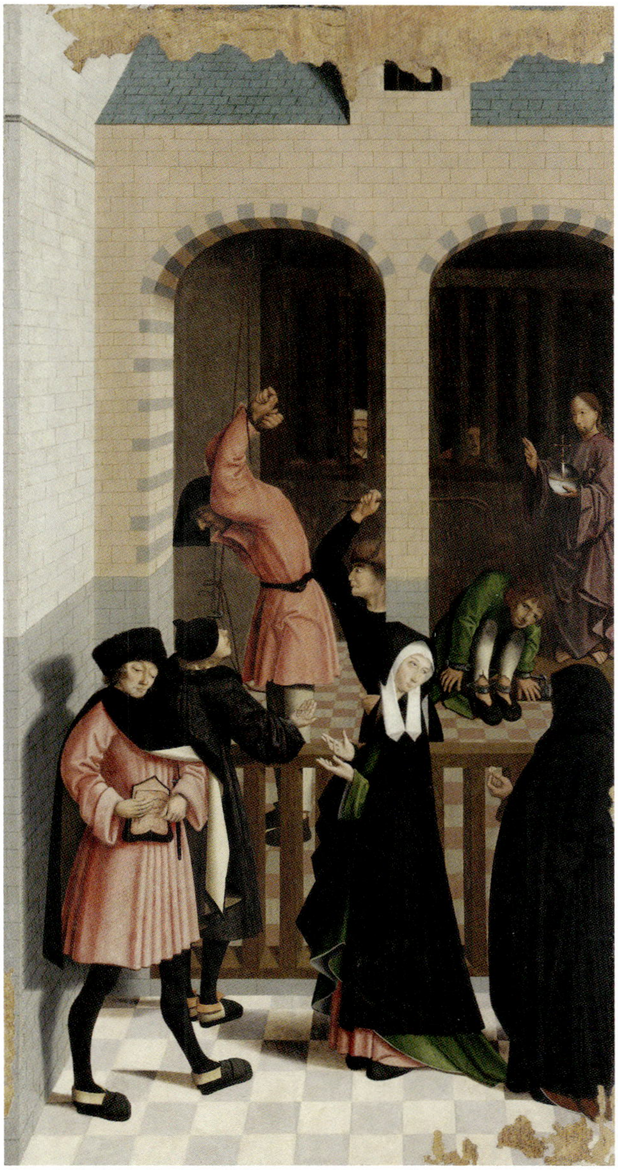

FIG. 5.7. Master of Alkmaar, *Visiting Prisoners*, from the *Polyptych with the Seven Works of Charity*, oil on panel, The Netherlands, Haarlem, 1504. Rijksmuseum, Amsterdam, SK-A-2815 (det.).

> For I was hungry, and you gave me to eat; I was thirsty, and you gave me to drink; I was a stranger, and you took me in: Naked, and you covered me: sick, and you visited me: I was in prison, and you came to me. . . . Amen I say to you, as long as you did it to one of these my least brethren, you did it to me.

The central burial scene includes a Last Judgment, suggesting that the charitable will be rewarded in heaven.

Throughout Europe, churches, hospitals, guilds, and confraternities collected money for charitable purposes in alms boxes (as many still do today). Designed in various shapes, surviving medieval examples are mostly of wood, but some are metal. One South Netherlandish brass alms box is cylindrically shaped, like others from the region, with a recessed slot at the top for coins (Fig. 5.8).[29] A padlock would have secured its cover, which is hinged to the body of the collection box. On the

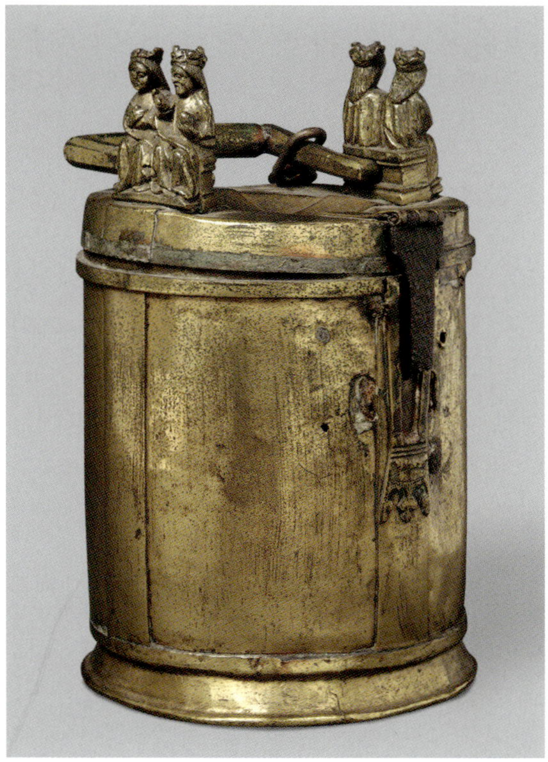

FIG. 5.8. Alms box, brass, South Netherlands, 15th century. The Metropolitan Museum of Art, New York, 47.101.59.

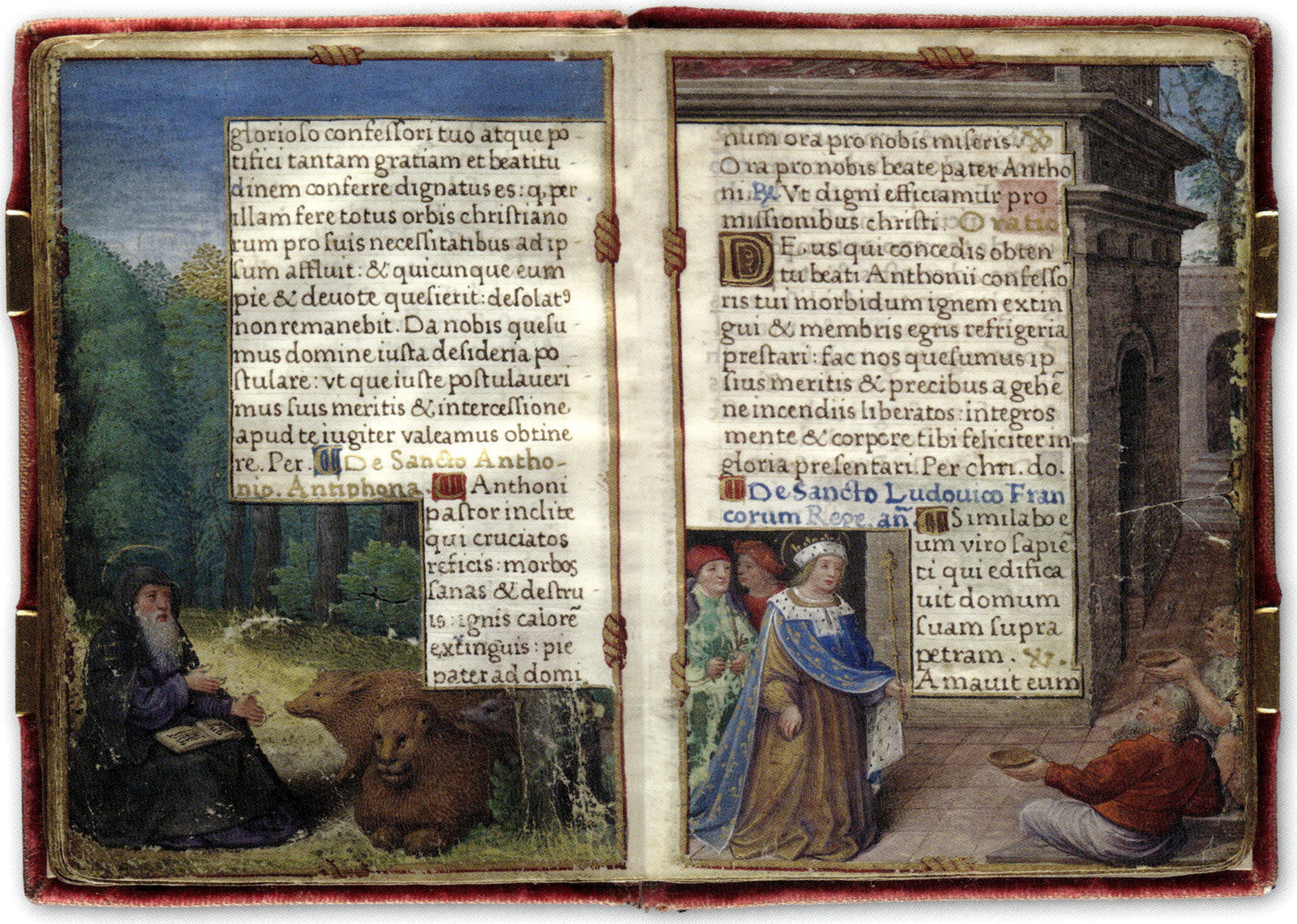

lid, the handle is attached to two pairs of cast figures, both crowned and seated on a bench. One, holding an orb, is presumably Christ; the other is the Virgin. Together they represent Mary's coronation in heaven. Such a scene on an alms box reminded Christians of the eternal rewards of charity.

Past rulers served as paragons of charity for present ones. For example, an illumination in a tiny prayer book, commissioned by Claude de France around the time of her coronation in 1517, shows Louis IX, king of France (d. 1270), famous for his generosity to the poor, approaching two paupers to distribute alms (Fig. 5.9).[30] Such an image would have reminded Queen Claude to do likewise. Crowned, haloed, holding a scepter and wearing a luxurious ermine-lined mantle decorated with the royal fleur-de-lis, the saint approaches the simply dressed paupers who extend their bowls. If Louis IX is a model almsgiver, these paupers are ideal beggars since they wait passively.[31] Although involuntary poverty was viewed as shameful, voluntary poverty was praised. On the facing page is St. Anthony Abbot, a model of voluntary poverty whose pose mirrors that of the paupers.

According to Matthew 2:11, wise men (Magi) from the East journeyed to adore the newborn Christ, bearing gifts of gold, frankincense, and myrrh. Almost from its earliest depictions, some scenes of the Adoration of the Magi show the oldest king giving the Christ Child gold coins.[32] These coins were multivalent.[33] They could be interpreted as tribute money to Christ the King or, marked with crosses, allude to the Eucharist, the sacred host consumed at the Mass. On the other hand, it has been argued that coins in the border of an Adoration of the Magi in the Hours of King Manuel I allude to

FIG. 5.9. Master of Claude de France, *St. Anthony in the Desert*; *St. Louis Giving Alms*, from the Prayer Book of Queen Claude de France, France, Tours, ca. 1517. The Morgan Library & Museum, New York, MS M.1166, fols. 36v–37r.

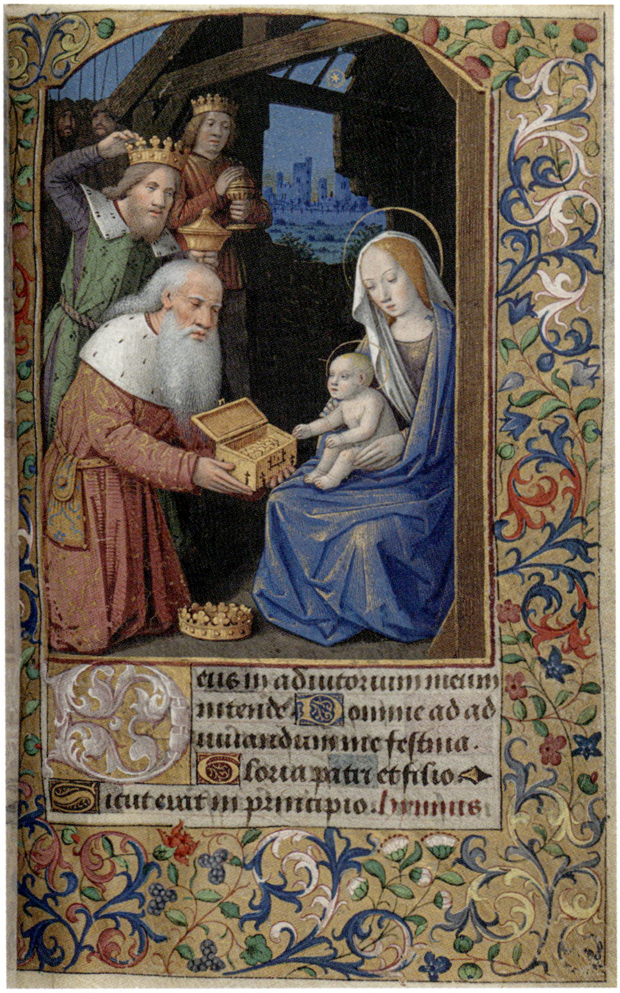

FIG. 5.10. Workshop of Jean Bourdichon, *Adoration of the Magi*, from a book of hours, France, Tours, ca. 1485–95. The Morgan Library & Museum, New York, MS M.380, fol. 59r.

Portugal's desire to become a global Christian power. Manuel had adopted the title "lord of the conquest, navigation, and commerce of India, Ethiopia, Arabia, and Persia," and the coins portrayed in the lower border show the inscription "in hoc signo vinces" (In this sign you will conquer) surrounding a cross, a reference both to Emperor Constantine and the Portuguese desire for Empire.[34]

The gift of gold also referred to alms. Augustine asserted that God "accepts as gold from the Magi what we give as alms."[35] When the Christ Child grasps coins, this is not simply a childish gesture; it shows that he accepts the Magi's gifts on behalf of the Church.[36] In 1486 the Florentine Neoplatonist Giovanni Nesi delivered a sermon at the Compagnia dei Magi (a lay confraternity with a spiritual devotion to the Magi) in which he stated that the star that had led the Magi to Christ was illuminated principally by Charity.[37] Similarly in the early fifteenth century, Bartolomeo Bolognini, supervisor of the Bolognese mint, commissioned a chapel adorned with an image of the Adoration of the Magi in part because he viewed his donation to the Church as similar to their gifts to Christ.[38] Rich and powerful donors, like Emperor Maximilian I, had themselves portrayed as the oldest king presenting a box of coins to the Christ Child.[39] That the Magi's gift of gold was interpreted as alms is underscored by an illumination that shows Mary distributing to paupers the coins brought by the kings.[40]

In an illumination in a book of hours painted in Tours between 1485 and 1495, the oldest king presents gold coins to Christ (Fig. 5.10). His wealth is evident from the large purse hanging from his belt and the gold crown that he has just removed in obeisance to Christ. Kneeling before the infant, he offers untold riches, an open coffer of gold coins, and Jesus, seated on his mother's lap, reaches for the money with his tiny hand outstretched. Depictions of the Adoration, like this one, suggest that a worthwhile use of wealth is to follow the Magi's example, and give to Christ, that is, to the Church.

FIG. 5.11. Master of St. Augustine (?), *St. Francis Renouncing His Worldly Goods*, oil on panel, Belgium, Antwerp (?), ca. 1500. Philadelphia Museum of Art, 2003-89-1.

Voluntary Poverty

In addition to charity, voluntary poverty was thought to save your soul. Christ and the apostles had embraced poverty, and Jesus had commanded his disciples, "Do not possess gold, nor silver, nor money in your purses: Nor scrip for your journey, nor two coats, nor shoes, nor a staff" (Matthew 10:9–10). Christ had also advised the rich young man to sell all he had if he wished to enter heaven (see Fig. 3.5).[41] The parable of Dives and Lazarus explains why poverty was deemed an ideal: the poor are closer to God (Figs. 4.18–4.21). This idea resonated throughout the Middle Ages. In 1189 Alain de Lille preached, "Where, then, will Christ live? Only among the paupers of Christ, of whom it is said, Blessed are the poor in spirit."[42] It should not be surprising, then, that even bankers sometimes wanted to associate themselves with the poor and so portrayed themselves as shepherds or commissioned works of the Adoration of the Shepherds.[43]

All monastic orders required a vow of poverty. Chapter 33 of the Rule of St. Benedict forbids a monk "to have anything as his own—anything whatever, whether book or tablets or pen or whatever it may be" without the permission of the abbot. The Rule instead advises that all possessions in monasteries be held in common.[44] Numerous reform movements throughout the Middle Ages tried periodically to revive the ideal of poverty. Some were deemed heretical, but others, such as the mendicant Franciscans and Dominicans, which arose in thirteenth-century Italy, were accepted by the Church. In the Low Countries, the Devotio Moderna embraced poverty, expelling members who "stained" the movement "with the infidelity of private property."[45] Hermits, mendicants, and some lay Christians shared a great desire to establish a sacred space beyond the material world of monetary negotiations and financial transactions.

The foremost medieval proponent of the ideal of voluntary poverty was St. Francis. In the early thirteenth century, Francis made a strong statement about the worthlessness of material goods when he rejected his family's wealth through the symbolic act of stripping off his clothes in a public square and returning them to his biological father, whom he renounced for his heavenly one.[46] The episode became part of the standard iconography of the saint. A Flemish panel from the turn of the sixteenth century, perhaps by the St. Augustine Master, portrays this scene, following closely St. Bonaventure's vita (biography) of the saint (Fig. 5.11). It shows the young Francis stripping off his shirt, which his father stoops to retrieve along with his son's opulent mantle (the saint's red hat lies nearby). Francis wears only a faintly visible hair shirt, a coarse garment that had lain against his skin beneath his clothes as a test of his spiritual fortitude. He and his father bend towards each other, but the empty space between them implies that no reconciliation will occur. Instead this gap is filled by the bishop, representing the Church. The bishop covers Francis with his cope in a gesture of protection and modesty that may derive from images of the Madonna of Mercy, which show the Virgin Mary sheltering supplicants beneath her cloak. Both the bishop and the priest beside him shield their eyes from Francis's nudity, underscoring the radical nature of the saint's act. Another man, holding the bishop's crosier, places his hand on his heart, a gesture expressing deep emotion. At the bishop's request, a

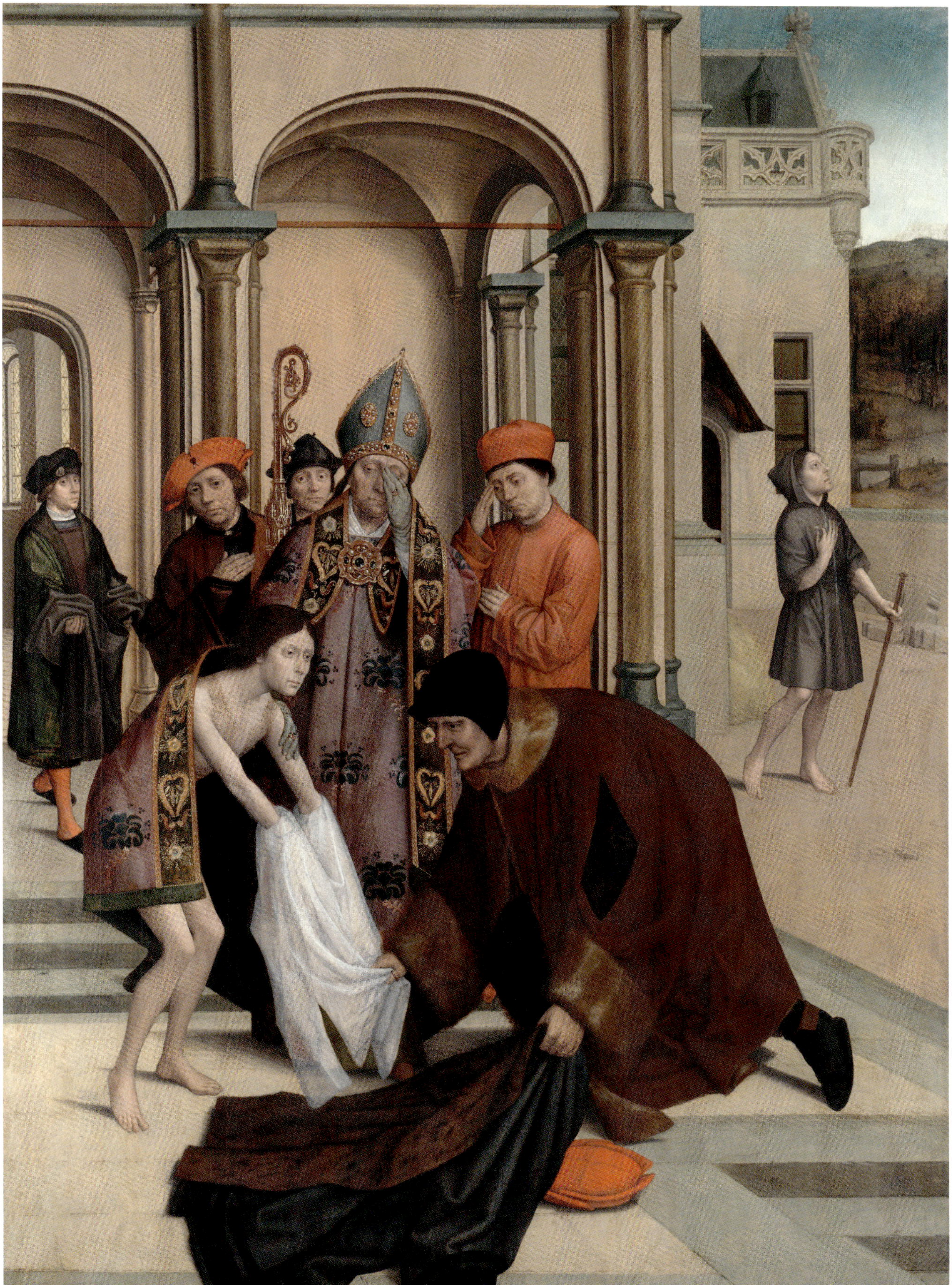

man, approaching at the left, brings a servant's clothes to cover the naked Francis.

Francis appears again at the right, wearing the servant's short hooded garment, on which he has drawn a white cross. Barefoot and holding a walking stick, he gazes towards heaven as he begins his life as a preacher, a founder of the Franciscan order, and a mendicant who embraced a life of poverty. A third incident appears in the background: thieves attack the saint, severely injuring him. According to his vita, this event strengthened his commitment to live according to the Gospels.

The architecture depicted in the painting serves to structure the composition, separating the sacred from the profane, and one incident from the next. It also adds narrative detail, while making clear that this episode represents a transitional moment in the saint's life. The elaborate church setting closes off the two main scenes from the rest of the city; no worldly elements enter this holy space. The renunciation scene is staged before a vaulted, open narthex, or porch; situated on the west facade of the church, this was a liminal space traditionally reserved for those who were not yet part of the congregation.[47] The altar, the holiest part of a church, is at the eastern end, and serves with the western porch as its two poles. As worshipers move from west to east they experience a sequence of spaces of increasing sacrality. It is not accidental, then, that Francis's father is furthest from the church, or that the saint is closer, situated just three steps away from the porch. More critically, the transitional space of the porch is invoked to underline that Francis is in the process of leaving the mundane world of his father and moving into the sacred space of the church. The bishop and his associates stand on the steps before the porch; its arch soars above the bishop, framing him. With its round arches and absence of Gothic ornament or sculpture, the porch may have suggested to northern viewers architecture from Francis's native Italy.

Francis's departure for the wilderness occurs in a separate space, before the transept of the church. Lying near the enclosure wall are intricately carved stones for constructing a compound pier or vault. They recall an earlier moment in his life when Francis wished to donate money to repair the church, but his father opposed this act of generosity. Although the ground of the renunciation scene is paved, Francis walks off on bare earth (note the rocks or clods of dirt). This suited his goal: to live in the wilderness, outside of society. Beyond the church wall at the far right a sliver of landscape indicates Francis's destination. This painting was almost certainly part of a multi-paneled ensemble, but neither its accompanying parts nor its original location have been identified.

A millennium earlier, St. Anthony Abbot had embraced poverty. He sold his possessions, distributed the proceeds to the poor (see Fig. 5.4), and withdrew to the wilderness to lead a solitary life of prayer and poverty. In the Prayer Book of Queen Claude de France, Anthony sits on the ground in a remote forest clearing, an old man with long white beard, reading a book and accompanied by a pig, his attribute, and a lion, which indicates the wilderness, although the animal is docile (see Fig. 5.9). The saint's black habit is that of the Hospitallers of St. Anthony, an order founded around 1095 that specialized in caring for the sick urban poor.

Anthony's vita relates that after he withdrew to the wilderness to avoid worldly temptations, the devil tested

FIG. 5.12. Fra Angelico, *St. Anthony Shunning the Mass of Gold*, tempera on panel, Italy, Florence, ca. 1435–40. Museum of Fine Arts, Houston, 44.550.

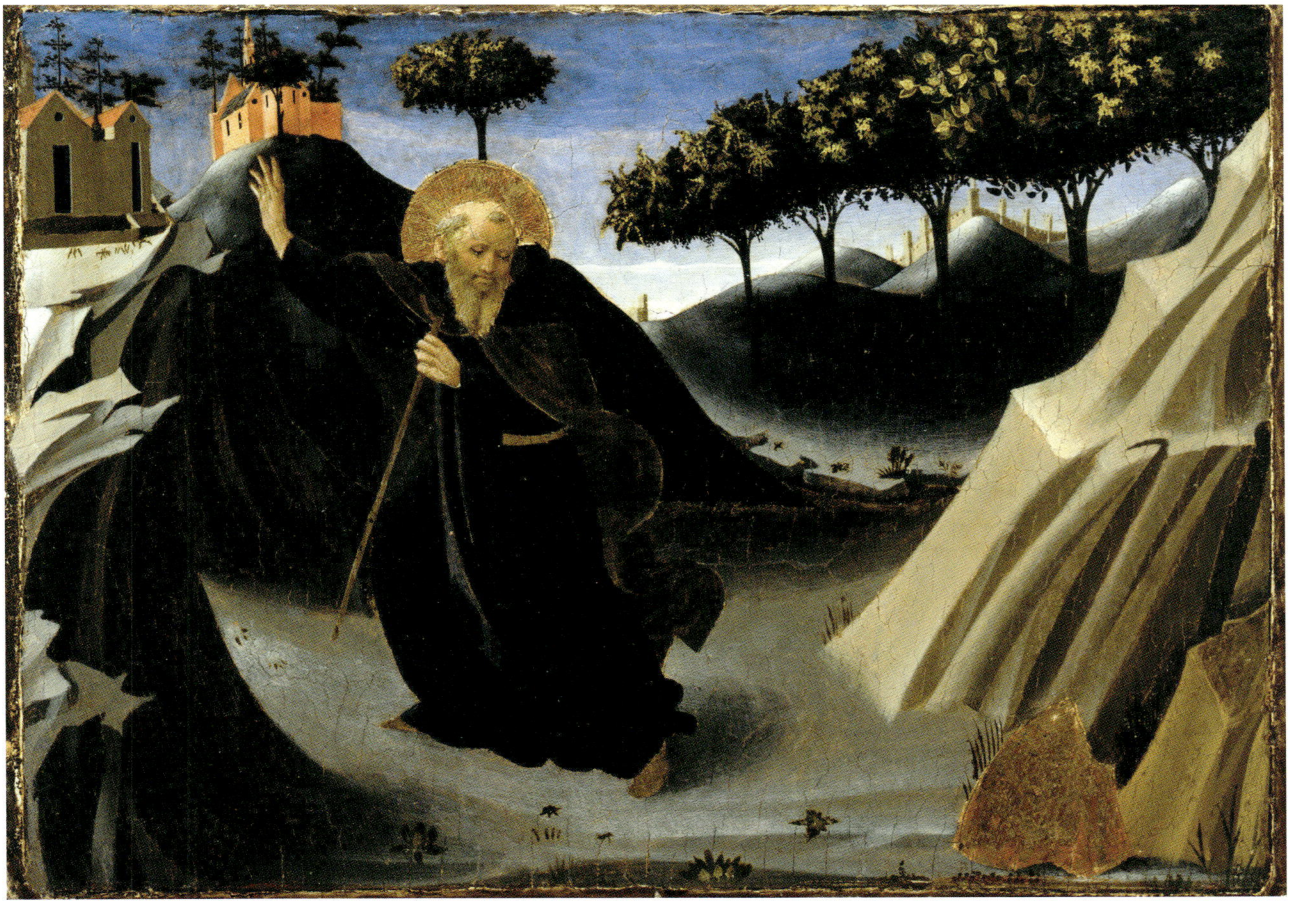

him with enticements and torments. Fra Angelico portrays one such episode: Anthony shunning a large mass of gold that the devil threw in his path to seduce him into committing the sin of avarice (Fig. 5.12).[48] Seeing the golden rock, Anthony throws up his arm in a gesture of alarm, raises his cane to gain freer movement, and flees so hastily that his robe flutters in the breeze created by his sudden actions. Anthony runs from the precious metal towards an abandoned mountain fortress that will become his refuge. According to his vita, this stronghold had been deserted so long that it had filled with serpents, which fled at the holy man's arrival. These evil reptiles are represented as mere lines painted on the ground before the fortress.

Fra Angelico, an Observant Dominican friar, infuses this work with brilliant colors and an other-worldly luminosity. The low foreground, the place of the devil, is filled with sharp, barren rocks; the elevated

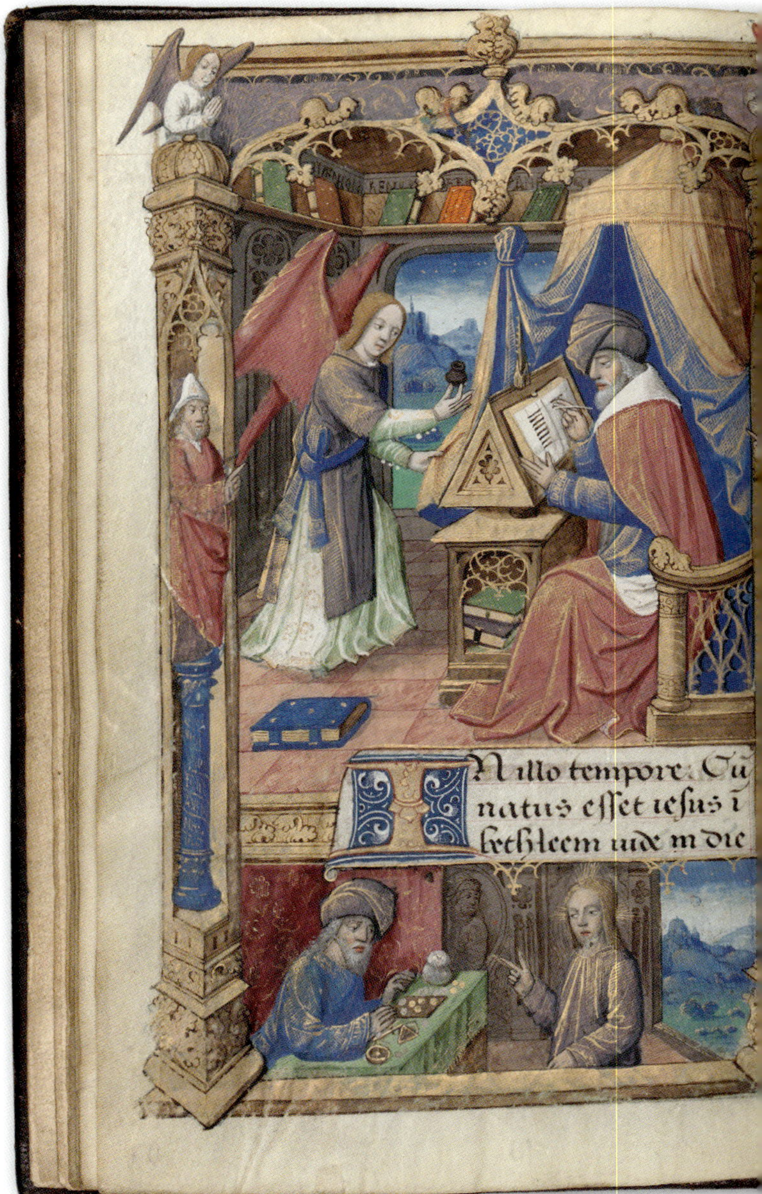

FIG. 5.13. ***St. Matthew Writing His Gospel*** **and** ***Calling of St. Matthew; Miracle Scenes,*** **from a book of hours, France, Paris, ca. 1500. The Morgan Library & Museum, New York, MS H.5, fols. 10v–11r.**

background, denoting the spiritual life of the hermit, shows gently rolling hills with verdant trees. This suggests a contrast between barren riches (the gold rock) and the fertility of Christian devotion. As the painting shows, Anthony, like Francis, rejected earthly riches in favor of spiritual ones.

Matthew did the same. The main miniature in a Parisian book of hours, datable around 1500, shows the saint writing, the traditional illustration for the lesson extracted from his Gospel (Fig. 5.13). In the margin below, Matthew, a tax collector, renounces the world of money to follow Christ. Patron saint of bankers and money changers, tax collectors, and accountants, Matthew sits at a counter on which lie a balance, gold and silver coins, and a moneybag. A rare subject in the early Middle Ages, the "Calling of Matthew" by Jesus, who encouraged him to become his disciple, became increasingly popular as the monetary system expanded, in part because it expressed ambivalence about the value of money.

The marginal images on the facing folio illustrate rarely depicted subjects, which are identified in the rhymed French verse written in blue between them: "When God was born everyone was amazed because the trees sprouted leaves and bore fruit and the lambs in the fields were sheared. Conclusion: everything was reborn."[49] The idea that all of creation bloomed or came alive in some way when Christ was born appears in Jacopus de Voragine's very popular *Golden Legend.*[50] The upper scene shows a man falling to his knees, his hands spread in a gesture of astonishment. The green trees bear the fruit mentioned in the verse, and the field of tall grain—not mentioned in the poem—highlights the theme of fertility. The lower miniature depicts

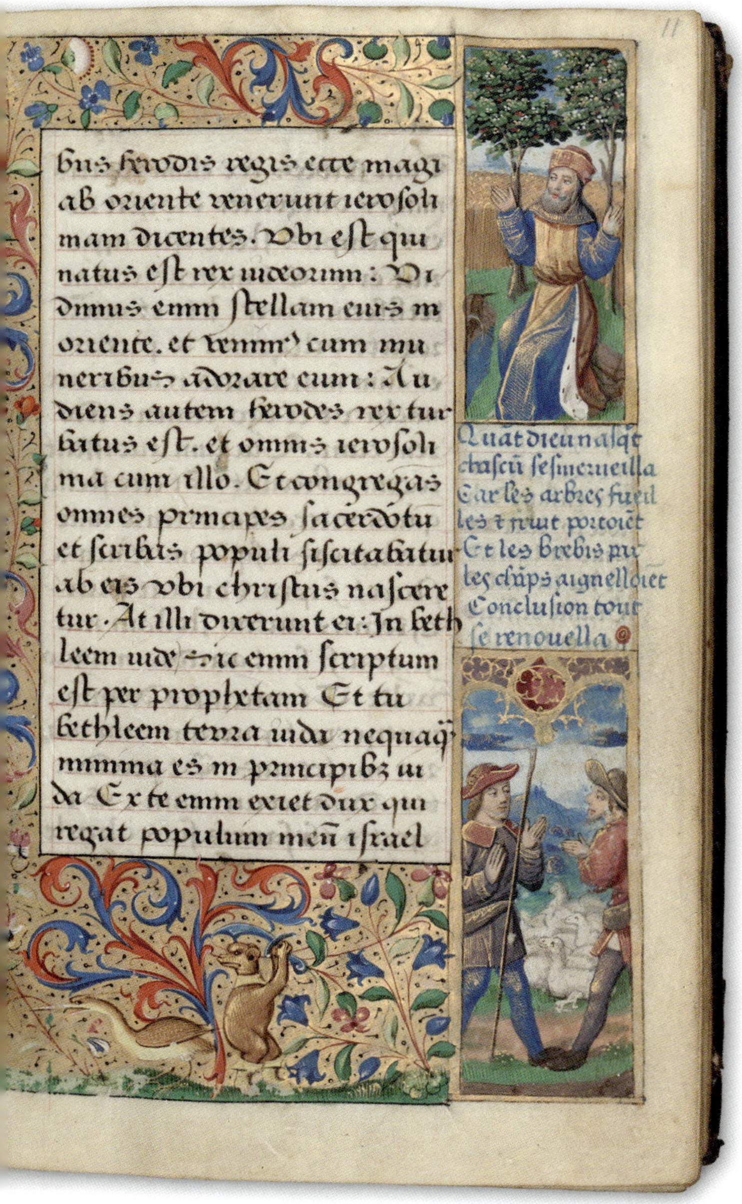

two shepherds, one of whom releases his crook as he separates his hands in wonderment. Behind are the lambs cited in the verse. Since the marginal images in this manuscript generally offer a gloss on the text on the facing folios, these miraculous scenes were probably sparked by the opening lines of Matthew's Gospel Lesson (Matthew 2:1), "At that time, when Jesus was born in Bethlehem." The marginal images and verse, especially its conclusion, may also comment on Matthew's rebirth as a disciple of Christ, shown in the facing lower border. They also serve to contrast the fruitfulness of Mary and nature with the sterility of money, an established topos (see Figs. 3.8–3.9, 5.12).

Secular tales also reinforced the ideal of voluntary poverty. One well-known story from classical antiquity—relayed by Cicero and Valerius Maximus—is the meeting between Alexander the Great and Diogenes the Cynic (d. ca. 323 BC).[51] Diogenes, an ancient Greek philosopher, so scorned worldly possessions that he lived in a barrel; he was the founder of the Cynic school, which advocated rejecting earthly pleasures and possessions in order to live a virtuous life of self-discipline. When Alexander came to speak to Diogenes, he asked the philosopher why he held him—a powerful king—in such low esteem. Diogenes responded that he was able to control his covetous desires whereas Alexander succumbed to them. In short, the philosopher was the master of avarice, which ruled Alexander. For that reason, Diogenes concluded that the king was Diogenes's servant's servant. Alexander offered to grant Diogenes anything he wanted, but the Cynic responded that he was richer than the king since he was content with what he had, whereas all of Alexander's wealth did not satisfy him.

FIG. 5.14. Master of the Harvard Hannibal, *Diogenes in Dialogue with Alexander the Great*, from Guillaume de Tignonville, *Les dits moraux des philosophes* (The Moral Sayings of the Philosophers), France, Paris, ca. 1400–1425. Harvard University, Houghton Library, Cambridge, MA, MS Typ 207, fol. 6r (det.).

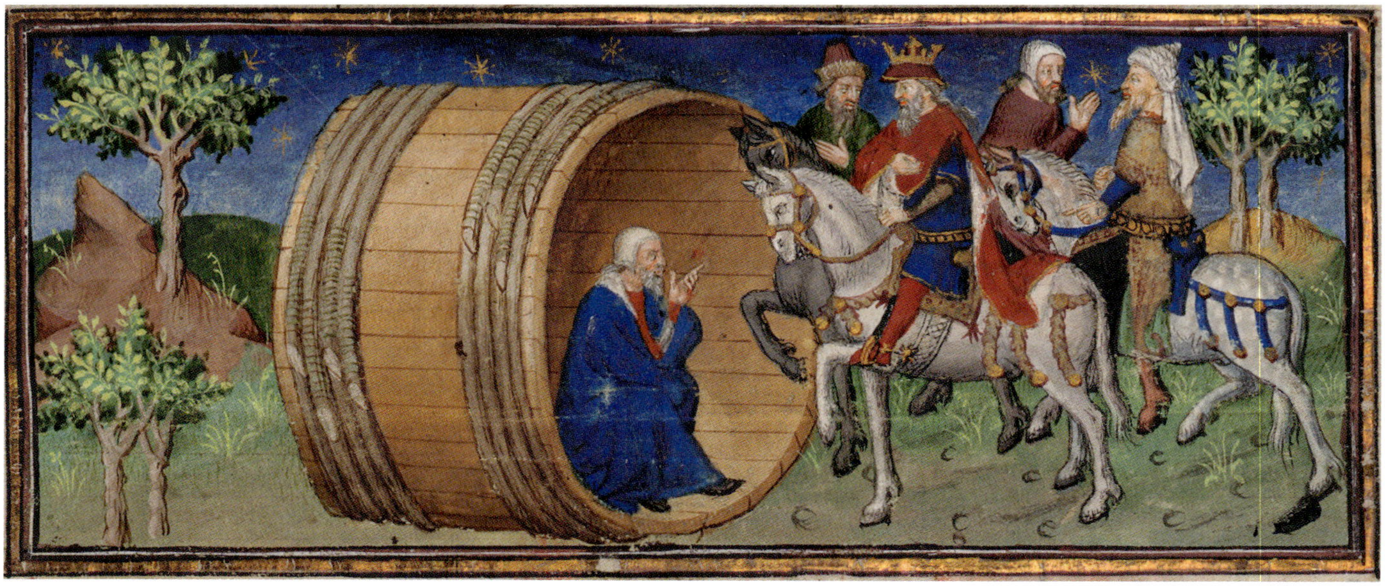

A Parisian manuscript, illuminated by the Master of the Harvard Hannibal around 1400–1425, depicts this tale (Fig. 5.14).[52] The text, Guillaume de Tignonville's *Les dits moraux des philosophes* (The Moral Sayings of the Philosophers), draws on Spanish and Latin versions of an eleventh-century Arabic compilation of sayings and biographies of famous philosophers.[53] The earliest dated manuscript of this work is inscribed 1402, when Tignonville was counselor and chamberlain to King Charles VI and provost of Paris.[54] This popular moralizing treatise survives in at least sixty-eight copies, almost all from northern France and the vast majority made for the upper nobility.[55]

Typical for this manuscript, the miniature focuses on conversation: the gestures of Diogenes and Alexander denote speech. The king is opulently dressed in a gold crown, spurs, and belt, and, riding a fine horse, he towers above the philosopher. Alexander and his courtiers animatedly discuss Diogenes's words, absorbing their meaning. The conical and turban-like hats worn by two courtiers signal the Eastern origins of the tale.

The story of Alexander and Diogenes appears in numerous texts, including Jacques Legrand's *Le livre de bonnes mœurs* (The Book of Good Morals), which was composed in 1404. The rubric for the chapter in which the tale appears could not be clearer: "The state of poverty is agreeable to God."[56] The text further describes Diogenes as "the wise philosopher who didn't value worldly goods."[57] The accompanying illumination in a manuscript dedicated to Jean, duc de Berry, includes the well-known vignette of Diogenes in his barrel but also the more obscure tale of Demetrius, another ancient Cynic (Fig. 5.15).[58] The text relates that Demetrius "threw all his riches in the sea," but the image suggests that he carefully packed his gold coins in sacks and chests before setting them afloat.[59]

This manuscript reflects the complexity of late medieval society. The dedicatee, Jean, duc de Berry, craved and amassed luxurious material goods, including precious jewels, sumptuous palaces, and profusely illuminated manuscripts.[60] Legrand, an Augustinian friar and preacher, employed tales about ancient Greek Cynics to remind Jean, uncle of the French king Charles VI, about the Christian ideal of voluntary poverty.

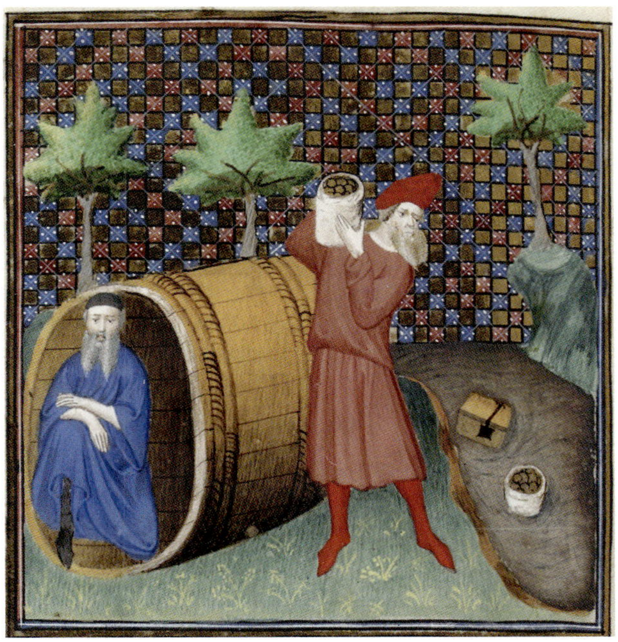

FIG. 5.15. Master of Luçon and workshop, *Diogenes and Demetrius*, from Jacques Legrand, *Le livre de bonnes mœurs* (The Book of Good Morals), France, Paris, ca. 1410. Bibliothèque nationale de France, Paris, MS fr. 1023, fol. 56v (det.).

Advice for Kings

Apostles, hermits, and mendicant saints could embrace voluntary poverty, but medieval European kings could not. The *Avis aus roys* (Advice to Kings), a manual for princes, probably composed for the sons of King John II of France around 1347, instead presents a very different economic ideal.[61] It may have been authored by the confessor (spiritual advisor) to Kings Philip VI and John II, Pierre de Treigny (d. 1356), who was probably also the instructor of the young Valois princes. This Aristotelian treatise explores the ideal qualities of a ruler. A profusely illustrated Parisian manuscript, datable around 1347–50, transmits the most faithful version of the text, whose multilayered economic teachings react to the new monetary economy in largely negative terms (Figs. 5.16–5.22).

Not surprisingly, the treatise advises princes to avoid avarice. It cautions that a king should not set his heart on "temporal riches" or "corporeal delights."[62] The accompanying illumination shows a king pointing both index fingers towards earthly pleasures—envisioned here as a beautiful woman, a platter of fowl, a golden vessel, and a large sack of gold coins (Fig. 5.16). Although he strides forward, the virtuous monarch turns his head away, renouncing these enticing temptations. The first sentence of the next chapter reads, "A good prince should never set his heart upon riches."[63]

The treatise also advises the prince to be charitable. One image shows a king giving clothes and drink to the needy (fol. 65r). A more unusual miniature illustrates a passage that admonishes the king to appoint an almoner (granter of alms) who is diligent, charitable, and compassionate (Fig. 5.17). He should fund

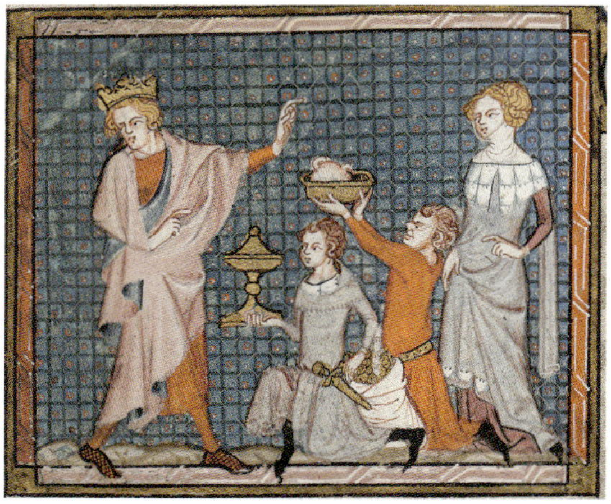

FIG. 5.16. *King Refusing Corporal Delights*, from *Avis aus roys* (Advice to Kings), France, Paris, ca. 1347–50. The Morgan Library & Museum, New York, MS M.456, fol. 10v (det.).

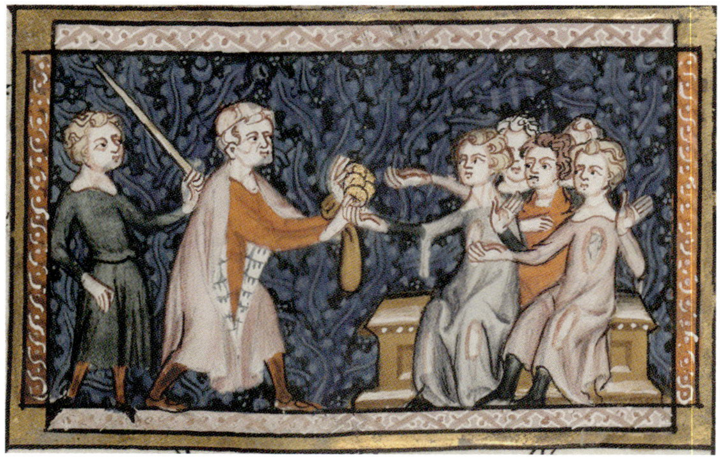

FIG. 5.17. *Almoner Distributing Alms*, from *Avis aus roys* (Advice to Kings), France, Paris, ca. 1347–50. The Morgan Library & Museum, New York, MS M.456, fol. 93r (det.).

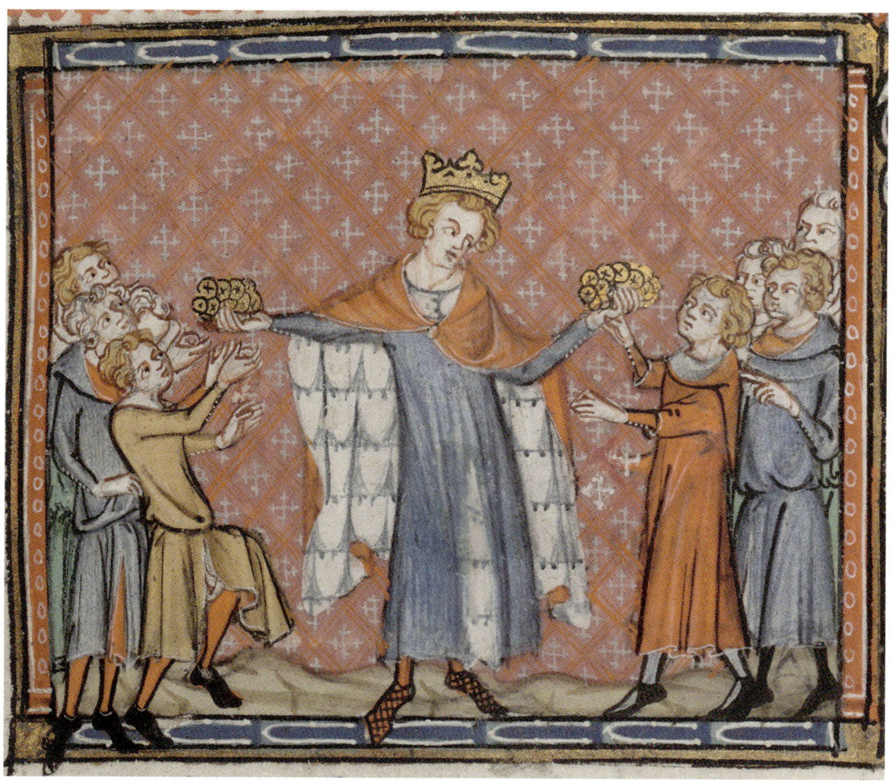

FIG. 5.18. *King's Liberality*, from *Avis aus roys* (Advice to Kings), France, Paris, ca. 1347–50. The Morgan Library & Museum, New York, MS M.456, fol. 39r (det.).

churches and hospitals, needy officials who have long served the king, and other indigent subjects. The treatise further advises almoners to speak gently and courteously as they dispense funds. The accompanying miniature shows an armed man protecting the almoner who distributes to five seated figures gold coins, each marked with a cross. All five are shown with outstretched hands and two wear patched clothes, indicative of their poverty.

The treatise also presents magnificence (the funding of great and noble projects) as a virtue. As an example, it shows the king ordering the construction of a church.[64] The manuscript further advises the king to practice liberality (Figs. 3.11, 5.18). Here it draws on Book IV of Aristotle's *Nicomachean Ethics*, which declares that the virtuous man "will give to the right people, the right amounts, and at the right time."[65] Book 1, chapter 28 of the treatise defines liberality as the ideal mean between avarice and "crazy generosity" (*fole largesce*).[66] Following Aristotle, the text notes that a good prince should choose carefully who will benefit from his generosity. He should bestow money on those who have served him long and loyally and on those who have helped the common good, including clergymen and mendicants. The accompanying illumination shows a king extending his arms to distribute fistfuls of gold coins (Fig. 5.18). Open palms reach to catch the falling coins. The recipients of liberality are not the deserving poor, but rather healthy, adult, and more well-to-do male subjects. Liberality, both in its moderation and its beneficiaries, is far from the radical acts of Sts. Anthony and Francis.

Conforming to the genre of manual for princes of which there were many versions, the treatise is fairly typical in its advice to avoid avarice and instead practice charity, magnificence, and liberality. But the manuscript is unusual in its conceptualizations of economic class. The manuscript opens, for example, with a striking image of a nude king as the body politic with his body parts representing different classes of the realm, all working harmoniously together in a hierarchical ordering.[67] While the king is at the top as the head, merchants ("who run all over the world") and laborers are at the bottom, associated respectively with the legs and the feet, the limbs closest to the earth.[68]

If this illumination assigns a lowly status to merchants, then the manuscript's other images of class distinctions omit them altogether. Book 3, chapter 10, defines classes by wealth: the very rich, the very poor, and those in between. In an Aristotelian mode, the treatise concludes that the middle class does the most for the common good. The author argues that the powerful despise and oppress the poor, and the poor envy the rich and think of ways to improperly seize their wealth. Only the middle class maintains "peace, love, and justice."[69] The accompanying illumination shows a seated man representing the middle class, to whom a king and a second man point (Fig. 5.19). Holding what is probably a shoe, this ideal citizen is an artisan. (The black strip hanging on a rail above is probably material for a matching shoe or the finished article; the white rectangle is a speech scroll that did not get inscribed.) Earlier scholars interpreted the figure as a merchant seated on a coffer, holding a purse.[70] But his seat does not resemble a coffer nor does the object in his hands look like a purse. His right hand seems to hold the toe of the shoe, while just beyond that is what appears to be a shoelace or strap.[71]

In fact, throughout this treatise, artisans are often praised, but merchants rarely. The idealization of artisans is also articulated in the anonymous ballads of the Four Estates, illuminated by Jean Bourdichon around 1500, where the artisan is a carpenter.[72] Having seen men ruined by poverty and riches alike, the carpenter asserts, "There is none better than the middle way" (*Il n'est cy bon que la moyenne voye*).[73]

Book 3, chapter 9, defines the classes necessary for a successful realm by the type of work each performs: peasants are needed to till the earth, artisans to produce goods, magistrates and scholars to interpret law, and soldiers to defend the commonwealth. Once again, the entire monetary class—merchants, moneylenders, investors, and bankers—is omitted. The image includes a laborer digging with a shovel, a worker repairing a roof, two learned men conversing, and a knight in armor holding a shield (Fig. 5.20).

Besides the omission or denigration of merchants, this manuscript also overtly resists the new monetary economy. Book 3, chapter 2, shows a king raising his index finger in a gesture of command (Fig. 5.21).[74] Before him are an underling and a usurer who displays on his table golden vessels and gold and silver coins. The usurer reaches for a bag from which silver coins spill. The underling, presumably at the order of the king, seems to be trying to remove the usurer's hand from the sack. The accompanying text states that good princes must not tolerate usury because it is both against nature (since it reproduces unnaturally) and against reason (since the proper function of money is to serve as a medium of exchange).[75]

A second passage condemns another aspect of the new monetary economy: wages. It follows Book 3, chapters 12 and 13, which champion feudal ideals, describing the relationship of vassal to king as "natural" and "just."[76] Both chapters are illustrated by vassals kneeling before a standing king.[77] Chapter 14 extends these ideas by asserting that only servitude based on loyalty is natural and desirable. The accompanying image shows four servants (Fig. 5.22). The first, on the left, is a blind man holding a beggar's bowl who strides out of the miniature guided by a cane and a dog. He illustrates those who must serve others because they are unable to care for themselves. The second figure, leaning to one side in an unstable pose, represents those who serve because they have been conquered and taken by force. The last two servants, at the right, are of greatest interest here. One of them is shown being paid, making clear that some work for money alone. By contrast, the last servant works only "for love and loyalty" (*pour amour et pour loyalté*).[78] The manual instructs the prince to "generously reward" only those who serve out of true devotion.[79] Those who are paid for their work, by contrast, are condemned.

The miniature reveals the tension between competing conceptions of labor. Do people work out of loyalty or for wages? The scholar Arnaud Montreuil has demonstrated that French vernacular literature of the twelfth and thirteenth century closely associated the service of a knight to his lord with love. He concludes that, in such texts, "service [was] not to be seen as a mercantile relationship."[80] But later, in the intermediate period when capitalism had not yet ascended, the feudal elite often felt an acute loss, the breakdown of traditional practices. It is not surprising, then, that a manual for princes presents an ideal vision of an economic system that was fading, while criticizing and

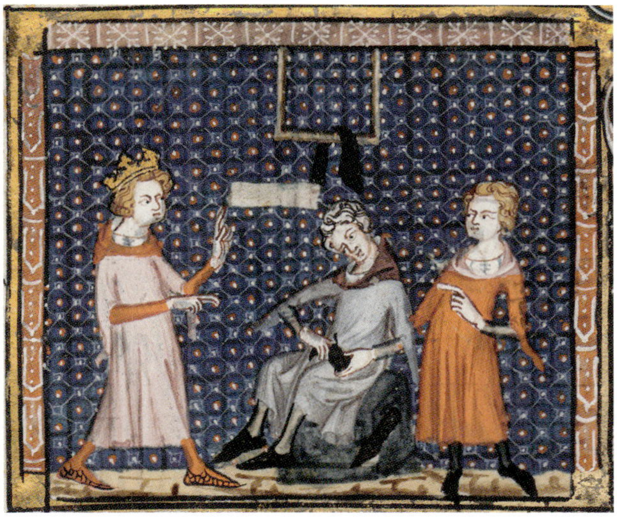

FIG. 5.19. *The Middle Class is Best*, from *Avis aus roys* (Advice to Kings), France, Paris, ca. 1347–50. The Morgan Library & Museum, New York, MS M.456, fol. 86v (det.).

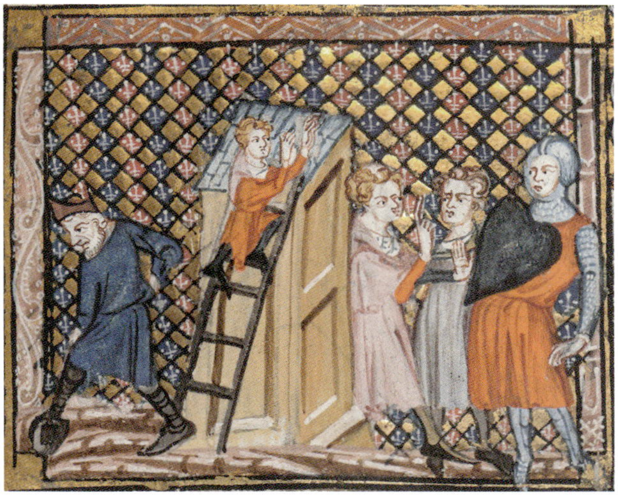

FIG. 5.20. *Four Economic Classes*, from *Avis aus roys* (Advice to Kings), France, Paris, ca. 1347–50. The Morgan Library & Museum, New York, MS M.456, fol. 86r (det.).

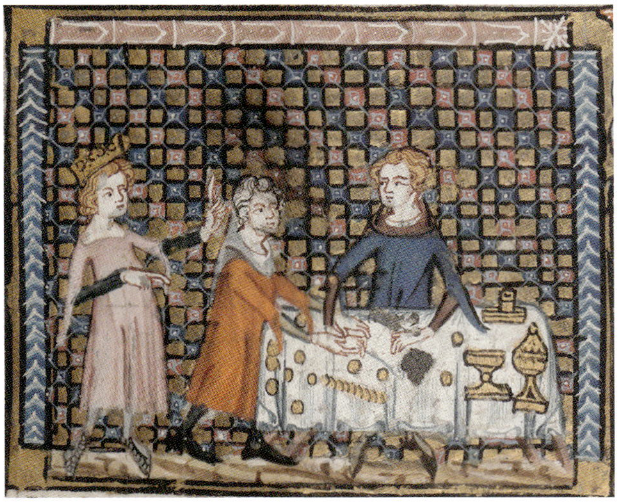

FIG. 5.21. *King Forbids Usury*, from *Avis aus roys* (Advice to Kings), France, Paris, ca. 1347–50. The Morgan Library & Museum, New York, MS M.456, fol. 87r (det.).

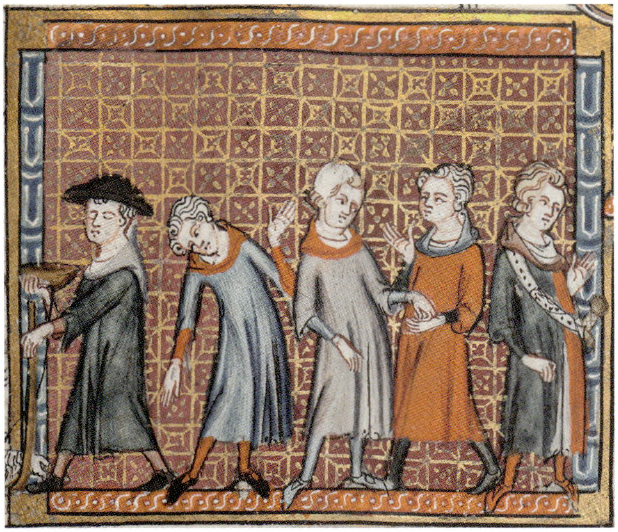

FIG. 5.22. *Four Types of Servants*, from *Avis aus roys* (Advice to Kings), France, Paris, ca. 1347–50. The Morgan Library & Museum, New York, MS M.456, fol. 89r (det.).

FIG. 5.23. Indulgence granted to the monastery of Santa Maria juxta Pontem Lapideum, France, Avignon, 1343. The Morgan Library & Museum, New York, MS M.697.

obscuring the commercial transactions, such as usury, that propped it up and were capable of enriching people of relatively low social standing. If the *Avis aus roys* teaches princes to avoid avarice and embrace charity, it also advises them to resist the new monetary economy and maintain the status quo.

Indulgences

If medieval Christians agreed that charity and voluntary poverty could save your soul, they debated whether the purchase of indulgences (spiritual pardons issued as certificates) was a good use of money.[81] By the thirteenth century, indulgences were granted for full or partial remission of punishment for sins if the sinner confessed, repented, and did penance. Penance could take various forms: prayer, fasting, almsgiving, crusading, pilgrimage, or contributing money or labor for the construction of the hospital, church, bridge, or road cited in the indulgence. Theologians believed that outward acts that benefited the Christian community expressed an interior state of true contrition. In this way, indulgences were central to both the sacrament of confession and social welfare. Indulgences promised time off from purgatory for the penitent or a deceased loved one if the conditions stipulated in the indulgence were fulfilled. Because of the good works of saints, martyrs, the Virgin, and Christ, Pope Clement VI declared in 1343 that the Church possessed an infinite "Treasury of Merit" that he could disperse through indulgences, which were sometimes referred to as payments. The scholar Robert W. Shaffern notes that "theologians and canonists increasingly imagined the benefits which indulgences conferred in arithmetic and mercantile imagery."[82]

Indulgences often had numerical values—a certain amount of money or a certain number of prayers would pay off a specified number of years in purgatory. In fact, Jacques Le Goff has proposed that the very idea of purgatory developed from new mercantile notions, such as the measurability of time, and new monetary practices, such as bookkeeping.[83]

In 1343 the papal court at Avignon issued an indulgence of forty days by three archbishops and fifteen bishops to the monastery of Santa Maria juxta Pontem Lapideum in the diocese of Spoleto (the structure has not survived).[84] The indulgence, with forty additional days added, was confirmed two months later by the bishop of Spoleto, Bartolomeo Bardi, as witnessed by this illuminated copy transcribed by Bardi's scribe, Gulielmus de Bonia (Fig. 5.23). Clergymen's seals were once appended to the document by the nineteen cords attached to it. In the large initial *U*, a Madonna nurses the Christ Child, perhaps a reference to Charity. The kneeling monk may be the person who requested the indulgence for the church. The standing haloed bishop may be St. Vincent, the first bishop of nearby Bevagna. Framing these figures are the symbols of the four Evangelists, while to the right are busts of St. Peter, Christ, and St. Paul.

The increased role of money in society led to abuses in the granting of indulgences. Some preachers who distributed indulgences kept a percentage of the money they collected and some misappropriated funds for purposes other than those stated on the indulgence. Such abuses contributed to an act that is often seen as the beginning of the Reformation: Martin

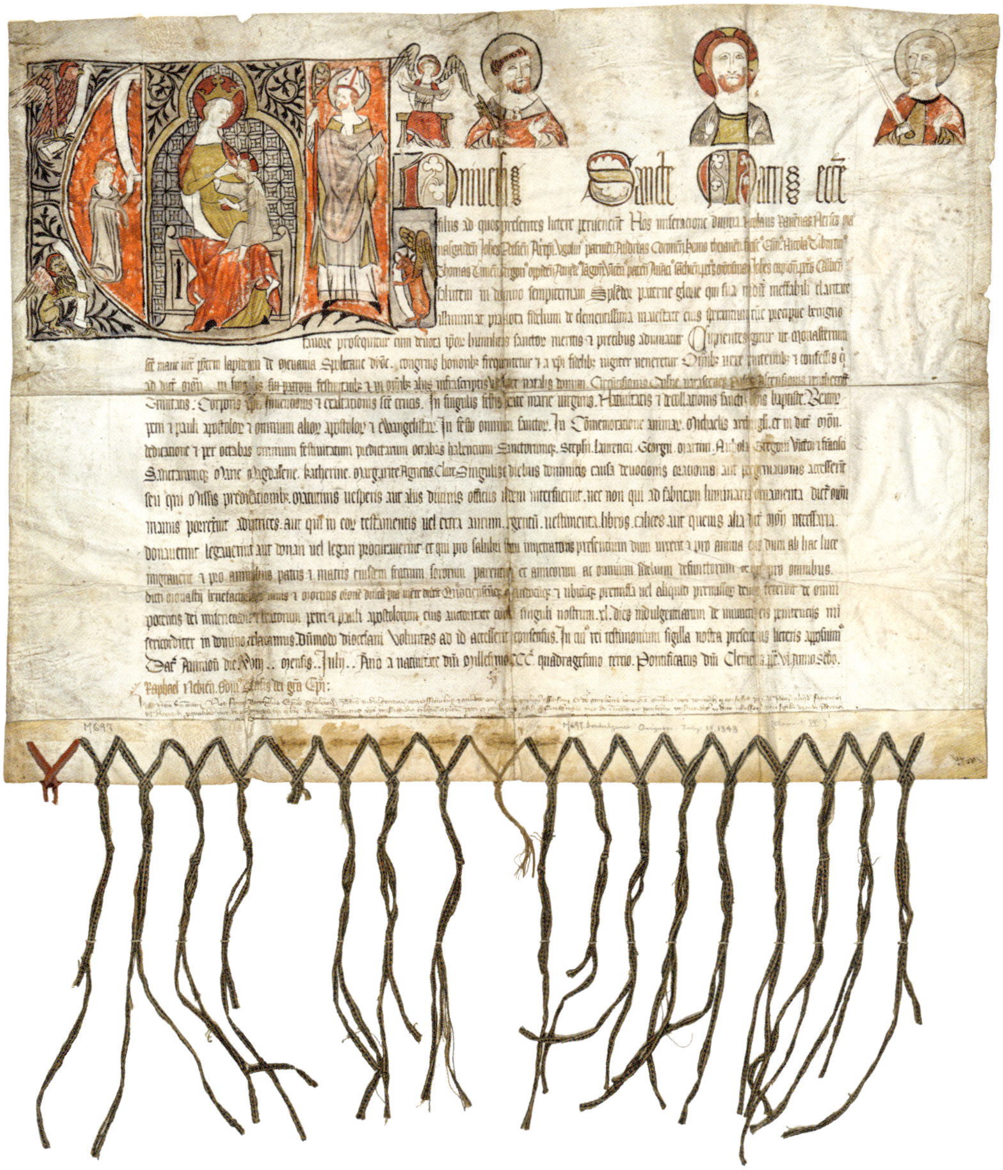

Luther posting his ninety-five theses in 1517. Luther was responding, in part, to the sale of indulgences to pay for the construction of St. Peter's in Rome by men such as the Dominican Johann Tetzel, who preyed on the poor and naive, using hard-sell tactics. In a sermon of 1517, Tetzel preached, "Don't you hear the voices of your wailing dead parents, and others who say, 'Have mercy upon me, have mercy upon me, because we are in severe punishment and pain. From this you could redeem us with a small alms and yet you do not want to do so'."[85] Several of Luther's criticisms of indulgences refer to monetary issues. Thesis 27 condemns the belief that "as the money clinks into the money chest, the soul flies out of purgatory." Thesis 43 proclaims, "Christians are to be taught that he who gives to the poor or lends to the needy does a better deed than he who buys indulgences." Luther argued that the pope should empty purgatory out of love, rather than for money, and that he should use his own wealth to build St. Peter's.[86]

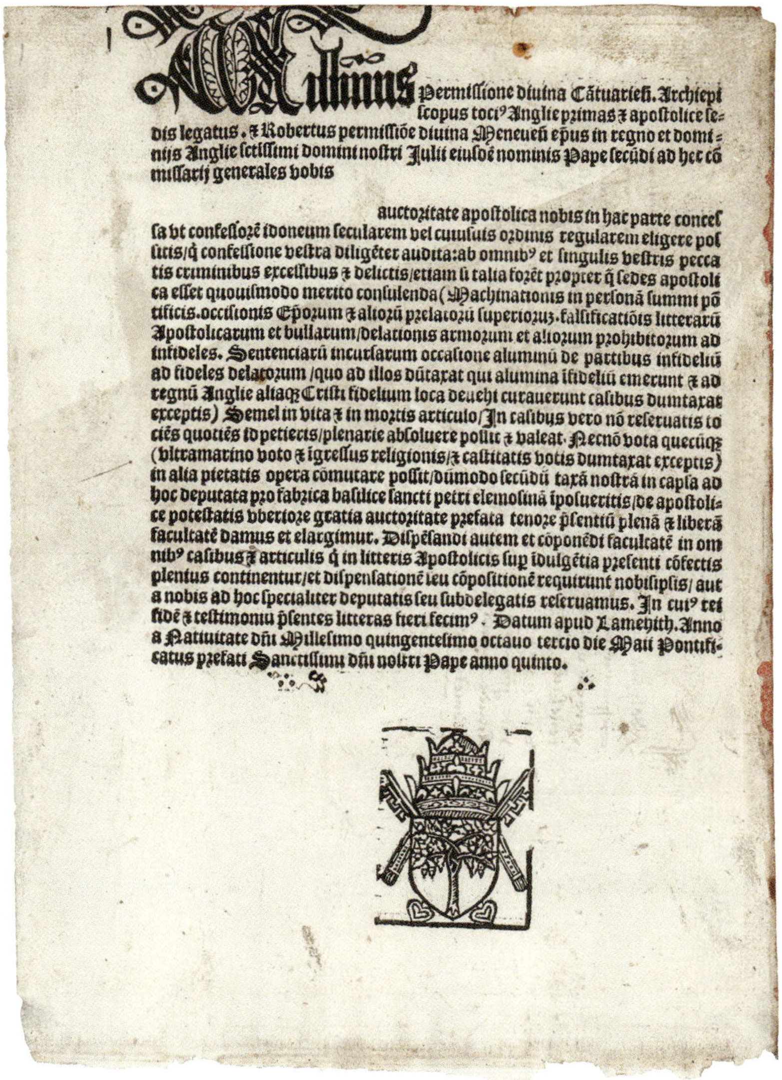

Willmus permissione diuina Cātuariē. Archiepiscopus toti⁹ Anglie primas ꝛ apostolice sedis legatus. ꝛ Robertus permissiōe diuina Meneueñ epūs in regno et dominijs Anglie sctissimi domini nostri Julii eiusdē nominis Pape secūdi ad hec cōmissarij generales vobis

auctoritate apostolica nobis in hac parte concessa vt confessorē idoneum secularem vel cuiusuis ordinis regularem eligere possitis/q̄ confessione vestra diligēter audita:ab omnib⁹ et singulis vestris peccatis criminibus excessibus ꝛ delictis/etiam si talia forēt propter q̄ sedes apostolica esset quouismodo merito consulenda (Machinationis in personā summi pōtificis.occisionis Eporum ꝛ aliorū prelatorū superiorū.falsificatiōis litterarū Apostolicarum et bullarum/delationis armorum et aliorum prohibitorum ad infideles. Sentenciarū incursarum occasione aluminū de partibus infideliū ad fideles delatorum /quo ad illos dūtaxat qui alumina īfideliū emerunt ꝛ ad regnū Anglie aliaq; Cristi fidelium loca deuehi curauerunt casibus dumtaxat exceptis) Semel in vita ꝛ in mortis articulo/In casibus vero nō reseruatis totiēs quotiēs id petieritis/plenarie absoluere possit ꝛ valeat. Necnō vota quecūq; (vltramarino voto ꝛ igressus religionis/ꝛ castitatis votis dumtaxat exceptis) in alia pietatis opera cōmutare possit/dūmodo secūdū taxā nostrā in capsa ad hoc deputata pro fabrica basilice sancti petri elemosinā iposueritis/de apostolice potestatis vberiore gratia auctoritate prefata tenore p̄sentiū plenā ꝛ liberā facultatē damus et elargimur. Dispēsandi autem et cōponēdi facultatē in omnib⁹ casibus ꝛ articulis q̄ in litteris Apostolicis sup idulgētia presenti cōfectis plenius continentur/et dispensationē seu cōpositionē requirunt nobisipsis/ aut a nobis ad hoc specialiter deputatis seu subdelegatis reseruamus. In cui⁹ rei fidē ꝛ testimoniū p̄sentes litteras fieri fecim⁹. Datum apud Lamehith. Anno a Natiuitate dñi Millesimo quingentesimo octauo tercio die Maii Pontificatus prefati Sanctissimi dñi nostri Pape anno quinto.

FIG. 5.24. **Indulgence for St. Peter's in Rome, England, London, 1508. The Morgan Library & Museum, New York, PML 18221.**

A printed indulgence of the type Luther criticized was granted by Pope Julius II, Archbishop William Warham of Canterbury, and Bishop Robert Sherborne of St. David's in exchange for a monetary contribution to the construction of St. Peter's (Fig. 5.24). Printed in London in 1508, it only survives because it was reused later to bind a book. As usual for printed indulgences, it bears the papal coat of arms but leaves a blank space for the recipient's name.[87] Huge sums were needed to construct St. Peter's, and indulgences were a major source of funding.[88] Luther was not alone in criticizing the practice. A tapestry woven for King Henry VIII of England in the 1530s, by which time he had renounced the Catholic Church and was feuding with Pope Clement VII, shows, among other avaricious figures, a personification of Simony holding several indulgences (Fig. 7.13). But for many faithful Catholics, buying indulgences was money well spent, since they believed it could save their souls. Medieval Christians did not reductively condemn money, but rather saw it as an opportunity. Properly used—through charity, voluntary poverty, and indulgences—it could be channeled to support the Church, public works, or the poor. Medieval Europeans explored the role of money in a thoughtful, nuanced way, considering both its positive and negative effects on society.

NOTES

1. Guest 1995; Mollat 1986.
2. Wood 2002, 55; Aquinas, *Summa Theologiae* II, ii, q. 66, a. 7.
3. For confessors' manuals, see Mollat 1986, 128.
4. Lesnick 1989, 126 n. 120; see also Brodman 2009, 36.
5. Wood 2002, 60.
6. Guest 1995, 176.
7. Horrox 1994, 289.
8. For this cutting, see Anderson 1993.
9. The inscription reads "qui me habet operit multitudinen [*sic*] p[e]cc[at]or[um]."
10. Faccin 1955, 205; Brodman 2009, 24; Osborne 2019, 157.
11. For this painting, see Boskovits 2016, 14–25. For its iconography, see Schiller 1980, 54–56.
12. Pestilli 2017, 49.
13. This image may have brought to mind the tithe, a tenth of a Christian's income that was given to the Church in kind or in money. A nominal portion of the tithe was supposed to be given to the poor, but, as Johannes Teutonicus (d. 1245), known for his glosses on Gratian's *Decretum*, observed, "Nowadays the bishops take everything for themselves." See Wood 2002, 57; Coulton 1925, 299. For tithing in Italy, see Boyd 1952. For England, see Swanson 2010.
14. Kent 2000, 172.
15. de Voragine 1993, vol. 1, 21–22.
16. Brodman 2009, 33.
17. Taylor 1982, 321.
18. Musacchio 2008, 17.
19. See Kaftal 1952, cols. 388–89.
20. Neff 2019, 163.
21. For doors and windows as metaphors for the orifices of a woman's body, see Wolfthal 2010, 75–119.
22. Deferrari 1952, 135–36.
23. For the painting, see Christiansen, Kanter, and Strehlke 1989, 111; Boskovits and Brown 2003, 481–90.
24. Koldeweij 2006, 80, fig. 5.1.
25. For this manuscript, see Sciacca 2012, 188–92; Sciacca and Fredericks 2015, especially 40–41.
26. The hill and tree are shorthand motifs for indicating the countryside; see, for example, Giotto's *Joachim in the Wilderness* in the Arena Chapel, Padua (1305).
27. For this manuscript, see Vanwijnsberghe 2007, 97, 156–59, 342.
28. For this altarpiece, see Filedt Kok 2008.
29. See, for example, Vandenberghe 1984, 42, 108.
30. For this manuscript, see Wieck 2010. For Louis, see Mollat 1986, 138.
31. See Acres 1998, 442.
32. To cite just two clear examples, both in the Metropolitan Museum of Art, New York: paintings after Hugo van der Goes (71.100) and by Gerard David, ca. 1520 (1982.60.17).
33. See de Voragine 1993, vol. 1, 83–84.
34. Museu Nacional de Arte Antiga, Lisbon, inv. 14/130 llum, fol. 87v; see Trexler 1997, 133–35.
35. For a variant translation, see Trexler 1997, 21; Migne 1845, col. 2007.
36. Trexler 1997, 24.
37. Hatfield 1970, 135, 161.
38. Drogin 2010, 304 n. 76.
39. Beer and Woelk 2014, 293.
40. Bibliothèque nationale de France, Paris, MS ital. 115, fol. 30v; see Flora 2008, 69, 71, fig. 12.
41. For biblical teachings praising poverty, see Wishart 1900, 193.
42. Alain de Lille 1965, 283; Mollat 1986, 112–13.
43. Burke 2004, 115; Wolfthal 2007.
44. Geary 2010, 174, ch. 33, verse 3.
45. Van Engen 1988, 168.
46. Bonaventure 2005, 14–19; Vitullo and Wolfthal 2010a, 2–3.
47. Viollet-le-Duc 1997, 239–61.
48. For the painting, see Wilson 1996, 130–45; Bowron and Morton 2000, 7–9; Roberts 2002, 13–134.
49. I thank Thelma Fenster for help with this translation.
50. For the miracle, see de Voragine 1993, vol. 1, 39, 41.
51. Eder 1915, 932–33; Sutton 2006. For an English illumination, see the *Confessio amantis*, Morgan, MS M.126, fol. 58r. See also Cary 1956, 83–85.
52. For this manuscript, see Hamburger et al. 2016, 227–28 (entry by Walter Cahn).
53. Hindman and Bergeron-Foote 2014, 78.
54. Cahn and Marrow 1978, 220.
55. Cahn 2014, 189, 191.
56. Eder 1915, 932–36; Châtelet 2002, 54.
57. Châtelet 2002, 54.
58. Beltran 1975, 406; Châtelet 2002.
59. Châtelet 2002, 54.
60. For the duke, see Camille 2001.
61. For this manuscript, see Lepot 2012.
62. Lepot 2014, vol. 2, 23, 25. Book 1, ch. 6. Book 1, ch. 7 (my translation).
63. Ibid, 25. Book 1, ch. 7 (my translation). See also Morgan, MS M.456, fol. 12v.
64. Morgan, MS M.456, fol. 41v.
65. Curzer 2012, 97 (*Nicomachean Ethics* IV.1, 1120a24-6).
66. For this quote, see Lepot 2014, vol. 2, 69.
67. Morgan, MS M.456, fol. 5r. See Lepot 2014, vol. 1, 267–70; vol. 2, 13.
68. For praise of merchants who travel, see Jackson 2018, 46.
69. Lepot 2014, vol. 2, 151. Book 3, ch. 10 (my translation).
70. Sherman 1995, 227; Lepot 2014, vol. 1, 270.
71. For a similar shoe, see van Buren and Wieck 2011, xii (lower left corner). See also Goubitz 2007. In shops, wares are often displayed this way; see Welch 2005, 25, fig. 21; 66, fig. 70; and Bibliothèque municipale, Rouen, MS 927, fol. 145r.
72. See Bibliothèque de l'École nationale supérieure des beaux-arts, Paris, Mn. Mas. 92.
73. See Husband 1980, 201.
74. For this gesture, see Garnier 1982, 167.
75. Aquinas, *Summa Theologiae* II, ii, q. 78, a. 1.
76. Lepot 2014, vol. 2, 155. Book 3, ch. 12 (my translation).
77. See Morgan, MS M.456, fols. 88r–88v.
78. Lepot 2014, 157. Book 3, ch. 14 (my translation).
79. Ibid. Book 3, ch. 14 (my translation).
80. Montreuil 2022, 50–51.
81. For indulgences, see Reynolds 1996; Swanson 2006; Rudy 2017, 38–51.
82. Shaffern 2007, 23.
83. Le Goff 1984.
84. Harrsen 1943, 320–21.
85. Hillerbrand 1964, 41.
86. Aland 1967, 52, 54, 56, 57.
87. Eisermann 2006, 313, 317.
88. Rice 1997, 8.

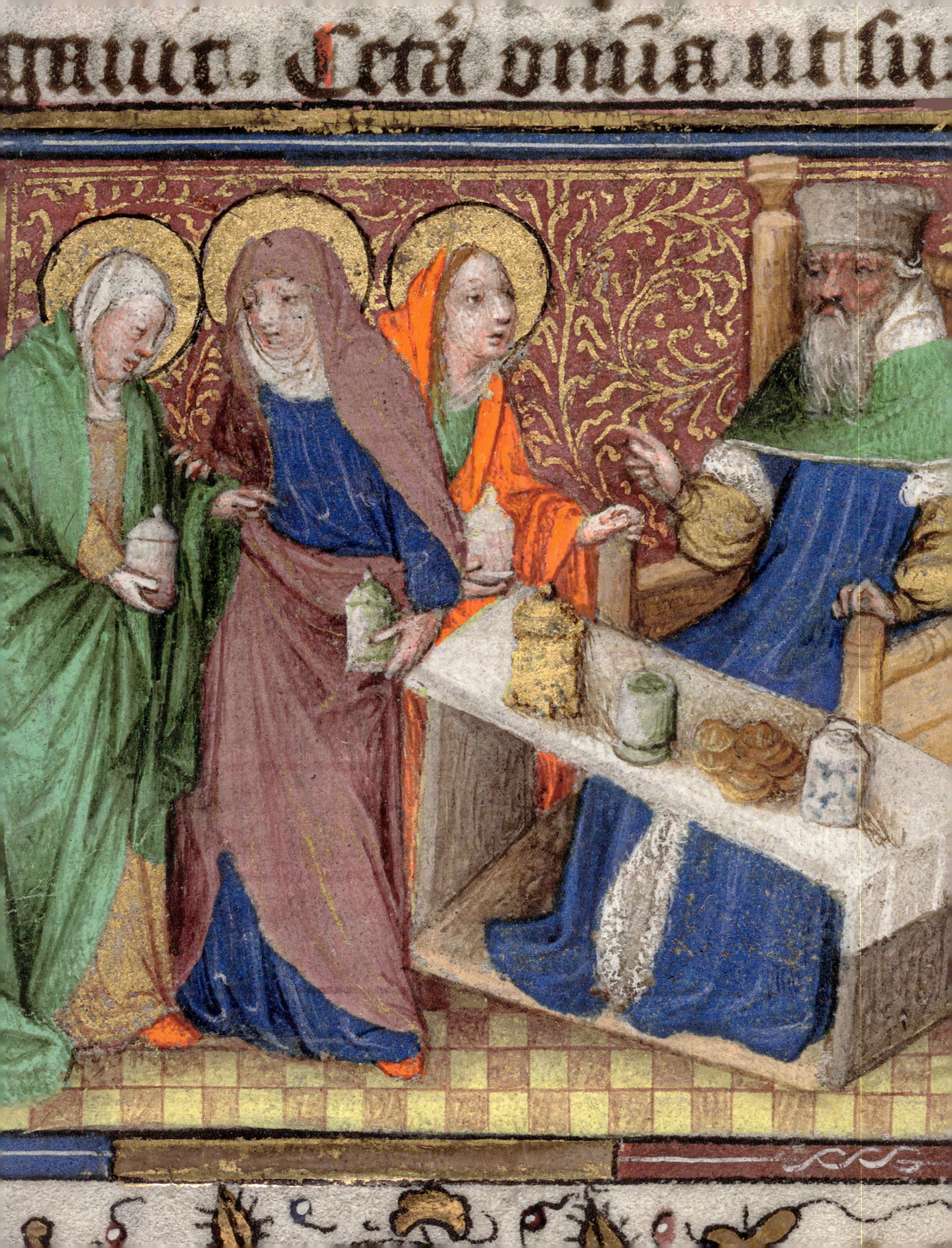

6

Merchants and the Material Culture of Money

DIANE WOLFTHAL

Morals versus Practices

As the monetary economy developed, the number of merchants, moneylenders, and money changers grew, and so did their anxiety about reconciling Christian morals with mercantile practices.[1] How could a man participate in the monetary economy and still follow the example of Christ and the apostles? Was the decision of St. Francis to voluntarily distance himself from both his family and the monetary economy the best model? Could one be both a good Christian and a successful merchant?

Some developed a new goal: to work not just for pure sustenance or to create a more comfortable life, but to make money grow in a methodical manner, at least in part through investment. This challenged many traditional Christian and classical notions of how men were supposed to work, creating a new class who, distanced from physical labor, learned to

Bressanone Master, *Holy Women Buying Spices*, from the Egmont Breviary, The Netherlands, Utrecht (?), ca. 1435–40. The Morgan Library & Museum, New York, MS M.87, fol. 202v. (Detail of Fig. 6.6.)

manipulate the monetary economy. Anxiety arose as capitalist values competed with traditional Christian and classical ethics, but Europeans responded to the new moral challenges in a range of creative ways.

Medieval Christians strove to distinguish merchants from usurers and to delineate the skills that allowed a merchant to earn a legitimate profit. According to Dominicans like Thomas Aquinas and Franciscans like Peter Olivi, both writing in the thirteenth century, what mattered was the civic utility of merchants' labor, that is, if their money contributed to the prosperity of a fruitful Christian community or instead encouraged sterile, selfish acts of usury and hoarding. Aquinas asserted that the desire for profit was not necessarily sinful, but rather depended on the end to which it would be put.[2]

Later writers continued this tradition, often in the vernacular, thereby making their ideas accessible to a wider audience. The fourteenth-century Frenchman Nicholas Oresme noted that money "belongs to the community" and was instituted for the "common good."[3] He condemned usury and "speculative" money changing, but praised merchants' usefulness, citing, for example, their travel over long distances to obtain goods that benefited the community.[4] (As outlined in the previous chapter, the *Avis aus roys* similarly describes the merchant "running" all over the world.) Oresme also justified merchants' profits if they were spent on meeting the needs of their family or contributing to the well-being of their community. The fifteenth-century Franciscan Bernardino of Siena similarly praised "fruitful merchants," citing many of the same arguments as Aquinas. So did contemporaneous merchants and humanists, such as Giovanni Morelli and Leon Battista Alberti.[5] Merchants understood the importance of depicting themselves as fruitful, industrious citizens whose labor and investments benefited the community, rather than as sterile, avaricious usurers who hoarded wealth for themselves.[6]

Portraits of Merchants

This new mercantile ideal is visualized in portraits made in the international trading centers of northern Europe. A comparison of a portrait of Duke Charles of Burgundy, the future Holy Roman emperor (Charles V), painted in the workshop of the Brussels artist Bernard van Orley in 1516, and that of an unidentified merchant, painted by the Antwerp artist Jan Gossart around fourteen years later, reveals the emergence of the new mercantile masculine ideal (Figs. 6.1–6.2).[7] Whereas Charles's aristocratic hand is idle, the merchant is busy writing in a ledger. While Charles's unfocused eyes and slightly open mouth create a dreamy expression, the merchant gazes intently at the viewer, his lips and jaw tightly clenched. Charles sits in an unspecified space and his main attribute is his huge collar of the chivalric Order of the Golden Fleece; the merchant works at his place of business, surrounded by the tools of his trade. On the back wall are two batches of papers (labeled "miscellaneous drafts" and "miscellaneous letters"), balls of twine, and a Hispano-Moresque dagger. In the foreground are a sand or talc shaker for blotting ink, scissors, an inkwell, coins, a book, a balance with a coin in one pan and a weight in the other, and a container for sealing wax, paper, and quill pens.

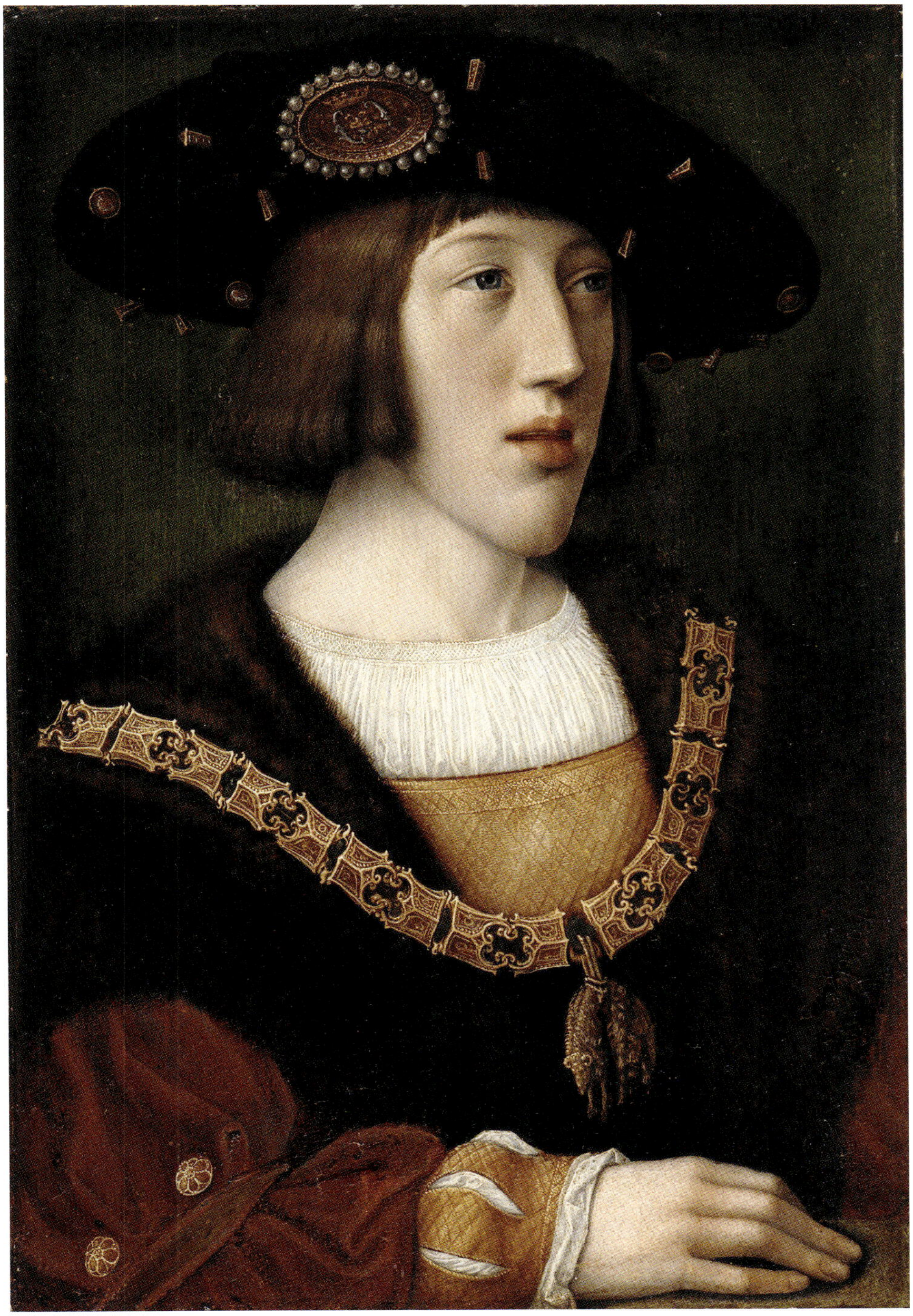

FIG. 6.1. Workshop of Bernard van Orley, *Portrait of Duke Charles of Burgundy*, oil on panel, Belgium, ca. 1516. Musée de Brou, Bourg-en-Bresse, D 980.15.

Both portraits emphasize their sitters' wealth, and both encourage the viewer to enjoy the splendor of their clothing and adornments. But only the merchant is alert and busy, and only he is shown writing, since literacy, unusual at the time, was a prerequisite for a successful career in commerce.[8] Indeed, his thriving business is international in nature, to judge by the Hispano-Moresque dagger and the gold coin featuring

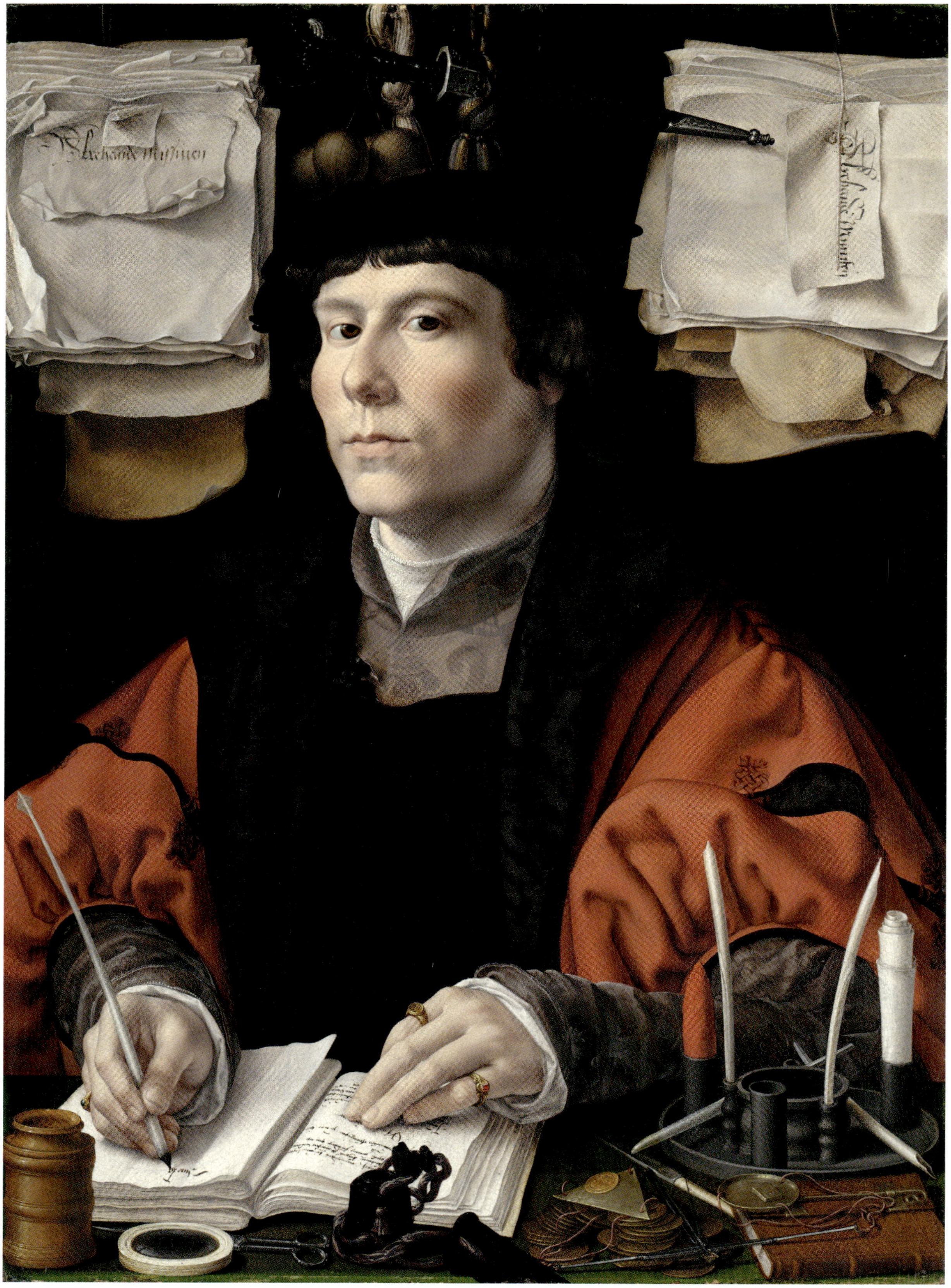

FIG. 6.2. Jan Gossart, *Portrait of a Merchant*, oil on oak, Netherlandish, ca. 1530. National Gallery of Art, Washington, DC, 1967.4.1.

Ferdinand and Isabella of Spain (Fig. 6.3).[9] In short, this portrait visualizes the new mercantile ideal. Presumably commissioned by the merchant himself, the painting idealizes his profession.

Success in business enabled more individuals to commission portraits, once the preserve of the royal and aristocratic elite. Similar examples include Hans Holbein's likeness of the Hanseatic merchant Georg Gisze, dated 1532, and Maerten van Heemskerck's *Portrait of a Man* of 1529.[10] In these portraits only a few coins are discreetly shown; those in Gossart's painting are placed next to the merchant's balance, suggesting that he is fair and honest. The sitters were not only merchants, but were also, as John Hand observes, "likely to be financiers and to deal with money in some manner as money changers, issuers of bills of exchange, or lenders of money."[11] For this reason, they were considered usurers, since they lent money for profit, either directly or through bills of exchange. By including only a few coins, these portraits downplay the merchants' involvement in practices that were viewed negatively, such as lending, investing, or changing money. But these sitters also needed to show that they earned their livelihood through labor. Labor, the legacy of Adam and Eve's disobedience, as recorded in Genesis, was deemed the proper way to earn a living, and the many objects that surround the merchants emphasize that they work for their money, rather than accruing wealth effortlessly. In these ways, painters counteract the negative perceptions of their sitters' trade.

James Murray has observed that "women as managers and owners of [money] exchanges were an almost common sight in Bruges."[12] Indeed women, especially in northern Europe, invested, lent, and exchanged money. For example, in the 1330s and '40s, Martha de Cabanis, a Montpellier widow, invested heavily in long-distance trade and local business, and the women of the Cosericghen family of Bruges

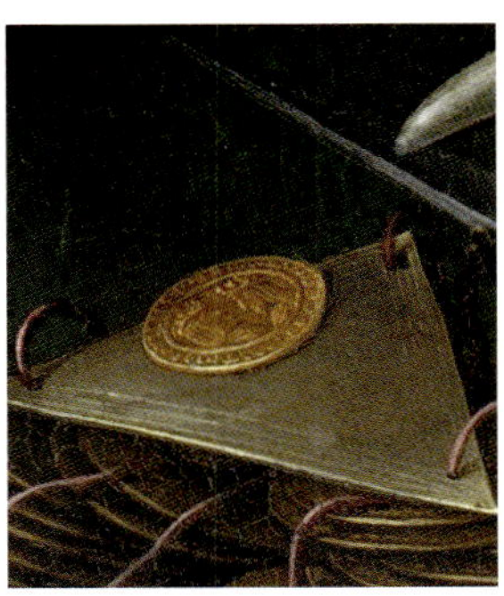

Detail of Fig. 6.2.

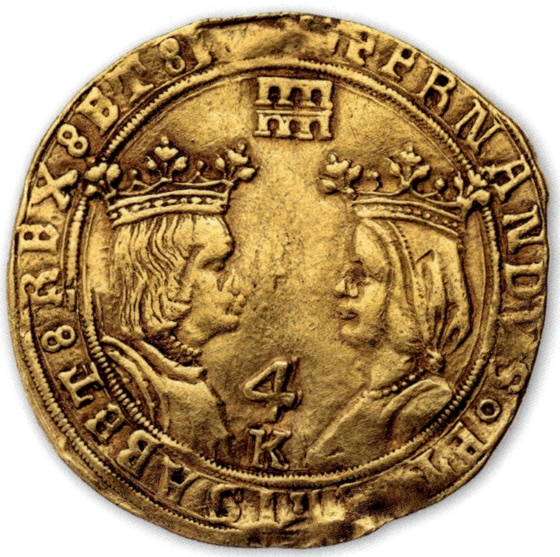

FIG. 6.3. Four-ducat gold coin, Ferdinand and Isabella, Spain, Castile (1497–1537, probably posthumous). American Numismatic Society, New York, 1954.237.146.

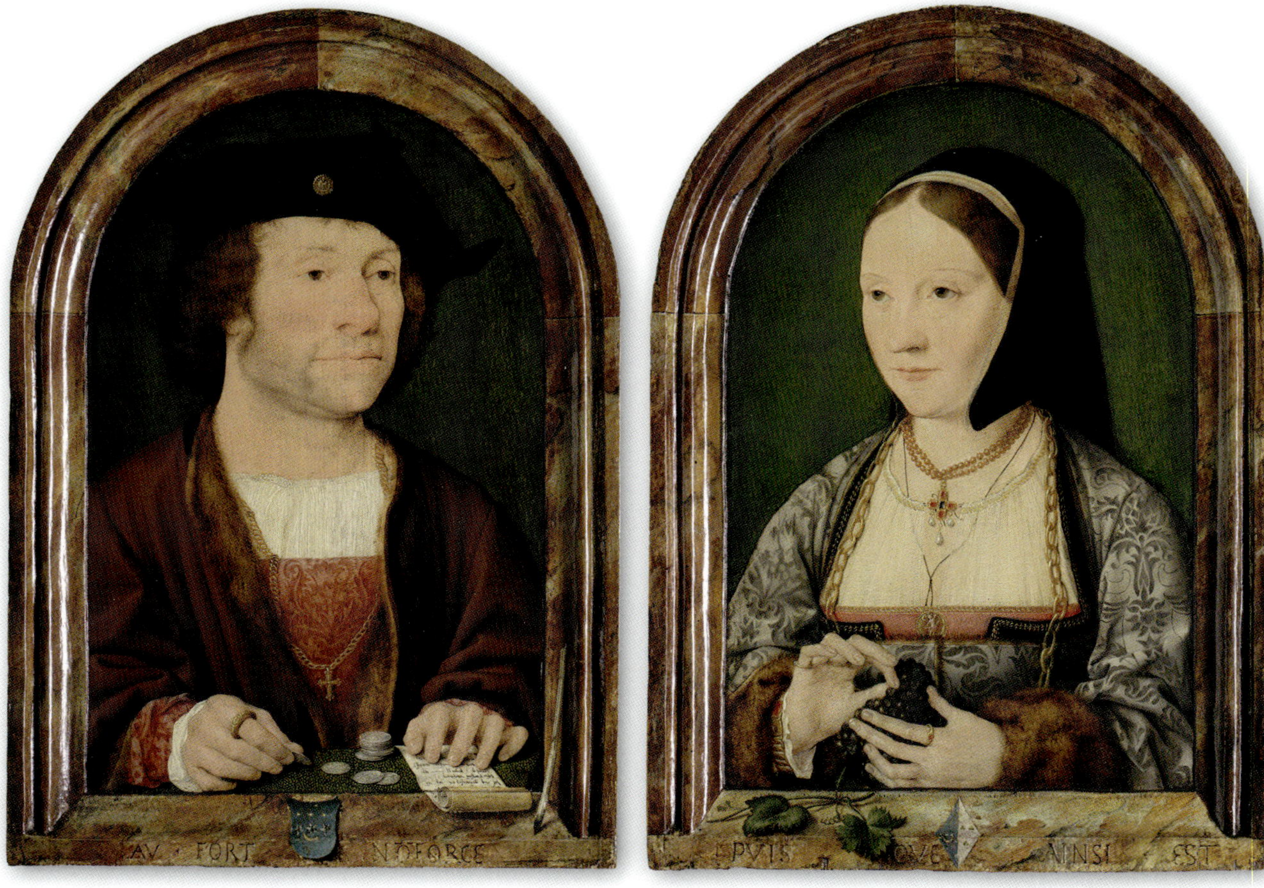

FIG. 6.4. Joos van Cleve, *Portrait of a Mercantile Couple*, oil on panel, Netherlandish, ca. 1530. Rijksmuseum Twenthe, Enschede, 0027 and 0028.

were active as moneylenders.[13] Yet women were rarely depicted in these roles. (Women sellers were occasionally portrayed, but then usually as minor figures; see Figs. 6.8–6.9.) Instead, the ideal merchant was gendered male. In double portraits of merchants and their wives, the husbands are shown counting or fingering money, while the wives are depicted as fertile or pious to counteract any negative associations that were linked to their husbands' trade. A portrait diptych by the Antwerp painter Joos van Cleve, dated around 1530, is typical (Fig. 6.4). The husband fingers a silver coin, and other coins lie nearby, as does an illegible handwritten note and a quill pen, which rests against the frame. By contrast, his wife holds a cluster of grapes, and grape leaves lie on the sill before her, a visual counterpart of her fertility since Psalm 128 reads, "The wife shall be as a fruitful vine." In this way, the fecund woman counteracts the negative view of money as sterile. Similarly, the numerous religious references (the husband's pin of the Virgin and Child, the wife's of St. Sebastian, and both their crosses) are intended to neutralize the unfavorable stereotype of the merchant.

Like Gossart, Adriaen Isenbrant painted an occupational portrait, that is, a work that depicts the sitter's profession (Fig. 6.5).[14] Isenbrant's subject, like Gossart's, must be a merchant, moneylender, or money changer since he holds a balance for coins. Both sitters were evidently well-to-do since they could afford to have their

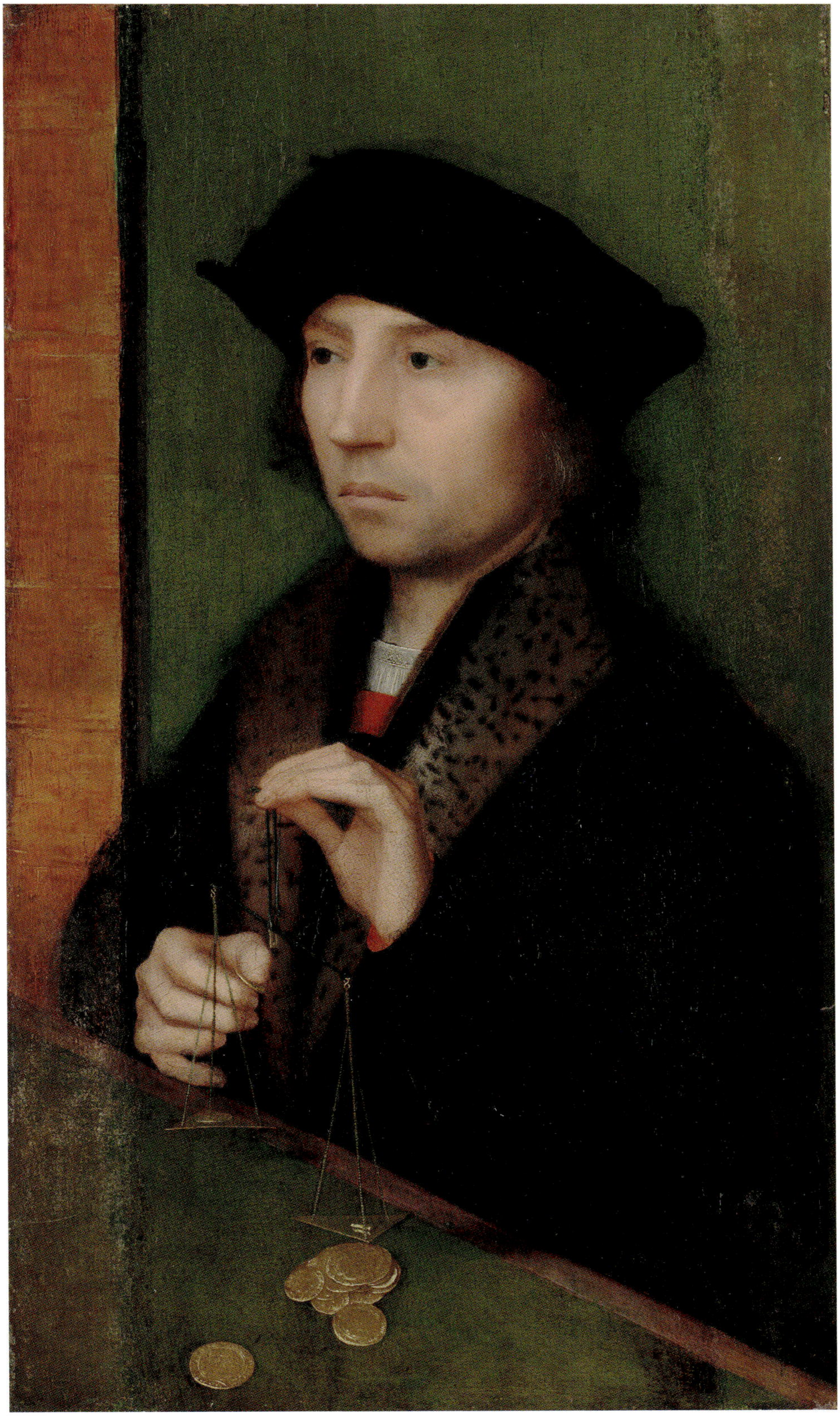

FIG. 6.5. Adriaen Isenbrant, *Man Weighing a Gold Coin*, oil on panel, Netherlandish, ca. 1515–20. The Metropolitan Museum of Art, New York, 32.100.36.

portraits painted by sought-after artists and to own expensive clothes; the mantle of Isenbrant's sitter, for example, is trimmed with fur. But Isenbrant's portrait differs in action, setting, and mood. The merchant is in the process of weighing a gold coin to evaluate its worth. At this time, the weight of coins mattered greatly. As Oresme observed, "merchants nowadays have more trouble in agreeing on the price and value of money than of the merchandise in which they deal."[15] The metal of coins wore away through normal use, especially gold, which is soft. Moreover, in the case of precious gold and silver currency, rulers sometimes debased coins in order to wring more value out of them, and the unscrupulous sometimes shaved off metal from coins while passing them off at face value.

It is not surprising that Isenbrant focuses on weighing money, since he was active in Bruges, a city termed "the cradle of capitalism."[16] The merchant holds the balance in the usual manner, between the thumb and index finger of one hand.[17] On one pan rests a coin, on the other a weight. Unlike Gossart's balance, both pans are triangular.[18] Although the standard form of German and Netherlandish balances was a bowl-shaped pan for the weight and a flat triangular one for the coin, Isenbrant joins Hans Holbein and Marinus van Reymerswaele, among other artists, in showing various combinations. With striking naturalism Isenbrant depicts not only the beam of the balance with arms of equal length, but even the three green strings that so often supported each pan. But the beam is not level as it would be if the coin was at its proper weight. Instead the weight is heavier, indicating that the coin is underweight.

Unlike Gossart's sitter, Isenbrant's has a far-away look and his action seems suspended in time. Furthermore, no other objects distract from his act of weighing coins. These elements suggest that the balance does not simply reflect reality, but has a deeper meaning. Guy Bauman has suggested that it was intended to encourage contemplation of the proper balance between worldly and spiritual values, or to recall St. Michael's judging souls at the Last Judgment.[19] But by choosing to place an underweight coin in the balance's pan, Isenbrant signals that the merchant is facing a moral decision: whether to honestly assess the coin or pass it off at its face value. The balance was often associated with fairness and justice.[20] Leviticus 19:35–36 warns, "Do not any unjust thing in judgment, in rule, in weight, or in measure. Let the balance be just and the weights equal." Proverbs 11:1 similarly declares, "A deceitful balance is an abomination before the Lord: and a just weight is his will." For these reasons Isenbrant's focus on the balance and the contemplative expression of his merchant combine to portray the sitter as someone who soberly considers the ethical dimensions of his trade. This portrait would have served to counteract the view that merchants are greedy misers.

Other aspects of the portrait advertise the merchant's success. In addition to the gold coin that he weighs, he holds another in his right hand; presumably it will be assessed next. A small pile of gold coins lies nearby on the table ready for weighing. One bears a cross *fleury* (a cross whose four arms end in one or more flowers), another an eight-lobed outline just inside the legend that circles the coin. Their decoration suggests they are probably from the Low Countries, but possibly French or German.[21] The coin on the table that is separated from the rest bears a male bust in profile, facing right, with an Italianate cap and haircut. The curving lower edge of the figure's bust overlaps and interrupts the coin's legend. Singled out by its isolated placement in the foreground, this coin was minted in northern Italy (see Fig. 1.9).[22] In his treatment of the coins, Isenbrant indicates not only their great value—they are all gold—but also that the merchant is engaged in international trade. Although it is impossible today to identify the coins precisely, Isenbrant was able to distinguish different types of currency as well as to suggest their material qualities: large and thin, they glitter in the light and their radiance animates the portrait. Their splendor would have been even more striking before wooden strips were added to either side of the painting to enlarge it.

A green cloth covers the merchant's counter. The hue is significant. When fourteenth-century members of the Arte del Cambio (Guild of Bankers and Money Changers) in Florence erected tables at their newly established Mercato Nuovo (New Market), only those who passed an examination and became members of the guild were permitted to cover their tables with green fabric.[23] Florentines were the greatest merchant bankers at this time, and hosted the most important European money market. For this reason their practices spread throughout Europe, including the custom of covering counters with green cloth, to judge by its frequent appearance in imagery (Figs. 3.7, 4.2, 4.26–4.27, 5.13, 6.2–6.5). The green cloth continued to be associated with merchants and finance into the sixteenth century, as attested by the portraits by Gossart, van Cleve, and Isenbrant, among many other paintings.[24]

In some images, the green cloth may have simply reflected reality; in others it may have been intended to lend legitimacy to the merchants portrayed. By contrast, representations of usurers generally lack a green fabric (see Figs. 4.9, 5.21). Why did Florentine bankers choose the color green? Associated with nature and fertility, this color could have served to counteract the association of money with sterility. Jan van Eyck may have dressed the wife of the banker Giovanni Arnolfini in green for this reason in the famous portrait of the pair in the National Gallery, London. Green was also the color of choice for the garments of pregnant women.[25] In the portraits by Gossart, van Cleve, and Isenbrant, the green cloth reflects the actual appearance of such tables. But it also would have served to counteract the association of money with barrenness and sterility, especially considering the understated portrayal of coins in these paintings compared to the large quantities included in images of Avarice (see Figs. 4.11, 4.17, 4.27).

Buying and Selling

As outlined above, with their foreign coins and Hispano-Moresque dagger, the portraits by Gossart and Isenbrant portray merchants who are engaged in international commerce. Another image that concerns global trade appears in the Egmont Breviary, illuminated in the northern Netherlands, perhaps in Utrecht, around 1435–40, for a duke of Guelders, probably Arnold von Egmont, the husband of Catherine of Cleves (see Figs. 4.8, 6.29).[26] It shows a rarely depicted subject: the three Holy Women buying spices (Fig. 6.6). Only one Gospel mentions this event, and then only briefly. Mark 16:1 relates, "When the Sabbath was past, Mary Magdalen, and Mary the mother of James, and

metipm queadmodũ ponti
fex intrat in scã p singulos
annos in sanguine alieno.
Hic autẽ vnã pro pccis offe
rens hostiã : in sempiternũ
sedet in dextera dei : de cetero ex
pectans donec ponant inimi
ci eius scabellũ pedũ eius.
Vna enĩ oblatione consũ
mauit in sempiternũ sãtifica
tos. Contestatur autẽ et nos
spũs scãs. Postq̃ enĩ dixit.
hoc est autẽ testamentũ qd
testabor ad illos. post dies
illos dicit dñs : dabo leges me
as in cordib; eor. et i menti
bus eor supscribam eas : et
pccor et iniquitatũ eor iã
non recordabor amplius.
Vbi autẽ hor remissio : iã
non oblatio pro pccõ. Ha
bentes itaq; frẽs fiduciã in
introitu scõr. in sanguine
xpi. quã initiauit nobis vi
am nouã et viuentẽ p vela
men id est carnẽ suã : et sa
cerdotẽ magnũ super domũ
dei : accedamus vero corde in
plenitudine fidei : aspsi cor
da a consciencia mala : et
abluti corpus aqua mũda :
teneamus spei nrẽ confessi
onẽ indeclinabilem. Fidelis
enĩ est qui repromisit. R.
Reuelabũt celi iniquitatẽ
iude et terra adũsus eũ consur
get et manifestũ erit pcc̃m illi
us in die furoris dñi. Cũ eis
qui dixerũt dño deo recede a
nobis sciẽciã viarũ tuarũ
nolumus. V. In diem pditio
nis seruabitur et ad diem vl
tionis ducetur. Cũ eis. Reue
labunt celi. Ad laudes añ.
O mors ero mors tua mor
sus tuus ero inferne. ps. Mise
re. A. In humilitate iudiciũ e
sublatũ est generationẽ eius
quis enarrabit. ps. Iudica me
ds et disc. A. O vos omñs qui
transitis p viã attendite et vi
dete si est dolor sicut dolor ms.
ps. Ds ds ms. Ds misereat. A.
Attendite vniũsi ppli et vide
te dolorem meũ. ps. Ego dixi.
Añ. Videbũt in quẽ transfixe
rũt et plangent se sup eũ oẽs
tribus terre. ps. Laudate dñm.
Ad bñd. A.
Dedit in morte aĩam suã et cũ sceleratis repu
tatus est et ipse pcc̃a multor
tulit et pro trãsgressoribus ro
gauit. Cetã omnia ut supra.

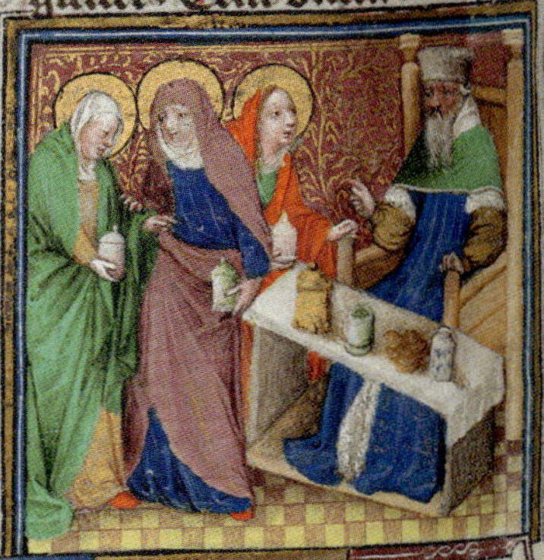

FIG. 6.6. **Bressanone Master, *Holy Women Buying Spices*, from the Egmont Breviary, The Netherlands, Utrecht (?), ca. 1435–40. The Morgan Library & Museum, New York, MS M.87, fol. 202v.**

Salome, bought sweet spices, that coming, they might anoint Jesus [in the tomb]." When they duly came to his sepulcher on Easter Sunday, it was empty; Christ had risen. The miniature, which accompanies the text for Lauds on Holy Saturday, originally appeared between illuminations of the Entombment (and its text for Matins on Holy Saturday), and the Resurrection (and its text for Easter Sunday, beginning with the vigil).[27]

The folio includes two half-length prophets in the left margin holding banderoles (speech scrolls) that allude to the Resurrection.[28] In the main miniature, the Holy Women discuss the wares that are for sale. One points to them, while her companion turns to her; the third woman converses with the merchant. Each woman holds an ointment jar. The magnificently dressed apothecary sits before a counter on which are displayed three vessels of different shapes and materials, and a pile of large circular objects, presumably coins.

Images of the Holy Women buying spices are extremely rare, as mentioned above, but the Egmont Breviary frequently shows iconographic innovation.[29] The biblical reference to this subject is too brief to have served as more than a general guide. Instead, this miniature may have been composed by combining an image of the Holy Women at Christ's Tomb (where they often stand holding ointment jars), and a depiction of a merchant from one of the many late medieval images that show vendors, including apothecaries, at their counters.[30] This merchant, however, is much more luxuriously dressed and is seated in a much more elegant chair than the typical vendor.

If the subject of the Holy Women buying spices is rare in art, it was quite common in Easter sepulcher dramas, and this may have sparked the idea for the subject.[31] By the thirteenth century this episode of Easter plays had become lengthy and elaborate, and included a lively exchange between the merchant and Holy Women about the price and quality of the ointment. The Egmont illumination shares with late medieval religious drama a propensity for including telling details from everyday life, such as this dialogue not mentioned in Mark's Gospel.

The unusual subject may also have been inspired by the contemporaneous spice trade. Spices are an integral part of the medieval biblical episode, but they were also a valued luxury commodity in the Middle Ages, used in cooking, medicine, and as aromatics.[32] They were believed to originate in the Garden of Eden, and then to flow from the rivers of paradise into Asia and Africa.[33] Imported from the East, spices were expensive, available only to the elite. They were a key driver of global trade, and Europeans' search for direct access to spices and other commodities, without Arab middlemen, greatly contributed to increased travel to the East and ultimately to the development of colonialism.[34] The Egmont Breviary evokes the high value placed on spices and the sums they commanded through the merchant's luxurious dress, his throne-like chair, and the coins piled on the counter. The coins are unrealistically portrayed since vendors would avoid displaying money in this way for fear of theft. Here, the pile of large gold coins serves to suggest not only the high cost of spices but also the presumed wealth of the East.

Another scene of merchants has a more direct connection to the East. In 1271 Marco Polo's father and uncle, both merchants, took seventeen-year-old Marco from Venice to the court of Kublai Khan, the Mongol emperor. Arriving in 1274, Polo spent more than sixteen years there until, in 1291, he traveled to India and Persia before returning home to Venice. He composed two versions of his travels, the first in 1298–99, the second between 1310 and 1320. Neither survives in its original language (probably Franco-Italian), but the account of Polo's travels immediately became popular.[35] At least 140 manuscripts are preserved, written in many European languages. They whetted the appetite for trade with the East, which Polo portrayed as a land of great riches. Among those riches were not only spices and textiles, but also enslaved persons, such as a Tartar named Peter whom Polo acquired in China and freed in his will.[36] He was particularly struck by the sophisticated economic practices of the Mongols. He reported, for example, that the entire empire used a single currency system, and that the khan had authorized the use of paper money—practices unknown in Europe.

An image of merchants appears in a French version of Polo's travelogue (Fig. 6.7). Profusely illustrated with pen and colored wash drawings, this manuscript was probably made in Paris around 1410–12 for a royal or noble patron. Polo relates that the Indian province of Lar is home to "the best merchants in the world and the most truthful."[37] The illumination shows two vendors behind a table, presumably the Brahmins, as Polo calls them, selling wares as potential customers approach, one bending forward with great interest. On the counter is an open box of round objects, perhaps pearls, and two unidentifiable items.[38] The unrelated background figure refers to an ascetic religious order of nudists who, Polo reports, tested recruits by tempting them with the attentions of a naked woman.

Manuscripts of Polo's travels construct a complex view of Asian merchants who are seen as familiar and civilized, yet also "wild and strange."[39] On the one hand, the illuminator minimizes differences between Asians and Europeans by showing the merchants from Lar as light-skinned and clothed in garments resembling European dress. Furthermore, they sell their merchandise at a counter, much like Europeans. On the other hand, the vendor at the right wears a "foreign" hat and, more critically, the two conduct business not in a city, but rather in the countryside, where a naked woman reminds the viewer of their exoticism. Such images nevertheless helped bridge the gap between East and West by emphasizing similarities and by visualizing the East, in this case India, as a culture that shared the European interest in trade. Manuscripts like this one helped to perpetuate the idea of an Asia teeming with natural resources and commercial markets and eager to trade with the West. The end of Mongolian rule, the restoration of a Chinese dynasty in 1368, the fragmentation of control over Central Asia, the rise of the Ottomans, and the ravages of the Black Death all contributed to the closing of the overland route to Asia. Some Europeans began to dream instead of reaching by ship the great marketplace in the East.

For most medieval Europeans, however, buying and selling occurred closer to home. Local trade is depicted, for example, in a Franciscan breviary created in Bruges around 1500–1510 and soon owned by Eleanor, dowager queen of Portugal. The office for the consecration of a church includes a miniature depicting such an event (Fig. 6.8). A procession circles around the church, one of the standard iconographies for this theme. Acolytes with banners of standing saints lead two rows: ecclesiastics at the front, laity (including children) at the rear (seen to the right of the building).

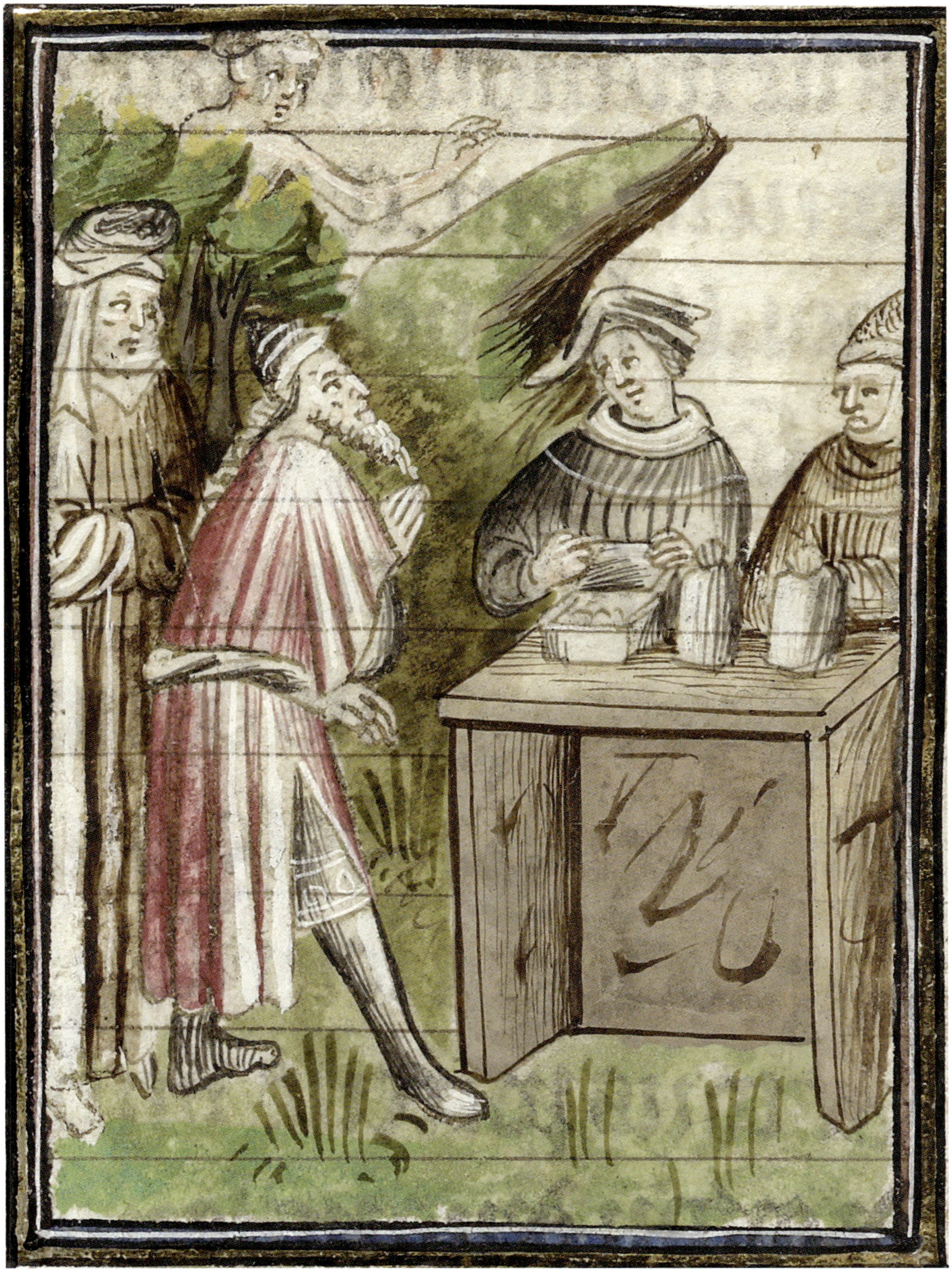

FIG. 6.7. Workshop of the Berry Apocalypse Master, *Merchants of Lar*, from Marco Polo, *Le livre des merveilles d'Asie* (The Book of the Marvels of Asia) (fols. 71–266), France, probably Paris, ca. 1410–12. The Morgan Library & Museum, New York, MS M.723, fol. 237r (det.).

desiderant qui thesaurũ pu
blice in via portant. Hoc
autē dico non ut proximi
opera nr͞a non videant cũ
scriptum sit. videant op͞a
vr͞a bona et glorificēt p͞rē
vr͞m qui in celis ē. Sed ut
p hoc q͞d agimus laudes
exterius non queramus.

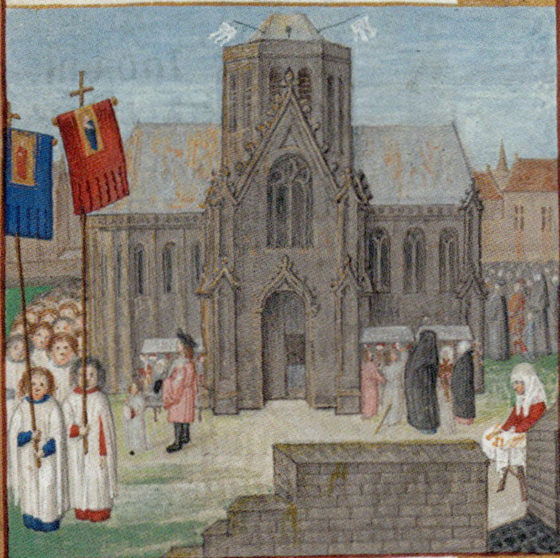

In dedicatione ecclesie. Ad
vs͞. a͞. Domũ tuam dn͞e. cu
reliq͞s de laudib3. p͞. Dixit
dn͞s. cu rel. In fine. lauda
ihr͞lm. Capitl͞m.

Vidi civitatē sc͞am
ihr͞lm novam
descendentem de celo a deo
paratam sicut sponsam
ornatam viro suo. Deo
gratias. Hymnus

Urbs beata ihr͞lm dicta
pacis visio. que con
struitur in celis vivis ex la
pidibus. & angelis coornata
ut sponsata comite.

Nova veniens e celo nup
tiali thalamo. preparata ut
sponsata copuletur dn͞o:
platee et muri eius ex auro
purissimo.

Porte nitent margari
tis aditis patentib3. et vir
tute meritorũ illuc itrodu
citur. omnis qui ob xp͞i no
men hic i mundo p͞mitur.

Tunsionib3 pressuris
expoliti lapides suis coaptã
tur locis p manũ artificis.
Disponuntur permansuri
sacris edificiis.

Gloria et honor deo usq3
quo altissimo. una p͞ri fili
oq3 inclito paraclito. cui
laus ē et potestas p immen
sa secula. Amen. V. Hec ē
domus dn͞i firmiter edificata.
Bene fundata est supra firmā
petram. Ad magn͞ a͞. Sc͞ificavit
dn͞s tabernaculum suũ. quia
hec ē domus dei in qua invo
cabitur nomē eius de quo scr͞p
tum est. et erit nomen meum

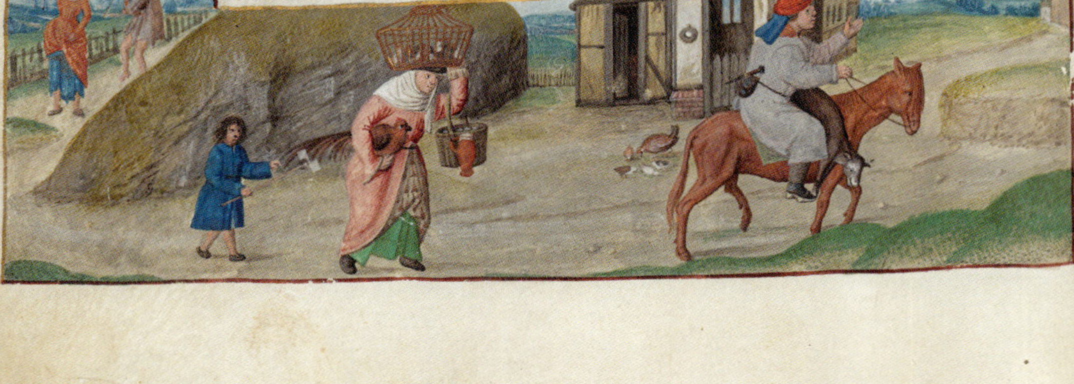

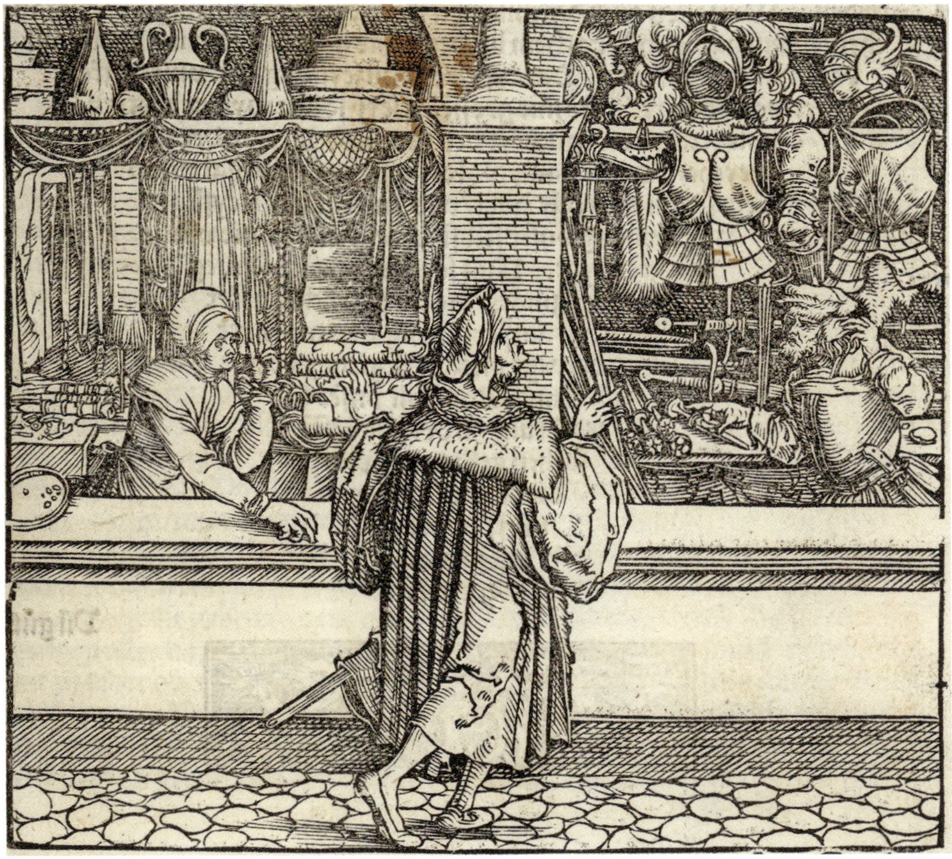

FIG. 6.8. ***Dedication of a Church*, from the Breviary of Eleanor of Portugal, Belgium, Bruges or Ghent, ca. 1500–1510. The Morgan Library & Museum, New York, MS M.52, fol. 578v.**

FIG. 6.9. Petrarch Master (Hans Weiditz?), *Shopping*, from Marcus Tullius Cicero, *De officiis* (On Obligations), trans. Johann Freiherr von Schwarzenberg and Johann Neuber, Germany, Augsburg: Heinrich Steyner, 1531. The Morgan Library & Museum, New York, PML 23007, leaf F1 recto (det.).

Although the illumination's iconography is conventional, its multiple references to commerce are unusual. In the main scene, women sell goods at three stalls alongside the church and at a table near the surrounding wall. In the lower border, men and women travel, presumably towards the church, where they will sell their produce and livestock. One man has flung the carcass of a calf over his horse. A woman carries a pheasant and a basket of eggs, while balancing on her head a wicker cage of live birds. They are followed by a boy with a whirligig, another woman with a cage on her head, and a man carrying a bird. This illumination is the only known image of a church dedication to include commercial activity. But fairs, which were held mostly for economic reasons and were essential for trade, were rooted in such church rituals.[40]

A small crowd gathers around the few stalls in the church dedication scene, but a much better sense of the experience of shopping is conveyed by the anonymous printmaker known as the Petrarch Master in the German-language translation of Cicero's *De officiis* (On Obligations), an artist much discussed in Chapter 3 (Fig. 6.9). The joy of shopping is visualized by a wealthy man, dressed in a long mantle with a fur collar, approaching two stalls crammed with goods. To the left, a woman sells purses, belts, fabric, and a variety of household vessels. To the right, a man specializes in armor and weapons. Both vendors try to attract the customer's attention—turning, leaning, and gesturing towards him. But he has eyes only for the armor. He moves towards the assortment, gazes up at it, and spreads his hands wide in a gesture of wonder. A dialogue, which immediately precedes the woodcut, was added to Cicero's text in this translation. It has the female seller cry, "Come here, don't pass by my wares. You will find a lot that will look good on you." The woman's words confirm that the late medieval city had become a consumer culture, and that stalls and counters were filled with commodities for sale that were meant to seduce the customer. This "culture of display," designed to solicit the eyes of passersby, was perfected in late medieval times.[41] It was only then that cities became populous enough to cater to great numbers of consumers, and even to niche markets, and that international commerce became strong enough to be able to offer a vast variety of consumer goods.

The customer replies to the saleswoman, "Whatever beauty and adornment belongs to the body is different for a man and a woman. Therefore sell your wares without me."[42] His response indicates that shopping was a gendered activity. If the merchant had become a masculinized ideal (see Figs. 6.2, 6.4, 6.5), so, too, was the shopper gendered. The Petrarch Master's stalls separate objects according to stereotypically gendered interests, and Cicero's accompanying text advises the reader, presumed to be male, to avoid anything effeminate or foppish. Thus the Petrarch Master shows the customer turning away from items associated with female fashion and the home and towards what late medieval society would have deemed manly: arms and armor.

Illuminated Registers

The monetary economy produced not only portraits of merchants and images of buying and selling, but also new types of illuminated financial records, including notable examples from Bologna in northern Italy. In 1376 Bologna established a new government, free from papal control. Soon the city took three important steps towards insuring its fiscal well-being. It began minting its own gold currency, it created a court in the commercial center of the city to adjudicate mercantile disputes, and it established the first consolidated public loans fund (*monte di pubbliche prestanze*). The word *monte* is used to describe an accumulation (literally, a mountain) of money, that is, a fund. Beginning in 1394, a series of registers was issued listing those Bolognese who had lent money to the city in exchange for the repayment of their principal plus 10 percent interest. Five codices were produced, one for each of the four quarters of the city and a fifth for clerical lenders throughout the commune. Each volume began with a richly illuminated folio, decorated in a strikingly similar manner in all surviving books.[43]

One volume is lost, but three others, all dated 1394 or 1395 and signed by an artist named Nicolò, remain in the State Archives of Bologna. A detached leaf, containing the manuscript's frontispiece and a headpiece, survives from the fifth codex (Figs. 6.10a–b).[44] Now in the Morgan Library, its recto shows, like the others, two rows of standing patron saints, whose names are inscribed at their feet. The same saints appear in all surviving examples, although in each case arranged in a different order. Here in the top row, left to right, are Bishop Petronius of Bologna, holding a

FIG. 6.10A. Nicolò di Giacomo di Nascimbene, called Nicolò da Bologna, *Sts. Petronius, Paul, Ambrose, Dominic, Francis, and Florian*, frontispiece from a register of creditors of a Bolognese lending society, Italy, Bologna, 1394–95. The Morgan Library & Museum, New York, MS M.1056r.

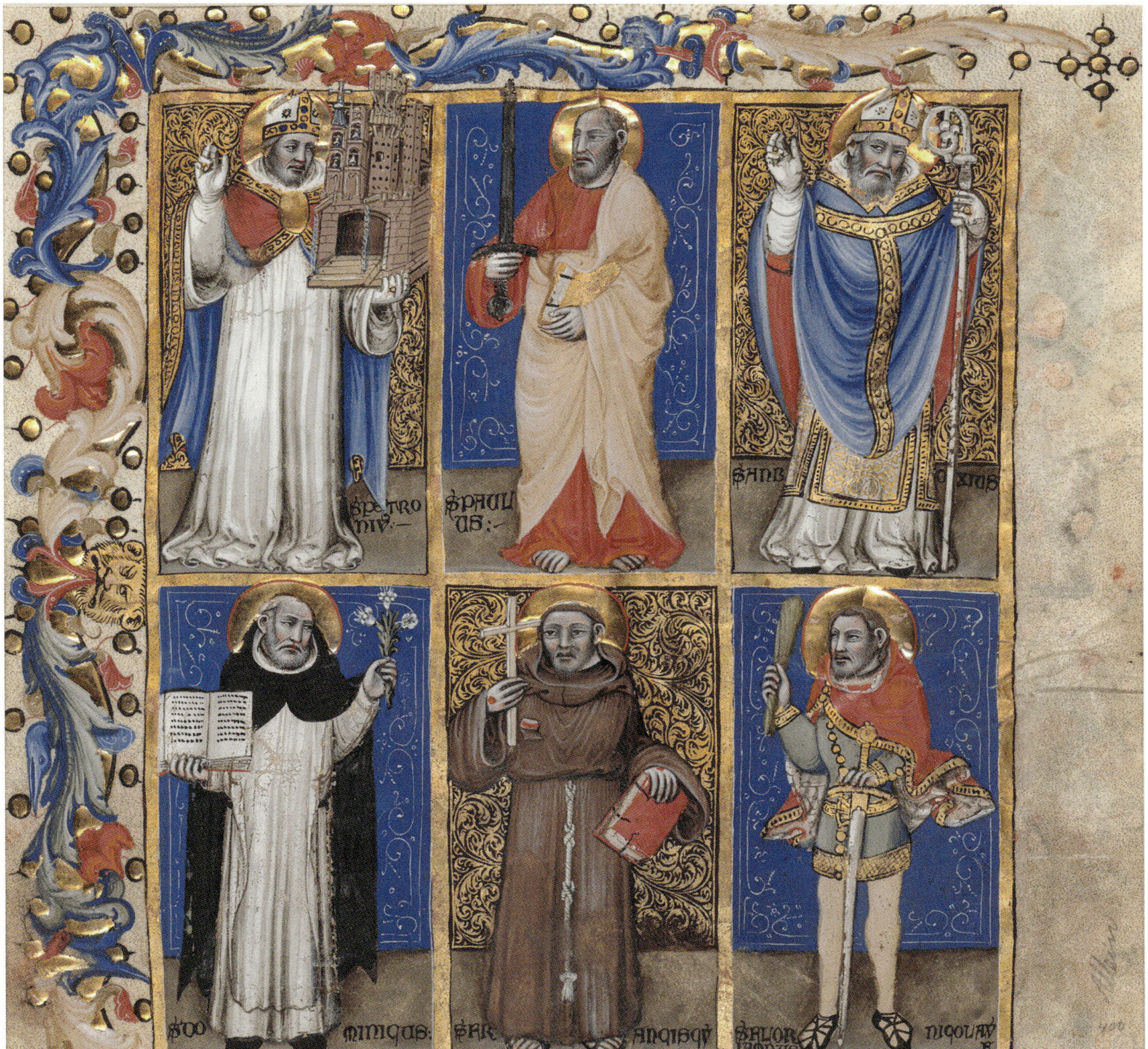

FIG. 6.10B. Nicolò di Giacomo di Nascimbene, called Nicolò da Bologna, *St. Peter* and *Goldbeating*, headpiece from a register of creditors of a Bolognese lending society, Italy, Bologna, 1394–95. The Morgan Library & Museum, New York, MS M.1056v.

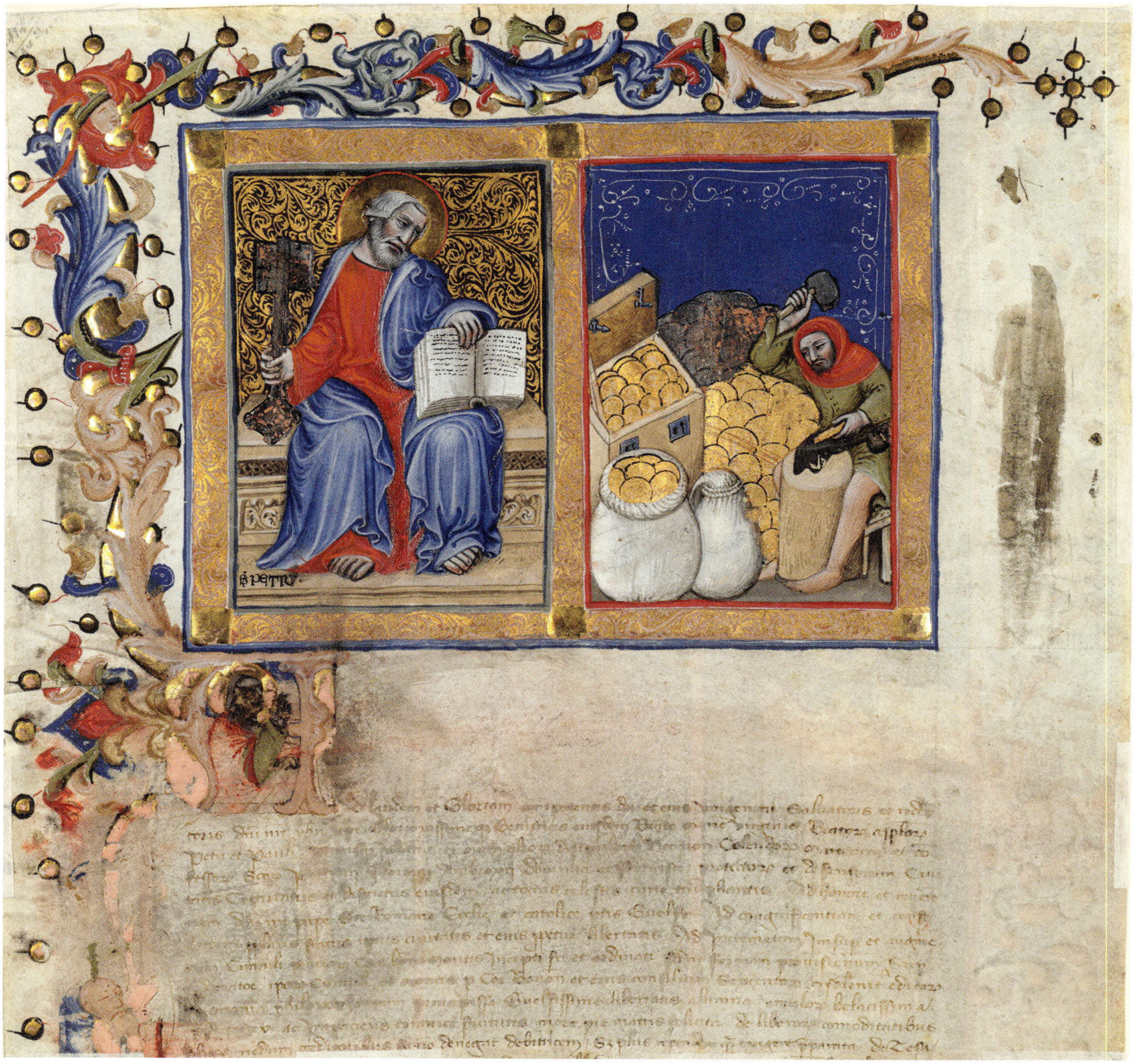

detailed model of the city; St. Paul with his sword; and Archbishop Ambrose of Milan. Below are St. Dominic, who died in Bologna, dressed as a Dominican friar; St. Francis, in a Franciscan habit and displaying three of the stigmata; and St. Florian, dressed as a soldier.

At Florian's feet, an inscription reads, "NICOLAV[S] F[ECIT]" (Nicholas made this). The folio has been universally attributed to the leading illuminator of Bologna, Nicolò di Giacomo di Nascimbene, often called Nicolò da Bologna.[45] Since he was the city's official illuminator and held a virtual monopoly on decorating communal manuscripts, it is not surprising that he received this commission. Part of the folio must be missing, since the other frontispieces show coats of arms below the saints, and this one probably originally did too.

On the bottom of the verso is a faded text, which can be reconstructed from the other registers (Fig. 6.10b). It begins by praising God, the Virgin, and the saints who are portrayed on the recto, and then discusses financial matters. The first letter, an *A*, frames a haloed, albeit faded, half-length figure of Christ raising his hand in blessing. Above the text, a two-part illumination shows, on the left, a seated St. Peter holding his attributes, a book and a key. Because he is the patron saint of the district of Porta San Pietro (St. Peter's Gate), this folio is probably the frontispiece of the register from that district.[46] Since Peter holds an enormous key on the *bolognino d'oro*, a gold coin produced in Bologna, he is also a particularly appropriate saint to feature in a book dedicated to loans to the commune.

To the right of Peter, a goldbeater raises his hammer as he steadies a gold ingot on an anvil, to make the thin sheets needed to produce new coins. This worker is much smaller than Peter; indeed, the scene focuses on the gold and silver coins that allude to the riches of Bologna. They fill the goldbeater's room, piled in sacks, in a chest, and on the floor. The juxtaposition of the gold and silver coins with Peter and Christ makes clear that medieval money and religion were inexorably intertwined.

Another illuminated monetary register confirms that truism. This manuscript, composed for successive officials of the Avignon mint around 1411, opens with miniatures of the Madonna and Child and the Crucifixion (Figs. 6.11a–b).[47] These illuminations are followed by a series of coats of arms of popes and others connected with the mint, from Gregory XI (r. 1370–78) to Julius III (r. 1550–55). The manuscript concludes with texts directly related to minting money: the minters' oath, a register of the mint's officials and employees from 1377 to 1591, and a list of sixteenth-century regulations. Although this is not the earliest minters' book—that distinction belongs to a Florentine codex begun in 1314—it is among the most beautifully illuminated.

Folio 2v shows a gentle, sweet Virgin and Child painted in exquisite colors (Fig. 6.11a). The composition seems modeled on an image that included a donor, since both the Virgin and Child turn to the left and Jesus tilts his head down and offers a blessing with his right hand. Below, in burnished gold letters, is the prayer "Beata es virgo maria" (Blessed are you, Virgin Mary). The facing folio, painted in the same refined colors, shows a Crucifixion with the grieving figures of the Virgin and St. John the Evangelist (Fig. 6.11b). In the upper corners are the sun and moon, referring to the darkness that fell over the earth at the moment

FIG. 6.11A. ***Madonna and Child,*** **from an oath of office for coiners and minters of Avignon and register of officials, France, Avignon, ca. 1411. The Morgan Library & Museum, New York, MS M.300, fol. 2v (det.).**

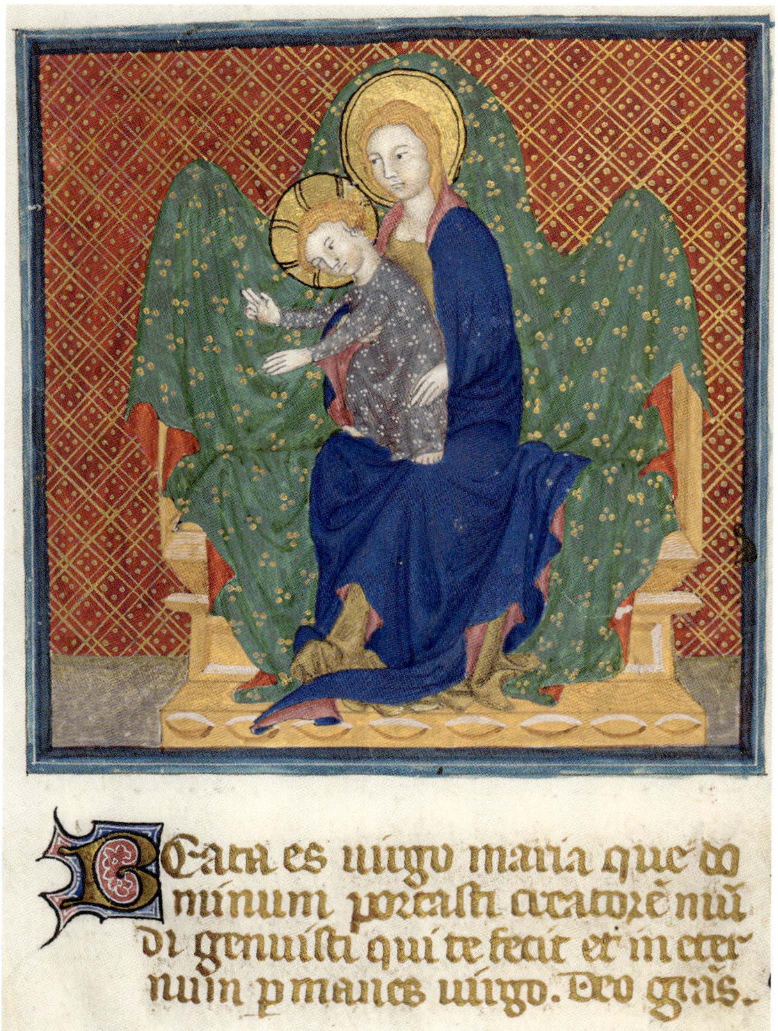

of Christ's death. Inscribed below, again in gold letters, is the "Ave verum corpus" (Hail true body), a short Eucharistic chant attributed to Innocent VI, the fifth Avignon pope (r. 1352–62). The hymn is a meditation on the belief that Christ is truly present in the sacrament of the Eucharist. The illumination shows white liquid issuing from Christ's side, the water mentioned in the prayer: "Hail true body . . . from whose pierced side flowed water and blood."[48] Theologically, this was the moment Christ gave birth to the Church.[49]

The minters' oath (fols. 18r–18v) must have been composed during the papacy of John XXIII, since it

FIG. 6.11B. ***Crucifixion with Virgin and St. John,*** **from an oath of office for coiners and minters of Avignon and register of officials, France, Avignon, ca. 1411. The Morgan Library & Museum, New York, MS M.300, fol. 3r (det.).**

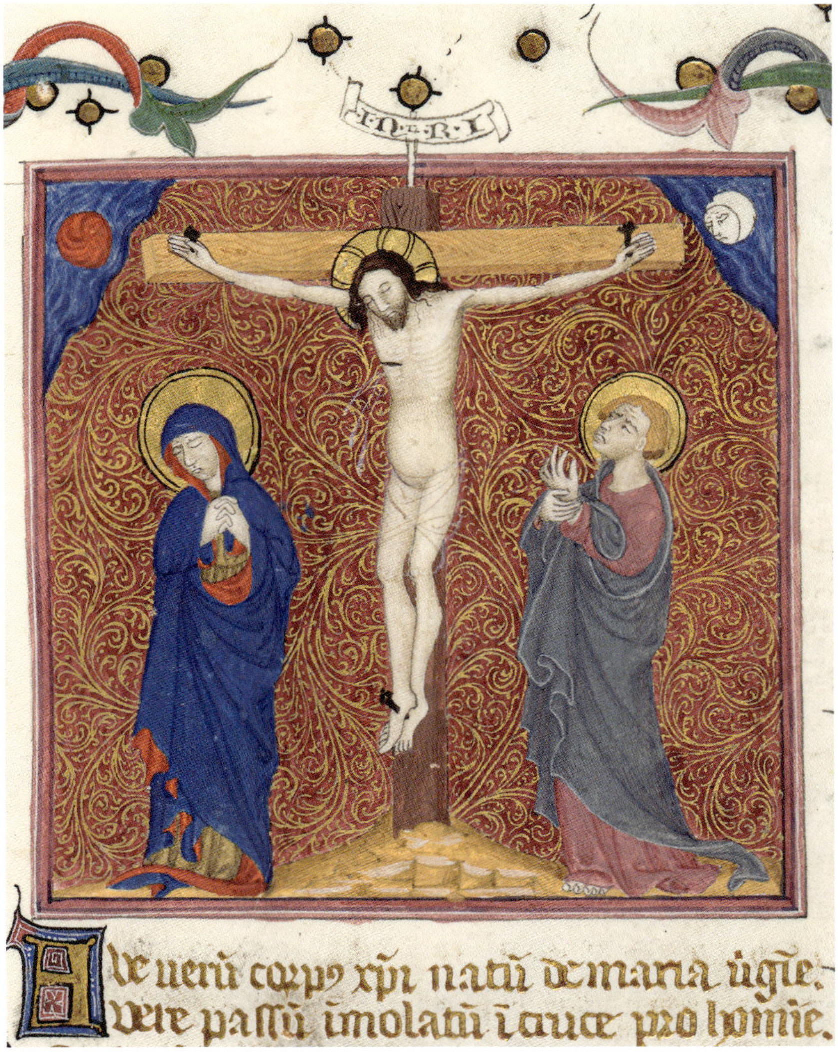

mentions him in the first line. Because he was pope in Avignon from 1410 to 1415 and the illuminations of the Virgin and Child and the Crucifixion date ca. 1411, the oath and miniatures were probably part of the same campaign. Although the oath mentions St. Peter twice, it never refers to the Madonna and Child or the Crucifixion, the subjects portrayed in the accompanying illuminations.

The intermingling of religion and money, seen on coins, in merchants' portraits, and in the Bologna creditors' book, recurs in the minters' oath. After swearing to be faithful to the pope "and all the laws of the

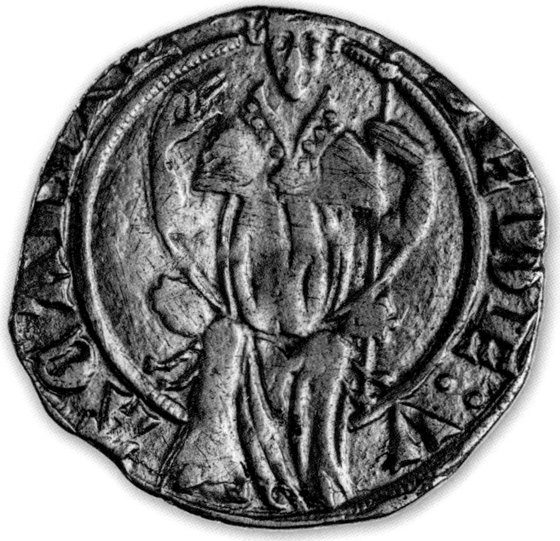

FIG. 6.12. Papal States *carlino*, France, Avignon, 1415–17. American Numismatic Society, New York, 1937.146.591.

Roman Church," the oath turns to economic matters. Each minter promises to prevent the debasement of coins, whether intentional or not. He also swears that if he learns of any deceit, he will prevent it and report it to the pope or the chamberlain. Particularly striking is that the minter promises six times to be trustworthy. Whereas the saints portrayed in the creditors' codex seem to serve as protectors of Bologna and its loan enterprise, in the Avignon minters' book Christ, the pope, the Church, and the saints seem to be invoked in order to strike fear into the minters' hearts in the hope of preventing any monetary wrongdoing.

One of the coins produced in Avignon in the second decade of the fifteenth century is the *carlino.* Pope John XXII (r. 1316–34) began minting the *carlino* at Avignon based on a silver coin from Naples. One small silver *carlino* dates from the *sede vacante* of 1415–17 (just a few years after the minters' book; Fig. 6.12). The period of time when cardinals cannot agree on a new pontiff is known in canon law as *sede vacante* (vacant seat). During such periods special coins are minted. They do not portray a particular pope with his arms or name, but a generic pontiff, who is often, as here, shown enthroned, blessing with one hand, and holding a scepter. The encircling legend reads "SEDE V/ACANTE." The legend on the reverse reads, in part, "SANTVS: PETRVS [ET PAULVS]," and the central field shows, tied by a cord, two crossed keys, symbolizing the keys to heaven that Christ gave St. Peter (Matthew 16:19) and, by the twelfth century, papal authority on earth. Although the minters' codex opens with images of the Virgin and Christ, this coin—like the minters' oath—focuses instead on St. Peter, who is traditionally held to be the first pope and is often invoked to represent papal authority.

The Material Culture of Money

Developing alongside the new mercantile economy was a material culture to support it: not just coins, books, and financial papers, but also purses, moneybags, portable balances to weigh coins, lockable chests for storage, merchant's stalls and tables, leather bindings for financial records, calendars to accurately date transactions, and even mechanical clocks to facilitate paying hourly wages. Late medieval artists explored both the material and immaterial qualities of these objects.

Merchants were often associated with the balance, the table, and coins or a purse (see Figs. 3.7, 5.13, 6.2,

6.4–6.5). One example of this association can be found in the *Liber de moribus hominum et officiis nobilium sive super ludo scacchorum* (Book of the Customs of Men and the Duties of Nobles or The Book of Chess). The Dominican friar Jacobus de Cessolis of Lombardy composed his treatise at the turn of the fourteenth century. In this frequently illustrated work, Jacobus uses the game of chess (introduced to western Europe from the Islamic world in the ninth or tenth century and popular throughout the continent by the twelfth century) to structure an ideal society of interdependent groups. His moralizing work explains each game piece and its attributes. Each pawn, for example, represents a different class of society, with the fourth pawn identified as a merchant. The Latin treatise was translated into numerous European languages, including at least three French versions. The earliest is Jean de Vignay's, datable between 1332 and 1350, when he was at the French royal court. Jean dedicates his *Jeu des échecs* (Game of Chess) to Duke John of Normandy (who became King John II "the Good"—Jean le Bon—of France in 1350). At least forty-eight manuscripts of his translation survive.[50]

One Parisian copy is datable to 1350–60, in other words shortly after Jean de Vignay's translation was composed.[51] Commissioned by a court patron, perhaps the king, it is filled with sensitively drawn grisaille miniatures (images rendered entirely in shades of gray).[52] One shows a merchant and king as elegant, slender figures with long torsos and straight backs sitting side by side (Fig. 6.13). Their difference in rank is made clear by the king's crown, his voluminous mantle, and ornate chair—a faldstool with animal-headed and -footed ornaments. More critical is the difference in their actions. Whereas the merchant weighs coins with his balance, the king performs no labor (for a similar contrast, see Figs. 6.1–6.2). Despite his lower status, the merchant is portrayed as a sympathetic and refined figure who holds his balance with great delicacy.

The merchant steadies the balance in his right hand, rests a plank (*table*) on his legs, and has a purse tucked into his belt.[53] Some manuscripts visualize the merchant carrying a board, but most images interpret the word *table* in its modern sense as a piece of furniture with four legs.[54] Here the artist adopts an intermediate position: a board functioning like a table.

For Jean, the balance, purse, and table are associated with specific mercantile activities. He relates that the table and balance denote money changing and money-lending. Indeed one definition of the Old French word *table* is a bureau for money changing.[55] He further states that the table and balance signify involvement with the king's income, loans, and revenues. By contrast, the purse indicates one who pays royal salaries. The close economic relationship between merchant and king that Jean de Vignay portrays is not surprising. Not only did the king need someone to oversee his accounts, but in the game of chess the fourth pawn is also placed immediately in front of the king. Unlike all but one of the pawns in this manuscript, the merchant is shown sitting beside the king. Jean also indicates that the merchant has other customers and performs other types of transactions, including selling cloth and various merchandise. The rubric confirms this, relating that the chapter will discuss "[t]he state and the office of changers and those who pay salaries and lend money and of cloth merchants and those who receive the taxes of the king."[56] Here Jean reflects a contemporary truth: many merchants functioned in multiple roles.

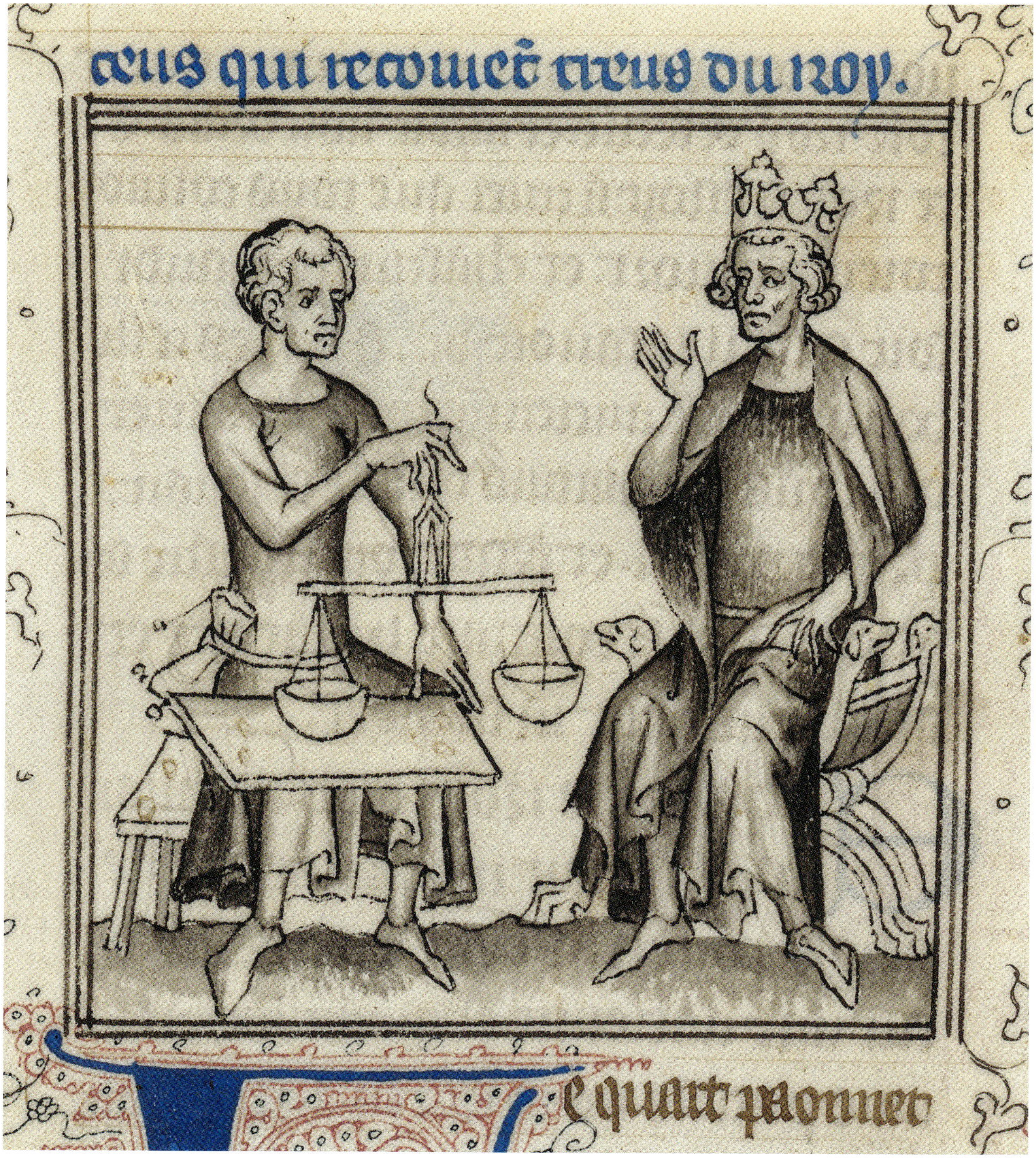

FIG. 6.13. *Merchant-Pawn and King*, from Jacobus de Cessolis, *Liber de moribus hominum et officiis nobilium sive super ludo scacchorum* (Book of the Customs of Men and the Duties of Nobles or The Book of Chess), trans. Jean de Vignay, France, probably Paris, 1350–60. The Morgan Library & Museum, New York, G.52, fol. 33v (det.).

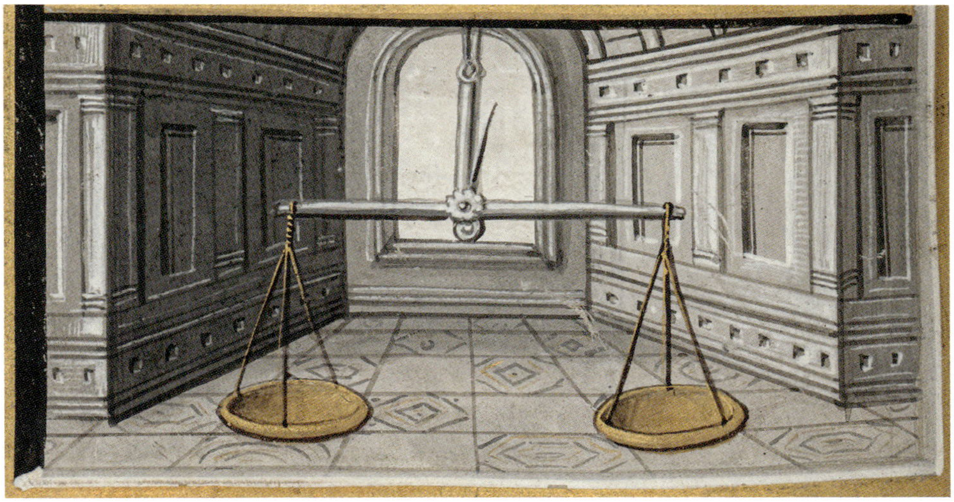

FIG. 6.14. ***Libra*, from a book of hours, France, Paris, ca. 1520. The Morgan Library & Museum, New York, MS M.632, fol. 9v (det.).**

The first paragraph in this section ends with a warning to merchants to keep their promises and to avoid avarice and debt. The rest of the chapter condemns greed, citing a series of ancient Roman sources to argue the case. In short, it offers an ambivalent picture of the merchant. On the one hand, the merchant is susceptible to avarice and participates in those mercantile activities deemed the most questionable—money changing and lending. On the other hand, he sells cloth, a perfectly honorable trade, and the king trusts him. The image under discussion, by contrast, is entirely positive. Far from avaricious, the merchant is depicted with no visible money, and his purse is discreetly tucked away. More importantly, he holds a balance, the focus of the composition. It is exaggerated in size, and no other object competes with it. How would viewers have interpreted this attribute?

Since antiquity, the balance has been viewed as an instrument that could ensure fairness. It is the attribute of Equity on ancient Roman coins, where it always appears with a horizontal beam, and this association was perpetuated into the Middle Ages.[57] Perhaps the most ubiquitous image of a balance in the Middle Ages is the zodiac sign for Libra (*libra* means scales in Latin). Astrological texts explicitly link Libra's balance with commerce; a late fifteenth-century Flemish manuscript advises that "When the sun is in this sign, it is a good time to travel to the east on trade business."[58] Some depictions show the balance alone, for example, in a Parisian book of hours, dated around 1520 (Fig. 6.14), where its pans are perfectly balanced in line with ancient Roman images of Equity. By contrast, medieval images of usurers generally exclude the balance (see Figs. 4.9, 5.21).

When the balance is portrayed, its meaning is inextricably tied to whether the pans hold equal weight, that is, whether the beam is level. When St. Michael weighs souls (or embodiments of virtue and sin) at the Last Judgment, the beam of his balance is rarely horizontal: sin and virtue do not equate. Whereas personifications of Justice (generally portrayed as a female figure) hold a balance whose beam is, as a rule, level, Injustice's balance is usually inclined.[59] This is depicted, for example, in *Der Wälsche Gast*, in images showing a lord choosing greed over generosity (Fig. 6.15).[60] Justice stands on the far left beside Generosity, and Injustice on the far right with Desire. Justice's pans are balanced, but the pans held by Injustice are tipped, and this imbalance is clearly associated with greed since she and Desire carry a beam from which hang three moneybags. Medieval viewers, then, could associate the balance with justice or injustice, generosity or greed, heaven or hell, fairness or inequity, depending on the context. The beam of Jean de Vignay's merchant (unlike Isenbrant's) is perfectly

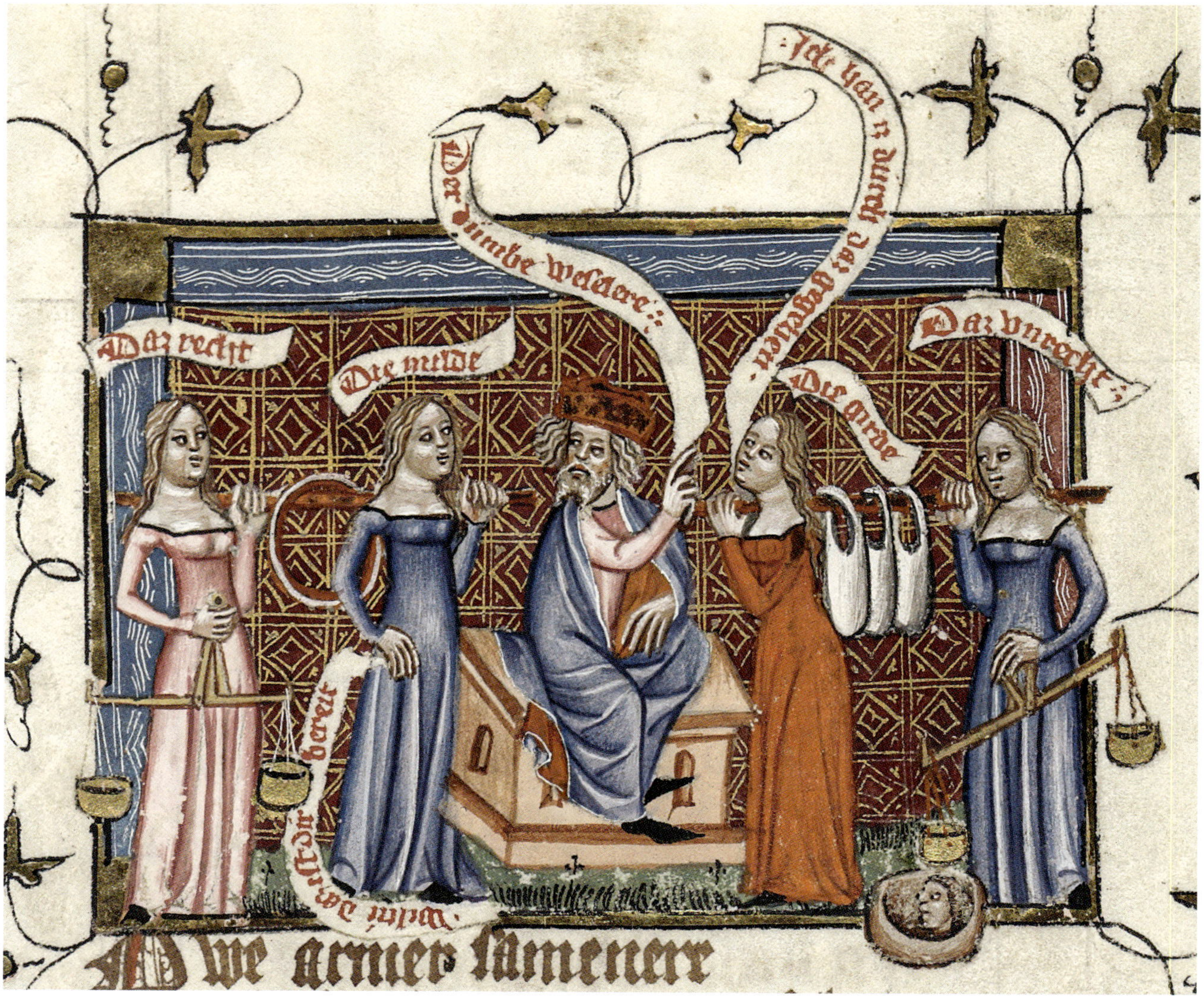

FIG. 6.15. ***Justice, Kindness, Money Changer, Desire, Injustice,*** **from Thomasin von Zirclaria,** ***Der Wälsche Gast*** **(The Italian Guest), Germany, Trier, ca. 1380. The Morgan Library & Museum, New York, MS G.54, fol. 49r (det.).**

horizontal, and the prong issuing from its fulcrum exactly vertical, indicating that the pans are flawlessly balanced and therefore the merchant is trustworthy.

Images of balances (Figs. 3.7, 5.13, 6.2, 6.5, 6.13–6.14, 6.35) served to counteract a difficult truth: that the value of coins was often unstable and difficult to determine with certitude. The word "trust," mentioned so often in the Avignon minters' oath, was a quality that merchants, moneylenders, and money changers wished to embody. The balance helped them to do that. But balances were not only attributes of immaterial qualities like trust, justice, and generosity—they were first and foremost material objects whose function was to check the weights of gold and silver coins. The beam was composed of arms of equal weight and length, and their pans, often suspended by three green silk cords, were also of equal weight even if dissimilar in shape. Portable balances were stored in small wooden boxes, together with a set of brass weights, each held in its own

FIG. 6.16. Berndt Odental (weights) and Jacob Heuscher (balance), boxed balance and weights, Germany, Cologne, 1699. American Numismatic Society, New York, 1930.179.1-24.

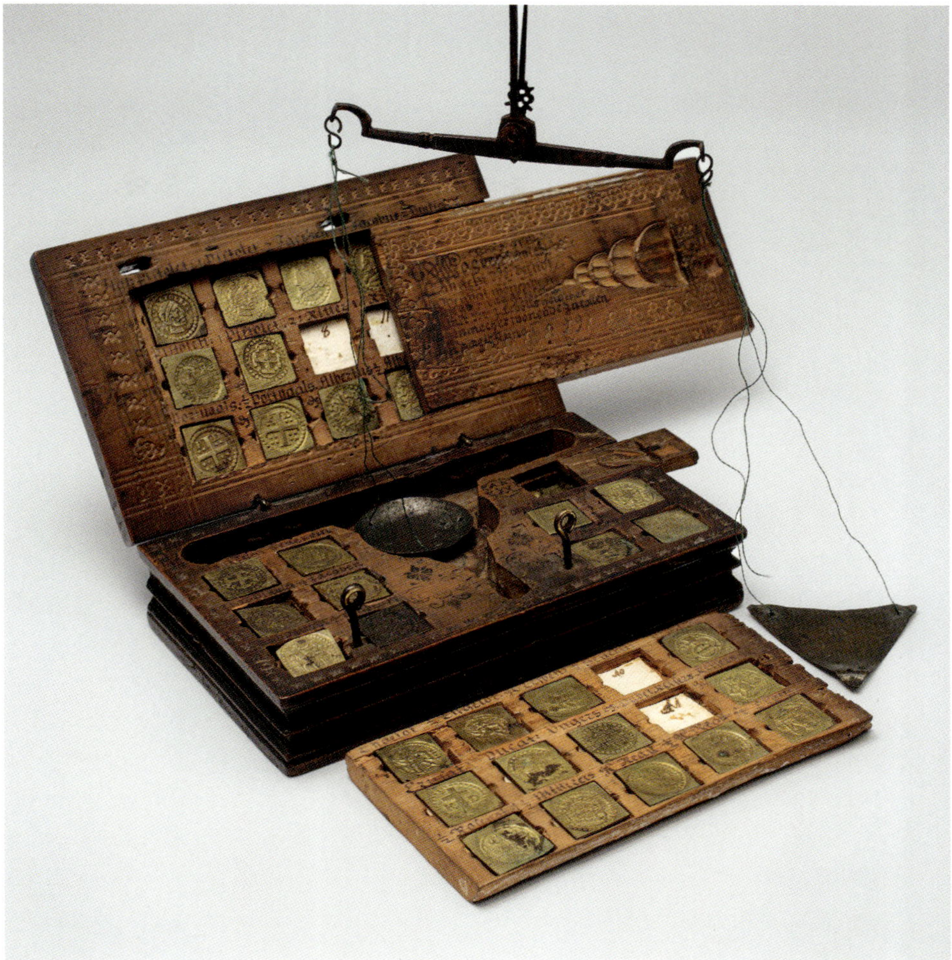

compartment. Some boxes had so many weights, each equivalent to a different international currency, that pull-out sections were needed to accommodate them (Fig. 6.16). These multiple weights attest to the range of international coins circulating in Europe.

Boxes containing weights and a balance for assessing coins have a long history. The earliest surviving European example was found in a seventh-century grave near Munich.[61] The oldest extant boxed balance with a date was produced in Nuremberg in 1497 for Hans II Harsdorf, who was appointed mintmaster there that year.[62] But undated fourteenth- and fifteenth-century northern European examples also survive. A wooden box produced in Cologne two centuries later includes the standard elements: a collapsible scale and set of weights (Fig. 6.16). This box is small, less than six inches long, yet it stores thirty-six large and nine small weights.[63] The large brass weights each nestle snugly in their own compartment. Notches on the side of each enclosure enabled the merchant to easily extract them. Each weight is cut in a rectangular shape to avoid confusion with the real coin whose image is reproduced on its face. These weights are stored in the hinged upper lid, in the body of the box, and in a removable drawer. They were used to assess coins from Great Britain, France, Germany, the Netherlands, Italy, Portugal, and

FIG. 6.17. Box for balance and weights, Germany, Cologne (pans from Middelburg), 1657. American Numismatic Society, New York, 0000.999.49450.

Spain, indicating the wide circulation of international coinage in Cologne. Like most German and Netherlandish coin balances, this one has a round bowl-like pan and a flat triangular pan, both hung with green cords. (French pans, by contrast, were often both bowl-shaped, as in Figs. 3.7 and 6.13.) Tiny weights in the Cologne box, used to balance the pans when a coin was underweight, are stored in a special compartment with a sliding door. If a coin weighed too little (as in Isenbrant's portrait), these small weights, called grain weights, would be added to the coin pan to determine how underweight the coin was. In the Cologne set, however, these grain weights are shaped both as flat rectangles and rounded bowls, suggesting that they may have been intended to be placed on either the flat or rounded pan. To close the box, prongs projecting from its body slide into slots in the upper lid, which is then firmly latched.

An inscription inside the lid dates the box to 1699 and attributes its contents to Berndt Odental, who made the weights, and Jacob Heuscher, whose name is etched on one of the pans.[64] The box also bears the stamp of the unidentified woodworker who made it. When closed, such boxes revealed their fine decoration, befitting their great expense and prestige. For example, a Cologne box, dated 1657, is outfitted with decorative latches that close the box, as well as several types of stamped decoration (Fig. 6.17).

Lockable boxes of all sorts held valuables, including money. A sixteenth-century steel coffer, most probably made by Michael Mann in Nuremberg, a major metal-working center, is reminiscent of the small chest that held the inheritance of the Prodigal Son represented in a contemporaneous glass roundel (Figs. 6.18, 6.35). The surfaces of the coffer are etched with personifications

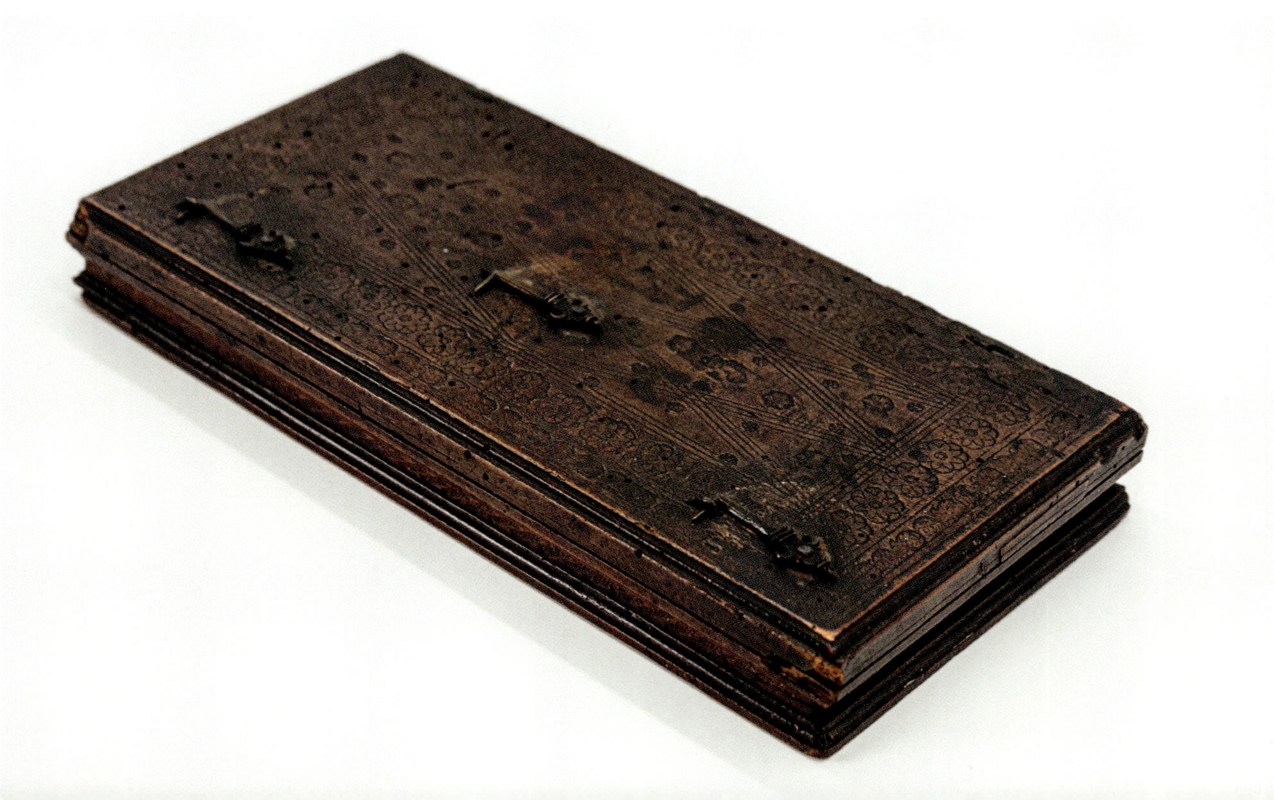

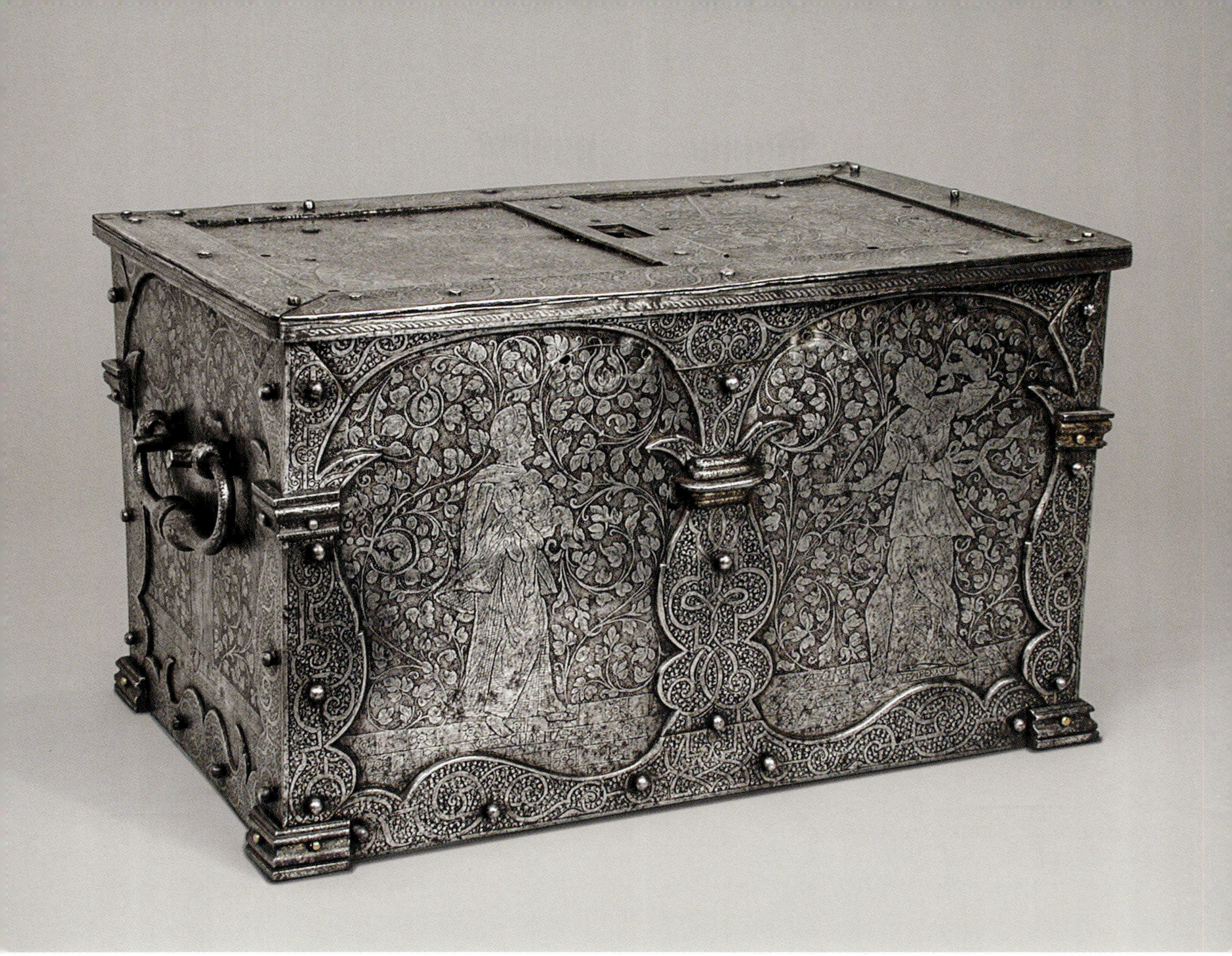

FIG. 6.18. Michael Mann, steel coffer, Germany, Nuremberg, late 16th century. The Metropolitan Museum of Art, New York, 23.29.

of the Virtues set against a swirling vegetal design. On the front, Temperance signifies moderation, especially regarding alcoholic drinks. Her act of diluting wine with water visualizes the virtue of restraint. Her companion is Charity, who holds a naked, squirming baby boy in her arms, as her billowing cape swings out around her. On the back are Hope and Patience, on the left side Faith, on the right Prudence, and on the hinged lid Justice and a second Patience. Mann distinguishes the Virtues and restless tendrils by raising their silvery forms above the darker, dotted background. He produced attractive strongboxes in a range of sizes, from small coffrets to large chests, like the one depicted in the Prodigal Son scene (Fig. 6.35).

This coffer, designed by Mann, has handles on both sides, and originally probably had four ball feet. Cut-steel bands reinforce the edges and center of the front and back, and the coffer's steel construction and state-of-the-art lock further enhance its security. Mann's strongboxes were known for their complicated

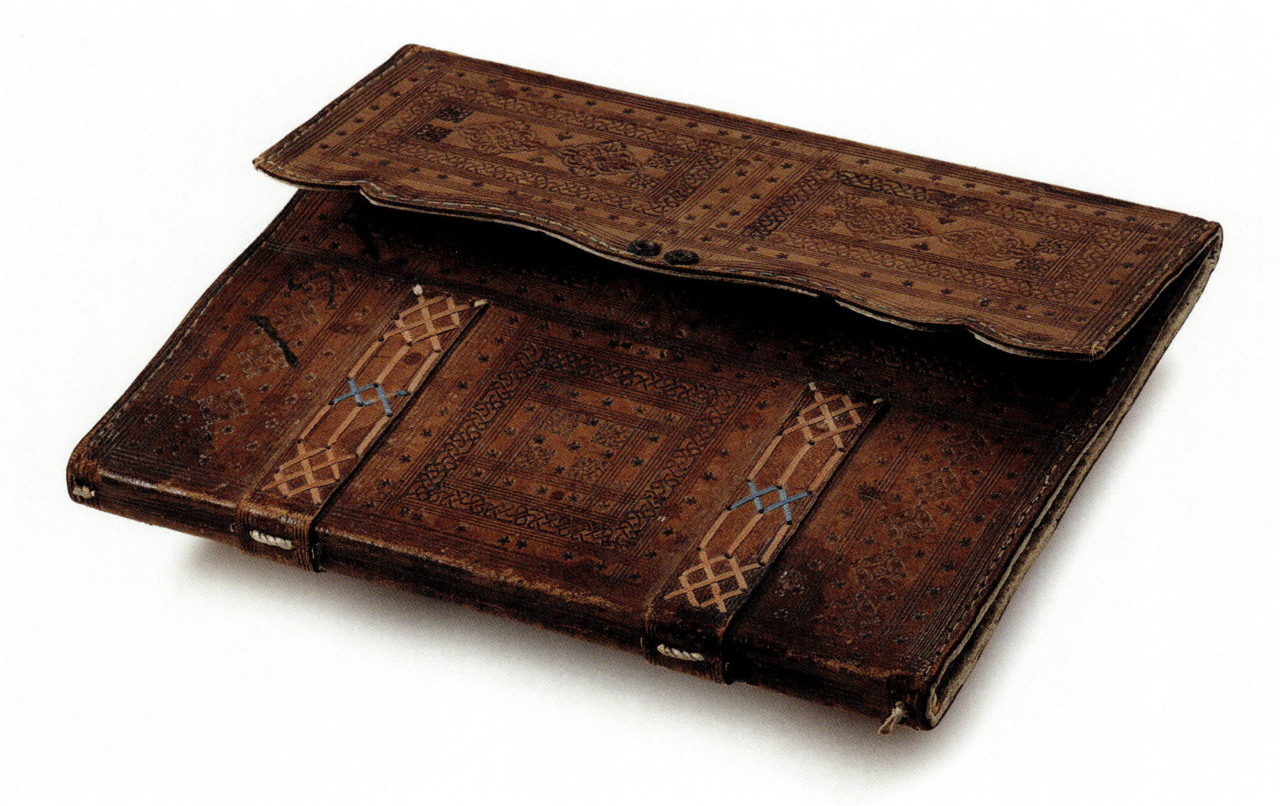

FIG. 6.19. Binding for Lanfredino Lanfredini's account ledger, goat skin, silk ribbons, blind tooled knotwork and arabesque tools, Italy, Florence, 1517–51. The Morgan Library & Museum, New York, PML 78802.

and sophisticated locks. As Edgar Frank observes, "There was a central keyhole in the lid, surrounded by wards [obstructions] and a system of levers and springs which actuated simultaneously four to twelve bolts which jutted out from three sides."[65] Such locks suggest the sophistication of medieval financial tools.

If the strongbox originally held money, would Charity have reminded the owner to give to the needy? Would Temperance have cautioned him to spend money moderately? Would Justice, next to the lock, have prompted moral spending? That such virtues were considered ideals appropriate for merchants is confirmed by the audience hall of the fifteenth-century Florentine Tribunale della Mercanzia, the high commercial court of the city, which Piero del Pollaiuolo painted with images of Faith, Hope, Charity, Prudence, and Justice.[66] We have seen the entanglement of religion and money in merchants' portraits, in the register of creditors from Bologna, in the Avignon minters' codex, and on coins that were stamped with crosses and saints.[67] A famous example of this link was recorded in 1253, when an Italian firm opened its account book with the phrase, "In the name of God and profit."[68]

Accounting ledgers developed in conjunction with the mercantile economy, and in Florence they were sometimes protected by luxurious bindings.[69] A particularly sumptuous and well-preserved example belonged to one of the wealthiest Florentine bankers, Lanfredino Lanfredini, a politically powerful ally of the Medici (Fig. 6.19). The goatskin binder encloses an account book for the years 1517–51 of Lanfredini's partnership with Giovanni di Agnolo Carducci, the manager of the firm, and three brothers from the Bartolini family, who were major merchant bankers at the time.[70] This is Lanfredini's private ledger (*libro segreto*), not the more

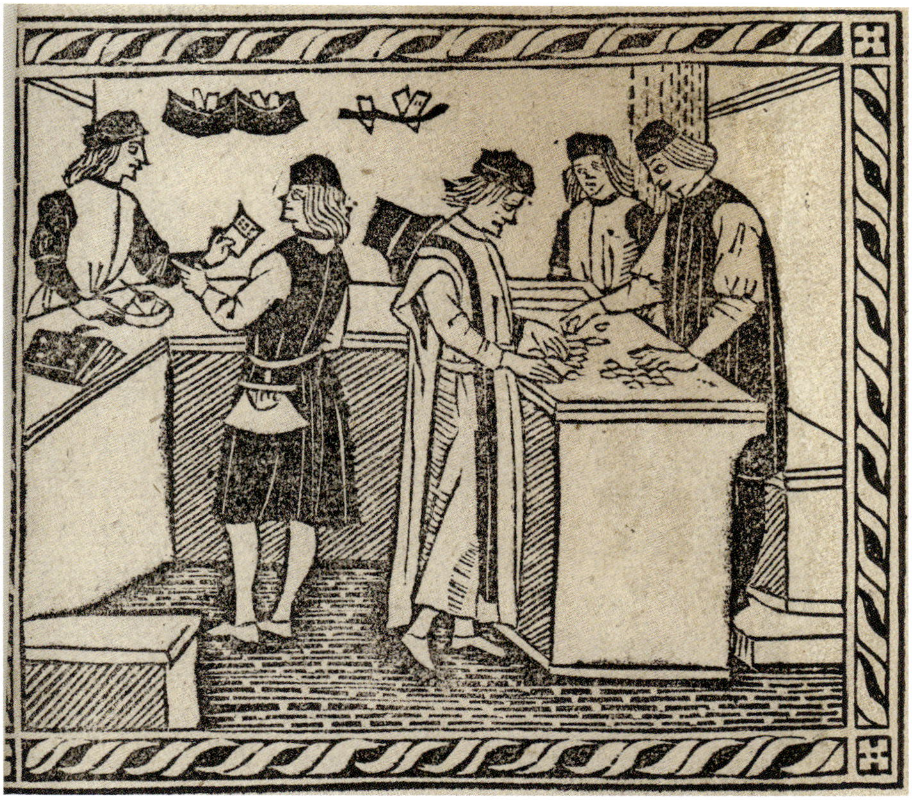

FIG. 6.20. ***Banking Scene,*** **frontispiece from** ***Libro che tratta di mercanzie et usanze dei paesi*** **(Book Concerning the Trade and Custom of Various Places Goods and Customs in Other Countries), Italy, Florence: Bartolommeo di Libri for Piero Pacini, ca. 1497. The Morgan Library & Museum, New York, PML 24748, leaf a1 recto (det.).**

extensive one belonging to the firm that recorded daily business activities. Lanfredini's book, recording debits on the left and profits on the right, reveals that the firm was engaged in a range of international transactions, from exchange operations routed through the Bartolini bank in Lyon to trade in wool, silk, pepper, and sugar.

Also international in origin is the form of the binding, which ultimately can be traced back to Islamic envelope-flap examples.[71] The overlapping, scalloped flap, which closes the binder, was secured with ties (now missing) that passed through the two eyelets at its center. Two strips of goatskin passing from front to back reinforce the binder. Such portable binders protected the enclosed pages from inclement weather and were designed so that, by opening string ties on the spine, blank pages could be added as needed, facilitating the ledger's day-to-day use. It now holds thirty-two leaves of paper, the last nine of which are blank. The binder was meant to be not only secure, but also beautiful, and so it is adorned with blue and pink silk ribbons and with blind-tooled panels of knot-work borders surrounding arabesques.

The *Libro che tratta di mercanzie et usanze dei paesi* (Book Concerning the Trade and Customs of Various Places), formerly attributed to Giorgio Chiarini and published in Florence around 1497, is a small manual for traveling merchants.[72] Its text declares that it includes all the customs dealing with coins, money exchange, weights and measures, and letters of exchange in different countries.[73] This bestselling guide for merchants supplied extensive information, from the types of merchandise sold in different commercial centers to shipping routes from Armenia and the Black Sea to Bruges and London.

The woodcut frontispiece shows a banking scene (Fig. 6.20). Commercial transactions take place around a U-shaped counter on which sit coins, a book, and an inkwell with quill pen. Two men are engaged with currency, while two others discuss a sheet with markings. Chits are affixed by a band or in pockets on

FIG. 6.21. Ring-framed purse, iron and red velvet, northern Europe, late 15th century. The Metropolitan Museum of Art, The Cloisters Collection, New York, 52.121.3.

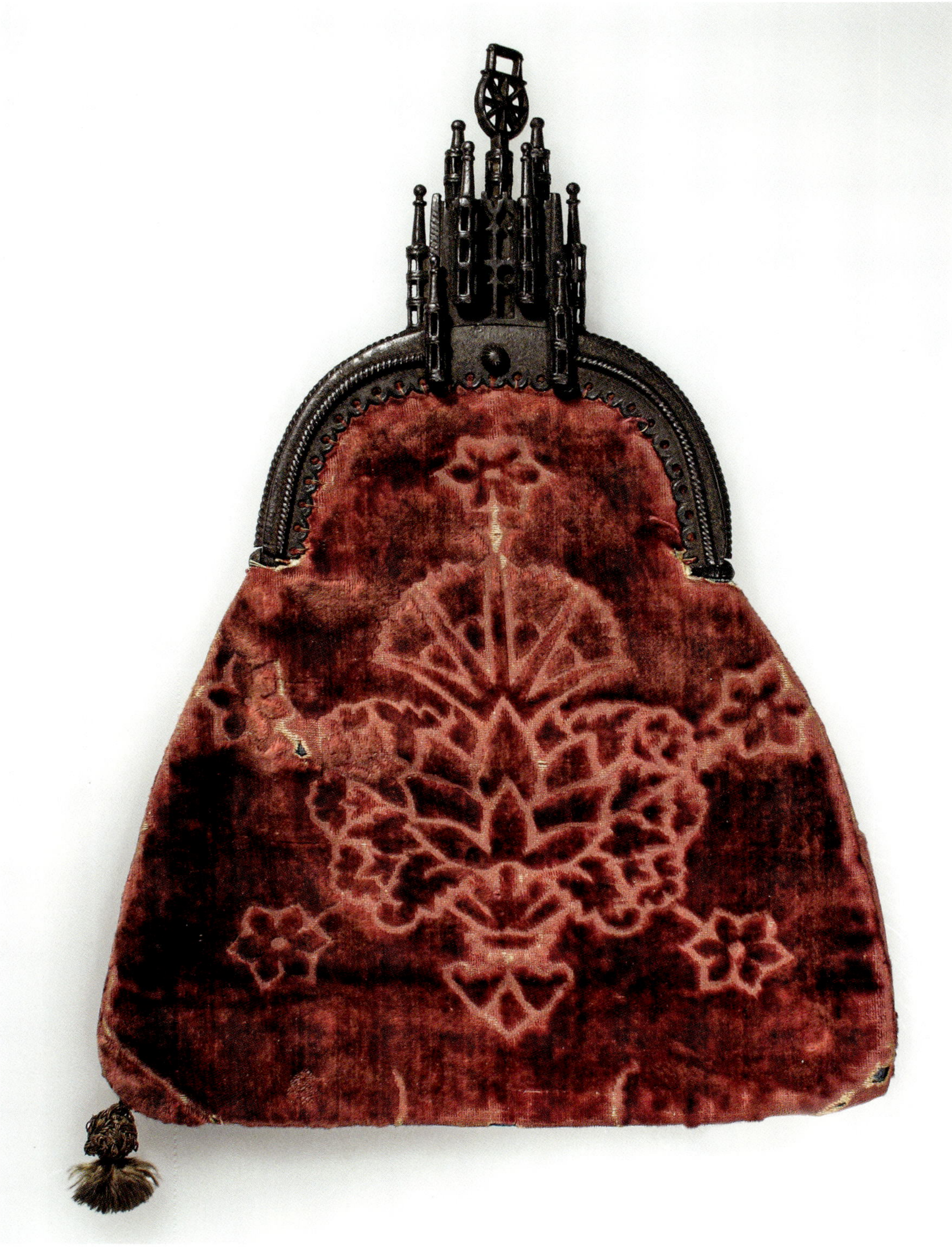

the back wall. As Richard Goldthwaite has observed—and the Lanfredini ledger confirms—"commerce and banking went hand in hand" in this era as they still do today.[74] Banks could grant loans, exchange currency, and transfer money abroad, while also investing in trade and even manufacturing.

Purses

One of the bank clients portrayed in the frontispiece prominently displays a framed purse suspended from his belt.[75] Many purses, like this one, consisted of a leather or cloth pouch attached to a metal frame surrounding the purse's mouth. Worn by men and women alike, such purses were both fashionable and functional, and could hold money as well as small personal items at a time before clothing had pockets. The bank client has a bar purse, that is, the pouch hangs from a horizontal bar.[76] But other purses had ring frames. A surviving fifteenth-century northern European example shows an elaborate castellated iron frame attached to a stylish velvet pouch (Fig. 6.21). The luxurious pouch is composed of cut and voided red velvet, a type in which some pile threads are woven back into the foundation of the cloth to create a pattern, in this case the stylized design known since the nineteenth century as the "pomegranate pattern." Found especially in contemporaneous Italian textiles, this pattern is composed, according to Melinda Watt, "of bold stylized floral and vegetal motifs that often resembled ripe pomegranate fruit, artichokes, or thistle blossoms."[77] One incredibly intricate tassel still adorns the purse's lower left corner.[78]

Like the purse worn by the bank client, this one would have originally had a metal extension (now lost) linking its iron frame to the owner's belt (Fig. 6.20; see Fig. 4.2).[79] This extension enhanced the security of the purse. As more and more coins circulated, purses became larger and more numerous, and had more safety features. Just as coffers were secured with increasingly sophisticated locks, so, beginning in the 1420s, purses began to be locked, and soon some locks had no visible keyhole, adding yet another layer of security.[80] The elegant iron frame of the velvet purse, which resembles a cluster of tiny turrets, is topped by a wheel that is the handle of a key. Once the key is released by pressing one of the turrets and a pin, it will fit a hole in the back of the iron frame to open the lock.[81] As a further safeguard, the side of the purse with the keyhole rested against the owner's body. The ingenious mechanism reflects contemporaneous technological advances in other spheres, such as coffer locks (see Fig. 6.18) and clocks.

Like the balance, the purse had both positive and negative associations in literature and the arts. When it holds money for indigent prisoners, it exemplifies charity (see Fig. 5.7), but Judas's purse signifies treachery and greed. His purse is singled out in a *Last Supper* produced at the Camaldolese monastery of Santa Maria degli Angeli in Florence (Fig. 6.22).[82] Once part of a manuscript commissioned for a monastery of the same order, San Michele di Murano (an island near Venice), the *Last Supper* is attributed to Silvestro dei Gherarducci, a monk at Santa Maria degli Angeli, who became its abbot in 1398 and died the next year.[83] Illuminated under Abbot Paolo Venier of San Michele, it dates sometime between 1392 and 1399.

The miniature belonged to a gradual (a choir book containing the text and music for Mass) and was part of the volume containing the feasts from Easter to the Twenty-fourth Sunday after Pentecost. The *Last Supper* appears in a letter *C* that begins the introit (the celebrant's entry into the sanctuary) for Corpus Christi, the feast celebrating the presence of Christ's body and blood in the Eucharist. The miniature accompanies the text, "Cibavit eos ex adipe frumenti, alleluia; et de petra, melle saturavit eos" (He fed them with the fat of wheat, alleluia; and filled them with honey out of the rock).[84] The image fittingly shows the Last Supper, when Christ instituted the Eucharist. Jesus is emphasized by being centrally placed, the tallest figure, and the only one isolated by empty space.

Towards the end of the meal, Christ announced that one of the apostles would betray him. When asked which one, he responded that it was the apostle to whom he would give a morsel of dipped bread. He then handed the sop to Judas, who accepted it and his role as traitor (John 13:25–27). Silvestro depicts this scene brilliantly. He harmoniously fills the large *C* by sitting the apostles around a circular table whose center is marked by a round bowl. He sensitively balances the colors, generously applying gold ground, which is richly and delicately tooled. Silvestro ingeniously foreshadows Judas's betrayal. The apostles gesture and turn to each other, wondering which of them will betray Christ, but Silvestro clearly indicates that it is Judas. He is easily identifiable, sitting opposite Christ in the foreground. He disrupts the harmony of the composition by sporting the only black halo, which is singularly adorned with scorpions, a common antisemitic motif.[85] Judas alone eats the sop that Jesus gave him, and he alone wears a purse, tucked into his belt, secured with a flimsy drawstring. Drawing attention to the purse are its central position and its blood-red color, the only red in the miniature. It is striking that the purse is not the fashionable ring type, but rather a rectangular drawstring pouch whose small size indicates that it was intended to hold only money.[86] In these ways Judas's greedy, traitorous nature is distinguished from that of the faithful apostles surrounding him.

A passage in Guillaume de Deguileville's *Le pèlerinage de l'âme* (The Pilgrimage of the Soul) similarly links greed and treason while confirming that the purse was not simply a fashion accessory, but rather held coins that could endanger one's soul. Deguileville's text is the second volume of his trilogy, datable to 1330–58, that began with *Le pèlerinage de la vie humaine* (The Pilgrimage of Human Life; see Fig. 4.4), and ended with *Le pèlerinage de Jésus Christ* (The Pilgrimage of Jesus Christ).[87] In *Le pèlerinage de l'âme*, after the narrator sees his death and burial in a dream, an angel guides his soul on a pilgrimage through purgatory, hell, and heaven. This text, which was often profusely illuminated, was extremely popular in England, France, and the Low Countries. Its English adaptation, called *The Pilgrimage of the Soul* or *Grace Dieu*, is dated 1413.

The fourth chapter of the third book of *Le pèlerinage de l'âme* paints a dramatic and gruesome vision of the punishment of two avaricious and treasonous officials. It relates how a disloyal chancellor and a treasurer built a huge wheel whose ostensible purpose was to fill the royal coffers. However, it had an underground component that enabled the officials to secretly siphon off funds for themselves. In hell, the traitors were

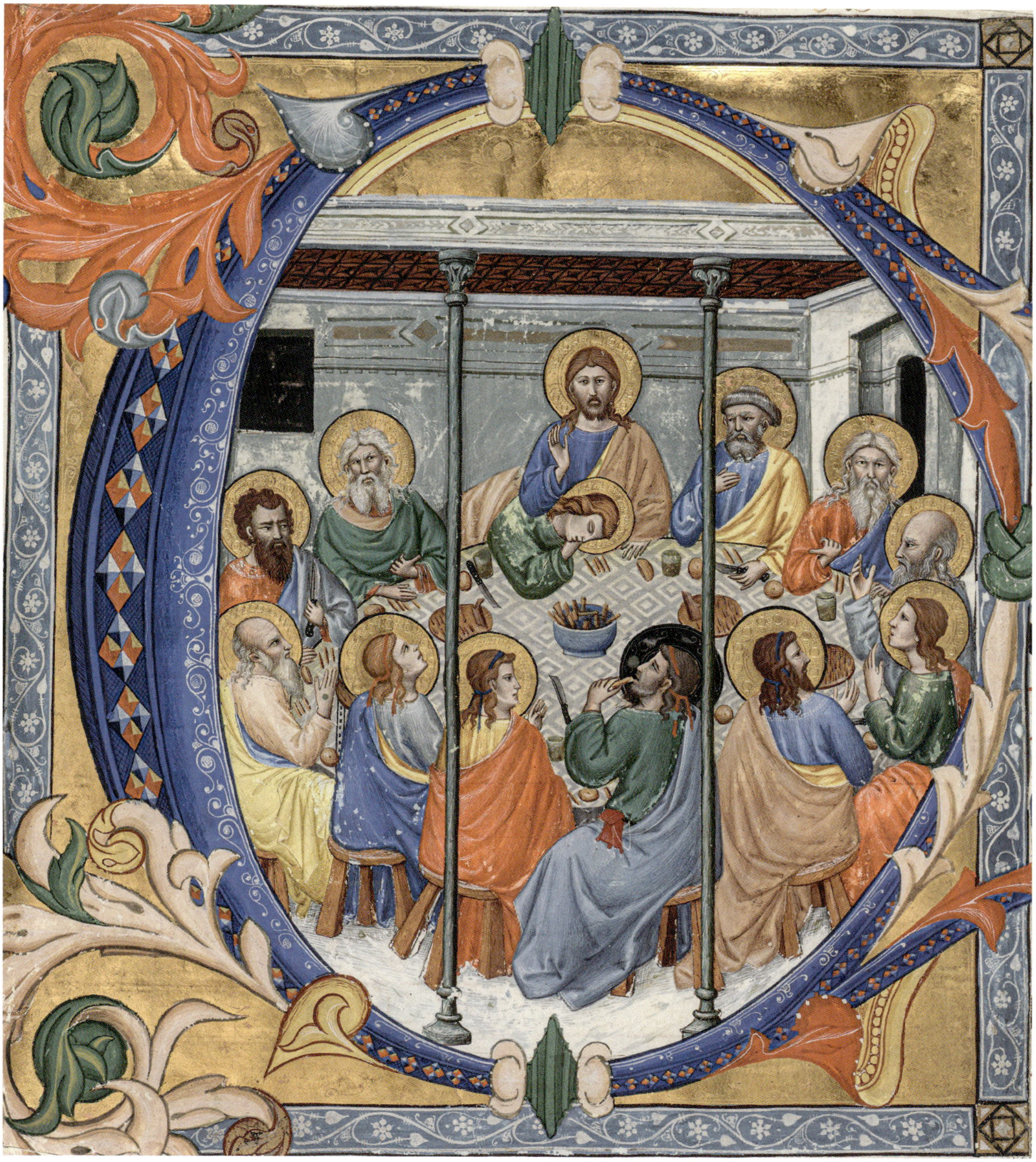

FIG. 6.22. **Silvestro dei Gherarducci, *Last Supper,* leaf from a gradual, Italy, Florence, 1392–99. The Morgan Library & Museum, New York, MS M.653.4 (det.).**

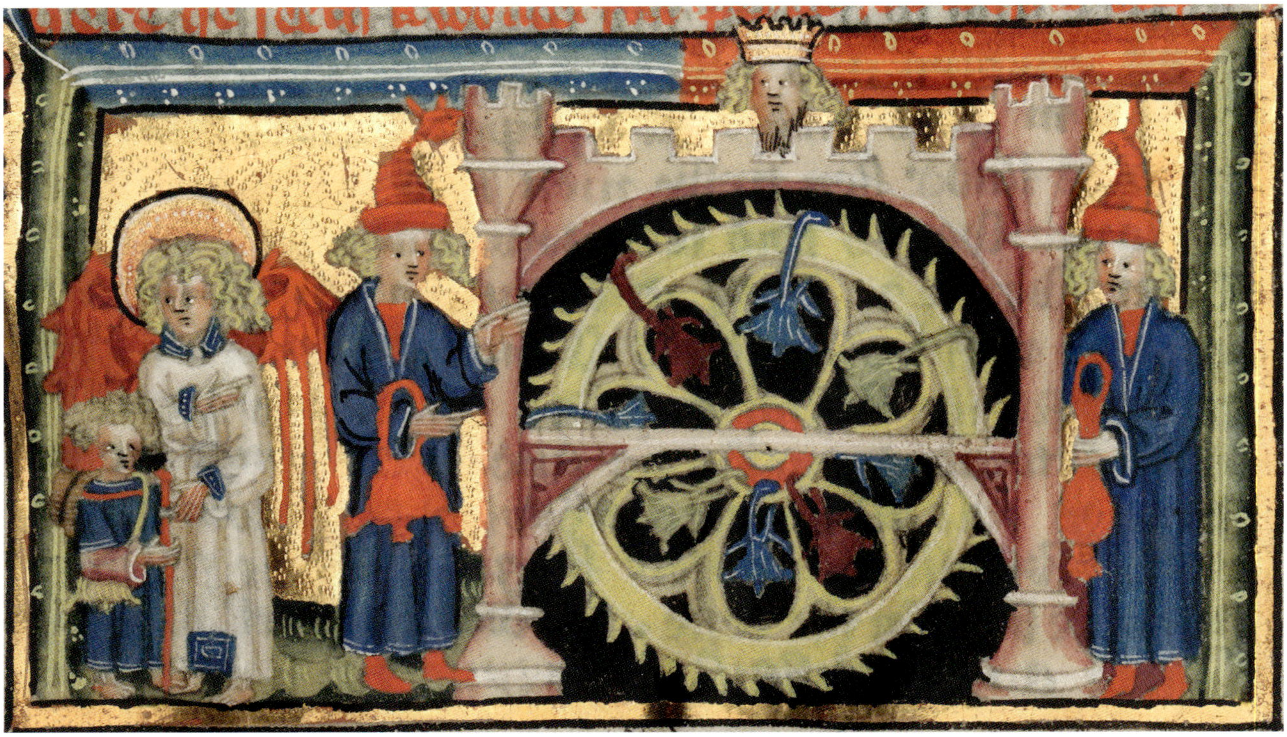

FIG. 6.23. ***Avaricious Courtiers and Spiked Wheel with Purses*, from Guillaume de Deguileville, *Le pèlerinage de l'âme* (The Pilgrimage of the Soul), in English, England, Lincolnshire (?), ca. 1430. The New York Public Library, Spencer 19, fol. 65r (det.).**

punished by an equally ingenious but different kind of wheel, whose circumference was spiked with iron hooks that ripped their flesh while they held "great bags of gold and silver."[88] Most of the chapter is devoted to the king's rancor towards his immoral, deceitful courtiers, whom he had trusted and loved. The king observes bitterly that the unscrupulous courtiers diverted for their own use money that he needed to run the government and defend the realm. They hid their theft and even betrayed government secrets in exchange for gifts. The king cries out, "You made this wheel and hung it full of bags. . . . Thus have you stolen my treasure, . . . and done me great harm with the plague of your wicked treason."[89]

One illustration for this chapter places an unusual emphasis on purses (Fig. 6.23).[90] It is found in a copy of *Le pèlerinage de l'âme* produced around 1430 that was owned and perhaps commissioned by Sir Thomas Cumberworth, high sheriff and member of Parliament for Lincolnshire (d. 1451). The miniature depicts a red-winged, haloed angel in ecclesiastical vestments pointing out the great wheel to the narrator's soul, which is personified as a small child carrying a walking stick and a pilgrim's bag over his shoulder. Standing to either side of the wheel are the chancellor and treasurer, each holding a purse, and the king is visible above the crenellated archway. All the figures—even the treasonous criminals—look sweet and gentle with their passive poses, childlike faces, flushed round cheeks, and innocent expressions. Moreover, although sharp spikes protrude from the wheel, the actual punishment is not portrayed. Instead, the focus is on the wheel hung with eight colorful purses with flaring sides, tassels at the base, and a loop for the arm or shoulder. Although the text is dramatic—for example, the king calls out, "Accursed be you of God and his saints"—the image is calm.[91] The only hint of the fate of the traitors is the background color behind the wheel, a deep black suggesting the abyss of hell. Although the text mentions once that the avaricious officials filled coffers and purses with the king's money, it more often cites moneybags as the container for their ill-gotten riches. Nevertheless, the illuminator chose to suggest deceitful greed by hanging the wheel with pretty purses.

Although numerous medieval images show men and women wearing purses, on at least one occasion a purse was intentionally excised. Infrared reflectography reveals that the *Virgin and Child with Chancellor Rolin*, datable to the mid-1430s, was originally planned to show the donor with a ring-framed purse. Jan van Eyck, however, painted over the object (Figs. 6.24–6.25). Scholars have debated whether this change occurred for aesthetic reasons or out of a desire to downplay Rolin's wealth.[92] It is noteworthy that his contemporaries condemned the way Rolin acquired his immense fortune. King Louis XI of France, when he learned of the chancellor's hospital foundation at Beaune, exclaimed, "It is only fitting that he who had made so many people poor during his lifetime, should leave a shelter for them after his death."[93] The chronicler Jacques Du Clercq (1420–1501) noted that Rolin "was reputed to be one of the wisest men in the kingdom, to speak temporally; with respect to the spiritual, I shall remain silent."[94] The Burgundian chronicler Georges Chastellain (1415–1475) described Rolin as a man who tried

> . . . to have everything passing through his own hands and at his own discretion, whether it concerned war, peace, or financial matters . . . there was no office and no sinecure, either in the city or the country, throughout his whole realm, not one gift or loan, that was not effected by him and executed by him and dependent on him as the one person who had charge of every matter. The confidence with which the whole world honored him brought him profits so inestimably great that none could name the figure, guess at it, or so much as believe it, so astounding was its size. . . . [He] strove to climb ever higher and multiply his wealth to the very end—dying sword in hand, in triumph over fortune.[95]

Rolin's contemporaries may have condemned him because of his avarice or because they were jealous of his wealth or power, especially since he was born a commoner. But their criticisms also fit a preconceived narrative, found, as we have seen, in the very popular *Pèlerinage de l'âme*, of a greedy and unscrupulous chancellor who improperly amasses huge sums of money and is, for that reason, tortured in hell. Duke Philip the Bold of Burgundy owned one copy of this text, and it was extraordinarily popular in England, France, and the Netherlands.[96] Rolin's purse in the underdrawing is not especially large (contrary to the view of some modern scholars), and a purse was a common attribute for a

FIG. 6.24. Jan van Eyck, *The Virgin and Child with Chancellor Rolin*, oil on panel, Belgium, Bruges, mid-1430s. Musée du Louvre, Paris, INV 1271.

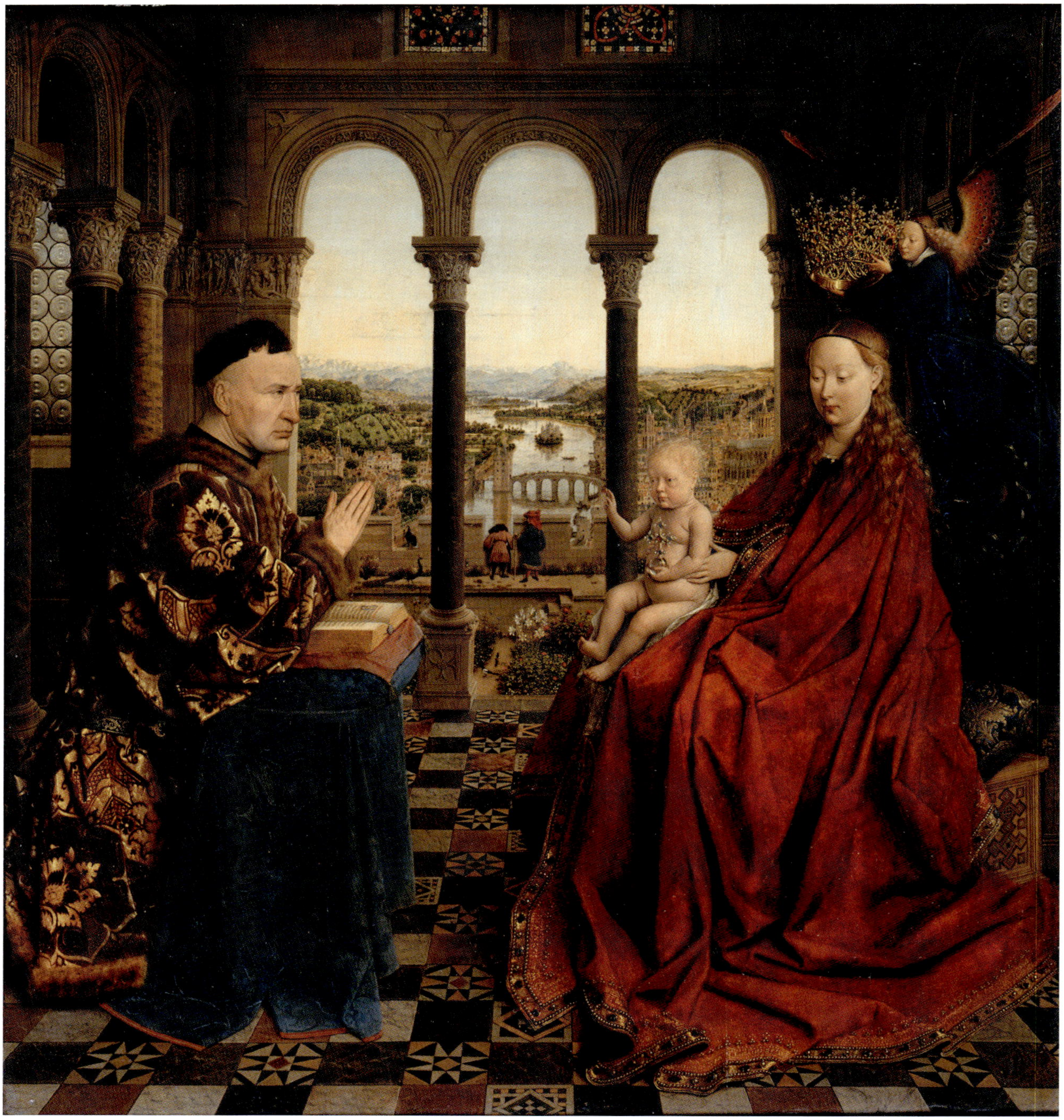

FIG. 6.25. Detail of Fig. 6.24: infrared reflectogram.

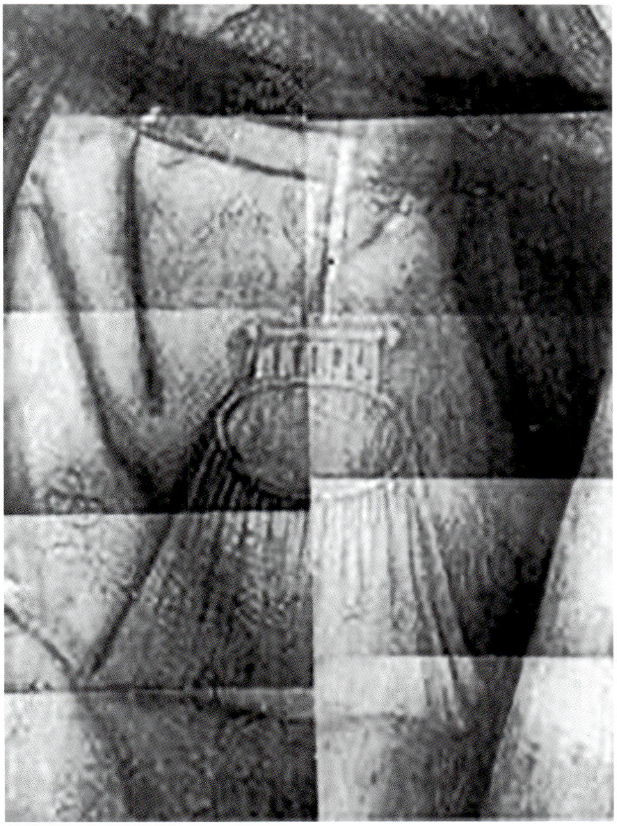

Detail of Fig. 6.24.

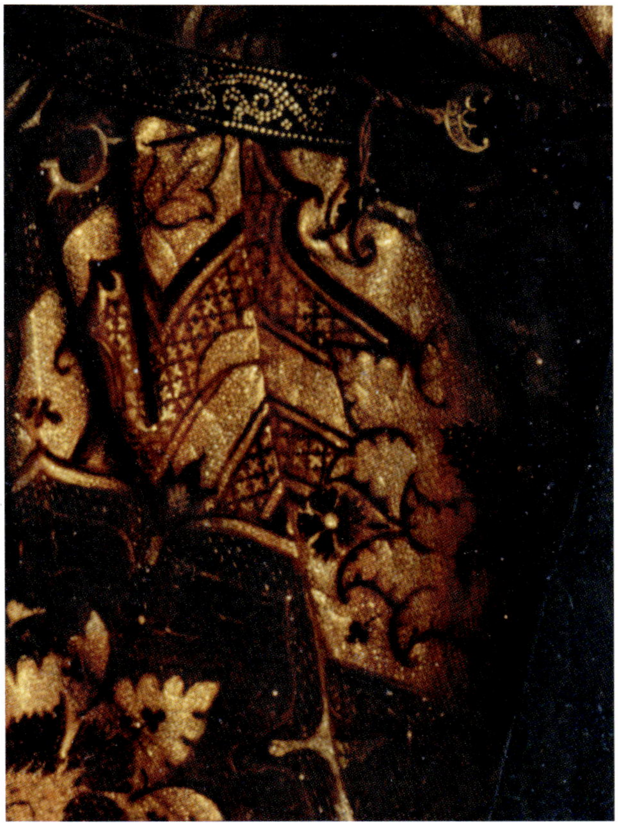

chancellor (it even appears as such on a playing card[97]). Yet the purse was probably eliminated to counteract its negative associations with wealth especially in the place where Rolin would be buried and where he would be remembered. After his death, the panel was hung as a memorial in the old Notre-Dame du Châtel church in Autun, France (since destroyed), where the chancellor had been baptized; it was placed in the St. Sebastian chapel where he funded a daily Mass. For these reasons, it was probably thought best to erase such a clear reminder of his earthly fortune. The painted-over purse in the Rolin *Virgin and Child* is yet another reminder that purses were not only fashionable and functional, but were also sometimes associated with avarice.

Coins

Most medieval images of money show precious gold and silver coins rather than less valuable denominations. Nicholas Oresme compares the two, noting that gold is better suited to "large transactions," silver for "buying goods of lower value."[98] The vast majority of medieval people came into contact only with "white"

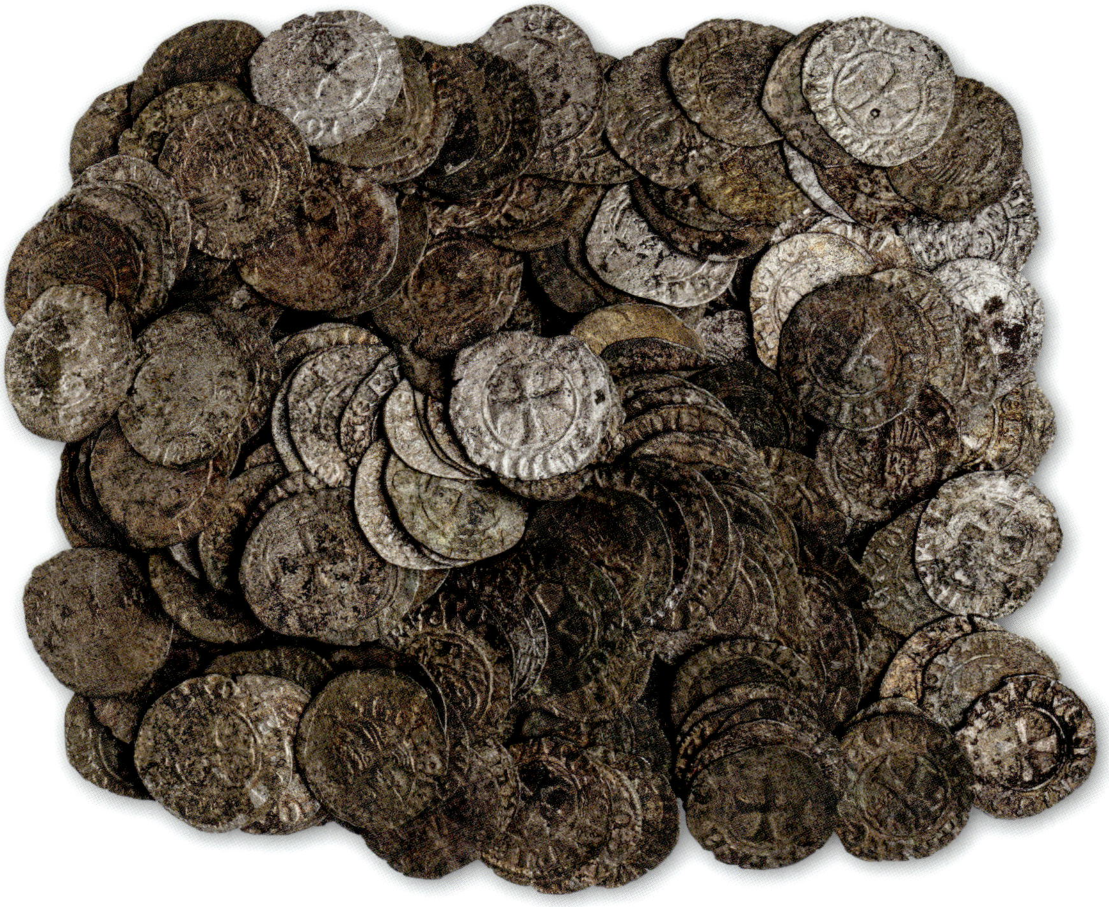

FIG. 6.26. **Chalkis Hoard: *torneselli* minted in Venice under Doge Antonio Vernier, 1382–1400, buried in 1470. American Numismatic Society, New York, 1985.58 (Doge Antonio Vernier box).**

money, which was composed of silver or a silver alloy, and "black" money, a less valuable currency composed mostly of base metal, and called black because copper darkens with use. The medieval currency system was triple-tiered in order to meet the needs of different classes of society, as outlined in David Yoon's essay in this volume.

Small "black" coins, used for daily transactions, are sometimes discovered in hoards, which were formed when medieval people hid their valuables, often during wartime, in the hope that they could later reclaim them. A large hoard of close to five thousand low-value Venetian coins, called the Chalkis Hoard, is believed to have come from the region of Negroponte, and to have been buried in response to the Turkish conquest of Chalkis in 1470 (Fig. 6.26).[99] The coins found in this hoard are the *tornesello*, a small, thin, inexpensive coin that was designed for use only in the Greek colonies; it shows the lion of St. Mark on one side, and a cross on the other. The hoard's *torneselli* that were minted during the reign of the doge Antonio Vernier (r. 1382–1400) are composed of eight parts copper to one part silver, and tend to be irregularly shaped and struck off-center, without much care. Minted at a rate of up to five and a half million coins a year, this was the type of currency used for everyday transactions.

Spectacular hoards of gold and silver coins have also been discovered, especially in recent years, when

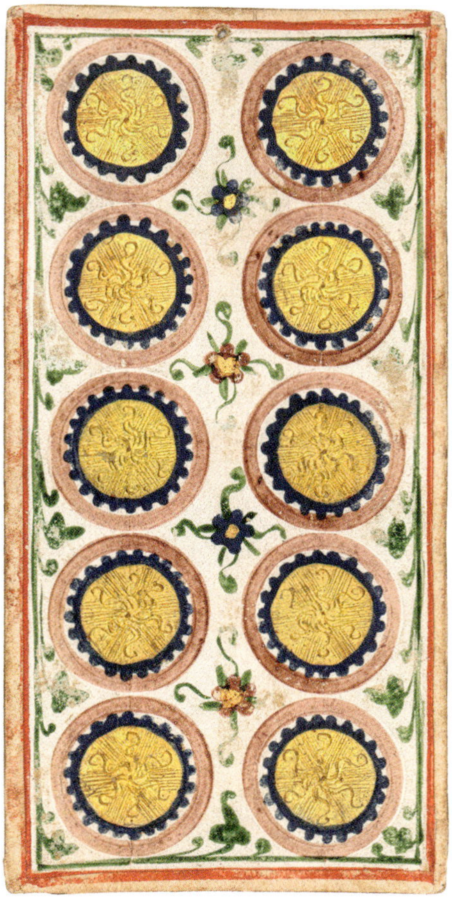

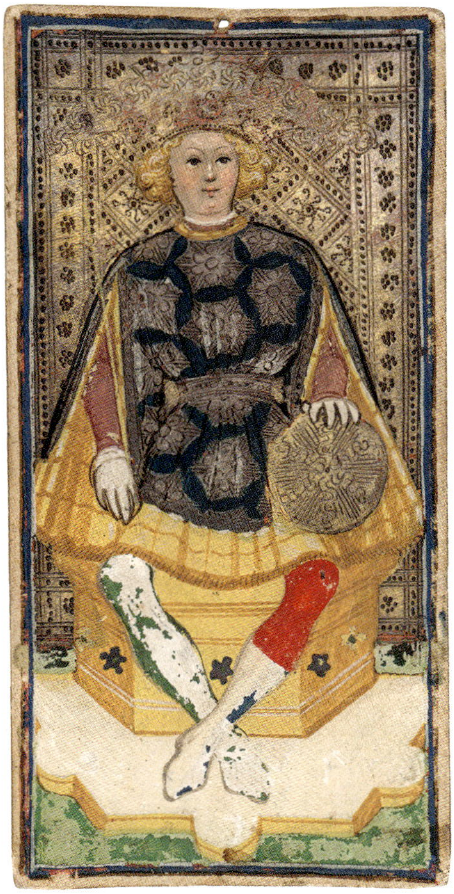

FIG. 6.27. Bonifacio Bembo, *Ten of Coins*, from the Visconti-Sforza tarot card deck, Italy, Milan, ca. 1450. The Morgan Library & Museum, New York, MS M.630.33.

FIG. 6.28. Bonifacio Bembo, *King of Coins*, from the Visconti-Sforza tarot card deck, Italy, Milan, ca. 1450. The Morgan Library & Museum, New York, MS M.630.20.

metal detectors have aided their recovery. In 2021, metal detectorists in Wales unearthed fourteenth-century gold coins, known as nobles, worth fifty days of wages for a skilled artisan.[100] In the same year, an archaeologist using a metal detector discovered 6,500 silver coins and silver ingots that had been wrapped securely in "three linen pouches, packed in a basket and then put in a ceramic vessel" before being buried in a Polish cornfield.[101] This hoard included Czech, Danish, Hungarian, and German coins, clear indications of foreign trade.

Coins were probably the most widely disseminated objects bearing images in the Middle Ages, and they permeated medieval visual culture. They even form one of the four suits of Italian playing cards. In an exceptional deck, probably made for Duchess Bianca Maria Visconti and Duke Francesco Sforza of Milan around 1450, coins are painted with their heraldic devices (Figs. 6.27–6.28).[102] In the Ten of Coins card, the gold pieces show the sun emanating wavy and straight rays, a Visconti emblem. The enthroned King of Coins holds a huge gold coin along with his scepter. It is certain that the ten-pip card always had the lowest value in the suit, but it is not known why coins were chosen for a suit of cards or how these cards were used to play a game.

Another striking representation of coins appears in the Hours of Catherine of Cleves, where St. Gregory (ca. 540–604) occupies the center of the folio, and gold and silver coins adorn the border, once again showing the intermingling of religion and money. The illuminator includes twenty-five images of eight coins from the Netherlands, Germany, and Denmark, dating from the first half of the fifteenth century (Fig. 6.29).[103] These coins include a Utrecht *postulaatgulden*, a Flemish

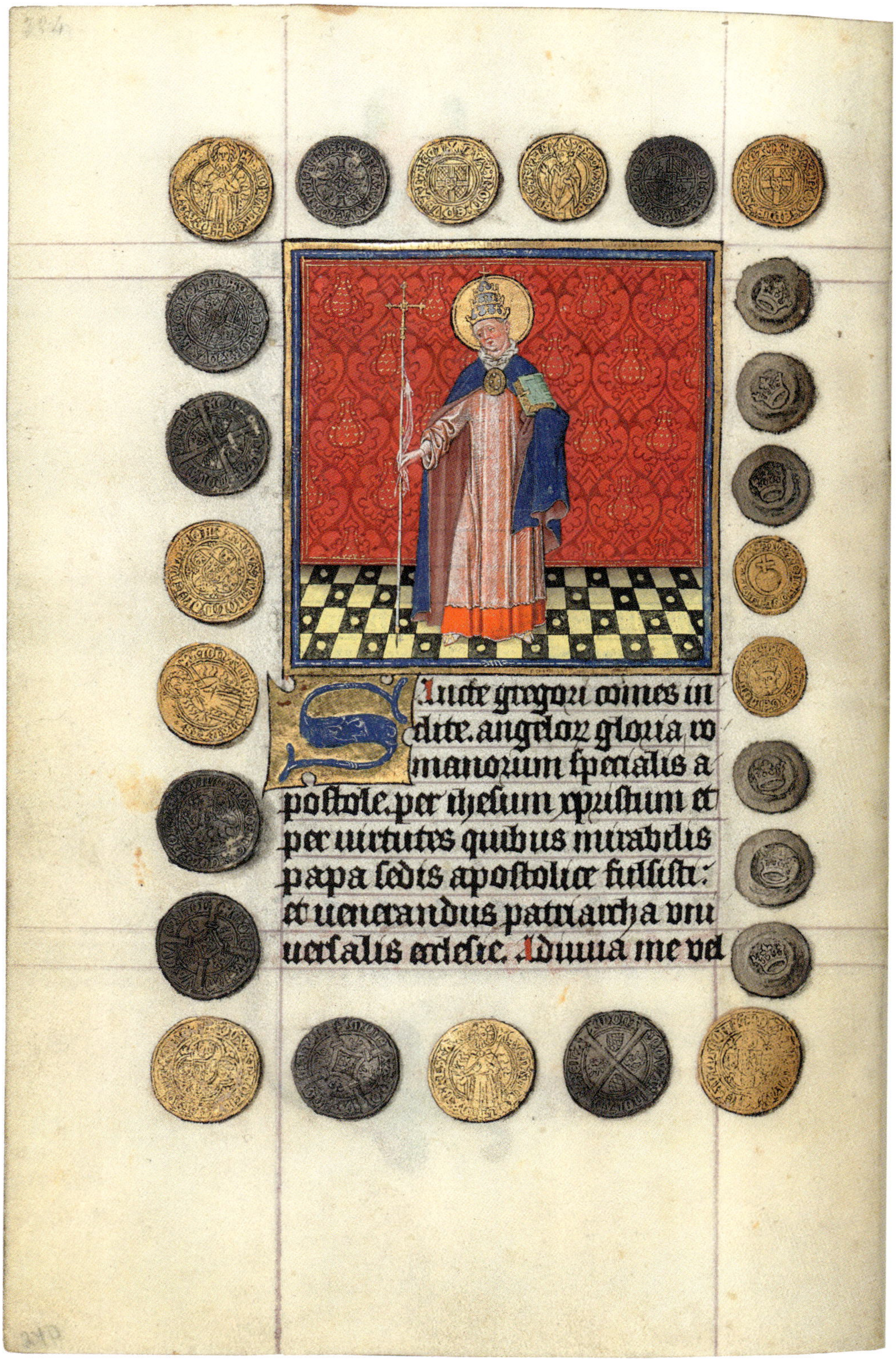

FIG. 6.29. Master of Catherine of Cleves, *St. Gregory the Great* and *Coins*, from the Hours of Catherine of Cleves, The Netherlands, Utrecht, ca. 1440. The Morgan Library & Museum, New York, MS M.917/945, p. 240.

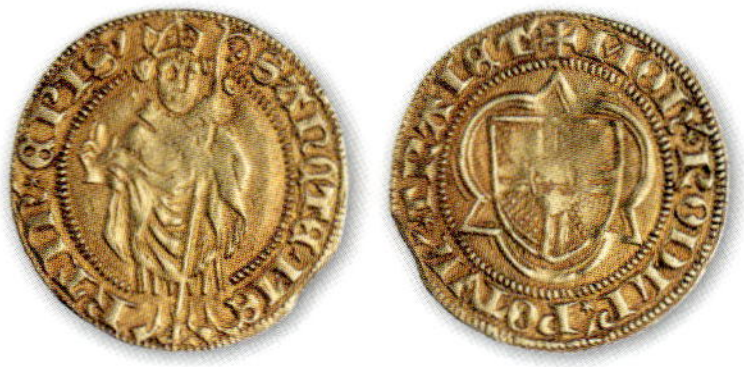

FIG. 6.30. **Gold florin, Utrecht, Rudolf of Diepholz, as postulate bishop, 1426–31. American Numismatic Society, New York, 1959.105.1.**

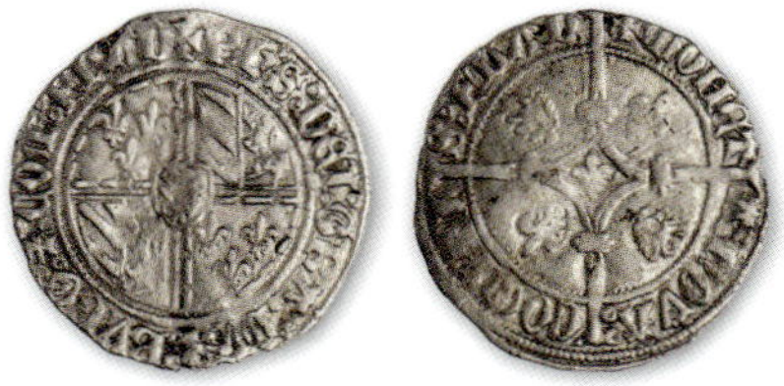

FIG. 6.31. **Billon *gros*, Flanders, Philip the Good, 1419–67, American Numismatic Society, New York, 1947.2.310.**

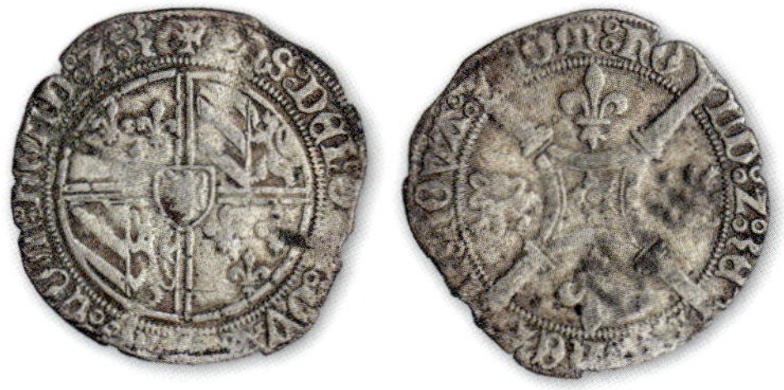

FIG. 6.32. **Billon double *gros*, Holland, Philip the Good, 1419–67. American Numismatic Society, New York, 1956.168.44.**

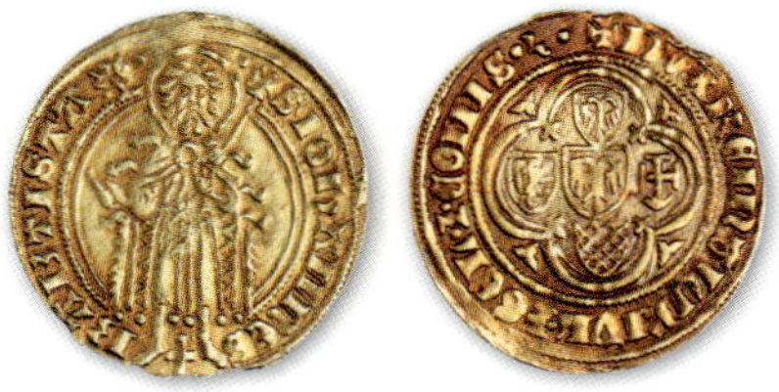

FIG. 6.33. **Gold florin, Gelderland, Reinald IV, 1402–23. American Numismatic Society, New York, 1951.67.172.**

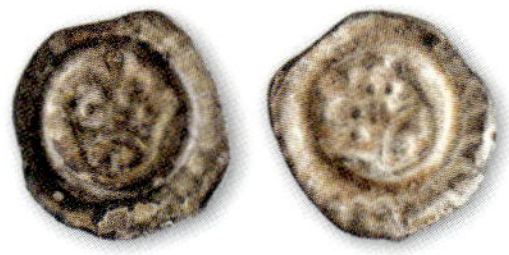

FIG. 6.34. **Silver *penning*, Denmark, Eric VII of Pomerania, 1396–1439. American Numismatic Society, New York, 1929.103.2054.**

quarter *groot*, a Holland half *groot*, a Gelderland *goldgulden*, and a Danish *penning* (for the same or similar coins, see Figs. 6.30–6.34). All these coins would have been widespread in the Netherlands, except for the Danish penny, which, ironically, is reproduced six times along the right margin. Both sides of some coins are shown. For example, the illuminator depicts the obverse of two gold Utrecht *gulden*, with St. John the Baptist carrying a crosier; an additional coin, featuring the reverse, appears in between them. These coins are remarkably convincing in their illusionism, showing irregularities of minting as well as traces of normal wear. In fact, it appears as if actual coins rest on the page since each casts a shadow. Yet at times the illuminator deviates from his models, transforming silver coins into gold ones and placing an inscription on the wrong side. Furthermore, each Danish penny is depicted larger than it is in reality, perhaps to create compositional harmony with the other, larger coins.

Several theories have been suggested to explain why St. Gregory is shown with coins.[104] An apocryphal story relates that his mother sent her newborn off to sea along with gold and silver coins to pay for his baptism and education. Jacobus de Voragine recounts that Gregory generously donated alms to a shipwrecked sailor, only to discover that he was actually an angel in disguise. Gregory also lived ascetically and gave generously to the needy. A possibility that has not been previously suggested is that the coins may refer to the saint's establishment, when he became pope, of a very effective administrative system of channeling donations to the Church to support the poor, especially refugees in Rome fleeing the violence of the Lombards, a Germanic people who had recently conquered much of Italy.[105] The coins might also have had personal associations for the patron. Most are local and contemporaneous, and so could have played a role in Catherine's daily life. In addition, her husband

FIG. 6.35. ***The Prodigal Receives His Share*****, from a series of eight scenes from the parable of the Prodigal Son, colorless glass, vitreous paint, and silver stain, Germany, 1532. The Metropolitan Museum of Art, The Cloisters Collection, New York, 41.190.442.**

minted one of the coins portrayed, bearing his name (DUX: ARNOLD': GELR). The duchess was estranged and alienated from her husband, and this is one of only three references to him—besides their combined arms—in the manuscript.[106]

The Color of Money in the Prodigal Son Roundels

A series of eight silver-stained glass roundels, produced in Germany in 1532, narrates the parable of the Prodigal Son (Luke 15:3–32).[107] They include the prodigal taking his share of the inheritance granted to him and his brother and gambling it away (Figs. 6.35, 4.13). This series is linked to the mercantile economy in several ways. The silver-stained glass roundel was a new type of object produced to meet the demand for windows from the growing class of wealthy merchants.[108] Earlier windows were generally large, intended for churches, and composed of pieces of colored glass. But, starting in the late thirteenth century, smaller decorated windows designed for domestic spaces began to be produced. These were composed of clear, colorless glass that was painted with a silver compound that, when fired, produced colors ranging from lemon yellow to deep amber. Such roundels were especially popular in the Netherlands and Germany in the first half of the sixteenth century.

Windows in merchants' rooms were smaller than those in churches, letting in less light. Transparent glass was needed to avoid a dark interior. Installed in small spaces, the roundels invited close looking, which encouraged artists to paint detailed scenes. The audience for these windows was generally private, unlike the broad audience for church windows. This encouraged glassmakers to paint more secular subjects and themes that explored personal ethical and spiritual matters.[109]

The Prodigal Son series is typical of this genre. The inheritance scene, for example, incorporates swirling patterns in its tiles and coins, an intricate tablecloth, and garments with varied textures. Large areas of the glass remain transparent, however, so that more light could enter the room. Finally, the theme is moralizing. Focusing on how the prodigal wasted his money on sinful pursuits, but was welcomed home nonetheless, it may have sparked thoughts about both forgiveness and the proper way to spend money and to conduct one's life.

This series is also filled with the material culture of merchants. The gambling scene includes four piles of coins and a moneybag (see Fig. 4.13). On the table of the inheritance scene are a balance, its traveling box, two tiny weights, a coffret (small chest), and piles of gold coins. The prodigal holds a moneybag, into which he shovels his coins, while on the floor rests a large strongbox.

The most striking aspect of these roundels is that because much of the glass is transparent, changing outdoor light and color would have constantly transformed not only the appearance of the roundels but also the room in which they were installed. This, in turn, could have affected the interpretation of the series.[110] Individual rays of sunlight, for example, would sometimes have highlighted the coins, making their glowing color the focus of the composition. This might make the coins more seductive to some viewers, while troubling the minds of others who might think instead about the right way to earn or spend money. In

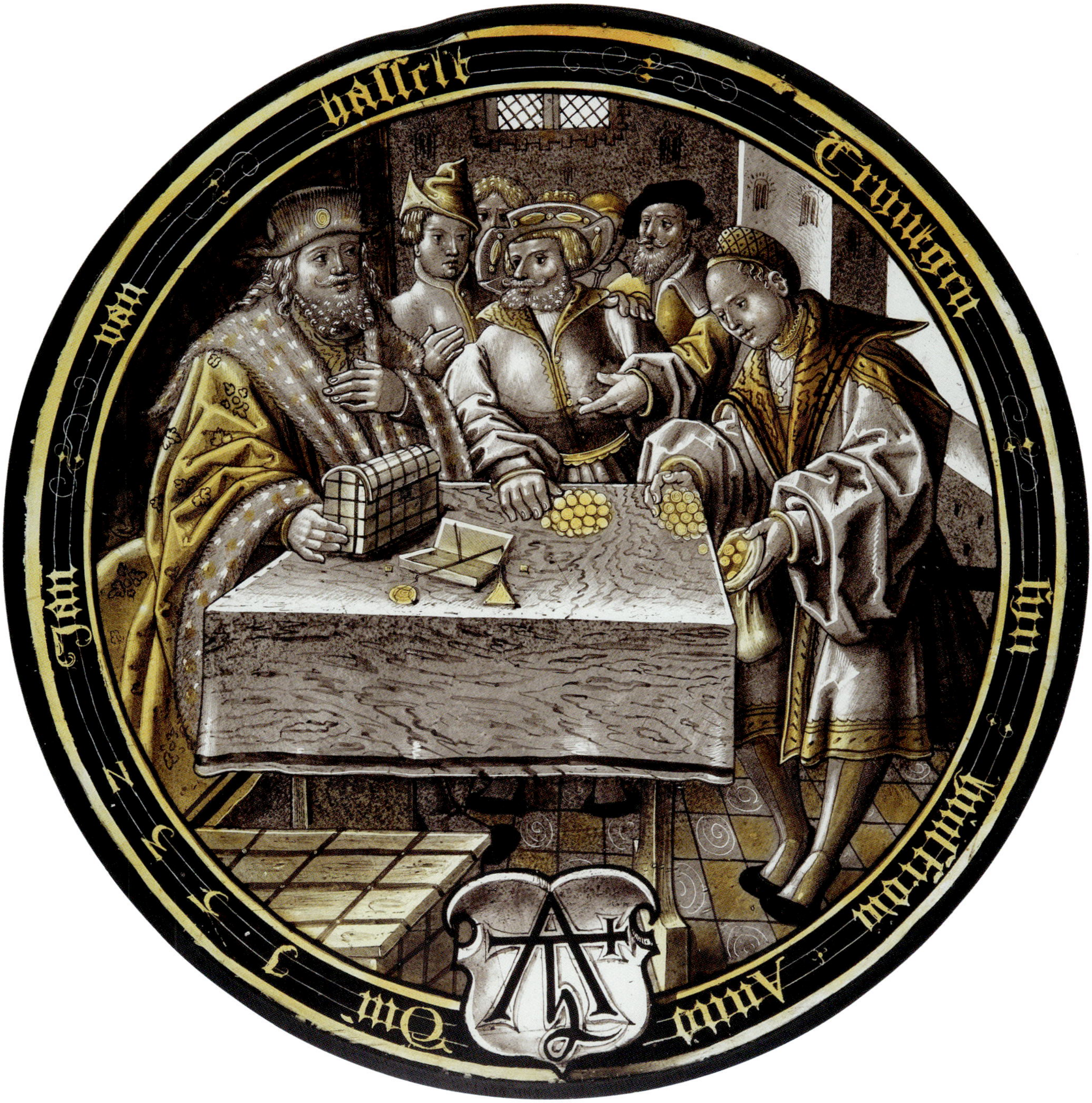

these roundels no color competes with the luminous, dazzling gold. In the inheritance scene, gold colors the coins on the table, the pans of the balance, the weights, the inscription circling the roundel, and aspects of the garments, hair, and floor. When the eight roundels were originally installed, sometimes golden light would have been cast on the walls, floor, and furniture of the merchant's room, suffusing it with a golden glow. The light would have sometimes been inchoate, but at other times it would have projected the shapes of the coins, balances, and weights pictured in the stained glass. Bissera Pentcheva has concluded that the walls of churches infused with "colored light" from stained-glass windows "became sites for emanating grace."[111] How, then, shall we describe the golden walls of wealthy merchants' homes? Was this, too, a moving experience, bringing them closer to their gold coins? Or did the color of money cause them to wonder about the state of their soul?

Material culture, so often overlooked, offers new insights into how medieval Europe viewed money and merchants. The vast numbers of lavish objects that developed around the new monetary economy did not simply serve to make homes more luxurious or celebrate merchants' success. Additionally, these works—merchants' portraits, illuminated financial records, coins, strongboxes, and images of purses and balances—reveal a widespread unease about the value of money and a concern that merchants would be associated with greed. To counter these ideas, merchants' portraits displayed only a few coins, their balances were depicted with horizontal beams, and numerous objects merged monetary and religious motifs. If the objects explored in this chapter often suggest a picture of the good life based on financial well-being, those in the next examine images of economic insecurity.

NOTES

1. See Vitullo and Wolfthal 2010a, 1–4; Vitullo and Wolfthal 2010b. I would like to thank David Yoon for his astute comments on this chapter.
2. Aquinas, *Summa Theologiae* II, ii, q. 77, a. 4; Vitullo and Wolfthal 2010b, 156, 189–90 n. 6.
3. Bales 1983, 106; Oresme 1956, 10–12.
4. Bales 1983, 107.
5. Bernardino da Siena 1934, 98; Vitullo and Wolfthal 2010b, 156, 190 n. 8.
6. See pp. 65, 110, 135, and 148 in this volume.
7. For Gossart's painting, see Ainsworth 2010.
8. Only 18 percent of sixteenth-century Europeans were literate. See Eskelson 2021, 112.
9. The coin is probably a one-ducat piece, since it lacks the minter's mark and denomination of ducats on the front. These were minted from 1497 to 1535 or 1537, which supports the date traditionally given the painting. See Crusafont, Balaguer, and Grierson 2013, 411. Imitations were minted in the Netherlands, but only decades after the painting was produced. See van Gelder and Hoc 1960, 141, no. 262–17A, pl. 22.
10. Holbein's portrait is in the Gemäldegalerie, Staatliche Museen, Berlin, Ident. nr. 586; Heemskerck's is in the Rijksmuseum, Amsterdam, SK-A-3518.
11. Hand and Wolff 1986, 104.
12. Murray 1988, 118 (quote), 300–326.
13. Reyerson 2018; Murray 2005, 309.
14. Ainsworth and Christiansen 1998, 194.
15. Oresme 1956, 97; Oresme 1864, iii.
16. Murray 2005.
17. See Huygebaert et al. 2016, 160; Kisch 1965.
18. In the infrared reflectography one pan is circular; see Koerkamp 2019.
19. Bauman 1986, 46; Sintobin 1998, 194. See further Vermeer's *Woman Holding a Balance*, ca. 1664, National Gallery of Art, Washington, DC, Widener Collection, 1942.9.97, which shows a *Last Judgment* in the background.
20. Huygebaert et al. 2016, 141, 143.
21. See van Gelder and Hoc 1960, pl. 7, no. 77–4; pl. 22, nos. 255–16A and 256–6A.
22. See Toffanin 2013 for similar busts (190, no. 215/2; 193, no. M4; 193, no. 217), and truncated legends (193, no. 217; 195, no. 219; 202, no. 229/2). It resembles especially the Bolognese *doppio ducato* of Giovanni II Bentivoglio; see Malaguzzi Valeri 1901, 271.
23. Horner and Horner 1873, 164–65.
24. See Quentin Massys's *Money Changer and his Wife* (1514; Musée du Louvre, Paris, INV 1444), Maarten van Heemskerck's *Portrait of a Man, possibly Pieter Gerritsz Bicker* (1529;

Rijksmuseum, Amsterdam, SK-A-3518), and the many paintings by Marinus van Reymerswaele.
25. For the varied meaning of green, see Pastoureau 2014, 65, 71, 118, 121–23. For green as the color of fertility, see also Mellinkoff 1993, vol. 1, 38. In medieval Italy, green cloth was often expensive, and therefore associated both with fashion and Judas. See Robson 2001, 74–75, 94, 137.
26. For this manuscript, see Bloem 2012; Bloem 2015, 245–67, 414–33.
27. The *Entombment* appears in Morgan, MS M.87, fol. 200v. The *Resurrection* is now in the Universiteitsbibliotheek, Utrecht, MS 12.C.17. See Dückers 2005, 79–80, cat. 126, illus.
28. The speech scrolls read "Christus resurgens" (Christ rising) and "Tercia die resurgens" (On the third day rising).
29. Bloem 2012.
30. Images of apothecaries include Bibliothèque municipale, Besançon, MS 463, fol. 1r; Bibliothèque nationale de France, Paris, MS lat. 9333, fol. 51v; The British Library, London, Sloane MS 1977, fol. 49v.
31. Chambers 1903, 306–10; Loewen 2004.
32. Freedman 2008.
33. Freedman 2008, 89, 91–92, 94–95, 225.
34. Freedman 2008, 3, 106, 108–10.
35. https://www.arlima.net/mp/marco_polo.html, accessed December 19, 2021.
36. See Polo 1875, 70.
37. Ibid., 350.
38. For similar pearls, see a *Livre des merveilles*, dated 1410–12, Bibliothèque nationale de France, Paris, MS fr. 2810, fol. 83r.
39. O'Doherty 2013, 127.
40. Löer 2017, 40.
41. Iskin 1995, 25; Welch 2005.
42. I thank Anne Marie Rasmussen for this translation. For this edition, see above, p. 86.
43. See Ceccanti and Castelli 1992, 380–82; D'Amico and Grandi 1987, 193–95; Medica 1999, 100.
44. For this folio, see Voelkle 1984, no. 7.
45. For this artist, see Norris 2021, 11; Turner 2021, 34, 36–38; Keene 2021, 81–83.
46. Two other surviving registers represent two other quarters (the Porta Stiera and the Porta Ravennate).
47. The only publication that mentions this work, Manzari 2006, 348–49, simply lists it among miniatures made in Avignon. The dating is based on style and a date found on fol. 21v of the manuscript.
48. Church Music Association of America 2012, 178–79.
49. See, for example, Bynum 1991, 97.
50. For Jean de Vignay's translation, see Thonon 2002, 207–17.
51. Ryskamp 1989, 88–89; Karlowska-Kamzowa 1997, 246–47.
52. Alexander 1997, 59; Leo 2013, 165, no 2.
53. The first definition of *table* in Old French is a plank or board; see Godefroy 1892, 615–16.
54. Bibliothèque nationale de France, Paris, Arsenal MS 5107, fol. 52v.
55. Godefroy 1892, 615–16.
56. My translation.
57. See Huygebaert et al. 2016, 160.
58. The quote appears in Universiteitsbibliotheek, Amsterdam, MS XXIII A 8, fol. 4r; see Meekes-van Toer 2013, 136 (thesis includes a translation of the entire text).
59. Huygebaert et al. 2016, 140–42.
60. For this manuscript, see above, pp. 87, 90; for this illumination, see Bismark and Hüpper 2018, 63.
61. de Graaf 1994, 75.
62. Sebregondi and Parks 2011, 165; de Graaf 1994, 75–76.
63. Cloisters 1975, 119, 130, no. 140.
64. For these craftsmen, see Kisch 1960, 88–89, 101–2, pl. II, and fig. 32a.
65. Frank 1950, 152.
66. Wright 2005, 228–49.
67. Naismith 2018b, 193.
68. de Roover 1974, 345.
69. For ledger bindings, see Szirmai 1999, 309–11.
70. Unpublished report by Richard A. Goldthwaite, dated December 5, 2004, The Morgan Library & Museum, New York.
71. Patton 2007.
72. See Fig. 2.9 for a manuscript version of this text at Temple University, Philadelphia. For a discussion of the copies of this text, see Spufford 2002a.
73. For a modern edition, see Borlandi 1936.
74. Goldthwaite 2009, 205. For images of similar counters, see the painted panels that served as covers of accounting registers in medieval Siena at http://www.archiviodistato.siena.it/museo-delle-biccherne/, accessed October 30, 2022.
75. For this type of purse, see Goubitz 2007, 47–54.
76. Ibid., 54–55.
77. Watt 2011. A very similar "pomegranate" design appears on the bodice of a portrait of a young woman painted by Antonio del Pollaiuolo, around 1460–65, and today in the Gemäldegalerie in Berlin, Ident. nr. 1614.
78. Early photos of the purse in the Metropolitan Museum show two tassels.
79. For this purse, see Hoffeld 1969, 171; Blanc 2004, 221–22; Goubitz 2007, 59.
80. Johnston 2011, 455; Blanc 2004, 221.
81. Rorimer 1953, 280; Goubitz 2007, 49.
82. Levi D'Ancona 1993, 14, 16, 31; Freuler 1994; Wieck 2014, 12.
83. For a dissenting voice on this attribution, see Bent 1992.
84 Lacoste et al. 2012.
85. Bulard 1935; Mellinkoff 1993, vol. 1, 46, 49, 106, 122; Capriotti 2014; Strickland 2019, 52.
86. Goubitz 2007, 61.
87. For the *Pèlerinage* and its illuminations, see Tuve 1966, 145–218; Emmerson 2009. For an English translation, see de Deguileville 1992.
88. Clubb 1953, 167 (my modernization of English).
89. Ibid., 167, 169 (my modernization of English).
90. For this manuscript, see McGerr 1990 and Sandler 2005. For its text, see Clubb 1953.
91. Clubb 1953, 167 (my modernization of English).
92. Lorentz 1994, 27; Harbison 1991, 10; van Asperen de Boer and Faries 1990, 47; Dhanens 1980, 276, 279.
93. d'Arbaumont 1865, 6 (my translation).
94. Rothstein 2000, 107; Du Clercq 1838, 194.
95. Chastellain 1836–66, 330–31; Albus 2000, 14–15.
96. Bibliothèque royale de Belgique, Brussels, MSS 10197–98. For its popularity, see Eichberger 1992, 130.
97. Husband 2015, 62, fig. 70.
98. Oresme 1956, 7.
99. Stahl 1985.
100. Geggel 2021b.
101. Geggel 2021a.
102. For playing and tarot cards, including this deck, see Husband 2015; Kaplan 1978; Dummett 1986.
103. For this folio, see Plummer 1966, no. 127; Gorissen 1973, 609–10, 693–99; Dückers and Priem 2009, nos. 3a and 115; Ijpelaar 2010, 26.
104. Gorissen 1973, 609; Voelkle 2006.
105. Dudden 1905, especially 316.
106. Marrow 2009, 23–24; Hand 2014, 143.
107. For these roundels, see Husband and Caviness 1991.
108. For these windows, see Husband 1991.
109. Husband and Caviness 1991, 16.
110. See Wolfthal 2022.
111. Pentcheva 2010, 147.

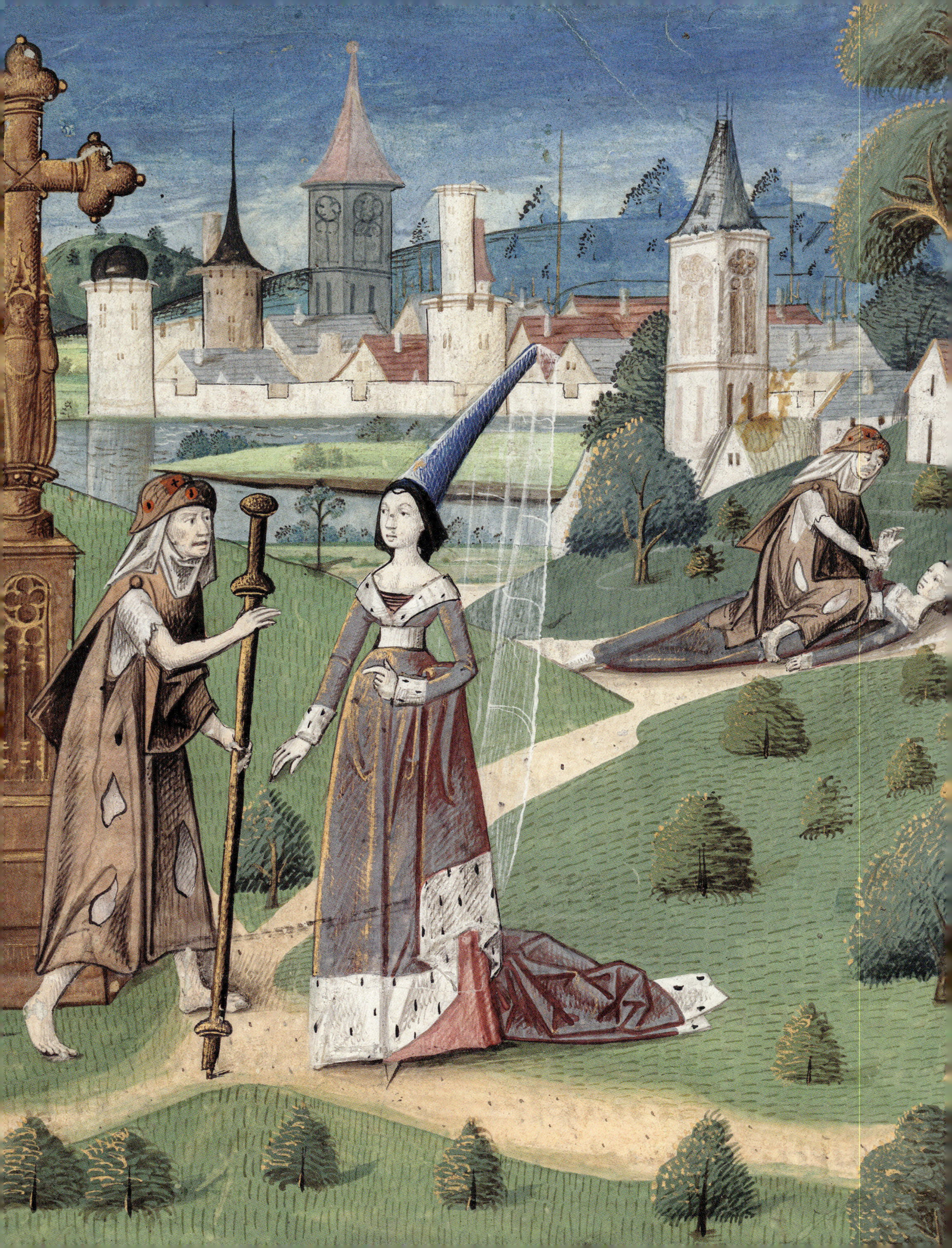

7

Money Management

DIANE WOLFTHAL

God and Fortune

MEDIEVAL EUROPEANS DEBATED WHETHER fortune alone determined economic class or whether human action could shape one's financial future. Medieval society envisioned Fortune as a powerful, capricious woman who turned an enormous upright wheel, arbitrarily changing the positions of those riding on it so that their fortunes rose or fell.[1] Although the motif was popularized by Boethius as early as the sixth century, the wheel of Fortune was an apt metaphor for the increased social mobility that accompanied the rise of the monetary economy. Suddenly some became rich, while others inexplicably fell into poverty. Fortune herself was seen as unpredictable and unstable, much like late medieval economic life. Christian doctrine taught that God—not Fortune—governed human destiny, yet Fortune remained very much alive in the medieval imagination since then, as

Workshop of Maître François (François le Barbier *père*), *Poverty and Fortune*, from Giovanni Boccaccio, *De casibus virorum illustrium* (Concerning the Fates of Famous Men and Women), trans. Laurent de Premierfait, France, Paris, ca. 1475. The Morgan Library & Museum, New York, MS M.342, fol. 77r. (Detail of Fig. 7.2.)

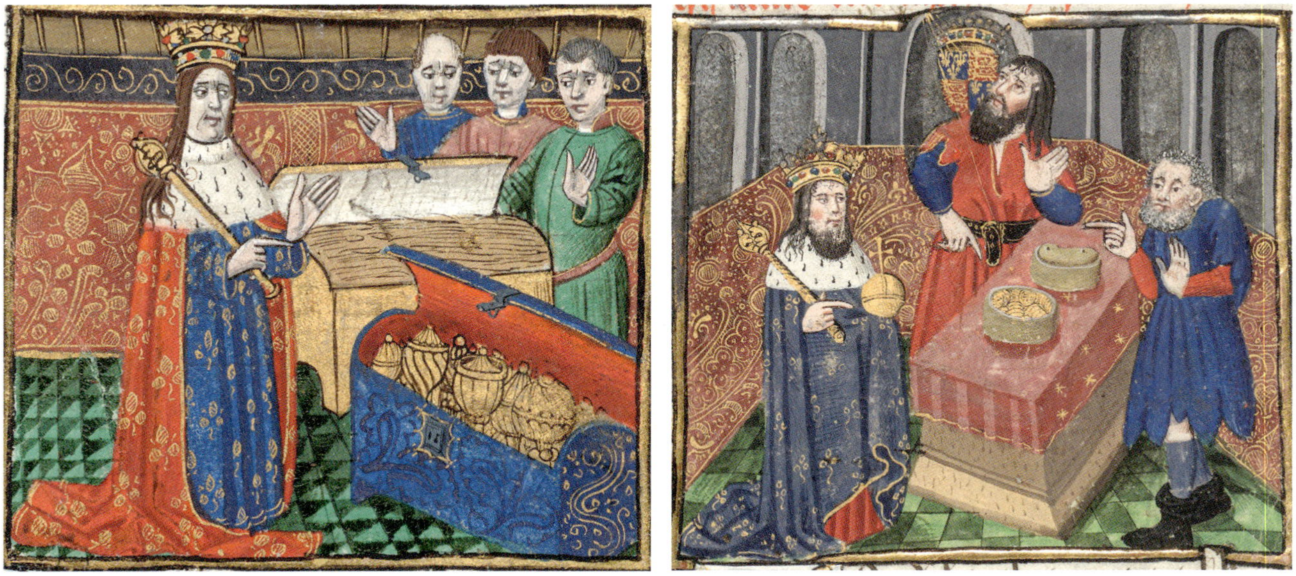

FIG. 7.1. *The Two Chests* and *Emperor Henry and the Two Beggars*, from John Gower, *Confessio amantis* (Lover's Confession), England, perhaps London, ca. 1470. The Morgan Library & Museum, New York, MS M.126, fols. 102v & 103r (dets.).

now, economic class was often determined by forces beyond one's control.

Two tales by John Gower exemplify the belief that Fortune determines economic class. They appear in his *Confessio amantis* (Lover's Confession), a Middle English poem written around 1393 and dedicated to King Richard II.[2] The *Confessio amantis* is at once a poem of consolation, a collection of tales, and an advice book for princes. It consists of a prologue and eight books. The first six are devoted to the sins of pride, envy, wrath, sloth, avarice, and gluttony. The seventh is a treatise on good kingship, and the last returns to the subject of sin by focusing on one aspect of lust: incest. The relevant stories appear in the fifth book, on avarice. In the first tale (5.2273–390), a king learns that several older courtiers have been complaining that they were not promoted as they deserved; instead, younger men were advanced. To teach them a lesson, the king asks them to choose one of two closed chests. When they select the coffer filled with worthless rocks and straw, rather than the one with golden treasure, the king blames Fortune alone for their predicament.[3]

A tale with a related theme follows (5.2391–441).[4] Emperor Frederick overhears two beggars arguing about the best way to attain wealth. One puts his faith in the generosity of kings, the other in God. The emperor then offers them the choice of one of two pies. The beggar who trusted in God selects the one filled with gold florins; the other beggar chooses the capon pie. The unlucky beggar then concludes, "How easily deceived is he / who trusts in man's help. / But well off is the man whom God helps" (5.2424–26).[5] The moral, as in the first story, is "No mite of profit shalt thou get / Beyond what fate intends for thee" (5.2450–51).[6] Taken together, these exempla suggest that Fortune determines class, and that complaining about one's lot is not only fruitless, but also a barrier to the good fortune that putting one's trust in God might bring.[7]

These tales are depicted in a lavishly illustrated manuscript thought to have been produced around 1470 for King Edward IV and his queen consort, Elizabeth Woodville (Fig. 7.1).[8] Part of an extensive picture cycle, the illuminations are treated as a pair, positioned on facing folios. In the first miniature, the unlucky courtiers spread their hands in amazement and knit their brows in consternation as the worthless straw is revealed. In the second, the lucky beggar raises his eyes up to God while pointing to the pie of gold coins, as his companion looks at and points to the emperor, who returns his gaze and gesture. Gold rays overlap a stained-glass window showing Edward IV's royal arms. Sonja Drimmer justly terms this "the visual conflation of divine grace and regnal beneficence."[9]

Gower was a wealthy landowner and investor; the initial version of the *Confessio amantis* was dedicated to one king (Richard II), and the illuminated copy under discussion, produced nearly eighty years later, was almost certainly made for another (King Edward IV).[10] It is not surprising, then, that these tales assert that Fortune determines our economic lot in life, and that God sanctions the class hierarchy.

If Fortune is an unseen force in the *Confessio amantis*, she is quite visible in another mirror-of-princes manuscript, Giovanni Boccaccio's *De casibus virorum illustrium* (Concerning the Fates of Famous Men and Women).[11] Initially written around 1355–60 and revised in 1373, its overarching theme is the vicissitudes of fortune, which Boccaccio illustrates through a series of tales about illustrious men and women whose vices caused their tragic ends. Here Fortune is envisioned less as an inevitable force of mutability than as divine justice.[12] At this time Italian sovereigns were mostly tyrannical despots, and Boccaccio's goal was to goad them to lead virtuous lives and rule wisely. *De casibus* became one of the most popular texts of the fifteenth century, surviving in almost ninety manuscripts and in early printed books, and translated into numerous vernacular languages. Laurent de Premierfait twice rendered *De casibus* into French, first in 1400 and then nine years later in a longer, more popular, and more loosely translated edition, known as *Du cas des nobles hommes et femmes*. The French translations, often commissioned by aristocrats, were generally more richly illustrated than the earlier Latin manuscripts.

In the third book of his second translation, Laurent de Premierfait describes an encounter between Fortune and Poverty.[13] Fortune addresses Poverty rudely, disparaging her solitary existence and miserable appearance, taking credit for causing her wretched condition, and arguing that if they fought, she would win. Poverty replies angrily that she has chosen a life of voluntary poverty, explaining:

> I would be your servant if I did not renounce the things of this world, but after I renounced them, I became free. I am out of your grasp because I have given up your gifts and your riches. You think that you knocked me down but you lifted me high because you didn't know that I didn't want to have anything to do with your gifts and your riches. You can threaten kings and princes who greatly desire the transitory goods that you give, but I have power, courage, boldness.[14]

The two then fight, and Poverty indeed wins. Because she has no desire for worldly things, Fortune cannot hurt her.

A large illumination of the encounter between Fortune and Poverty appears in a Parisian luxury manuscript of Laurent de Premierfait's second translation. Made around 1475 for Louis III de Bournel, seigneur

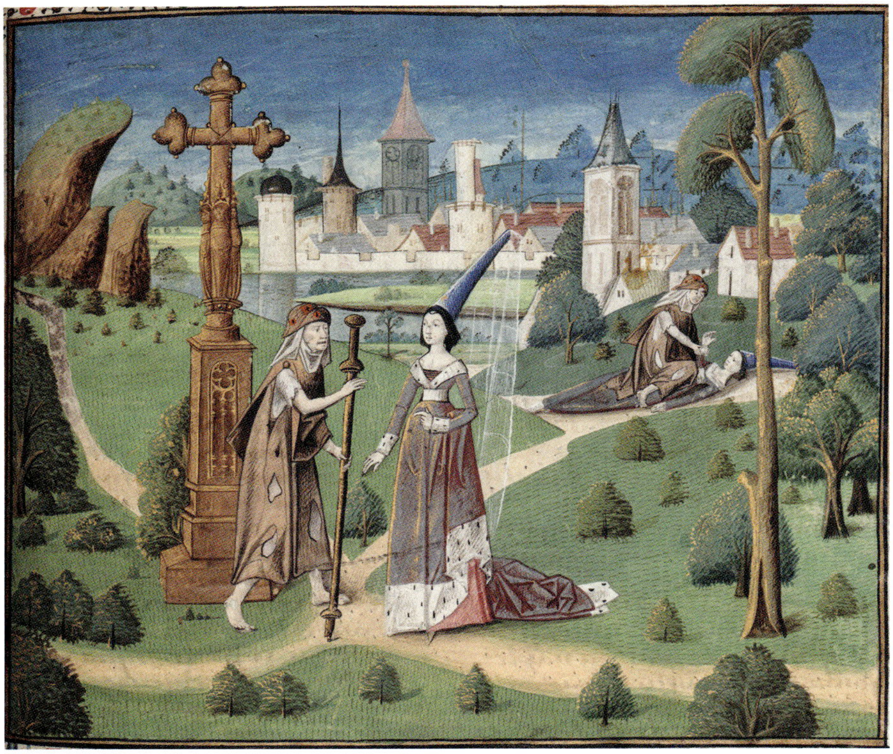

FIG. 7.2. Workshop of Maître François (François le Barbier *père*), *Poverty and Fortune*, from Giovanni Boccaccio, *De casibus virorum illustrium* (Concerning the Fates of Famous Men and Women), trans. Laurent de Premierfait, France, Paris, ca. 1475. The Morgan Library & Museum, New York, MS M.342, fol. 77r (det.).

de Thiembronne, the manuscript's illuminations have been attributed to the workshop of Maître François, recently identified as François le Barbier *père* (Fig. 7.2).[15] The image shows a verdant, peaceful landscape, an attribute of voluntary poverty. As Boccaccio notes, "O how an exceedingly beautiful and holy thing [it is] to engage in simple tasks with you [poverty]. To choose country places, to honor solitary places, to despise superfluities, to contemplate heavenly things under the shade of the trees by silvery streams."[16] In this idyllic setting, Poverty and Fortune meet at a junction, near a large cross. They gesture in conversation. Fortune, a young woman in fashionably pointed shoes, a blue turret with transparent veil, and an ermine-trimmed purple gown, faces Poverty, an older, barefoot woman with a torn brown garment and a pilgrim's hat and staff. The pilgrim's garb makes clear her voluntary poverty. In the middle ground, before a cityscape, Poverty defeats Fortune. Straddling her opponent, Poverty grasps her by the wrist, and, as specified in the text, places a knee against her chest. The text explains the moral: those who renounce worldly goods, fame, and power have little to lose from bad fortune. One way to control one's economic fate, then, was to embrace poverty.

At first glance two biblical parables seem to endorse the opposite strategy: invest money to turn a profit. The Parable of the Talents (Matthew 25:14–30) and its variant, the Parable of the Pounds (Luke 19:12–27), relate how a master left his servants money while he traveled, instructing them to invest it in trade. Upon his return, he rewarded the servants who made a profit, but punished the one who saved the money without taking financial risks. Early Christians interpreted the absent master as Christ, who had ascended to heaven but would return; the money referred to divine gifts that should be employed to serve God. The servants' punishments and rewards denoted the Last Judgment.[17] The idea that the Parable of the Pounds foreshadowed the Last Judgment became widespread when it appeared in the *Speculum humanae salvationis* (Mirror of Human Salvation), composed between 1309 and 1324.[18] This text became a bestseller, surviving in several hundred manuscripts.

FIG. 7.3. ***Last Judgment*** **and** ***Parable of the Ten Pounds,*** **from** ***Speculum humanae salvationis*** **(Mirror of Human Salvation), England, Yorkshire (?), ca. 1400. The Morgan Library & Museum, New York, MS M.766, fol. 61v (det.).**

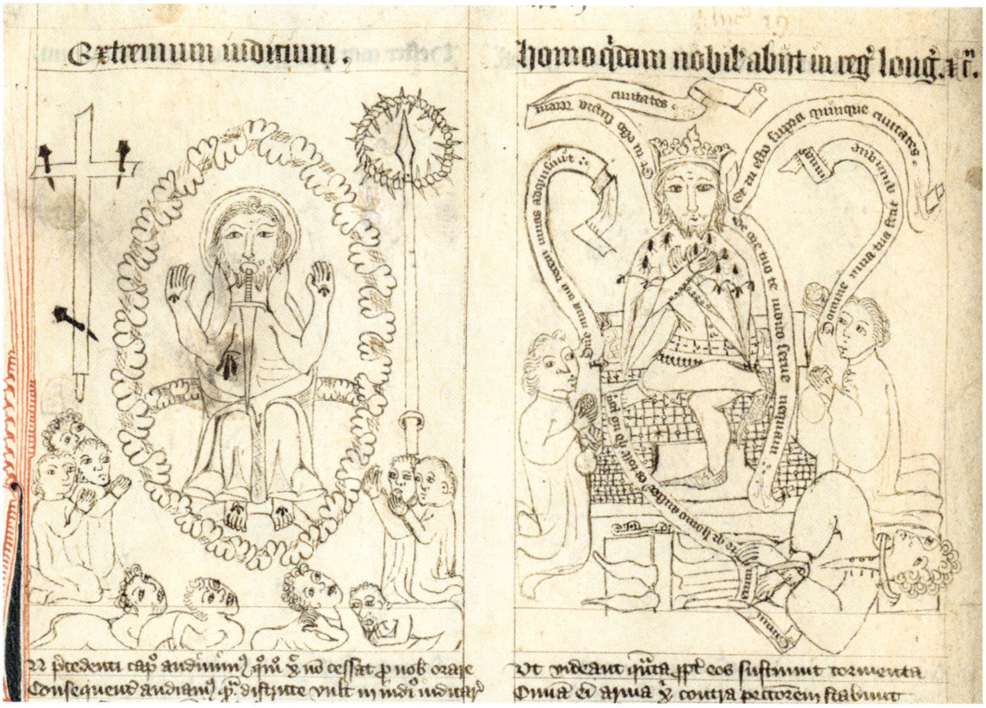

One illustration of this typology appears in a charming Yorkshire *Speculum*, datable shortly after 1400 (Fig. 7.3).[19] Folio 61v shows the Last Judgment beside the Parable of the Pounds. An inscription identifies the latter's biblical source (Luke 19) and the other inscriptions quote the Gospel writer. The caption relates that a nobleman went on a journey. The scrolls inform us that one servant invested a mina (an amount of coin) and produced another ten, that another invested a mina and produced another five, and that the lord rewarded them with ten and five cities respectively. A scroll describes the third servant who failed to invest as "wicked." In his version of the same story, the Evangelist Matthew relates that the third servant was "cast . . . out into the exterior darkness. There shall be weeping and gnashing of teeth" (Matthew 25:30). The darkness, sorrow, and terror of this punishment would have suggested to medieval Christians a vision of hell, which may, in turn, have sparked the idea that the parable foreshadows the Last Judgment.

The crowned lord wearing an ermine cape is flanked by the servants who made a profit. They kneel, each holding a moneybag in one hand and a single coin in the other. Below, stocks secure the feet of the "wicked" servant, and straps bind his wrists and neck, a punishment not mentioned in the Gospels. Through their similar compositions, the parable is shown to prefigure the Last Judgment. The crowned lord appears at the same level as Christ; both are seated and stare straight ahead. To either side kneel virtuous figures, the servants and the saved. Below both, the "wicked" servant and the damned are recumbent as they look up at their judge.

Although this parable was generally not interpreted in the Middle Ages as recommending investment as a path towards securing one's economic future, a few manuscripts did suggest ways to achieve that goal. One example is a small Parisian book of hours, illuminated by Jean Pichore's workshop in 1510–20 for Philibert de Clermont, seigneur de Montoison, chamberlain to two kings.[20] This manuscript has a remarkable set of calendar images showing the Twelve Ages of Man. The rhyming quatrain for August recommends that when a man approaches the age of forty-eight, he

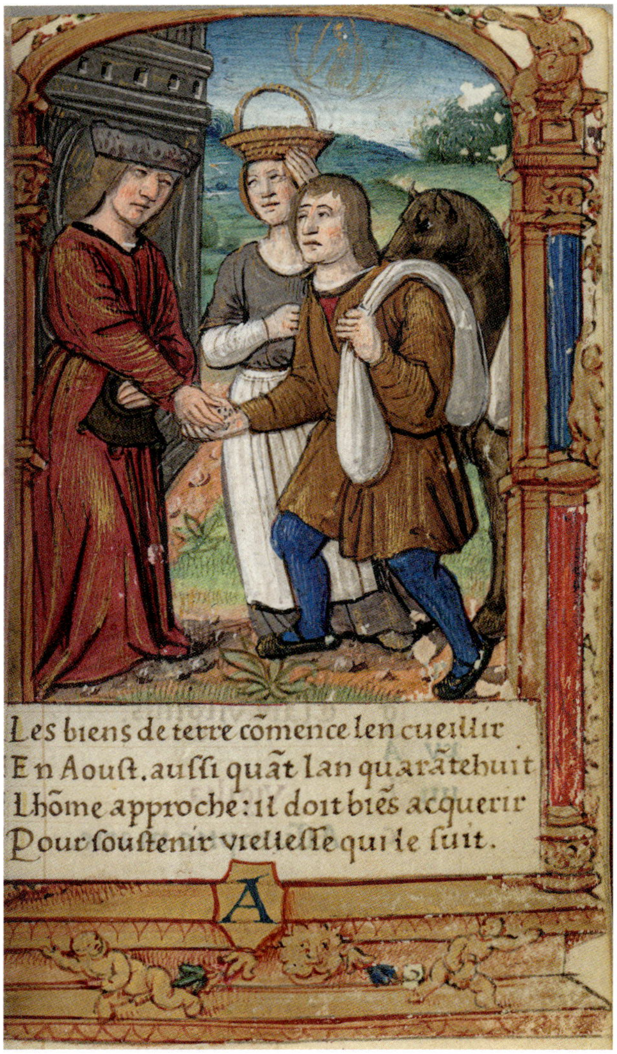

FIG. 7.4. Workshop of Jean Pichore, *Man Preparing for His Old Age*, from a book of hours, France, Paris, 1510–20. The Morgan Library & Museum, New York, MS M.813, fol. 13r.

should acquire goods to sustain him in his old age, an act of proper money management (Fig. 7.4).[21] The illumination shows a man reaching with one hand into his purse and with the other paying a farmer for the goods that he has brought in sacks, one slung over his shoulder, the other across his horse's back. A woman balances on her head a basket, presumably filled with produce. In August, food is harvested, and, if it is not purchased then, it will be too late to procure supplies for the autumn and winter. Indeed the illumination for September illustrates a fifty-four-year-old man whose barn and wine barrel are empty: he failed to plan well.

A Newlywed's Financial Nightmare

Planning, hard work, and a virtuous life are the prescription for financial independence offered by Jacques Bruyant's *Livre du chastel de labour de povreté et de richesse* (Book of the Castle of Labor, of Poverty, and of Wealth), composed in Paris in 1342.[22] One of eleven surviving manuscripts of this work, a relatively small number, is a deluxe codex, produced in the 1430s, profusely illuminated by the Master of Sir John Fastolf. It consists of forty-seven chapters, all but one introduced by a large illumination. Bruyant's poem was inspired by the *Roman de la rose*. In both texts an author-narrator relates an allegorical dream that takes the form of a journey to a better place. But rather than a dream of love, Bruyant's dream is, in fact, a nightmare, rooted in a newlywed's worries about the financial consequences of his recent marriage. His anxiety is assuaged by his guide, a personification of Reason, who shows him the path that will insure successful money management. Five aspects of Bruyant's text concern money: the newlywed's fear of poverty; Reason's recommendation that he should avoid avarice and embrace charity; her conviction that one can shape one's economic fate; her belief that one should earn only enough to support oneself; and, finally, the book's implicit claim that women need not trouble themselves with money management.

The first section of the manuscript portrays the physical and psychological torments of the narrator and his fears of impoverishment. The second illumination shows the newlyweds in bed surrounded by personifications of Want and his sisters, Necessity, Suffering, and Hunger. This foursome, in torn and

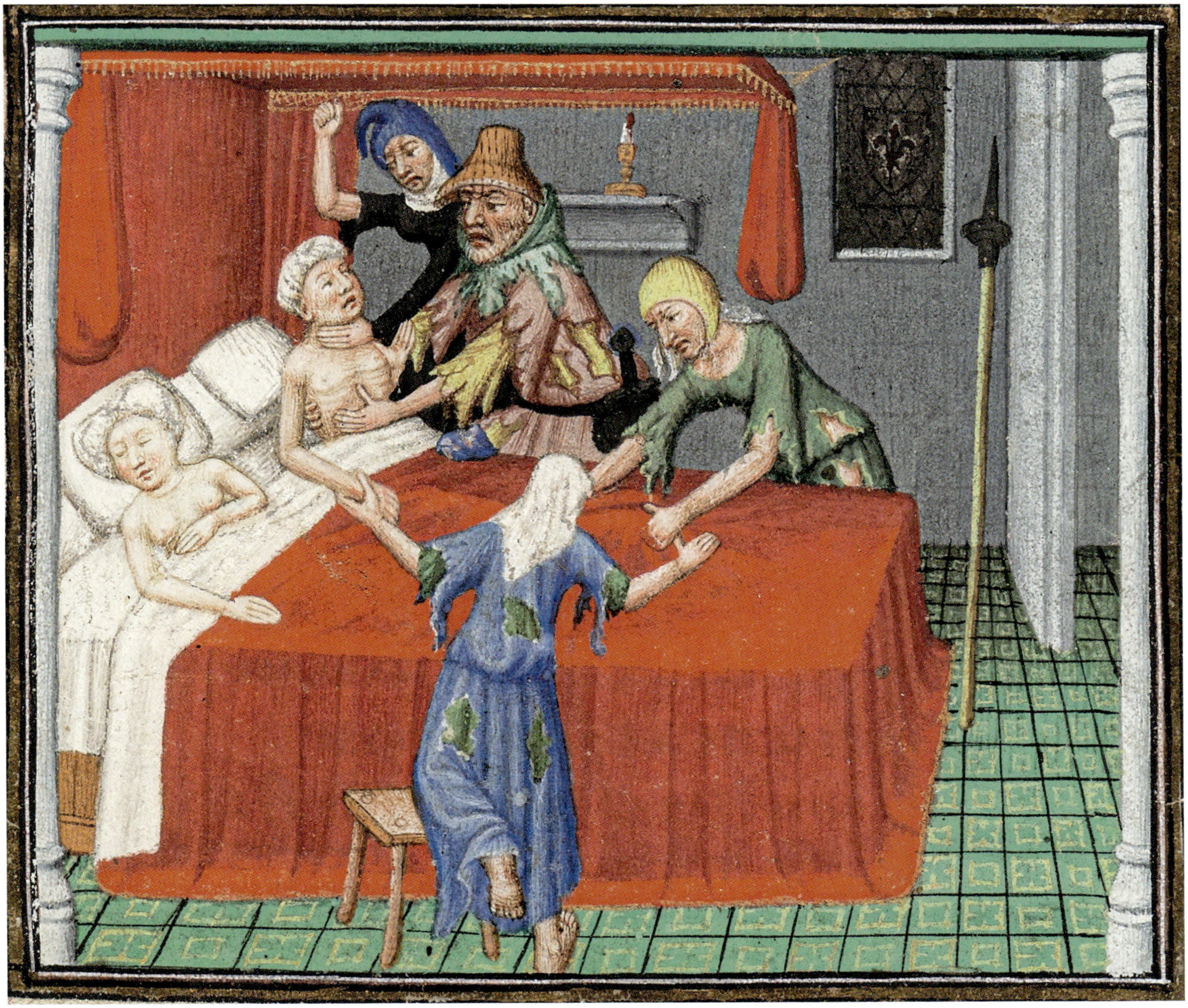

patched clothes, assaults the hapless narrator (Fig. 7.5). Want has set aside his spear to grab the husband's torso with both hands, while Necessity, with her fist raised threateningly, seizes his neck. Another sister grasps his wrist, while the third sister pulls the newlywed's legs. The illuminator effectively expresses the man's anxiety, convincingly portraying the visitors to his bedchamber as violent and frightening. Throughout this attack—and in all the scenes of the dream sequence—the husband is awake, his eyes open, while the wife's remain closed. Asleep, she is oblivious to her husband's tormentors and, later, to the advice Reason gives him.

FIG. 7.5. Master of Sir John Fastolf, *Newlyweds with Want, Necessity, Suffering and Hunger*, from Jacques Bruyant, *Le livre du chastel de labour de povreté et de richesse* (The Book of the Castle of Labor, of Poverty, and of Wealth), France, Paris, 1430s. The Free Library of Philadelphia, Rare Book Department, Widener 1, fol. 2r (det.).

Personifications of Anxiety, Care, Discomfort, and Despair express the husband's acute anxiety. Discomfort gives voice to his anxiety, ". . . what will you do? . . . You have nothing and you owe a lot."[23] The newlywed, however, is not portrayed in dire economic straits. Instead, the images place him in a well-appointed room with a tiled floor, curtained bed, stained-glass window, and stone walls. But the man, according to the text, worries about his debts until, distraught, he considers dishonest means of obtaining a livelihood. Then Reason steps in, expelling Despair and advising the husband to live a virtuous life.

Avarice and its corresponding virtue, Charity, play major roles in Bruyant's text. One illumination shows, on the left, a young woman at a counter receiving with one hand a sack of money and with the other distributing alms in the form of a small, round loaf of bread, the *miche ronde* (Fig. 7.6).[24] More moneybags and loaves rest on the counter. The recipients of the charity represent the deserving poor: a woman leaning on a cane and an old man on crutches, with an amputated foot. On the right, a luxuriously dressed woman fingers large piles of gold and silver coins displayed on the green cloth of moneylenders and money changers.[25] The scroll overlapping her table reads, "Let us overcome poverty with largesse."[26] As if in response, a more simply dressed woman drops coins into the palm of a needy man. Behind this group, a thief readies his dagger to cut the cords of a man's purse hanging from his neck, and a gray-haired Covetousness, brandishing a sword, carries a banner adorned with two moneybags, a motif with often negative connotations.[27] In the distance, the newlywed and Reason (identifiable by her triple mirror, symbolizing self-reflection and wisdom) observe the scene.[28] The accompanying rubric reads, "How Reason speaks to the newlywed and explains the sin of Greed, Looting, and Usury, and also Charity and Largesse and other virtues contrary to that damnable and evil sin."[29] According to Reason, to keep greed at bay, charity is essential.

Bruyant's chapter 27 features Fraud, who tells the newlywed that if he follows him he will become rich. Fraud advises him to flatter the rich and ignore the poor, to be stingy, to cheat and steal, and to refuse to pay his debts.[30] Bruyant clearly understands the negative consequences of avarice at the dawn of capitalism. In one image, Reason shows the newlywed the heavenly reward for those who follow her and the hellish punishment for those who do not.

Bruyant, unlike Gower in the tales recounted at the start of this chapter, argues that one's economic future is not preordained; he repeatedly has Reason recommend diligence as a means to gain wealth. In this respect he follows Boccaccio and others who saw virtue as the only bulwark against bad fortune. The illumination for chapter 19 shows the road to the castle of riches (Fig. 7.7). Reason shows the newlywed a fork in the road where one path, labeled laziness, leads to poverty, and the other, labeled diligence, to wealth. A hunched figure on crutches stands on the path to poverty; a queen, a king, and two other elegantly dressed figures mark the road to riches, which leads to the castle. The text argues that destiny—or fate—is not responsible for how people act. Rather, individuals are responsible for their financial well-being; if they ignore reason and embark on the wrong path, that is their choice. In this way, Bruyant condemns the poor for their poverty.[31] If diligence can make one wealthy, then economic class

FIG. 7.6. Master of Sir John Fastolf, *Charity, Largesse, and Avarice,* from Jacques Bruyant, *Le livre du chastel de labour de povreté et de richesse* (The Book of the Castle of Labor, of Poverty, and of Wealth), France, Paris, ca. 1430. The Free Library of Philadelphia, Rare Book Department, Widener 1, fol. 15v (det.).

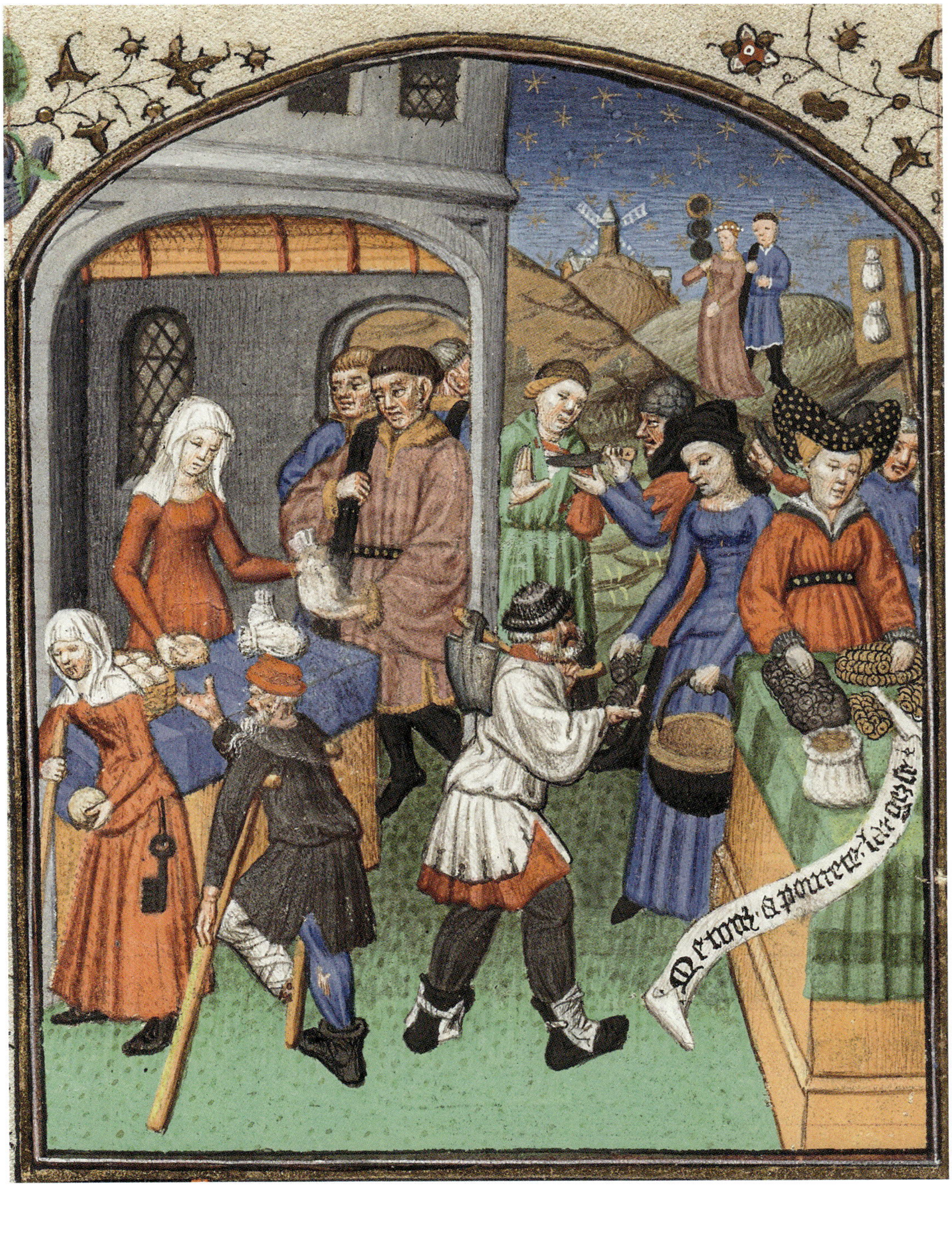

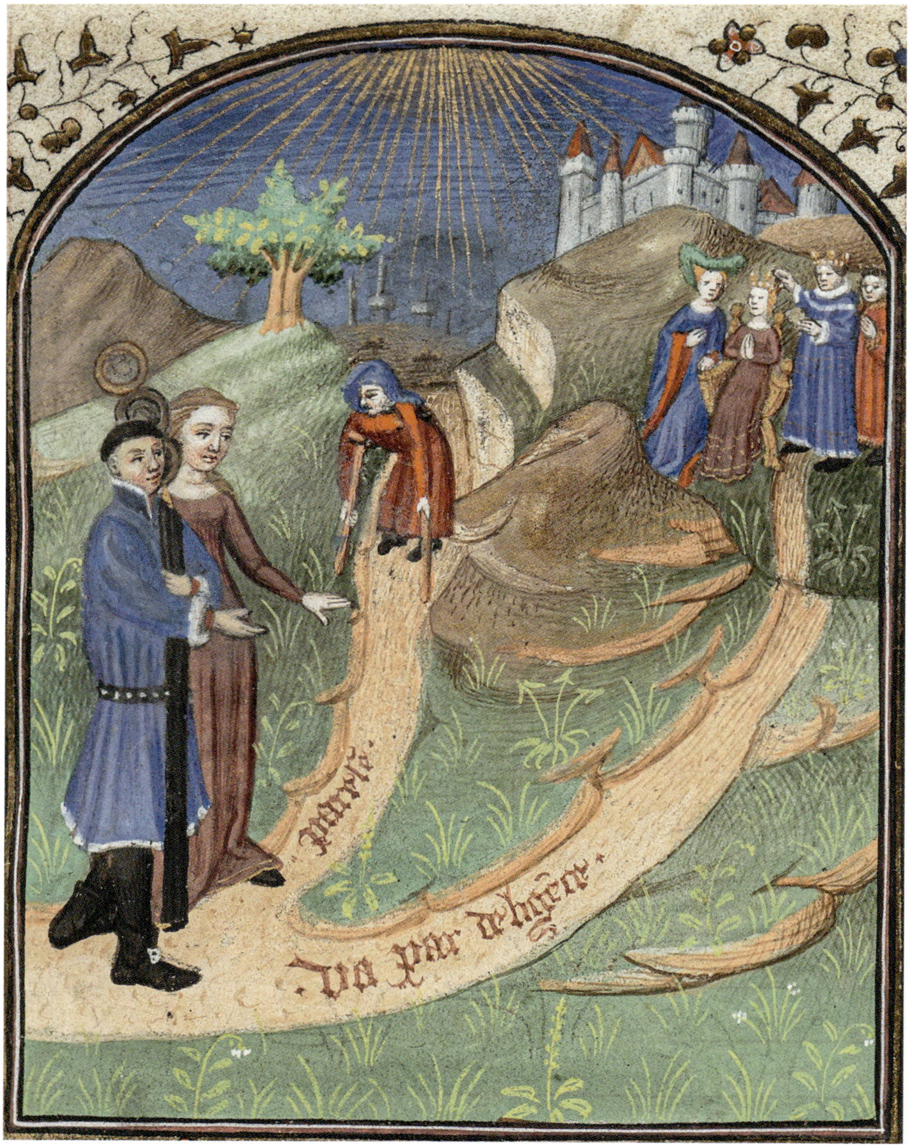

FIG. 7.7. Master of Sir John Fastolf, *Reason Shows Newlywed the Fork in the Road*, from Jacques Bruyant, *Le livre du chastel de labour de povreté et de richesse* (The Book of the Castle of Labor, of Poverty, and of Wealth), France, Paris, ca. 1430. The Free Library of Philadelphia, Rare Book Department, Widener 1, fol. 28r (det.).

FIG. 7.8. Master of Sir John Fastolf, *The Castle of Labor*, from Jacques Bruyant, *Le livre du chastel de labour de povreté et de richesse* (The Book of the Castle of Labor, of Poverty, and of Wealth), France, Paris, ca. 1430. The Free Library of Philadelphia, Rare Book Department, Widener 1, fol. 61v.

is malleable, but would it be preferable if poverty were eliminated? In the Middle Ages some argued, as mentioned in Chapter 5, that the poor were needed to help the rich atone for their sins through charity, but Bruyant sees no positive value in poverty, hunger, and despair.[32]

Guided by its lord and lady, Hard Work and Pains (Fig. 7.8), the newlywed visits the Castle of Labor, where he sees more than 100,000 workers engaged in various tasks. He, too, works day and night before he is finally allowed to rest. In the miniature men construct a building; in the margins they and a woman toil in the fields. Bruyant once again urges diligence upon his readers to avoid poverty.

With Reason as his guide, the husband becomes confident that he can achieve this goal. The objective, as explained by Reason, is not to become rich, but rather to earn enough to support oneself and one's family. Bruyant was not alone in arguing this position. As discussed in Chapter 5, many theologians maintained that any excess income should be donated to the Church or the poor.[33] The idea of removing oneself

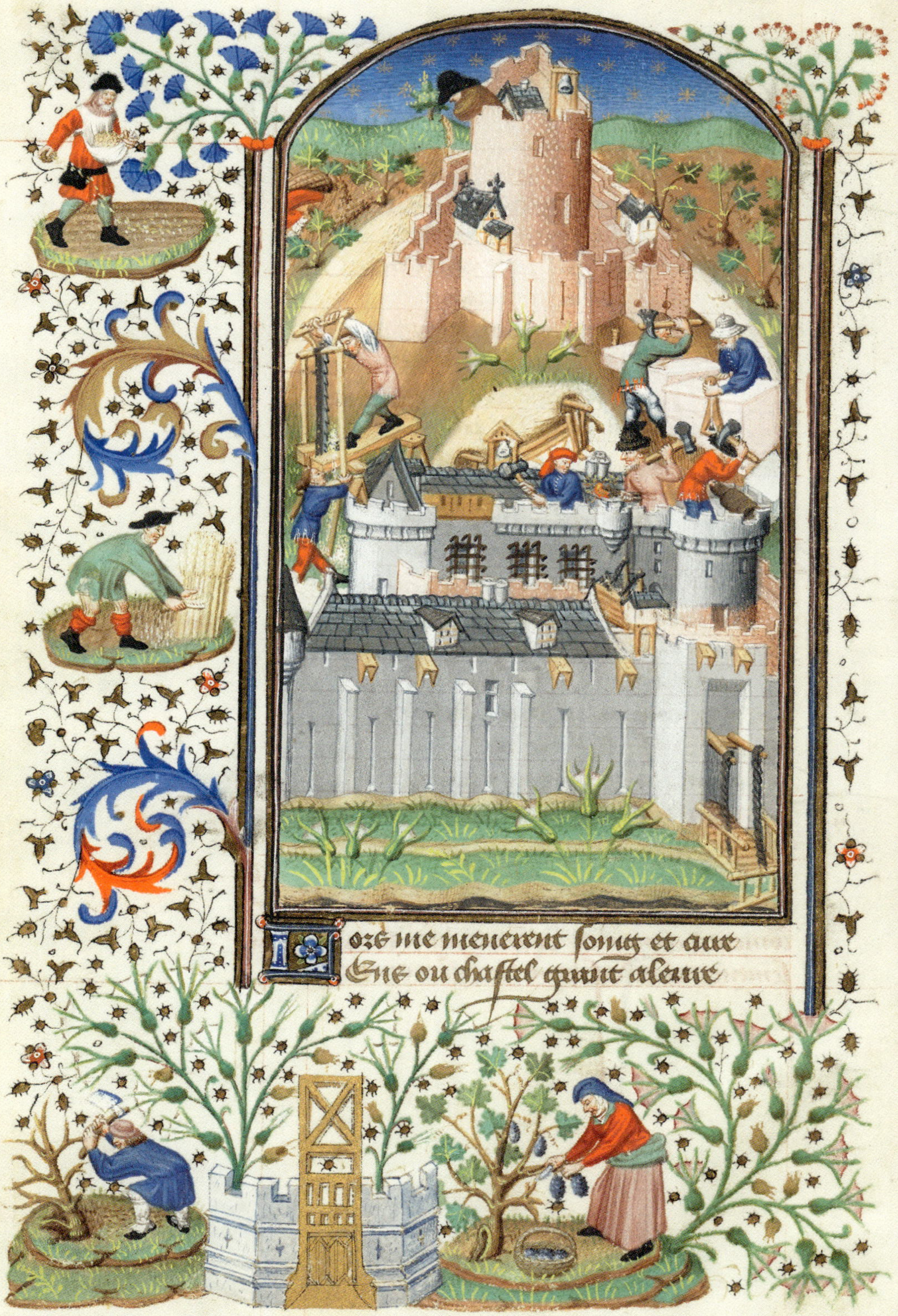
Lors me menerent soing et cure
Ens ou chastel quavoit aleure

FIG. 7.9. Albrecht Dürer, *The Prodigal Son amid Swine*, engraving, Germany, Nuremberg, ca. 1496. The Metropolitan Museum of Art, New York, 19.73.35.

from the economic cycle entirely, and being content with essentials, also had its advocates. A self-sufficient Wildman, living simply in the forest, expresses this sentiment in a stanza of late medieval French verse:

> For mighty castles, grand palaces I do not care.
> In a hollow tree I make my home.
> I do not delight in fancy food
> Or in strong drink.
> I live upon fresh fruit alone,
> And so I have, thank God, enough.[34]

Bruyant warns the newlywed about a second fork in the road to the Castle of Riches. There he should choose "enough," rather than covetousness. The text states that having enough "makes men truly rich and happy, and without which no man were really so, even were he king of France." But those who take the road of Covetousness "are not satisfied even when they reach the fair Castle of Riches."[35] This statement is reminiscent of the popular story of Diogenes, who told Alexander that he would never be satisfied because he always wanted more (see Figs. 5.14–5.15).

With the rise of the monetary economy, one's economic future was increasingly unstable. This luxury manuscript was obviously made for someone with considerable wealth: forty-seven of its seventy-three folios are illuminated with high-quality miniatures adorned with gold and silver leaf. It is ironic, then, that its primary goal is to teach the ideal of sufficiency, not wealth.

Significantly, as recounted by Bruyant, the wife sleeps through her husband's vivid and sometimes violent dream; missing all the action, she is only awake in the last two scenes. In the penultimate chapter, the newlywed relates his entire dream to his wife over dinner. The accompanying image shows her setting the table. The final chapter includes a long misogynist passage, inspired by the wife scolding her husband for what she terms his idle dreams. The image, however, shows that the husband has learned the lesson of his dream, since he displays a box of silver coins to his wife (an act not mentioned in the text).[36] But she pulls away. An implicit message of the manuscript, then, is that women need not trouble themselves with money management.

Bruyant's newlywed was not alone in dedicating himself to the path of virtue in order to achieve economic solvency. The Parable of the Prodigal Son (Luke 15:11–32) is a much more famous example. Its complex narrative often unfolds over several scenes (see Figs. 4.13, 6.35), but Albrecht Dürer's engraving of ca. 1496 focuses on one moment, when the young man decides to end his dissolute life, which has impoverished him and alienated him from God and his family (Fig. 7.9).[37] Now a swineherd, he falls to his knees, beseeching God for forgiveness while vowing to make amends to his father, whose inheritance he has squandered. Leaning against his body is a large club, which is neither part of the biblical narrative nor appropriate to the role of swineherd. It may refer to the club of Hercules, who chose the hard road of virtue over the easy path of vice.[38]

But what happened to those who never turned their lives around? As we have seen, medieval society viewed voluntary poverty as a virtue (see Figs. 5.4, 5.9, 5.11, 7.2), but involuntary poverty was not perceived in a favorable light. The deserving poor—women

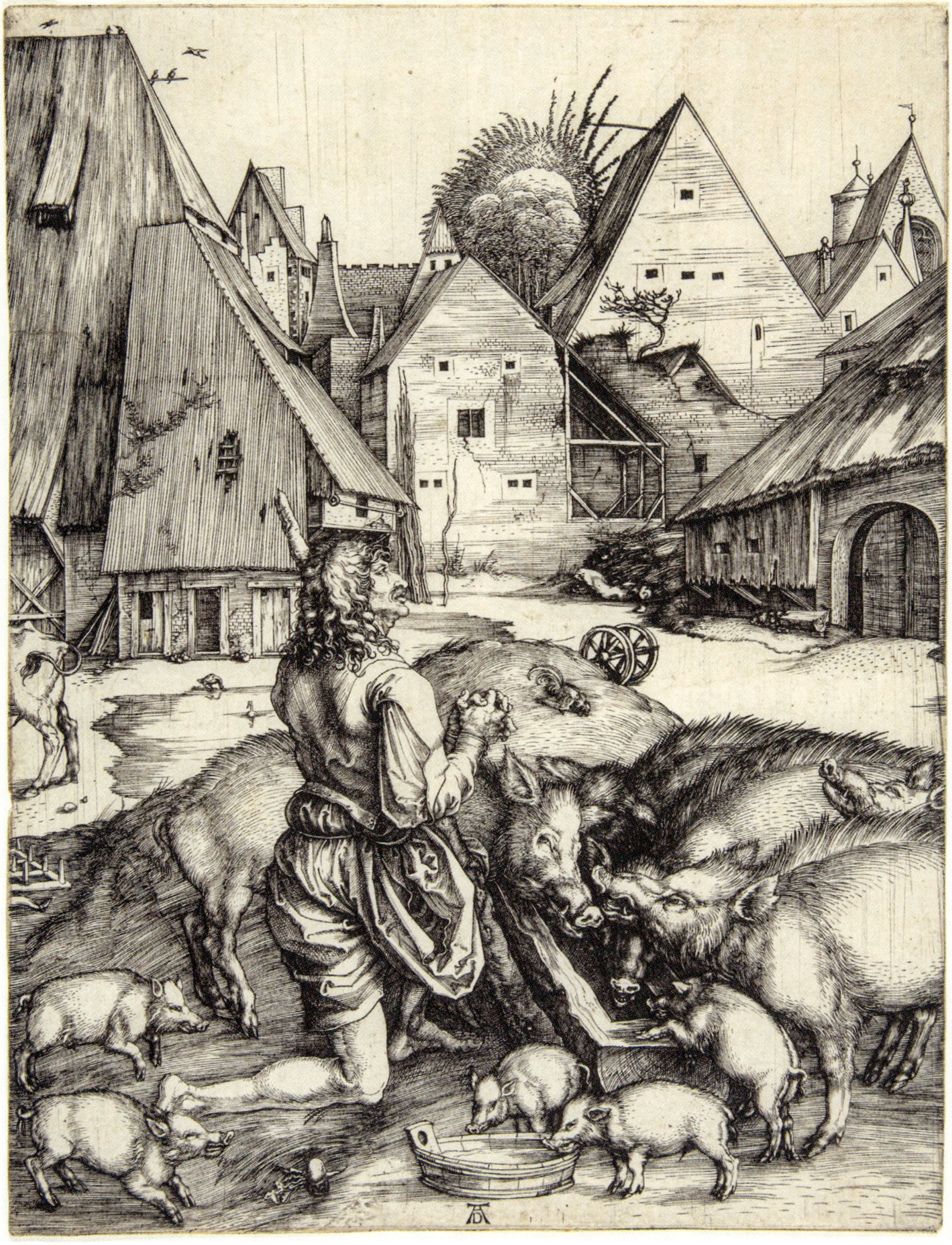

with young children, the blind, the lame, young women without a dowry—were considered worthy of charity. But poverty due to dissolute living—to drunkenness, gambling, immoderate spending, or laziness—was condemned. Sorgheloos (meaning "carefree" in medieval Dutch) is such a figure. The tragic figure of a popular Netherlandish morality tale, Sorgheloos, like the Prodigal Son, is a young wastrel

FIG. 7.10. ***Sorgheloos,*** **colorless glass, vitreous paint, and silver stain (photographed in photographer's studio), Netherlandish, 1510–20. The Metropolitan Museum of Art, The Cloisters Collection, New York, 1999.243.**

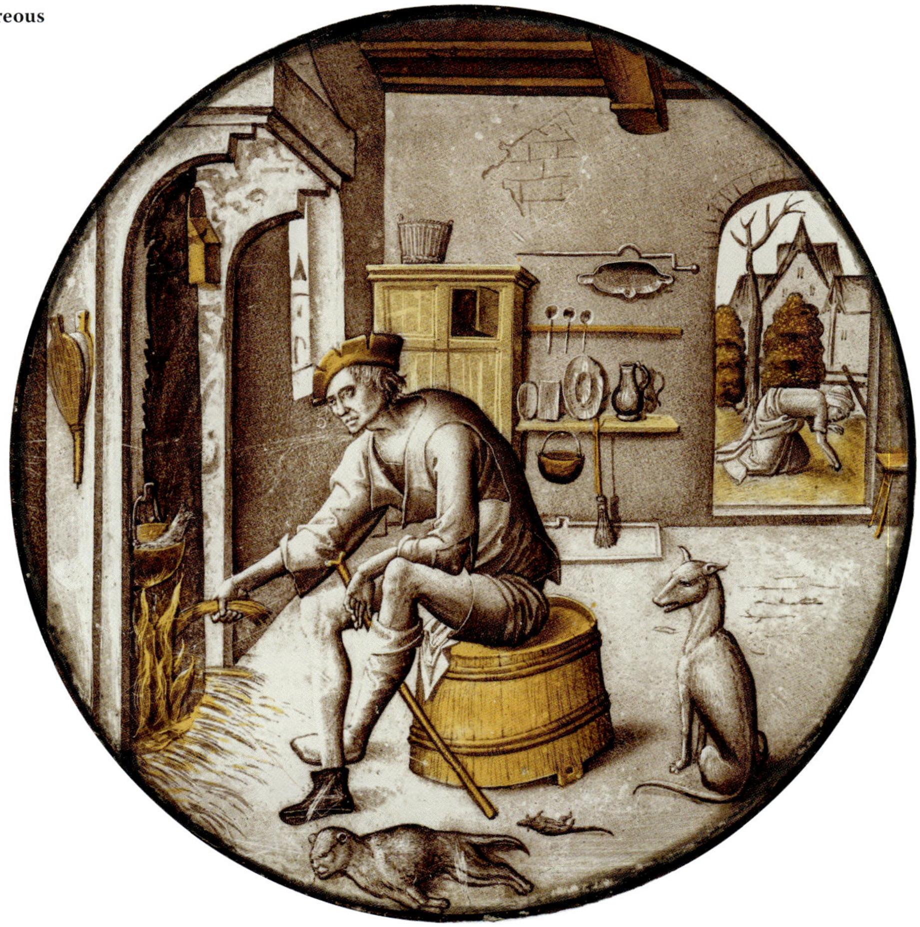

whose sinful indulgence leads to destitution and social isolation.[39] But unlike the biblical prodigal, Sorgheloos, who is not as carefree as his ironic name implies, does not change his behavior, and his story has no happy ending, no homecoming, no forgiveness. Instead, he is condemned to a miserable life of unremitting loneliness and poverty. The moral of the tale, which attributes Sorgheloos's misfortune to his bad choices, is that prodigality leads to poverty—physical, spiritual, and moral. Yet aspects of the tale may well have aroused sympathy. A poem printed in 1541, for example, has Sorgheloos cry, "Indigence bites me, yea Poverty smites me / Oh would that I had a morsel to eat."[40] In the end, Sorgheloos, a pathetic and tragic figure, recognizes his foolishness, but it is too late.

A Netherlandish glass roundel, datable to 1510–20, depicts the last act of the tale (Fig. 7.10).[41] Sensitively painted, it may well have aroused both pity and condemnation. An impoverished Sorgheloos sits on an overturned washtub in a dilapidated cottage with a peeling wall. Unable to afford wood, he feeds a fire with straw as he cooks a solitary fish, perhaps the "rancid herring" of the poem.[42] His empty cupboard, torn clothes, missing shoe and legging, emaciated dog, and dead cat and mouse further attest to the household's poverty.[43] Quite touching are the sadness in his eyes and the grim expression of his mouth. Visible through the open door is the figure of Poverty, his constant companion, gleaning straw. When viewers saw this roundel as part of a series, they might have focused on the moral: that Sorgheloos caused his own downfall. But contemplated in isolation, the roundel may have aroused sympathy, since it so movingly depicts the hunger, misery, and despair of the chronically poor.

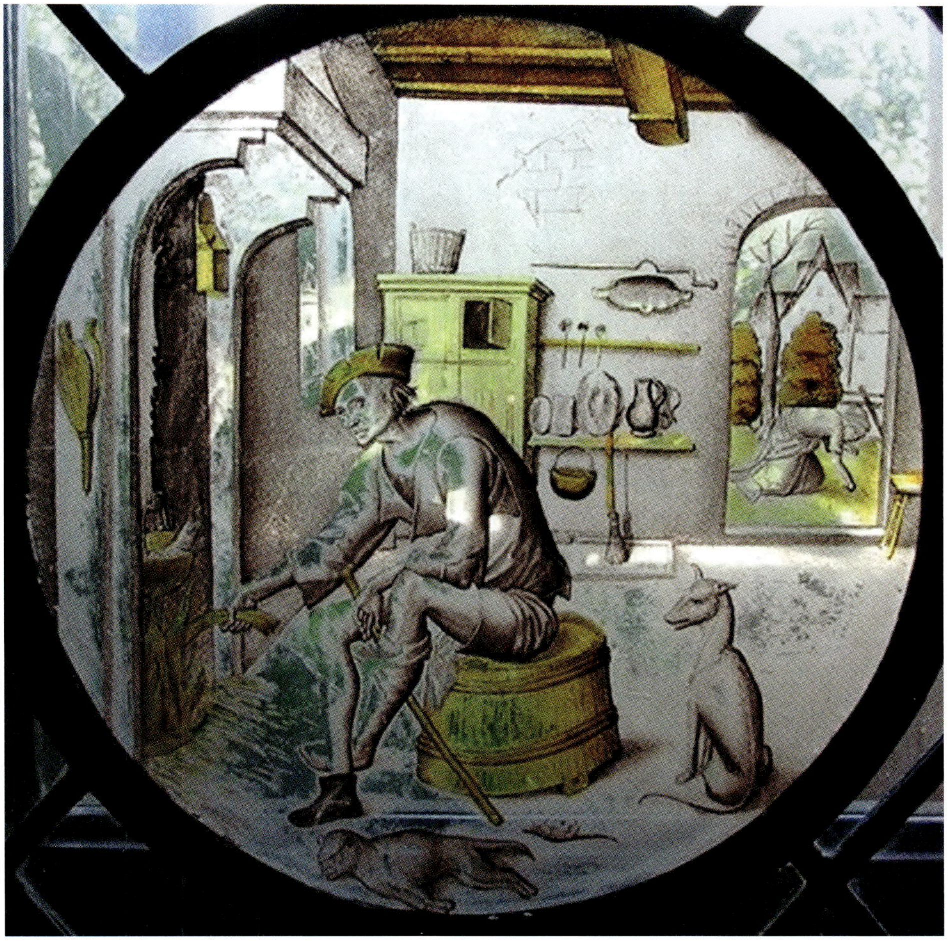

FIG. 7.11. Same as Fig. 7.10 (photographed with outdoor light).

This reaction would have been accentuated when color from the outside—the green of the trees or the blue of the sky—infused the roundel's transparent passages, making Sorgheloos and his home appear even more ominous and desolate (Fig. 7.11).

The figure of Poverty in the *Roman de la rose* also serves as a touchstone for the mixed feelings that the poor aroused in medieval Europe. On the one hand, Poverty is included among the sins outside the walled garden in which the narrator's beloved is confined (Fig. 7.12; see Fig. 4.3).[44] On the other hand, the description of Poverty's misery may well have aroused the reader's pity. Guillaume de Lorris begins by relating that Poverty could not even afford a rope to hang herself. He notes that if the weather turned cold, Poverty would die because she wears only an old, thin, patched sack, and is otherwise "naked as a worm." She shivers alone, cowering in a corner like a dog, "always shamed and despised." Unlike in the story of Sorgheloos, in the *Roman de la rose* poverty is not caused by the actions of the poor. Rather, those who are born poor remain so: "Cursed be the hour in which a poor man was conceived, for he will never be well fed, well clothed, nor well shod."[45] Guillaume, in short, paints a picture of Poverty as a social outcast who will forever live a miserable and pitiable existence.

The accompanying illumination confirms this bleak view (Fig. 7.12).[46] Poverty forms a striking contrast to Hypocrisy, who appears on the same folio. The large figure of Hypocrisy is depicted as a nun praying within an arcade at her *prie dieu* (prayer desk). Thin Poverty, by contrast, occupies little space as she sits on the bare earth, far from town or indeed any structure at all. The trees that frame her are a conventional sign of social

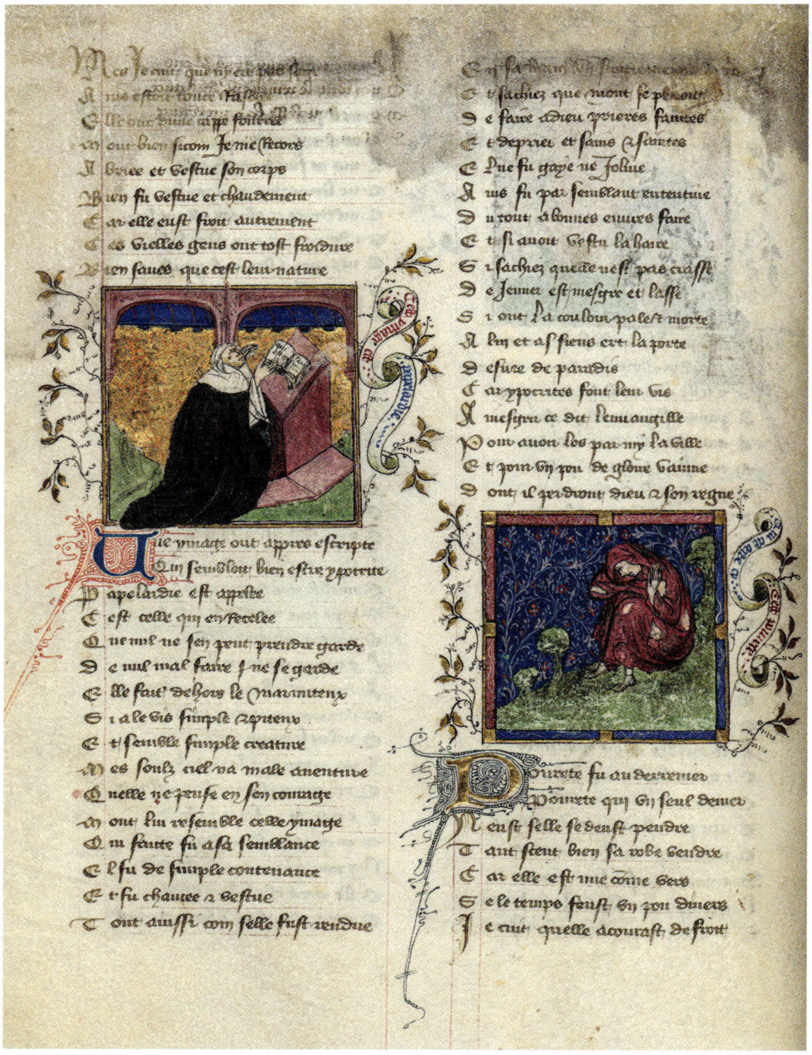

FIG. 7.12. ***Hypocrisy* and *Poverty*, from Guillaume de Lorris and Jean de Meun, *Le roman de la rose* (The Romance of the Rose), France, possibly Paris, ca. 1405. The Morgan Library & Museum, New York, MS M.245, fol. 4v.**

alienation.[47] Indeed, as mentioned in Chapter 5, many civic authorities tried to keep beggars outside their walls.[48] Poverty is dressed in a formless cloth whose large holes reveal her bare skin. Her head bends in a mournful pose, her mouth is downturned, and the upraised gesture of her left hand signals distress.[49]

By evoking the grinding poverty and social isolation of the poor, images of Sorgheloos and Poverty—together with those of the biblical beggar, Lazarus (see Figs. 4.18, 4.20–4.21)—form a striking contrast to contemporaneous paintings of wealthy merchants. Medieval society debated how to deal with the poor, especially those deemed "undeserving." By the late Middle Ages vagrancy laws that severely punished beggars existed side by side with charitable programs. One possible reaction to these images is voiced by the beggar in *Dives and Pauper*, a prose commentary on the Ten Commandments in the form of a dialogue, datable to 1405–10: "If any man or woman dies for lack of help, then all who should have helped, or might have helped, or who knew of the person's plight, but who would not help are guilty of manslaughter."[50] Such haunting representations as those of Sorgheloos, Poverty, and Lazarus serve as a powerful reminder that destitution, hunger, and despair exist in the midst of great wealth, then as now.

The Triumph of Avarice

At the close of the Middle Ages a series of tapestries explored the conflict between the virtues and vices for control of the human soul. Woven in Brussels after designs by Pieter Coecke van Aelst of Antwerp, it is datable to 1532–36. A humanist scholar composed the iconographic program, which survives in a mid-sixteenth-century manuscript. But the artist deviated from this program by downplaying the virtuous protagonists, and emphasizing the sinners. Each sin is represented by a winged woman riding a triumphal cart as part of a procession of biblical, mythological, and

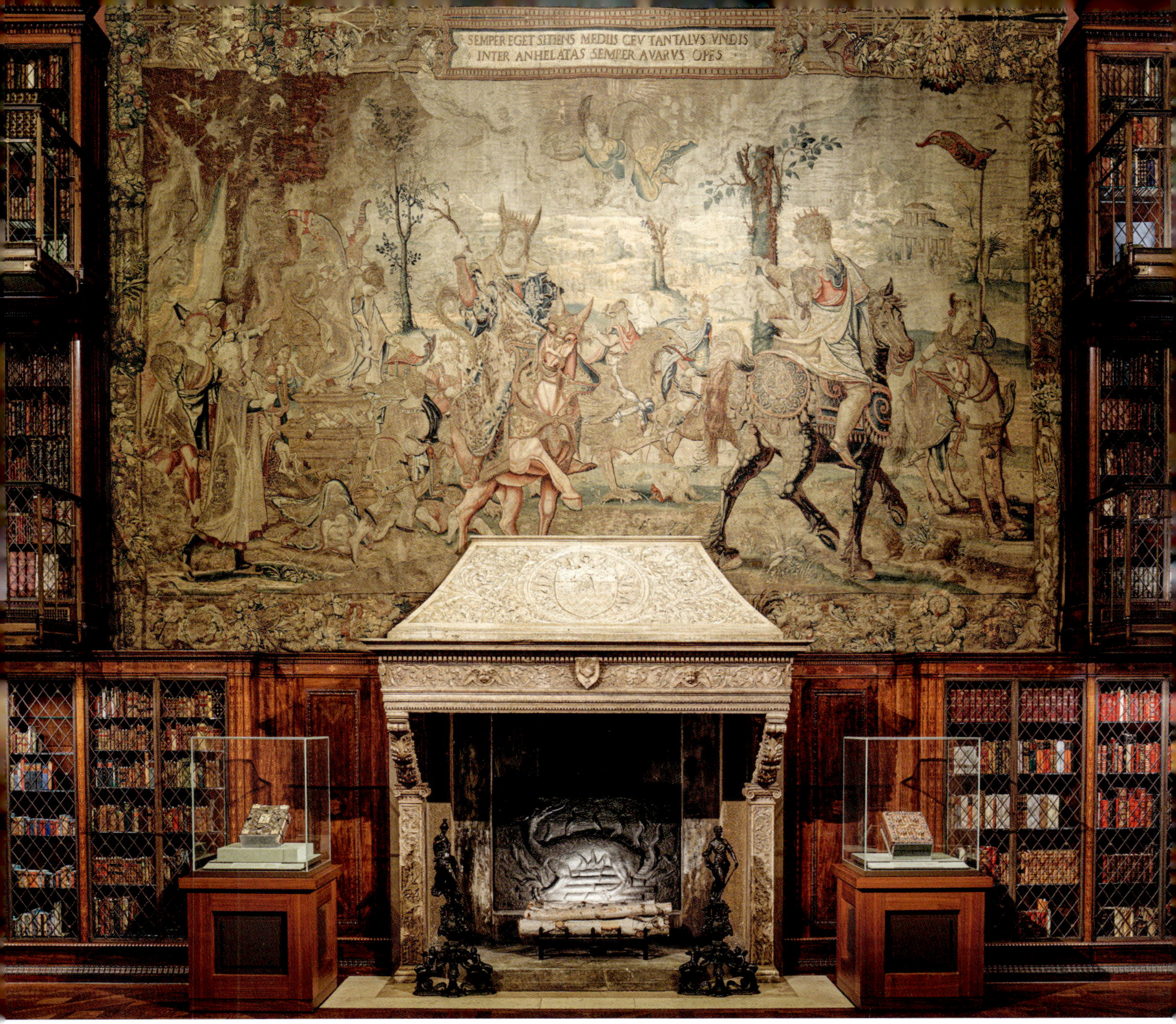

FIG. 7.13. Willem de Pannemaker (weaver) and Pieter Coecke van Aelst (designer), *The Triumph of Avarice*, tapestry, Netherlandish, 1532–36. The Morgan Library & Museum, New York, AZ 130.

historical figures that exemplify that vice. At least five sets of the series were woven; one entered the English royal collection in 1535–36. The tapestry that concerns us here, the *Triumph of Avarice*, first recorded in the collection of King Henry VIII, was purchased nearly four hundred years later by J. Pierpont Morgan, and is today on view in the library and museum that bear his name (Fig. 7.13).[51]

This enormous tapestry, over twenty-four feet wide, was extravagantly woven with wool, silk, and gilt-covered threads. Here a monstrous Avarice, with wings, horns, and talons, rides a chariot pulled by a gigantic vulture.[52] With extended claw-like fingernails, she crouches, grasping fistfuls of gold coins from an open coffer. Four crowned figures on horseback gather before her: Midas with enormous donkey ears holding a golden branch; Pygmalion clutching his statue with both hands; and, in the background, King Croesus, whose name was synonymous with wealth, and King Polymnestor, who killed out of greed. One other figure stands out from the crowd: Simony who follows the chariot clutching a monstrance and illustrated indulgences. The Latin inscription in the cartouche states that greed is never satisfied, "[a]s Tantalus is ever thirsty in the midst of water, so is the miser always desirous of riches."[53] While Liberality flies in the heavens, accompanied by angels, a fiery image of hell at the left, whence the procession originates, serves as a warning to the avaricious. Virtue is here a small presence. Overwhelmed by Avarice and her triumphant horde of followers, Liberality nonetheless offers viewers a clear alternative.

Henry VIII probably commissioned the series.[54] Tapestry was a favorite art form for the king, who amassed an unparalleled collection. Henry must have admired the beauty and power of this weaving, and also supported the anti-clerical message implied by the figure of Simony. The king was in an introspective mood in the 1530s, reeling from his failure to produce a male heir, and the tapestry probably caused him to think about the moral choice that it presented.[55] Its four crowned misers may have especially encouraged him to consider the role greed played in his own life. Henry may have agreed that the Vices dupe mankind and that he was, as Thomas Campbell asserts, "a woeful sinner who had now seen the error of his ways."[56]

What drew the wealthy financier and banker J. Pierpont Morgan to the tapestry? Since he acquired it in 1906, the immediate impetus may have been the desire to decorate his new office and library, which Charles Follen McKim completed that year. Indeed, the tapestry was hung above the fireplace in the library. Morgan was undoubtedly drawn to it because of its fine quality, sumptuous materials, and impressive provenance.[57] (It had belonged not only to an English king, but also to a Dutch count and a Spanish monarch.) This was clearly an important acquisition for Morgan. Although he donated numerous tapestries to museums, he kept this one for himself. But did the tapestry cause Morgan, like so many merchant bankers before him, to be concerned about the state of his soul? Morgan rarely commented on why he acquired a particular work of art.[58] But evidence suggests that he may not have paid much attention to its subject. An exchange with his librarian Belle da Costa Greene reveals that he failed to recognize another work that he saw daily. (When Morgan asked Greene where the recently purchased bust of a crying infant attributed to Michelangelo was, she replied, "This bronze Bust is in your library and faces you when sitting in your chair. It has been there about a year."[59]) Moreover, because he was such a voracious collector (spending over the course of twenty years more than 900 million in today's dollars), he was probably on to his next purchase before he had a chance to savor his last one.[60]

Should magnificent works of art, like the tapestry, be appreciated solely on the basis of their beauty, their exquisite materials, their illustrious provenance, or their astounding size? Or can the ideas that they were intended to communicate still speak to us today? The medieval categorization of some poor people as "undeserving" is still pervasive. So, too, is the invocation of religious narrative and symbols to justify the extraordinary wealth of a few as well as the abject poverty of others. But other medieval ideas are less prevalent: to question our dependence on material things, to give generously to our community and the poor, to contemplate the morality of how we earn and spend money, to reflect on the forces that seem to lock some of our neighbors into poverty, in short, to consider more deeply the role that money plays in our lives and our society. We have much to learn from the medieval past.

NOTES

1. For a recent article on Fortune, see Jackson 2018.
2. For the *Confessio amantis*, see Gower 1963, Gower 2004, and Galloway 2010. For the tales under discussion see also Gallacher 1975, 153–54; Nicholson 2005, 261–62; Gower 2004, 85–88; Gower 1963, 185–88.
3. Gower 1963, 188.
4. The tale does not appear in Gower 1963. For the Middle English version see Gower 2004, 88–89.
5. Gower 2004, 88 (my translation).
6. Gower 1963, 188.
7. Gallacher 1975, 154.
8. For this manuscript, see Scott 1996, vol. 2, 322–25; Drimmer 2011. For illustrations in Gower's works, see Griffiths 1983; Pearsall 2004.
9. Drimmer 2011, 254.
10. Gower's political views are disputed. See Ferster 1996, 108.
11. For Boccaccio's *De casibus*, see Boccaccio 1962.
12. Ibid., x.
13. For Laurent de Premierfait's translation, see Smith 1934. For a transcription of his section on Poverty, see Thompson 1994, 399–400. For the original Latin, see Boccaccio 1962, 70–72.
14. My translation of Thompson 1994, p. 400.
15. For images of the combat between Fortune and Poverty, see Thompson 1994; Wüstefeld and Morcos 2015, 194. For this image, see Thompson 1994, 172. For François le Barbier, see Deldicque 2014.
16. Boccaccio 1962, xi (I, 15).
17. Hultgren 2000, 274, 278, 279.
18. For other examples in the *Speculum humanae salvationis*, see Appuhn 1989, 74–75, 115; Wilson and Lancaster Wilson 1984, 198–99, pl. III–22; Morgan, MSS M.385, fol. 42v, and M.140, fol. 42v.
19. For this manuscript, see Scott 1996, vol. 2, 138, 267; Wilson and Lancaster Wilson 1984, 46.
20. For Morgan, MS M.813, see Wieck 2004, 249–50, 253 n. 14; Hofmann 2004, 57, 60; Zöhl 2004, 560, 188.
21. For the poem's sources, see Sears 1986, 116–18.
22. For this manuscript, see Bruyant 1909; König and Bartz 2005.
23. König and Bartz 2005, vol. 2, 242 (my translation).
24. See above, p. 122, for this standard type of charity.
25. See above, p. 155.
26. "Metons a pourete largezce."
27. See above, p. 114.
28. The meaning and origin of this attribute have never been determined. See König and Bartz 2005, vol. 2, 70. Reason's mirror is often a symbol of self-reflection and wisdom. See McWebb 2001.
29. König and Bartz 2005, vol. 2, 266 (my translation).
30. Ibid., 324, 326.
31. Scott 2012, 269.
32. See above, p. 120, for this function of the poor.
33. See pp. 119–20.
34. Husband 1980, 201 (translation and original).
35. Bruyant 1909, 31; König and Bartz 2005, vol. 2, 304.
36. See König and Bartz 2005, vol. 2, 125–26, for this interpretation. The coins can be clearly seen, but Bruyant 1909, 19, misinterprets this object as a tinderbox.
37. Panofsky 1971, 76.
38. Witcombe 1998, 10.
39. For Sorgheloos see Husband 1989; Husband 1995, 88–97; Wolfthal 1989, 77–79.
40. Husband 1989, 188; de Jong 1977–78, 119, lines 96–97.
41. For this roundel, see Husband 1989. For the other versions of the composition, see Husband 1995, 97, figs. 1–2, no. 37.
42. Husband 1989, 188; de Jong 1977–78, 119, line 120.
43. Hoogewerff 1939, 333. The dog, dead cat, missing shoe, and walking stick are all standard attributes of personifications of involuntary poverty; see Tuttle 1981.
44. For the text accompanying the image of Poverty, see de Lorris and de Meun 1965–75, vol. 1, 14–25; de Lorris and de Meun 1971, 36–37; de Lorris and de Meun 1994, 9.
45. See de Lorris and de Meun 1971, 36–37; de Lorris and de Meun 1965–75, vol. 1, 14, line 442, and 15, lines 455–59.
46. For the iconography of images of Poverty in the *Roman de la rose*, see Ménard 1984, McMunn 2000, and Blamires and Holian 2002, 61–63.
47. Blamires and Holian 2002, 62.
48. See, for example, Terpstra 2019, 149–50.
49. Blamires and Holian 2002, 62. For the gesture, see fol. 13r (Lover pierced by Eros).
50. Barnum 1980, 13–14, lines 1–5; Wood 2002, 56.
51. See Cleland et al. 2014, 187–212 for this series.
52. For the tapestry's iconography, see Bauer and Steppe 1981, 67–68.
53. "SEMPER EGET SITIENS MEDIIS CEV TANTALVS VNDIS / INTER ANHELATAS SEMPER AVARVS OPES."
54. For Henry VIII's tapestry collection, see Campbell 2007, 222–26.
55. Ibid., 224.
56. Ibid., 226.
57. For Morgan's love of sumptuous materials, see Strouse 2000, 22, 28.
58. Strouse 2000, 4.
59. Ibid., 22.
60. For Morgan's art expenses, see ibid., 6.

Bibliography

Acres 1998
David Acres, "The Columba Altarpiece and the Time of the World," *Art Bulletin* 80, no. 3 (1998): 422–51.

Ainsworth 2010
Maryan Ainsworth, "Jan Gossart, Portrait of a Man (Jan Jacobsz. Snoek?)," in *Man, Myth, and Sensual Pleasures: Jan Gossart's Renaissance. The Complete Works*, edited by Maryan Ainsworth, Stijn Alsteens, and Nadine M. Orenstein, New York: The Metropolitan Museum of Art, 2010, 290–92.

Ainsworth and Christiansen 1998
Maryan Ainsworth and Keith Christiansen, eds., *From Van Eyck to Bruegel: Early Netherlandish Painting in the Metropolitan Museum of Art*, New York: The Metropolitan Museum of Art, 1998.

Alain de Lille 1965
Alain de Lille, *Textes inédits*, vol. 52, edited by M.-T. d'Alverny, Paris: Librairie philosophique Duckale, 1965.

Alain de Lille 1973
Alain de Lille, *Anticlaudianus; or, The Good and Perfect Man*, translated and with a commentary by James J. Sheridan, Toronto: Pontifical Institute of Mediaeval Studies, 1973.

Alain de Lille 2004
Alain de Lille (Alanus de Insulis), *Anticlaudianus*, edited by Massimo Sannelli, Trent: La Finestra, 2004.

Aland 1967
Kurt Aland, ed., *Martin Luther's 95 Theses*, Saint Louis and London: Concordia, 1967.

Albus 2000
Anita Albus, *The Art of Arts: Rediscovering Painting*, New York: Knopf, 2000.

Alexander 1997
Jonathan J. G. Alexander, "Art History, Literary History, and the Study of Medieval Illuminated Manuscripts," *Studies in Iconography* 18 (1997): 51–66.

Allen 2012
Martin Allen, *Mints and Money in Medieval England*, Cambridge: Cambridge University Press, 2012.

Anderson 1993
Barbara C. Anderson, "A Fifteenth-Century Illumination and the Work of Pedro de Toledo," *J. Paul Getty Museum Journal* 21 (1993): 11–28.

Appuhn 1989
Horst Appuhn, *Heilsspiegel: Die Bilder des mittelalterlichen Andachtsbuches "Speculum humanae salvationis,"* Dortmund: Harenberg, 1989.

Aquinas 1951
Thomas Aquinas, *Super evangelium s. Mattaei lectura*, edited by Raffaele Cai, Turin: Marietti, 1951.

d'Arbaumont 1865
Jules d'Arbaumont, "Nicolas Rolin, Chancelier de Bourgogne," in *Nicolas Rolin, Chancelier de Bourgogne: notice historique sur sa famille*, edited by l'abbé Boullemier, Paris: J. B. Dumoulin, 1865, 1–53.

***Archivio Stato di Siena: Museo delle Biccherne* 2014**
Accessed October 30, 2022, http://www.archiviodistato.siena.it/museobiccherne/it/5/home.

Armour 1994
Peter Armour, "Gold, Silver, and True Treasure: Economic Imagery in Dante," *Romance Studies* 23 (1994): 7–30.

van Asperen de Boer and Faries 1990
J. R. J. van Asperen de Boer and Molly Faries, "*La Vierge au Chancelier Rolin* de Van Eyck: examen au moyen de la réflectographie à l'infrarouge," *Revue du Louvre* (1990): 37–49.

Baird 1896
Henry Martyn Baird, *History of the Rise of the Huguenots of France*, vol. 1, New York: Scribner, 1896.

Bales 1983
Kevin B. Bales, "Nicole Oresme and Medieval Social Science: The Fourteenth Century Debunker of Astrology Wrote an Early Monetary Treatise," *American Journal of Economics and Sociology* 42 (1983): 101–11.

Barasch 1987
Moshe Barasch, *Giotto and the Language of Gesture*, Cambridge and New York: Cambridge University Press, 1987.

Barnum 1980
Priscilla Heath Barnum, ed., *Dives and Pauper*, vol. 1, part 2, Oxford: Oxford University Press, 1980.

Bauer and Steppe 1981
Rotraud Bauer, with Jan Karel Steppe, *Tapisserien der Renaissance nach Entwürfen von Pieter Coecke van Aelst: Ausstellung im Schloss Halbturn*, Eisenstadt: Schloss Halbturn, 1981.

Baulant 1968
Micheline Baulant, "Le prix des grains à Paris de 1431 à 1788," *Annales: Économies, Sociétés, Civilisations* 23 (1968): 520–40.

Baulant 1971
Micheline Baulant, "Le salaire des ouvriers du bâtiment à Paris de 1400 à 1726," *Annales: Économies, Sociétés, Civilisations* 26 (1971): 463–83.

Bauman 1986
Guy C. Bauman, "Early Flemish Portraits, 1425–1525," *Metropolitan Museum of Art Bulletin* 43, no. 4 (1986): 4–64.

Baumann 1996
Priscilla Baumann, "Miser and Usurer Iconography in Romanesque Auvergne: Variations on a Theme," *Misericordia International* 5, *The Profane Arts of the Middle Ages* 2 (1996): 151–60.

Beer and Woelk 2014
Manuela Beer and Moritz Woelk, eds., *The Magi: Legend, Art and Cult*, Munich: Hirmer, 2014.

Beltran 1975
E. Beltran, "Un passage du *Sophilogium* emprunté par Michault dans le *Doctrinal*," *Romania* 96 (1975): 405–12.

Bent 1992
George R. Bent, "The Scriptorium at S. Maria degli Angeli and Fourteenth Century Manuscript Illumination: Don Silvestro

dei Gherarducci, Don Lorenzo Monaco, and Giovanni del Biondo," *Zeitschrift für Kunstgeschichte* 55 (1992): 507–23.

Bernardino da Siena 1934
Bernardino da Siena, *Le prediche volgari*, vol. 1, edited by Ciro Cannarozzi, Pistoia: Alberto Pacinotti, 1934.

Bernardino da Siena 1950
Bernardino da Siena, *Opera omnia*, vol. 1, Florence: Ad Claras Aquas, 1950.

Bertolet and Epstein 2018
Craig E. Bertolet and Robert W. Epstein, eds., *Money, Commerce, and Economics in Late Medieval English Literature*, London: Palgrave MacMillan, 2018.

Bismark and Hüpper 2018
Heike Bismark and Dagmar Hüpper, "Text-Bild Kommentar," in *Der Welsche Gast, Universitäts- und Forschungsbibliothek Erfurt/Gotha: Kommentar zur Faksimile-Edition*, edited by Heike Bismark et al., Lucerne: Quaternio Verlag, 2018, 31–75.

Black 2017
Robert Black, "Dante and Avarice: Some Historical Context," in *Dante and the Seven Deadly Sins: Twelve Literary and Historical Essays*, edited by John C. Barnes and Daragh O'Connell, Dublin: Four Courts Press, 2017, 179–98.

Blamires and Holian 2002
Alcuin Blamires and Gail C. Holian, *The Romance of the Rose Illuminated: Manuscripts at the National Library of Wales*, Cardiff: University of Wales, 2002.

Blanc 2004
Monique Blanc, "L'argent, le pouvoir, l'apparat: le sac de prestige au Moyen Âge," in *Le cas du sac: histoires d'une utopie portative*, Paris: Hermès, 2004, 207–27.

Blöcker 1993
Susanne Blöcker, *Studien zur Ikonographie der Sieben Todsünden in der niederlandischen und deutschen Malerei und Graphik von 1450–1560*, Bonner Studien zur Kunstgeschichte 8, Münster and Hamburg: LIT, 1993.

Bloem 2012
Miranda Bloem, "New Light on Three Miniatures from the Egmond Breviary," *Oud Holland* 125, nos. 2–3 (2012): 69–80.

Bloem 2015
Miranda Bloem, "De Meesters van Zweder van Culemborg. De werkplaatspaktijken van een groep Noord-Nederlandse verluchters, ca. 1415–1440," PhD diss., University of Amsterdam, 2015.

Blumenkranz 1966
Bernhard Blumenkranz, *Le juif médiéval au miroir de l'art chrétien*, Paris: Études Augustiniennes, 1966.

Boccaccio 1962
Giovanni Boccaccio, *De casibus illustrium virorum*, introduced by Louis Brewer Hall, Gainesville: Scholars' Facsimiles & Reprints, 1962.

Bonaventure 1867
Bonaventure, *Opera omnia*, vol. 11, edited by A. C. Peltier, Paris: Ludovicus Vives, 1867.

Bonaventure 2005
Bonaventure, *The Life of St. Francis*, foreword by Donna Tartt, translated by Ewert Cousins, San Francisco: Harper Collins, 2005.

Boreczky 2017
Anna Boreczky, *The Budapest "Concordantiae caritatis": The Medieval Universe of a Cistercian Abbot in the Picture Book of a Viennese Councilman*, Budapest: Schöck Artprint, 2017.

Borlandi 1936
Franco Borlandi, ed., *El libro di mercatantie et usanze de' paesi*, Turin: Lattes, 1936.

Boskovits 2016
Milós Boskovits, *Italian Paintings of the Thirteenth and Fourteenth Centuries*, Collections of the National Gallery of Art Systematic Catalogue, Washington: National Gallery of Art, 2016.

Boskovits and Brown 2003
Milós Boskovits and David Alan Brown, eds., *Italian Paintings of the Fifteenth Century*, Collections of the National Gallery of Art Systematic Catalogue, Washington: National Gallery of Art, 2003.

Botticini and Eckstein 2012
Maristella Botticini and Zvi Eckstein, *The Chosen Few: How Education Shaped Jewish History, 70–1492*, Princeton: Princeton University Press, 2012.

Boulton 2014
Maureen Boulton, "The Life of Christ in Meditative Texts in Late Medieval France," in *Devotional Culture in Late Medieval England and Europe: Diverse Imaginations of Christ's Life*, edited by Stephen Kelly and Ryan Perry, Medieval Church Studies 31, Turnhout: Brepols, 2014, 127–46.

Bowron and Morton 2000
Edgar Peters Bowron and Mary G. Morton, *Masterworks of European Painting in the Museum of Fine Arts, Houston*, Houston: Museum of Fine Arts, 2000.

Boyd 1952
Catherine E. Boyd, *Tithes and Parishes in Medieval Italy: The Historical Roots of a Modern Problem*, Ithaca, NY: Cornell University Press for the American Historical Association, 1952.

Brant 1872
Sebastian Brant, *Das Narrenschiff*, edited by Karl Goedeke, Leipzig: F. U. Brockhaus, 1872.

Brieger, Meiss, and Singleton 1969
Peter Brieger, Millard Meiss, and Charles S. Singleton, *Illuminated Manuscripts of the Divine Comedy*, 2 vols., Princeton: Princeton University Press, 1969.

Brodman 2009
James Brodman, *Charity and Religion in Medieval Europe*, Washington: Catholic University of America Press, 2009.

Browning 1840
William Shergold Browning, *A History of the Huguenots*, London: Whittaker, 1840.

Bruyant 1909
Jean Bruyant, *Le livre du Chastel de Labour. A Description of an Illuminated Manuscript of the Fifteenth Century, Belonging to P.A.B. Widener, Philadelphia, with a Short Account and Synopsis of the Poem*, Philadelphia: Published privately, 1909.

Bulard 1935
Marcel Bulard, *Scorpion: symbole du peuple juif dans l'art religieux des XIVᵉ, XVᵉ, XVIᵉ siècles*, Paris: E. de Boccard, 1935.

Burckhardt 1892
Jacob Burckhardt, *The Civilisation of the Renaissance in Italy*, translated by S. G. C. Middlemore, London: Swan Sonnenschein, 1892.

van Buren and Wieck 2011
Anne H. van Buren and Roger S. Wieck, *Illuminating Fashion: Dress in the Art of Medieval France and the Netherlands, 1325–1515*, New York and London: The Morgan Library & Museum in association with D Giles Limited, 2011.

Burke 2004
Jill Burke, *Changing Patrons: Social Identity and the Visual Arts in Renaissance Florence*, University Park, PA: Penn State University Press, 2004.

Bynum 1991
Caroline Walker Bynum, *Fragmentation and Redemption: Essays on Gender and the Human Body in Medieval Religion*, New York: Zone Books, 1991.

Cabanel 2012
Patrick Cabanel, *Histoire des protestants en France (XVIᵉ-XVIᵉ siècle)*, Paris: Fayard, 2012.

Caferro 2018
William Caferro, *Petrarch's War: Florence and the Black Death in Context*, Cambridge: Cambridge University Press, 2018.

Cahill et al. 2020
Nicholas Cahill et al., "Depletion Gilding of Lydian Electrum Coins and the Sources of Lydian Gold," in *White Gold: Studies in Early Electrum Coinage*, edited by Peter van Alfen and Ute Wartenberg, New York: American Numismatic Society and The Israel Museum, Jerusalem, 2020, 291–336.

Cahn 2014
Walter Cahn, "A Late Medieval Compendium of Ancient Wisdom: Guillaume de Tignonville's 'Dits moraux des philosophes'," in *Manuscripta Illuminata: Approaches to Understanding Medieval and Renaissance Manuscripts*, edited by Colum Hourihane, Princeton and University Park, PA: Pennsylvania State University Press, 2014, 86–206.

Cahn and Marrow 1978
Walter Cahn and James Marrow, "Medieval and Renaissance Manuscripts at Yale: A Selection," *Yale University Library Gazette* 52 (1978): 173–284.

Cahn and Seidel 1979
Walter Cahn and Linda Seidel, *Romanesque Sculpture in American Collections*, vol. 1, *New England Museums*, New York: Burt Franklin, 1979.

Cahn et al. 1999
Walter Cahn et al., *Romanesque Sculpture in American Collections*, vol. 2, *New York and New Jersey, Middle and South Atlantic States, the Midwest, Western and Pacific States*, Turnhout: Brepols, 1999.

Camille 2001
Michael Camille, "'For Our Devotion and Pleasure': The Sexual Objects of Jean, Duc de Berry," *Art History* 24, no. 2 (2001): 169–94.

Campbell 2016
Bruce M. S. Campbell, *The Great Transition: Climate, Disease and Society in the Late-Medieval World*, Cambridge: Cambridge University Press, 2016.

Campbell 1995
Jeffrey Campbell, "The *Ars Moriendi*: An Examination, Translation, and Collation of the Manuscripts of the Shorter Latin Version," MA thesis, School of Graduate Studies, University of Ottawa, 1995.

Campbell 2007
Thomas P. Campbell, *Henry VIII and the Art of Majesty: Tapestries at the Tudor Court*, New Haven: Yale University Press, 2007.

Capriotti 2014
Giuseppe Capriotti, *Lo scorpione sul petto: iconografia antiebraica tra XV e XVI secolo alla periferia dello Stato Pontifcio*, Rome: Gangemi, 2014.

Cary 1956
George Cary, *The Medieval Alexander*, edited by D. J. A. Ross, Cambridge: Cambridge University Press, 1956.

Ceccanti and Castelli 1992
Melania Ceccanti and Maria Cristina Castelli, *Il codice miniato: rapporti tra codice, testo e figurazione*, Storia della miniatura: studi e documenti 7, Florence: Leo S. Olschki, 1992.

Chambers 1903
Edmund Kerchever Chambers, *The Mediæval Stage*, vol. 2, London: Oxford University Press, 1903.

Charron, Gautier, and Girault 2013
Pascale Charron, Marc-Édouard Gautier, and Pierre-Gilles Girault, eds., *Trésors enluminés des musées de France: pays de la Loire et Centre*, Angers: Musée des beaux-arts / Paris: Institut national d'histoire de l'art, 2013.

Chastellain 1836–66
Georges Chastellain, *Œuvres*, vol. 3, *Grande Chronique des Ducs de Burgoyne*, edited by M. le baron Kervyn de Lettenhove, Brussels: F. Heussner, 1836–66.

Châtelet 2002
Albert Châtelet, "Un traité de bonnes mœurs écrit et illustré dans une période tourmentée," *Art de l'enluminure* 1 (Summer 2002): 40–62.

Christiansen, Kanter, and Strehlke 1989
Keith Christiansen, Laurence B. Kanter, and Carl Brandon Strehlke, *Painting in Renaissance Siena 1420–1500*, New York: The Metropolitan Museum of Art, 1989.

Church Music Association of America 2012
Church Music Association of America, *The Parish Book of Chant: A Manual of Gregorian Chant and a Liturgical Resource for Scholars and Congregations; Including Order of Sung Mass for both Ordinary and Extraordinary Forms of the Roman Rite; with a Complete Kyriale, along with Chants and Hymns for Occasional and Seasonal Use and their Literal English Translations*, Richmond, VA: Church Music Association of America, 2012.

Cicero 1928
Cicero, *De officiis*, translated by Walter Miller, Loeb Classical Library, London and New York: William Heinemann and G. P. Putnam's, 1928.

Cicero 1966
Cicero's Offices, with Laelius, Cato Maior, and Select Letters, introduced by John Warrington, London: Dent / New York: Dutton, 1966.

Cipolla 1956
Carlo M. Cipolla, *Money, Prices and Civilisation in the Mediterranean World: Fifth to Seventeenth Century*, Princeton: Princeton University Press, 1956.

Cipolla 1994
Carlo M. Cipolla, *Before the Industrial Revolution: European Society and Economy, 1000–1700*, 3rd edition, New York: Norton, 1994.

Clark and Sponsler 1999
Robert Clark and Claire Sponsler, "Othered Bodies: Racial Cross-Dressing in the *Mistere de la Sainte Hostie* and the Croxton Play of the Sacrament," *Journal of Medieval and Early Modern Studies* 29, no. 1 (1999): 61–87.

Clark 1997
Stuart Clark, *Thinking with Demons: The Idea of Witchcraft in Early Modern Europe*, Oxford and New York: Oxford University Press, 1997.

Cleland et al. 2014
Elizabeth H. Cleland et al., *Grand Design: Pieter Coecke van Aelst and Renaissance Tapestry*, New York: The Metropolitan Museum of Art, 2014.

Cloisters 1975
The Cloisters, Metropolitan Museum of Art, *The Secular Spirit: Life and Art at the End of the Middle Ages*, New York: E. P. Dutton and The Metropolitan Museum of Art, 1975.

Clubb 1953
Merrel Dare Clubb, Jr., "The Middle English 'Pilgrimage of the Soul': An Edition of Manuscript Egerton 615," PhD diss., University of Michigan, 1953.

Cohn 2002
Samuel K. Cohn, Jr., *The Black Death: Disease and Culture in Early Renaissance Europe*, New York: Oxford University Press, 2002.

Cohn 2018
Samuel K. Cohn, Jr., *Epidemics: Hate and Compassion from the Plague of Athens to AIDS*. Oxford: Oxford University Press, 2018.

Cottret 2000
Bernard Cottret, *Calvin: A Biography*, Grand Rapids, MI: Wm. B. Eerdmans / Edinburgh: T & T Clark, 2000.

Coulton 1925
George C. Coulton, *The Medieval Village*, Cambridge: Cambridge University Press, 1925.

Cribb 1986
Joe Cribb, ed., *Money: From Cowries to Credit Cards*, London: British Museum, 1986.

Cribb 2004
Joe Cribb, "The Origins of Money: Evidence from the Ancient Near East and Egypt," in *La banca premonetale: contributi culturali e storici intorno alle prime forme di transazione monetaria*, edited by Guido Crapanzano, Milan: Art Valley, 2004, 79–122.

Cribb 2005
Joe Cribb, "Money as Metaphor 1—Money is Justice: The Origins of Money and Coinage," Royal Numismatic Society Presidential Address 2005, *Numismatic Chronicle* (2005): 417–38.

Cribb and Williams 1997
Joe Cribb and Jonathan Williams, "Who Made the First Coins?" *British Museum Magazine* 27 (1997): 18–20.

Crusafont, Balaguer, and Grierson 2013
Miquel Crusafont, Anna M. Balaguer, and Philip Grierson, *Medieval European Coinage with a Catalogue of the Coins in the Fitzwilliam Museum, Cambridge*, vol. 6, *The Iberian Peninsula*, Cambridge: Cambridge University Press, 2013.

Curzer 2012
Howard J. Curzer, *Aristotle and the Virtues*, Oxford: Oxford University Press, 2012.

D'Amico and Grandi 1987
Rosalba D'Amico and Renzo Grandi, eds., *Il tramonto del medioevo a Bologna: il cantiere di San Petronio*, Bologna: Nuova Alfa Editoriale, 1987.

Dante 2000
Dante, *The Inferno*, edited and translated by Robert and Jean Hollander, New York: Random House, 2000.

Davies 2005
Glyn Davies, *A History of Money: From Ancient Times to the Present Day*, 3rd revised edition, Cardiff: University of Wales Press, 2005.

Deferrari 1952
Roy J. Deferrari, ed., *The Fathers of the Church: The Early Christian Biographies*, vol. 15, translated by Roy J. Ferrari et al., New York: Fathers of the Church, 1952.

de Deguileville 1992
Guillaume de Deguileville, *The Pilgrimage of Human Life (Le Pèlerinage de la vie humaine)*, translated by Eugene Clasby, Garland Library of Medieval Literature 76, series B, New York and London: Garland, 1992.

Delcorno 2018
Pietro Delcorno, *In the Mirror of the Prodigal Son: The Pastoral Uses of a Biblical Narrative (c. 1200–1550)*, Leiden and Boston: Brill, 2018.

Deldicque 2014
Mathieu Deldicque, "L'enluminure à Paris à la fin du XVᵉ siècle: Maître François, le Maître de Jacques de Besançon et Jacques de Besançon identifiés," *Revue de l'art* 183, no. 1 (2014): 9–18.

Derbes and Sandona 2008
Anne Derbes and Mark Sandona, *The Usurer's Heart: Giotto, Enrico Scrovegni, and the Arena Chapel in Padua*, University Park, PA: Pennsylvania State University Press, 2008.

Dhanens 1980
Elisabeth Dhanens, *Hubert and Jan van Eyck*, New York: Alpine, 1980.

Dorin 2015
Rowan William Dorin, "Banishing Usury: The Expulsion of Foreign Moneylenders in Medieval Europe, 1200–1450," PhD diss., Harvard University, 2015.

Dorin 2020
Rowan Dorin, "On Myths and Moneylenders," *Marginalia*, May 22, 2020, accessed June 5, 2022, https://themarginalireview.com/on-myths-and-moneylenders/.

Douteil 2010
Herbert Douteil, *Die "Concordantiae caritatis" des Ulrich von Lilienfeld: Edition des Codex Campililiensis 151 (um 1355)*, edited by Rudolf Suntrup, Arnold Angenendt, and Volker Honemann, 2 vols., Münster: Verlag Aschendorff, 2010.

Drimmer 2011
Sonja Drimmer, "The Visual Language of Vernacular Manuscript Illumination: John Gower's 'Confessio Amantis' (Pierpont Morgan Ms. M. 126)," PhD diss., Columbia University, 2011.

Drogin 2010
David J. Drogin, "Art, Patronage, and Civic Identities in Renaissance Bologna," in *The Court Cities of Northern Italy*, edited by Charles M. Rosenberg, Cambridge: Cambridge University Press, 2010, 244–324.

Dückers 2005
Rob Dückers, "The Limbourg Brothers and the North: Book Illumination and Panel Painting in the Guelders Region 1380–1435," in *The Limbourg Brothers: Nijmegen Masters at the French Court, 1400–1416*, edited by Rob Dückers and Pieter Roelofs, Ghent: Ludion, 2005, 65–83.

Dückers and Priem 2009
Rob Dückers and Ruud Priem, eds., *The Hours of Catherine of Cleves: Devotions, Demons and Daily Life in the Fifteenth Century*, Antwerp: Ludion, 2009.

Du Clercq 1838
Jacques Du Clercq, *Choix de chroniques et mémoires sur l'histoire de France / XVᵉ siècle*, edited by J. A. C. Buchon, Paris: Auguste Desrez, 1838.

Dudden 1905
Frederick Homes Dudden, *Gregory the Great: His Place in History and Thought*, vol. 1, London: Longmans & Co., 1905.

Dummett 1986
Michael A. E. Dummett, *The Visconti-Sforza Tarot Cards*, New York: G. Braziller, 1986.

Duplessy 1988
Jean Duplessy, *Les monnaies françaises royales, de Hugues Capet à Louis XVI (987–1793)*, vol. 1, *Hugues Capet–Louis XII*, Paris and Maastricht: Maison Platt and A. G. van der Dussen, 1988.

Ebrey, Schirokauer, and Hansen 2022
Patricia Ebrey, Conrad Schirokauer, and Valerie Hansen, "The Song Economic Revolution," in *China in 1000 CE: The Most Advanced Society in the World*, 2022, accessed August 26, 2022, http://afe.easia.columbia.edu/songdynasty-module/econ-rev-money.html.

Eder 1915
Robert Eder, "Tignonvillana inedita," *Romanische Forschungen* 33 (1915): 851–1022.

Edwards 2018
Elizabeth Edwards, "Money and Literature," in *Money and Coinage in the Middle Ages*, edited by Rory Naismith, Leiden and Boston: Brill, 2018, 264–86.

Eichberger 1992
Dagmar Eichberger, "Image Follows Text? *The Visions of Tondal* and Its Relationship to Depictions of Hell and Purgatory in Fifteenth-Century Illuminated Manuscripts," in *Margaret of York, Simon Marmion, and "The Visions of Tondal,"* edited by Thomas Kren, Malibu: The J. Paul Getty Museum, 1992, 129–40.

Einzig 1966
Paul Einzig, *Primitive Money in Its Ethnological, Historical and Economic Aspects*, 2nd edition, Oxford and New York: Pergamon Press, 1966.

Eisermann 2006
Falk K. Eisermann, "The Indulgence as a Media Event: Developments in Communication through Broadsides in the Fifteenth Century," in *Promissory Notes on the Treasury of Merits: Indulgences in*

Late Medieval Europe, edited by Robert N. Swanson, Leiden and Boston: Brill, 2006, 309–30.

Ellard 1943
Gerald Ellard, "Bread in the Form of a Penny," *Theological Studies* 4 (1943): 319–46.

Emmerson 2009
Richard K. Emmerson, "Translating Images: Images and Poetic Reception in French, English, and Latin Versions of Guillaume de Deguileville's *Trois pèlerinages*," in *Poetry, Place and Gender: Studies in Medieval Culture in Honor of Helen Damico*, edited by Catherine E. Karkov, Kalamazoo, MI: Medieval Institute Publications, 2009, 275–301.

Epstein 1991
Steven A. Epstein, *Wage Labor and Guilds in Medieval Europe*, Chapel Hill: University of North Carolina Press, 1991.

Epstein 2009
Steven A. Epstein, *An Economic and Social History of Later Medieval Europe, 1000–1500*, Cambridge: Cambridge University Press, 2009.

Eskelson 2021
Tyrel C. Eskelson, "States, Institutions, and Literacy Rates in Early-Modern Western Europe," *Journal of Education and Learning* 10, no. 2 (2021): 109–23.

Faccin 1955
Dominic Faccin, *Spiritual Exercises according to Saint Bonaventure*, New York: Franciscan Institute, 1955.

Falkenburg 2006
Reindert Falkenburg, "Speculative Imagery in Petrarch's *Von der Artzney Bayder Glueck* (1532)," in *Petrarch and His Readers in the Renaissance*, edited by Karl A. E. Enenkel and Jan Papy, Leiden and Boston: Brill, 2006, 171–89.

Feliu 2018
Gaspar Feliu, "Money and Currency," in *Money and Coinage in the Middle Ages*, edited by Rory Naismith, Leiden and Boston: Brill, 2018, 21–40.

Ferster 1996
Judith Ferster, *Fictions of Advice: The Literature and Politics of Late Medieval England*, Philadelphia: University of Pennsylvania Press, 1996.

Filedt Kok 2008
J. P. Filedt Kok, "Master of Alkmaar, Polyptych with the Seven Works of Charity, 1504," in *Early Netherlandish Paintings*, edited by J. P. Filedt Kok, Rijksmusuem Amsterdam online collection catalogue, 2008, accessed March 14, 2019, hdl.handle.net/10934/RM0001.COLLECT.9048.

Fisher 2013
Will Fisher, "The Erotics of Chin Chucking in Seventeenth-Century England," in *Sex before Sex: Figuring the Act in Early Modern England*, edited by James M. Bromley and Will Stockton, Minneapolis and London: University of Minnesota Press, 2013, 141–69.

Flora 2008
Holly Flora, "The Charity of the Virgin Mary in the Paris *Meditations of the Life of Christ* (BnF ital. 11)," *Studies in Iconography* 29 (2008): 55–89.

Fox 1909
J. Shirley Fox, "Die-Making in the Twelfth Century," *British Numismatic Journal* 6 (1909): 191–96.

Frank 1950
Edgar B. Frank, *Old French Ironwork: The Craftsman and His Art*, Cambridge, MA: Harvard University Press, 1950.

Freedman 2008
Paul Freedman, *Out of the East: Spices and the Medieval Imagination*, New Haven: Yale University Press, 2008.

Freuler 1994
Gaudenz Freuler, "Don Silvestro dei Gherarducci," in *Painting and Illumination: Early Renaissance Florence, 1300–1450*, edited by Laurence B. Kanter et al., New York: The Metropolitan Museum of Art, 1994, 124–76.

Friedel 2007
Robert Friedel, *A Culture of Improvement: Technology and the Western Millennium*, Cambridge, MA: MIT Press, 2007.

Frühmorgen-Voss, Ott, and Bodemann 1996
Hella Frühmorgen-Voss, Norbert H. Ott, and Ulrike Bodemann, *Katalog der deutschsprachigen illustrierten Handschriften des Mittelalters*, vol. 2, fascicle 4, Munich: Verlag C. H. Beck, 1996.

Frühmorgen-Voss, Ott, and Bodemann 2008
Hella Frühmorgen-Voss, Norbert H. Ott, and Ulrike Bodemann, *Katalog der deutschsprachigen illustrierten Handschriften des Mittelalters*, vol. 4/1, fascicle 1/2, Munich: Verlag C. H. Beck, 2008.

Galbraith 1975
John Kenneth Galbraith, *Money: Whence It Came, Where It Went*, Boston: Houghton Mifflin, 1975.

Gallacher 1975
Patrick J. Gallacher, *Love, the Word, and Mercury: A Reading of John Gower's "Confessio Amantis,"* Albuquerque: University of New Mexico Press, 1975.

Galloway 2010
Andrew Galloway, "John Gower," in *Oxford Bibliographies*, last modified December 15, 2010, accessed August 8, 2019, https://www.oxfordbibliographies.com/view/document/obo-9780195396584/obo-9780195396584-0017.xml?rskey=y4qYeX&result=1&q=John+Gower#firstMatch.

Garnier 1982
François Garnier, *Le langage de l'image au moyen âge: signification et symbolique*, Paris: Le Léopard d'Or, 1982.

Geary 2010
Patrick J. Geary, ed., *Readings in Medieval History*, 4th edition, Toronto: University of Toronto Press, 2010.

Geggel 2021a
Laura Geggel, "6,500 Medieval Coins and Rare Gold Rings Unearthed in Polish Cornfield," *Live Science*, January 26, 2021, accessed December 23, 2021, https://www.livescience.com/medieval-polish-hoard.html.

Geggel 2021b
Laura Geggel, "Medieval Gold Coin Hoards and Skull Ring Discovered in Wales," *Live Science*, April 7, 2021, accessed December 23, 2021, https://www.livescience.com/uk-metal-detector-medieval-treasures.html.

van Gelder and Hoc 1960
Hendrik Enno van Gelder and Marcel Hoc, *Les monnaies des Pays-Bas bourguignons et espagnols, 1434–1713: répertoire général*, Amsterdam: J. Schulman, 1960.

Gilomen 1990
Hans-Jörg Gilomen, "Wucher und Wirtschaft im Mittelalter," *Historische Zeitschrift* 250 (1990): 265–301.

Gilomen 2010
Hans-Jörg Gilomen, "Kredit und Innovation im Spätmittelalter," *Aufbruch im Mittelalter – Innovation in Gesellschaften der Vormoderne: Studien zu Ehren von Rainer C. Schwinges*, edited by Christian Hesse and Klaus Oschema, Ostfildern: Universitätsbibliothek, 2010, 35–68.

Goddard 2014
Richard Goddard, "The Merchant," in *Historians on Chaucer: The "General Prologue" to the "Canterbury Tales,"* edited by Stephen Henry Rigby, Oxford: Oxford University Press, 2014, 170–86.

Godefroy 1885
Frédéric Godefroy, *Dictionnaire de l'ancienne langue française*, vol. 4, Paris: F. Vieweg, 1885.

Godefroy 1892
Frédéric Godefroy, *Dictionnaire de l'ancienne langue française*, vol. 7, Paris: Émile Bouillon, 1892.

Goldberg 2012
Jessica L. Goldberg, *Trade and Institutions in the Medieval Mediterranean: The Geniza Merchants and Their Business World*, Cambridge: Cambridge University Press, 2012.

Goldthwaite 2009
Richard A. Goldthwaite, *The Economy of Renaissance Florence*, Baltimore: Johns Hopkins University Press, 2009.

Gorissen 1973
Friedrich Gorissen, *Das Stundenbuch der Katharina von Kleve: Analyse und Kommentar*, Berlin: Gebr. Mann Verlag, 1973.

Goubitz 2007
Olaf Goubitz, *Purses in Pieces: Archaeological Finds of Late Medieval and Sixteenth-Century Leather Purses, Pouches, Bags, and Cases in the Netherlands*, Zwolle: SPA Uitgevers, 2007.

Gower 1963
John Gower, *Confessio Amantis (The Lover's Shrift)*, translated by Terence Tiller, Baltimore: Penguin Books, 1963.

Gower 2004
John Gower, *Confessio amantis*, vol. 3, ed. Russell A. Peck, translated by Andrew Galloway, Kalamazoo: Medieval Institute Publications, 2004.

de Graaf 1994
Cor de Graaf, "Muntmeesters en muntschenners, vervalsers en wisselaars: muntgewichten en muntweegapparatus in de Nederlanden," in *Gewogen of bedrogen: het wegen van geld in de Nederlanden*, edited by Marloes Huiskamp and Cor de Graaf, Leiden: Waanders, 1994, 57–94.

Grebe 2001
Anja Grebe, "The Art of the Edge: Frames and Page-Design in Manuscripts of the Ghent-Brussels School," in *The Metamorphosis of Marginal Images*, edited by Nurith Kenaan-Kedar and Asher Ovadiah, Tel Aviv: Tel Aviv University, 2001, 83–102.

Greif 2006
Avner Greif, *Institutions and the Path to the Modern Economy: Lessons from Medieval Trade*, Cambridge: Cambridge University Press, 2006.

Grierson 1975
Philip Grierson, *Numismatics*, London: Oxford University Press, 1975.

Grierson 1977
Philip Grierson, *The Origins of Money*, London: Athlone Press, 1977.

Griffiths 1983
Jeremy Griffiths, "Gower's 'Confessio Amantis': The Poem and Its Pictures," in *Gower's "Confessio Amantis": Responses and Reassessments*, edited by A. J. Minnis, Cambridge: D. S. Brewer, 1983, 163–78.

Grunzweig 1931
A. Grunzweig, *Correspondance de la filiale de Bruges des Medici*, Brussels: Maurice Lamertin, 1931.

Guest 1995
Gerald Guest, "A Discourse on the Poor: The Hours of Jeanne d'Evreux," *Viator* 26 (1995): 153–80.

Halbertal 2021
Moshe Halbertal, "Medieval Judaism and the Roots of the Welfare State," *Sapir: A Journal of Jewish Conversations* 1 (Spring 2021), accessed January 18, 2022, https://sapirjournal.org/social-justice/2021/05/medieval-judaism-and-the-roots-of-the-welfare-state/.

Hamburger 2005
Jeffrey F. Hamburger, "Biblia Pauperum," in *The Splendor of the Word: Medieval and Renaissance Illuminated Manuscripts at the New York Public Library*, edited by Jonathan J. G. Alexander, James H. Marrow, and Lucy Freeman Sandler, New York: New York Public Library, 2005, 128–32.

Hamburger et al. 2016
Jeffrey F. Hamburger et al., eds., *Beyond Words: Illuminated Manuscripts in Boston Collections*, Boston: McMullen Museum of Art, Boston College, 2016.

Hamburger, Suckale, and Suckale-Redlefsen 2018
Jeffrey F. Hamburger, Robert Suckale, and Gude Suckale-Redlefsen, eds., *Painting the Page in the Age of Print: Central European Manuscript Illumination of the Fifteenth Century*, Toronto: PIMS, 2018.

Hand and Wolff 1986
John Oliver Hand and Martha Wolff, *Early Netherlandish Painting*, Washington: National Gallery of Art, 1986.

Hand 2014
Joni M. Hand, *Women, Manuscripts and Identity in Northern Europe, 1350–1550*, London: Routledge, 2014.

Harbison 1991
Craig Harbison, *Jan van Eyck: The Play of Realism*, London: Reaktion Books, 1991.

Harrsen 1943
Meta Harrsen, "Figural Grisaille Ornament on a Historiated Initial of about 1400, and the Derivation of this Style from the Indulgences of Avignon," in *Bookmen's Holiday: Notes and Studies Written and Gathered in Tribute to Harry Miller Lydenberg*, New York: New York Public Library, 1943, 316–22.

Hatfield 1970
Rab Hatfield, "The Compagnia de' Magi," *Journal of the Warburg and Courtauld Institutes* 33 (1970): 107–61.

Hayes 1999
Dawn Marie Hayes, "Mundane Uses of Sacred Places in the Central and Later Middle Ages, with a Focus on Chartres Cathedral," *Comitatus: A Journal of Medieval and Renaissance Studies* 30, no. 1 (1999): 11–37.

Heck and Cordonnier 2018
Christian Heck and Rémy Cordonnier, *The Grand Medieval Bestiary: Animals in Illuminated Manuscripts*, New York: Abbeville Press, 2018.

Heng 2018
Geraldine Heng, *The Invention of Race in the European Middle Ages*, Cambridge and New York: Cambridge University Press, 2018.

Herrad of Landsberg 1977
Herrad of Landsberg, *Hortus Deliciarum (Garden of Delights)*, commentary and notes by A. Straub and G. Keller, edited and translated by Aristide D. Caratzas, New Rochelle, NY: Caratzas Brothers, 1977.

Hillerbrand 1964
Hans J. Hillerbrand, *The Reformation: A Narrative History Related by Contemporary Observers and Participants*, London: SCM Press, 1964.

Hinckeldey 1980
Christoph Hinckeldey, *Strafjustiz in alter Zeit: Schriftenreihe des Mittelalterlichen Kriminalmuseums Rothenburg ob der Tauber*, vol. 3, Rothenburg ob der Tauber: Mittelalterliches Kriminalmuseum, 1980.

Hindman and Bergeron-Foote 2014
Sandra Hindman and Ariane Bergeron-Foote, *Flowering of Medieval French Literature*, Paris: Les Enluminures, 2014.

Hirsch, Kett, and Trefil 2002
Eric Donald Hirsch, Joseph F. Kett, and James Trefil, *The New Dictionary of Cultural Literacy*, Boston and New York: Houghton Mifflin, 2002.

Hoffeld 1969
Jeffrey M. Hoffeld, "The Art of the Medieval Blacksmith," *Metropolitan Museum of Art Bulletin*, new series, 28, no. 4 (Dec. 1969): 161–73.

Hoffmann 2014
Richard C. Hoffmann, *An Environmental History of Medieval Europe*, Cambridge: Cambridge University Press, 2014.

Hofmann 2004
Mara Hofmann, *Jean Poyer: Das Gesamtwerk*, Ars Nova 7, Turnhout: Brepols, 2004.

Hoogewerff 1939
G. J. Hoogewerff, *De Noord-Nederlandsche Schilderkunst*, part 3, The Hague: Martinus Nijhoff, 1939.

Horner and Horner 1873
Joanna Horner and Susan Horner, *Walks in Florence*, vol. 1, London: Strahan, 1873.

Horrox 1994
Rosemary Horrox, ed. and trans., *The Black Death*, Manchester Medieval Sources, Manchester and New York: Manchester University Press, 1994.

Howgego 1995
Christopher Howgego, *Ancient History from Coins*, 2nd edition, Oxford and New York: Routledge, 1995.

Hultgren 2000
Arland J. Hultgren, *The Parables of Jesus: A Commentary*, Grand Rapids, MI, and Cambridge: William B. Eerdmans, 2000.

Husband 1980
Timothy Husband, *The Wild Man: Medieval Myth and Symbolism*, New York: The Metropolitan Museum of Art, 1980.

Husband 1989
Timothy Husband, "'Ick Sorgheloose ...': A Silver-Stained Roundel in The Cloisters," *Metropolitan Museum of Art Bulletin* 24 (1989): 173–88.

Husband 1991
Timothy Husband, "Introduction," in *Stained Glass before 1700 in American Collections: Silver-Stained Roundels and Unipartite Panels*, edited by Timothy Husband and Madeline Caviness, Washington: National Gallery of Art, 1991, 15–33.

Husband 1995
Timothy Husband, *The Luminous Image: Painted Glass Roundels in the Lowlands, 1480–1560*, New York: The Metropolitan Museum of Art, 1995.

Husband 2015
Timothy Husband, *The World in Play: Luxury Cards 1430–1540*, New York: The Metropolitan Museum of Art, 2015.

Husband and Caviness 1991
Timothy Husband and Madeline Caviness, eds., *Stained Glass before 1700 in American Collections: Silver-Stained Roundels and Unipartite Panels*, Corpus Vitrearum Checklist IV, Studies in the History of Art 39, Washington: National Gallery of Art, 1991.

Huygebaert et al. 2016
Stefan Huygebaert et al., eds., *The Art of Law: Three Centuries of Justice Depicted*, translated by Myra Wilkinson, Tielt: Lannoo, 2016.

Ifft Decker 2020
Sarah Ifft Decker, "Complicating Myths: Moneylending in Iberia," *Marginalia*, May 22, 2020, accessed June 5, 2022, https://themarginaliareview.com/complicating-myths-moneylending-in-iberia/.

Ijpelaar 2010
Linda Ijpelaar, "De randversiering in het getijdenboek van Katherina van Kleef: een onderzoek naar de interpretatieverschillen," BA thesis, University of Amsterdam, 2010.

Iskin 1995
Ruth E. Iskin, "Selling, Seduction, and Soliciting the Eye: Manet's *Bar at the Folies Bergère*," *Art Bulletin* 77 (1995): 25–44.

Jackson 2010
Deirdre Jackson, *Lion*, London: Reaktion Books, 2010.

Jackson 2015
Deirdre Jackson, *Medieval Women*, London: British Library, 2015.

Jackson 2018
Deirdre Jackson, "The Colours of Fortune," in *Manuscripts in the Making: Art and Science*, edited by Stella Panayotova and Paolo Ricciardi, London and Turnhout: Harvey Miller / Brepols, 2018, 43–53.

Jacobi 2019
Lauren Jacobi, *The Architecture of Banking in Renaissance Italy: Constructing the Spaces of Money*, Cambridge and New York: Cambridge University Press, 2019.

"Jew, v[*erb*]." 2019
"Jew, *v.*," OED Online, Third Edition, 2019 (modified 2022), accessed August 24, 2022, https://www.oed.com/view/Entry/101211.

Johansen and Mann 2000
Bruce E. Johansen and Barbara A. Mann, eds., *Encyclopedia of the Haudenosaunee*, London: Greenwood Press, 2000.

Johns 1907
Claude H. W. Johns, "A Marriage Contract from Chabour," *Proceedings of the Society of Biblical Archaeology* 29 (1907): 177–84.

Johnston 2011
Ruth A. Johnston, *All Things Medieval: An Encyclopedia of the Medieval World*, Santa Barbara, CA: Greenwood, 2011.

Jones 1987
E. L. Jones, *The European Miracle: Environments, Economies, and Geopolitics in the History of Europe and Asia*, 2nd edition, Cambridge: Cambridge University Press, 1987.

de Jong 1977–78
P. J. de Jong, "Sorgheloos, een zestiende eeuwse rijmprentenreeks: tekst en commentaar," *Spektator* 7, no. 2 (1977–78): 104–20.

Jordan 1996
William Chester Jordan, *The Great Famine: Northern Europe in the Early Fourteenth Century*, Princeton: Princeton University Press, 1996.

Kaftal 1952
George Kaftal, *Iconography of the Saints in Tuscan Painting*, Florence: Le Lettere, 1952.

Kaplan 1978
Stuart R. Kaplan, *The Encyclopedia of Tarot*, vol. 1, Stamford, CT: U.S. Games Systems, 1978.

Karlowska-Kamzowa 1997
Alicja Karlowska-Kamzowa, "L'évolution des illustrations du *Jeu des Echecs* de Jacques de Cessols à Paris, dans la IIe moitié du XIVe siècle," translated by Katarzyna Dybel, in *Jeux de la variante dans l'art et la littérature du Moyen Âge: mélanges offerts à Anna Drzewiecka par ses collègues, ses amis et ses élèves*, Krakow: Bartosz, 1997, 242–49.

Kauffmann 1994
C. M. Kauffmann, "Art and Popular Culture: New Themes in the Holkham Bible Picture Book," in *Studies in Medieval Art and Architecture Presented to Peter Lasko*, edited by D. Buckton and T. A. Heslop, Stroud and London: Alan Sutton, 1994, 46–69.

Kedar 1976
Benjamin Z. Kedar, *Merchants in Crisis: Genoese and Venetian Men of Affairs and the Fourteenth-Century Depression*, New Haven: Yale University Press, 1976.

Keene 2021
Bryan C. Keene, "Bolognese Narrative Painting around the Time of Papal Legate Bertrand du Pouget (1327–1334)," in *Medieval Bologna: Art for a University City*, edited by Trinita Kennedy, Nashville: Frist Art Museum, 2021, 73–85.

Kelsey 2019
Penelope Myrtle Kelsey, *Reading the Wampum: Essays on Hodinöhsö:ni' Visual Code and Epistemological Recovery*, Syracuse, NY: Syracuse University Press, 2019.

Kent 2000
Dale Kent, *Cosimo de' Medici and the Florentine Renaissance: The Patron's Oeuvre*, New Haven: Yale University Press, 2000.

Kent 1978
John Kent, *2000 Years of British Coins and Medals*, London: British Museum Publications, 1978.

Kerschner and Konuk 2020
Michael Kerschner and Koray Konuk, "Electrum Coins and Their Archaeological Context: The Case of the Artemision of Ephesus," in *White Gold: Studies in Early Electrum Coinage*, edited by Peter van Alfen and Ute Wartenberg, New York: American Numismatic Society and The Israel Museum, Jerusalem, 2020, 83–190.

Kisch 1960
Bruno Kisch, *Gewichte- und Waagemacher im alten Köln*, Cologne: Verlag der Löwe, 1960.

Kisch 1965
Bruno Kisch, *Scales and Weights: A Historical Outline*, New Haven and London: Yale University Press, 1965.

Koerkamp 2019
Joyce Klein Koerkamp, "Man Weighing Gold," last modified 2019, accessed January 1, 2020, https://www.metmuseum.org/art/collection/search/436722.

Koldeweij 2006
Jos Koldeweij, *Geloof en geluk: sieraad en devotie in middeleeuws Vlaanderen*, Arnheim: Terra Vanno, 2006.

König and Bartz 2005
Eberhard König and Gabriele Bartz, *Das Buch vom erfüllten Leben: Jacques Bruyant, Le livre du Chastel de labour*, 2 vols., Lucerne: Faksimile Verlag, 2005.

Koslow 1975
Susan Koslow, "Frans Hals's Fisherboys: Exemplars of Idleness," *Art Bulletin* 57, no. 3 (1975): 418–32.

Kren 1983
Thomas Kren, *Renaissance Painting in Manuscripts: Treasures from the British Library*, New York: Hudson Hills Press, 1983.

Kren and McKendrick 2003
Thomas Kren and Scot McKendrick, *Illuminating the Renaissance: The Triumph of Flemish Manuscript Painting in Europe*, Los Angeles: J. Paul Getty Museum, 2003.

Kumler 2011
Aden Kumler, "The Multiplication of the Species: Eucharistic Morphology in the Middle Ages," *RES* 59/60 (Spring/Autumn 2011): 179–91.

Kuroda 2020
Akinobu Kuroda, *A Global History of Money*, Oxford and New York: Routledge, 2020.

Lacoste et al. 2012
Debra Lacoste et al., eds., *Cantus: A Database for Latin Ecclesiastical Chant – Inventories of Chant Sources*, 2012, accessed August 24, 2022, https://cantus.uwaterloo.ca/.

Lacroix 1890
Abbé E. Lacroix, *Le Miracle de la Sainte Hostie de 1290, à Paris*, Paris: Dumoulin, 1890.

Lafaurie 1951
Jean Lafaurie, *Les monnaies des rois de France: Hugues Capet à Louis XII*, Paris and Basel: Émile Bourgey / Monnaies et Médailles, 1951.

Lammertse 2016
Friso Lammertse, "The Pilgrimage of Life Triptych," in *Bosch: The 5th Centenary Exhibition*, edited by Pilar Silva Maroto, Madrid: Museo Nacional del Prado, 2016, 292–301.

Landau and Parshall 1994
David Landau and Peter Parshall, *The Renaissance Print, 1470–1550*, New Haven and London: Yale University Press, 1994.

Langholm 1983
Odd Inge Langholm, *Wealth and Money in the Aristotelian Tradition: A Study in Scholastic Economic Sources*, Bergen: Universitetsforlagen, 1983.

Langholm 2015
Odd Inge Langholm, "A Herald of Scholasticism: Alan of Lille on Economic Virtue," in *Money and the Church in Medieval Europe, 1000–1200: Practice, Morality, and Thought*, edited by Giles E. M. Gasper and Svein H. Gullbekk, Farnham, England, and Burlington, VT: Ashgate, 2015, 93–104.

Leclercq-Marx 2007
Jacqueline Leclercq-Marx, "Le rapport au gain illicite dans la sculpture romane: entre réalités socio-économiques, contacts de culture et réseaux métaphoriques," *Cahiers de civilisation médiévale* 50 (2007): 43–63.

Le Goff 1984
Jacques Le Goff, *The Birth of Purgatory*, translated by Arthur Goldhammer, Chicago : University of Chicago Press, 1984.

Le Goff 1988
Jacques Le Goff, *Your Money or Your Life: Economy and Religion in the Middle Ages*, translated by Patricia Ranum, New York: Zone Books, 1988.

Lehnertz et al. forthcoming
Andreas Lehnertz et al., eds., *Jewish Craftspeople in the Middle Ages*, Berlin and Boston: De Gruyter, forthcoming.

Lemaire 1993
Claudine Lemaire, "Les manuscrits de Jean II, comte d'Oettingen, ou la fin d'une légende," in *Miscellanea Martin Wittek: album de codicologie et de paléographie offert à Martin Wittek*, edited by Anny Raman and Eugène Manning, Louvain and Paris: Peeters, 1993, 243–53.

Leo 2013
Dominic Leo, "The Pucellian School and the Rise of Naturalism: Style as Royal Signifier?," in *Jean Pucelle: Innovation and Collaboration in Manuscript Painting*, edited by Kyunghee Pyun and Anna D. Russakoff, London and Turnhout: Harvey Miller, 2013, 149–69.

Lepot 2012
Julien Lepot, "Le prince justicier dans l'*Avis aus roys*, un 'miroir au prince' enluminé du XIVe siècle," in *Le roi fontaine de justice: pouvoir justicier et pouvoir royal au Moyen Âge et à la Renaissance*, edited by Silvère Menegaldo and Bernard Ribémont, Paris: Klincksieck, 2012, 193–207.

Lepot 2014
Julien Lepot, "Un miroir enluminé du milieu du XIVème siècle: l'Avis aus roys," PhD diss., Université d'Orléans, 2014, 2 vols., accessed April 7, 2019, https://tel.archives-ouvertes.fr/tel-01128082.

Lesnick 1989
Daniel R. Lesnick, *Preaching in Medieval Florence: The Social World of Franciscan and Dominican Spirituality*, Athens, GA, and London: University of Georgia Press, 1989.

Levi D'Ancona 1993
Mirella Levi D'Ancona, *The Choir Books of Santa Maria degli Angeli in Florence*, vol. 2, *The Reconstructed "Diurno Domenicale" from Santa Maria degli Angeli*, Florence: Centro Di, 1993.

Little 1971
Lester K. Little, "Pride Goes before Avarice: Social Change and the Vices in Latin Christendom," *American Historical Review* 76, no. 1 (1971): 16–49.

Little 1978
Lester K. Little, *Religious Poverty and the Profit Economy in Medieval Europe*, Ithaca, NY: Cornell University Press, 1978.

Löer 2017
Ulrich Löer, "Das Motiv Kirchweih (Dedicatio) in mittelalterlicher Buchmalerei: zum Verhältnis von Bild und Text in illuminierten Choralbüchern des Dominikanerinnenklosters Paradiese bei Soest," *Soester Zeitschrift. Zeitschrift des Vereins für Geschichte und Heimatpflege Soest* 129 (2017): 33–60.

Loewen 2004
Peter Loewen, "The Conversion of Mary Magdalene and the Musical Legacy of Franciscan Piety in the Early German Passion Plays," in *Speculum Sermonis: Interdisciplinary Reflections on the Medieval Sermon*, edited by G. Donavin, C. Nederman, and R. Utz, Turnhout: Brepols, 2004, 235–59.

Loewen 2021
Peter Loewen, "A Rudder for the Ship of Fools? Franciscan Song in Pre-Reformation Europe," *Speculum* 96, no. 4 (2021): 1079–138.

Long 2016
Michael Long, "The Sound of Money in Late Medieval Music," in *Money, Morality, and Culture in Late Medieval and Early Modern Europe*, edited by Diane Wolfthal and Juliann Vitullo, Farnham, England, and Burlington, VT: Ashgate, 2016, 87–109.

Lopez 1976
Robert S. Lopez, *The Commercial Revolution of the Middle Ages, 950–1350*, Cambridge: Cambridge University Press, 1976.

Lorentz 1994
Philippe Lorentz, "Les Rolin et les 'primitifs flamands'," in *La bonne étoile des Rolin: mécénat et efflorescence artistique dans la Bourgogne du XVᵉ siècle*, edited by Corinne Charles, Autun: Musée Rolin, 1994, 23–29.

de Lorris and de Meun 1965–75
Guillaume de Lorris and Jean de Meun, *Le roman de la rose*, edited by Félix Lecoy, 3 vols., Paris: Champion, 1965–75.

de Lorris and de Meun 1971
Guillaume de Lorris and Jean de Meun, *The Romance of the Rose*, translated by Charles Dahlberg, Princeton: Princeton University Press, 1971.

de Lorris and de Meun 1994
Guillaume de Lorris and Jean de Meun, *The Romance of the Rose*, translated and edited by Frances Horgan, Oxford: Oxford University Press, 1994.

Macfarland 1999
Joseph C. Macfarland, "Machiavelli's Imagination of Excellent Men: An Appraisal of the Lives of Cosimo de' Medici and Castruccio Castracani," *American Political Science Review* 93, no. 1 (1999): 133–46.

Machiavelli 1988
Niccolò Machiavelli, *Florentine Histories*, translated by Laura F. Banfield and Harvey C. Mansfield, Jr., Princeton: Princeton University Press, 1988.

Malaguzzi Valeri 1901
Francesco Malaguzzi Valeri, *La zecca di Bologna*, Milan: L. F. Cogliati, 1901.

Mâle 1972
Émile Mâle, *The Gothic Image: Religious Art in France of the Thirteenth Century*, translated by Dora Nussey, New York: Harper & Row, 1972.

Mann and Syson 1998
Nicholas Mann and Luke Syson, *The Image of the Individual: Portraits in the Renaissance*, London: British Museum Press, 1998.

Manzari 2006
Francesca Manzari, *La miniatura ad Avignone al tempo dei papi, 1310–1410*, Modena: Franco Cosimo Panini, 2006.

Marrow 1984
James Marrow, "Simon Bening in 1521: A Group of Dated Miniatures," in *Liber Amicorum Herman Liebaers*, edited by Frans Vanwijngaerden, Brussels: Crédit Communal de Belgique, 1984, 537–59.

Marrow 2009
James Marrow, "Multitudo et varietas: The Hours of Catherine of Cleves," in *The Hours of Catherine of Cleves: Devotions, Demons and Daily Life in the Fifteenth Century*, edited by Rob Dückers and Ruud Priem, Antwerp: Ludion, 2009, 19–31.

McGerr 1990
Rosemary Potz McGerr, ed., *The Pilgrimage of the Soul: A Critical Edition of the Middle English Vision*, New York and London: Garland, 1990.

McMunn 2000
Meradith T. McMunn, "Programs of Illustration in *Roman de la rose* Manuscripts Owned by Patrons and Friends of Christine de Pizan," in *Au champ des escriptures: IIIᵉ Colloque international sur Christine de Pizan*, edited by Eric Hicks, Paris: Honoré Champion, 2000, 737–53.

McWebb 2001
Christine McWebb, "Christine de Pizan's Lady Reason and the Book in Beinecke MS 427," *Florilegium* 18, no. 1 (2001): 83–96.

Medica 1999
Massimo Medica, *Haec sunt statuta: le corporazioni medievali nelle miniature bolognesi*, Modena: F. C. Panini, 1999.

Meekes-van Toer 2013
Irene Meekes-van Toer, *"Als die maen is inden weder*: Practical Advice in a Late-Fifteenth-Century Astrological Calendar Manuscript, Amsterdam UB MS XXIII A 8," MA thesis, University of Amsterdam, 2013, accessed August 24, 2022, https//studenttheses.uu.nl/bitstream/handle/20.500.12932/13161/Final%20Master%20Thesis%20Irene.pdf?sequence=1&isAllowed=y.

Meiss 1951
Millard Meiss, *Painting in Florence and Siena after the Black Death*, Princeton: Princeton University Press, 1951.

Mell 2017–18
Julie L. Mell, *The Myth of the Medieval Jewish Moneylender*, 2 vols., New York: Palgrave Macmillan, 2017–18.

Mellinkoff 1993
Ruth Mellinkoff, *Outcasts: Signs of Otherness in Northern European Art of the Late Middle Ages*, 2 vols., Berkeley: University of California Press, 1993.

Ménard 1984
Philippe Ménard, "Les représentations des vices sur les murs du verger du 'Roman de la rose': le texte et les enluminures," in *Texte et image. Actes du colloque international de Chantilly, 13 au 15 octobre 1982*, Paris: Les Belles Lettres, 1984, 177–90.

Migne 1845
J.-P. Migne, ed., *Patrologiae cursus completus. Series Latina*, vol. 39, Paris: Garnier, 1845.

Migne 1995
J.-P. Migne, ed., *Patrologia Latina*, vol. 210, Alexandria, VA: Chadwyck-Healey, 1995.

Mills 2015
Robert Mills, *Seeing Sodomy in the Middle Ages*, Chicago and London: University of Chicago Press, 2015.

Milton 2011
Gregory B. Milton, "Jews and Finance in Medieval Iberia," in *The Jew in Medieval Iberia, 1100–1500*, edited by Jonathan Ray, Brookline, MA: Academic Studies Press, 2011, 227–56.

Mollat 1986
Michel Mollat, *The Poor in the Middle Ages*, translated by Arthur Goldhammer, New Haven and London: Yale University Press, 1986.

Montreuil 2022
Arnaud Montreuil, "'Qui pour armes servoient': Service and Knighting in the Vernacular Courtly Literature of the 12th and 13th Centuries," in *"We are all servants": The Diversity of Service in Premodern Europe*, edited by Isabelle Cochelin and Diane Wolfthal, Toronto: Centre for Reformation and Renaissance Studies, 2022, 37–80.

Mormando 1999
Franco Mormando, "What Happens to Us When We Die? Bernardino of Siena on 'The Four Last Things'," in *Death and Dying in the Middle Ages*, edited by Edelgard E. DuBruck and Barbara I. Gusick, New York: Lang, 1999, 109–42.

Mousseaux 1962
M. Mousseaux, "Note sur Jean Vallière," *Bulletin de la Société de l'histoire du protestantisme français* 108 (January–March 1962): 18–21.

Muir 1995
Lynette Muir, *The Biblical Drama of Medieval Europe*, Cambridge: Cambridge University Press, 1995.

Muller 2007
Kathryn V. Muller, "The Two 'Mystery' Belts of Grand River: A Biography of the Two Row Wampum and the Friendship Belt," *American Indian Quarterly* 31 (2007): 129–64.

Munscheck 2000
Hedwig Munscheck, *Die "Concordantiae caritatis" des Ulrich von Lilienfeld*, Frankfurt am Main and New York: Peter Lang, 2000.

Murillo-Barroso and Martinón-Torres 2012
Mercedes Murillo-Barroso and Marcos Martinón-Torres, "Amber Sources and Trade in the Prehistory of the Iberian Peninsula," *European Journal of Archaeology* 15, no. 2 (2012): 187–216.

Murray 1988
James M. Murray, "Family, Marriage, and Moneychanging in Medieval Bruges," *Journal of Medieval History* 14 (1988): 115–25.

Murray 2005
James M. Murray, *Bruges, Cradle of Capitalism, 1280–1390*, Cambridge: Cambridge University Press, 2005.

Musacchio 2008
Jacqueline Marie Musacchio, *Art, Marriage, and Family in the Florentine Renaissance Palace*, New Haven: Yale University Press, 2008.

Naismith 2018a
Rory Naismith, "Introduction," in *Money and Coinage in the Middle Ages*, edited by Rory Naismith, Leiden and Boston: Brill, 2018, 1–18.

Naismith 2018b
Rory Naismith, "Money and Society," in *Money and Coinage in the Middle Ages*, edited by Rory Naismith, Leiden and Boston: Brill, 2018, 179–202.

Neff 2019
Amy Neff, *A Soul's Journey: Franciscan Art, Theology, and Devotion*, Toronto: PIM, 2019.

Nelson 1969
Benjamin Nelson, *The Idea of Usury: From Tribal Brotherhood to Universal Otherhood*, 2nd edition, Chicago and London: University of Chicago Press, 1969.

Nicholson 2005
Peter Nicholson, *Love and Ethics in Gower's "Confessio Amantis,"* Ann Arbor: University of Michigan Press, 2005.

Noonan 1957
John T. Noonan, Jr., *The Scholastic Analysis of Usury*, Cambridge: Harvard University Press, 1957.

Norris 2021
Michael Byron Norris, "Medieval Bologna through Its Books," in *Medieval Bologna: Art for a University City*, edited by Trinita Kennedy, Nashville: Frist Art Museum, 2021, 1–13.

O'Doherty 2013
Marianne O'Doherty, *The Indies and the Medieval West: Thought, Report, Imagination*, Turnhout: Brepols, 2013.

Ogilvie 2011
Sheilagh Ogilvie, *Institutions and European Trade: Merchant Guilds 1000–1800*, Cambridge: Cambridge University Press, 2011.

Ogilvie 2019
Sheilagh Ogilvie, *The European Guilds: An Economic Analysis*, Princeton: Princeton University Press, 2019.

Opll and Roland 2006
Ferdinand Opll and Martin Roland, *Wien und Wiener Neustadt im 15. Jahrhundert: unbekannte Stadtansichten um 1460 in der New Yorker Handschrift der "Concordantiae caritatis" des Ulrich von Lilienfeld*, Innsbruck: Studienverlag, 2006.

Oresme 1864
Nicholas Oresme, *Traictie de la première invention des monnoies de Nicole Oresme*, edited by Louis Wolowski, Paris: De Guillaumin, 1864.

Oresme 1956
Nicholas Oresme, *The "De Moneta" of Nicholas Oresme and English Mint Documents*, edited by Charles Johnson, London and New York: Nelson, 1956.

Origo 1957
Iris Origo, *The Merchant of Prato, Francesco di Marco Datini, 1335–1410*, New York: Alfred A. Knopf, 1957.

Osborne 2019
Thomas M. Osborne, Jr., "Virtue," in *The Cambridge Companion to Medieval Ethics*, edited by Thomas Williams, Cambridge: Cambridge University Press, 2019, 50–171.

Panofsky 1971
Erwin Panofsky, *The Life and Art of Albrecht Dürer*, 4th edition, Princeton: Princeton University Press, 1971.

Parks 2005
Tim Parks, *Medici Money: Banking, Metaphysics, and Art in Fifteenth-Century Florence*, New York and London: W. W. Norton, 2005.

Parshall 2001
Peter Parshall, "Hans Holbein's 'Pictures of Death'," *Studies in the History of Art* 60 (2001): 82–95.

Pastoureau 2014
Michel Pastoureau, *Green: The History of a Color*, translated by Jody Gladding, Princeton and Oxford: Princeton University Press, 2014.

Patton 2007
Pamela A. Patton, "An Islamic Envelope-Flap Binding in the Cloister of Tudela: Another 'Muslim Connection' for Iberian Jews?," in *Spanish Medieval Art: Recent Studies*, edited by Colum Hourihane, Tempe, AZ: ACMRS, 2007, 65–88.

Pearsall 2004
Derek Pearsall, "The Manuscripts and Illustrations of Gower's Works," in *A Companion to Gower*, edited by Siân Echard, Cambridge: D. S. Brewer, 2004, 73–97.

Pentcheva 2010
Bissera V. Pentcheva, *The Sensual Icon: Space, Ritual, and the Senses in Byzantium*, University Park, PA: Pennsylvania State University Press, 2010.

Persson 2010
Karl Gunner Persson, *An Economic History of Europe: Knowledge, Institutions, and Growth, 600 to the Present*, Cambridge: Cambridge University Press, 2010.

Pestilli 2017
Livio Pestilli, *Picturing the Lame in Italian Art from Antiquity to the Modern Era*, London and New York: Routledge, 2017.

Petrarch 1991
Petrarch's "Remedies for Fortune Fair and Foul," edited by Conrad H. Rawski, 5 vols., Bloomington and Indianapolis: Indiana University Press, 1991.

Petrarch 2002
Petrarch, *Les remèdes aux deux fortunes*, vol. 1, translated by Christophe Carraud, Grenoble: Jérôme Millon, 2002.

Petryszcze 2020
Le Mistere de la Saincte Hostie, edited and introduced by Camille Salatko Petryszcze, MA thesis supervised by D. Hüe, 2020, accessed July 31, 2022, https://sites-recherche.univ-rennes2.fr/cetm/Edition%20Hostie/ostie.html.

Phelps Brown and Hopkins 1955
E. H. Phelps Brown and Sheila V. Hopkins, "Seven Centuries of Building Wages," *Economica* 22 (1955): 195–206.

Pirenne 1936
Henri Pirenne, *Economic and Social History of Medieval Europe*, translated by I. E. Clegg, London: K. Paul, Trench, Trubner & Co., 1936.

Plummer 1966
John Plummer, *The Hours of Catherine of Cleves: Introduction and Commentaries*, New York: George Braziller, 1966.

Pollard 2001
A. J. Pollard, *The Wars of the Roses*, 2nd edition, Basingstoke: Palgrave, 2001.

Polo 1875
Marco Polo, *The Book of Ser Marco Polo the Venetian*, translated by Henry Yule, 2nd edition, London: John Murray, 1875.

Powell 1996
Marvin A. Powell, "Money in Mesopotamia," *Journal of the Economic and Social History of the Orient* 39, no. 3 (1996): 224–42.

Ray 1997
Meredith Kennedy Ray, "Settling the Debt: Veronica Franco's Literary Economics," *Romance Language Annual* 8 (1997): 303–10.

Reid-Schwartz 1994
Alexandra Reid-Schwartz, "Economies of Salvation: Commerce and the Eucharist in *The Profanation of the Host* and the Croxton *Play of the Sacrament*," *Comitatus: A Journal of Medieval and Renaissance Studies* 25, no. 1 (1994): 1–20.

Renger 1970
Konrad Renger, *Lockere Gesellschaft: zur Ikonographie des Verlorenen Sohnes und von Wirtshausszenen in der niederländischen Malerei*, Berlin: Gebr. Mann Verlag, 1970.

Reyerson 2018
Kathryn L. Reyerson, *Mother and Sons, Inc.: Martha de Cabanis in Medieval Montpellier*, Philadelphia: University of Pennsylvania Press, 2018.

Reynolds 1996
Philip Lyndon Reynolds, "Indulgences," in *The Oxford Encyclopedia of the Reformation*, vol. 2, edited by Hans J. Hillerbrand, New York: Oxford University Press, 1996, 314–15.

Rice 1997
Louise Rice, *The Altars and Altarpieces of New St. Peter's: Outfitting the Basilica, 1621–1666*, Cambridge: Cambridge University Press, 1997.

Roberts 2002
Perri Lee Roberts, *Sacred Treasures: Early Italian Paintings from Southern Collections*, Athens: Georgia Museum of Art, 2002.

Robson 2001
Janet Robson, "*Speculum imperfectionis*: The Image of Judas in Late Medieval Italy," PhD diss., vol. 1, The Courtauld Institute of Art, University of London, 2001, accessed January 18, 2022, https://www.academia.edu/40958597/Speculum_Imperfectionis_The_Image_of_Judas_in_Late_Medieval_Italy_VOLUME_ONE_TEXT.

Robson 2002
Janet Robson, "Fear of Falling: Depicting the Death of Judas in Late Medieval Italy," in *Fear and Its Representations in the Middle Ages and the Renaissance*, edited by Anne Scott and Cynthia Kosso, Arizona Studies in the Middle Ages and the Renaissance 6, Turnhout: Brepols, 2002, 33–65.

Robson 2004
Janet Robson, "Judas and the Franciscans: Perfidy Pictures in Lorenzetti's Passion Cycle at Assisi," *Art Bulletin* 86, no. 1 (2004): 31–57.

Rogers 1882
J. E. Thorold Rogers, *A History of Agriculture and Prices in England from the Year after the Oxford Parliament (1259) to the Commencement of the Continental War (1793)*, vol. 3, *1401–1582*. Oxford: Clarendon Press, 1882.

de Roover 1944
Raymond de Roover, "Early Accounting Problems of Foreign Exchange," *Accounting Review* 19 (1944): 381–407.

de Roover 1948
Raymond de Roover, *Money, Banking, and Credit in Mediaeval Bruges: Italian Merchant-Bankers, Lombards, and Money Changers. A Story of the Origins of Banking*, Cambridge, MA: Mediaeval Academy of America, 1948.

de Roover 1974
Raymond de Roover, "The Scholastic Attitude toward Trade and Entrepreneurship," in *Business, Banking, and Economic Thought*, edited by Julius Kirschner, Chicago and London: University of Chicago Press, 1974, 336–45.

Rorimer 1953
James J. Rorimer, "Acquisitions for the Cloisters," *Metropolitan Museum of Art Bulletin*, new series, 11, no. 10 (June 1953): 265–85.

Rosenthal and Volovici 2019
Joanne Rosenthal and Marc Volovici, eds., *Jews, Money, Myth*, London: Jewish Museum, 2019.

Rössner 2018
Philipp Rössner, "From the Black Death to the New World (c.1350–1500)," in *Money and Coinage in the Middle Ages*, edited by Rory Naismith, Leiden and Boston: Brill, 2018, 151–75.

Rothstein 2000
Bret Rothstein, "On Devotion as Social Ornament: Jan van Eyck's *Virgin and Child with Chancellor Nicolas Rolin*," *Dutch Crossing* 24 (2000): 96–132.

Rubin 1999
Miri Rubin, *Gentile Tales: The Narrative Assault on Late Medieval Jews*, London: Yale University Press, 1999.

Rudy 2017
Kathryn M. Rudy, *Rubrics, Images and Indulgences in Late Medieval Netherlandish Manuscripts*, Library of the Written Word – The Manuscript World 55, Leiden: Brill, 2017.

Ryskamp 1989
Charles Ryskamp, ed., *The Twenty-first Report to the Fellows of the Pierpont Morgan Library 1984–1986*, New York: The Pierpont Morgan Library, 1989.

Sandler 2005
Lucy Freeman Sandler, "Guillaume Deguileville, *The Pilgrimage of the Soul*, or *Grace Dieu*," in *The Splendor of the Word: Medieval and Renaissance Illuminated Manuscripts at the New York Public Library*, edited by Jonathan J. G. Alexander, James H. Marrow, and Lucy Freeman Sandler, New York: New York Public Library, 2005, 400–404.

Sargent and Velde 2002
Thomas J. Sargent and François Velde, *The Big Problem of Small Change*, Princeton: Princeton University Press, 2002.

Schaps 2004
David M. Schaps, *The Invention of Coinage and the Monetization of Ancient Greece*, Ann Arbor: University of Michigan Press, 2004.

Schefer 2007
Jean Louis Schefer, *L'hostie profanée: histoire d'une fiction théologique*, Paris: P.O.L., 2007.

Scheidig 1955
Walter Scheidig, *Die Holzschnitte des Petrarca-Meisters zu Petracas Werk "Von der Artzney bayder Glück des guten and widerwärtigen" (Augsburg, 1532)*, Berlin: Deutsche Akademie der Künste, 1955.

Scher 2000
Stephen Scher, ed., *Perspectives on the Renaissance Medal*, New York: Garland Publishing and American Numismatic Society, 2000.

Schiller 1972
Gertrud Schiller, *Iconography of Christian Art*, vol. 2, translated by Janet Seligmann, Greenwich: New York Graphic Society, 1972.

Schiller 1980
Gertrud Schiller, "Maria," in *Ikonographie der christlichen Kunst*, vol. 4, pt. 2, Gütersloh: Gerd Mohn, 1980.

Schreckenberg 1996
Heinz Schreckenberg, *The Jews in Christian Art: An Illustrated History*, New York: Continuum, 1996.

Sciacca 2012
Christine Sciacca, ed., *Florence at the Dawn of the Renaissance: Painting and Illumination, 1300–1350*, Los Angeles: J. Paul Getty Museum, 2012.

Sciacca and Fredericks 2015
Christine Sciacca and Maria Fredericks, *Pacino di Bonaguida's Picture Book*, Simbach: Müller und Schindler, 2015.

Scott 2012
Anne M. Scott, "*Le Chastel de Labour, La Voie de Povreté ou de Richesse* and a Luxury Book, Widener 1, Free Library of Philadelphia," in *Experiences of Poverty in Late Medieval and Early Modern England and France*, edited by Anne M. Scott, Farnham, England, and Burlington, VT: Ashgate, 2012, 243–77.

Scott 1996
Kathleen L. Scott, *Later Gothic Manuscripts, 1390–1490*, 2 vols., London: Harvey Miller, 1996.

Sears 1986
Elizabeth Sears, *The Ages of Man: Medieval Interpretations of the Life Cycle*, Princeton: Princeton University Press, 1986.

Sebregondi and Parks 2011
Ludovica Sebregondi and Tim Parks, eds., *Money and Beauty: Bankers, Botticelli and the Bonfire of the Vanities*, Florence: Palazzo Strozzi, 2011.

Shaffern 2007
Robert W. Shaffern, *The Penitents' Treasury: Indulgences in Latin Christendom, 1175–1375*, Scranton: University of Scranton Press, 2007.

Sherman 1995
Claire Richter Sherman, *Imagining Aristotle: Verbal and Visual Representation in Fourteenth-Century France*, Berkeley: University of California Press, 1995.

Simpson and Weiner 1989
J. A. Simpson and E. S. C. Weiner, eds., *The Oxford English Dictionary*, vol. 20, Oxford: Clarendon Press, 1989.

Sintobin 1998
Véronique Sintobin, "Adriaen Isenbrant," in *From Van Eyck to Bruegel: Early Netherlandish Painting in the Metropolitan Museum of Art*, edited by Maryan W. Ainsworth and Keith Christiansen, New York: The Metropolitan Museum of Art, 1998, 194–95.

Skrine 1990
Peter Skrine, "Images of the Merchant in German Renaissance Literature," *Bulletin of the John Rylands Library* 72, no. 1 (1990): 185–97.

Smil 2017
Vaclav Smil, *Energy and Civilization: A History*, Cambridge, MA: MIT Press, 2017.

Smith 1992
Elise Lawton Smith, *The Paintings of Lucas van Leyden: A New Appraisal, with Catalogue Raisonné*, Columbia, MO, and London: University of Missouri Press, 1992.

Smith 1934
Florence Smith, "Laurent de Premierfait's French Version of the *De casibus* with Some Notes on Its Influence in France," *Revue de littérature comparée* 14 (1934): 512–26.

Smith 2012
Kathryn A. Smith, "The Monk Who Crucified Himself," in *Thresholds of Medieval Visual Culture: Liminal Spaces*, edited by Elina Gertsman and Jill Stevenson, Woodbridge: Boydell & Brewer, 2012, 44–72.

Sobré 1989
Judith Berg Sobré, *Behind the Altar Table: The Development of the Painted Retable in Spain, 1350–1500*, Columbia, MO: University of Missouri Press, 1989.

Spufford 1970
Peter Spufford, *Monetary Problems and Policies in the Burgundian Netherlands, 1433–1496*, Leiden: E. J. Brill, 1970.

Spufford 1988
Peter Spufford, *Money and Its Use in Medieval Europe*, Cambridge: Cambridge University Press, 1988.

Spufford 2002a
Peter Spufford, "Late Medieval Merchants' Notebooks: A Project," in *Kaufmannsbücher und Handelspraktiken vom Spätmittelalter bis zum beginnende 20. Jahrhundert*, edited by Markus A. Denzel, Jean Claude Hocquet, and Harald Witthöft, Stuttgart: Franz Steiner, 2002, 47–61.

Spufford 2002b
Peter Spufford, *Power and Profit: The Merchant in Medieval Europe*, New York: Thames and Hudson, 2002.

Stahl 1985
Alan M. Stahl, *The Venetian Tornesello, a Medieval Colonial Coinage*, Numismatic Notes and Monographs 163, New York: American Numismatic Society, 1985.

Stahl 2000
Alan M. Stahl, *Zecca: The Mint of Venice in the Middle Ages*, Baltimore: Johns Hopkins University Press, 2000.

Starkey 2013
Kathryn Starkey, *A Courtier's Mirror: Cultivating Elite Identity in Thomasin von Zerclaere's "Welscher Gast,"* Notre Dame, IN: University of Notre Dame Press, 2013.

Steenbock 1990
Frauke Steenbock, "Largesse – Münzen, Blüten, und Mannaregen: eine Motivstudie," in *Festschrift für Peter Bloch*, edited by Hartmut Krohm and Christian Theuerkauff, Mainz am Rhein: Philipp von Zabern, 1990, 135–42.

Steinberg 1996
Leo Steinberg, *The Sexuality of Christ in Renaissance Art and in Modern Oblivion*, 2nd edition, Chicago and London: University of Chicago Press, 1996.

Stephen of Bourbon 1877
Stephen of Bourbon, *Anecdotes historiques, légendes et apologues tirés du recueil inédit d'Étienne de Bourbon, dominicain du XIIIe siècle*, edited by A. Lecoy de la Marche, Paris: Henri Loones, 1877.

Strickland 2003
Debra Higgs Strickland, *Saracens, Demons, and Jews: Making Monsters in Medieval Art*, Princeton and Oxford: Princeton University Press, 2003.

Strickland 2019
Debra Higgs Strickland, "Monsters, Demons, and Jews in the Painting of Hieronymus Bosch," in *Monsters and Monstrosity in Jewish History: From the Middle Ages to Modernity*, edited by Iris Idelson-Shein and Christian Wiese, London: Bloomsbury, 2019, 42–68.

Strouse 2000
Jean Strouse, "J. Pierpont Morgan: Financier and Collector," *Metropolitan Museum of Art Bulletin* 57, no. 3 (2000): 3–65.

Stuard 2006
Susan Mosher Stuard, *Gilding the Market: Luxury and Fashion in Fourteenth-Century Italy*, Philadelphia: University of Pennsylvania Press, 2006.

Stumpf 2010
Béatrice Stumpf, *Guillaume de Digulleville, "Pèlerinage de Vie humaine," transcrit d'après le manuscrit BNF, fr. 1818*, last modified July 13, 2010, accessed October 31, 2022, https://hal.archives-ouvertes.fr/hal-00502099.

Suckale 1987
Robert Suckale, "Die Regensburger Buchmalerei von 1350 bis 1450," in *Regensburger Buchmalerei: von frühkarolingischer Zeit bis zum Ausgang des Mittelalters. Ausstellung der Bayerischen Staatsbibliothek München und der Museen der Stadt Regensburg*, edited by Florentine Mütherich and Karl Dachs, Munich: Prestel, 1987, 93–110.

Sutton 2006
James William Sutton, ed., *The Dicts and Sayings of the Philosophers*, Kalamazoo, MI: Medieval Institute Publications, TEAMS, 2006.

Swanson 2006
Robert N. Swanson, ed., *Promissory Notes on the Treasury of Merits: Indulgences in Late Medieval Europe*, Leiden and Boston: Brill, 2006.

Swanson 2010
Robert N. Swanson, "Pay Back Time? Tithes and Tithing in Late Medieval England," *Studies in Church History* 46 (2010): 124–33.

Szirmai 1999
J. A. Szirmai, *The Archaeology of Medieval Bookbinding*, Aldershot, England: Ashgate, 1999.

Taylor 1982
Michael D. Taylor, "Gentile da Fabriano, St. Nicholas, and an Iconography of Shame," *Journal of Family History* (Winter 1982): 321–32.

Terpstra 2019
Nicholas Terpstra, ed., *Lives Uncovered: A Sourcebook of Early Modern Europe*, Toronto, Buffalo, and London: University of Toronto Press, 2019.

Thomas à Kempis 1905
Thomas à Kempis, *The Founders of the New Devotion*, translated by J. P. Arthur, London: Kegan Paul, 1905.

Thomas à Kempis 1922
Thomas à Kempis, *Opera omnia*, vol. 7, Freiburg im Breisgau: Herder, 1922.

Thomasin von Zirclaria 1852
Thomasin von Zirclaria, *Der wälsche Gast des Thomasin von Zirclaria*, edited and translated by Heinrich Rückert, Quedlinburg and Leipzig: Gottfried Basse, 1852.

Thomasin von Zirclaria 2009
Thomasin von Zirclaria, *Der Welsche Gast (The Italian Guest)*, translated and introduced by Marion Gibbs and Winder McConnell, Kalamazoo: Western Michigan University, 2009.

Thomasin von Zirclaria 2018
Thomasin von Zirclaria (Thomasin von Zerclaere), *Der Welsche Gast* [facsimile of Gotha, Schloss Friedenstein, Forschungsbibliothek, Memb. I 120], Lucerne: Quaternio Verlag, 2018.

Thompson 1994
Phyllis Anna Nitze Thompson, "The Triumph over Fortune: Illuminations from Boccaccio's *De casibus virorum illustrium*," PhD diss., Boston University, 1994.

Thonon 2002
Sandrine Thonon, "Les métiers sur l'échiquier: leurs représentations littéraires et figurées dans les traductions françaises de l'œuvre de Jacques de Cessoles," in *Le verbe, l'image et les représentations de la société urbaine au Moyen Âge. Actes du colloque international tenu à Marche-en-Famenne du 24 au 27 octobre 2001*, edited by Marc Boone, Élodie Lecuppre-Desjardin, and Jean-Pierre Sosson, Antwerp and Apeldoorn: Garant, 2002, 207–17.

Toch 2003
Michael Toch, *Peasants and Jews in Medieval Germany*, Studies in Cultural, Social and Economic History, Aldershot, England, and Burlington, VT: Ashgate, 2003.

Todeschini 2005
Giacomo Todeschini, "La riflessione etica sulle attività economiche," in *Economie urbane ed etica economica nell'Italia medievale*, edited by R. Greci, G. Pinto, and G. Todeschini, Rome: Laterza, 2005, 153–228.

Todeschini 2010
Giacomo Todeschini, "The Incivility of Judas: 'Manifest' Usury as a Metaphor," in *Money, Morality, and Culture in Late Medieval and Early Modern Europe*, edited by Juliann Vitullo and Diane Wolfthal, Farnham, England, and Burlington, VT: Ashgate, 2010, 33–52.

Todeschini 2018
Giacomo Todeschini, "Jewish Usurers, Blood Libel, and the Second-Hand Economy: The Medieval Origins of a Stereotype (from the Thirteenth to the Fifteenth Century)," in *The Medieval Roots of Antisemitism: Continuities and Discontinuities from the Middle Ages to the Present Day*, edited by Jonathan Adams and Cordelia Hess, Andover: Routledge, 2018, 341–51.

Toffanin 2013
Alessandro Toffanin, *Monete italiane regionali*, vol. 10, *Milano*, Pavia: Edizioni Numismatica Varesi, 2013.

Tomei 2002
Alessandro Tomei, *Le biccherne di Siena: arte e finanza all'alba dell'economia moderna*, Rome: Retablo, 2002.

Travaini 2004
Lucia Travaini, "Saints and Sinners: Coins in Medieval Italian Graves," *Numismatic Chronicle* 164 (2004): 159–81.

Travaini 2015
Lucia Travaini, "Saints, Sinners and. . . a Cow: Offerings, Alms, and Tokens of Memory," in *Money and the Church in Medieval Europe, 1000–1200: Practice, Morality, and Thought*, edited by Giles E. M. Gasper and Svein H. Gullbekk, Farnham, England, and Burlington, VT: Ashgate, 2015, 209–21.

Trexler 1997
Richard Trexler, *The Journey of the Magi: Meanings in History of a Christian Story*, Princeton: Princeton University Press, 1997.

Tudor-Craig 1987
Pamela Tudor-Craig, "The Hours of Edward V and William Lord Hastings: British Library Manuscript Additional 54782," in *England in the Fifteenth Century. Proceedings of the 1986 Harlaxton Symposium*, edited by Daniel Williams, Woodbridge: Boydell, 1987, 351–69.

Tünde 2000
Wehli Tünde, "Magyar Anjou Legendárium," in *Három Kódex. Az Országos Könyvtár millenniumi kiállítás*, edited by Karsay Orsolya, Wehli Tünde, and Mikó Arpád, Budapest: Az Országos Széchényi Könyvtár, 2000, 73–120 (with English summary).

Turner 1983
Derek H. Turner, *The Hastings Hours*, London: Thames and Hudson, 1983.

Turner 2021
Nancy Turner, "Bringing Honor to That Art Called Illumination: Bolognese Manuscript Painting Techniques, ca. 1250–1400," in *Medieval Bologna: Art for a University City*, edited by Trinita Kennedy, Nashville: Frist Art Museum, 2021, 27–39.

Tuttle 1981
Virginia G. Tuttle, "Bosch's Image of Poverty," *Art Bulletin* 63 (1981): 88–95.

Tuve 1966
Rosemond Tuve, *Allegorical Imagery: Some Mediaeval Books and Their Posterity*, Princeton: Princeton University Press, 1966.

Van Cleve 1991
John Van Cleve, *The Problem of Wealth in the Literature of Luther's Germany*, Columbia, NC: Camden House, 1991.

Van Cleve 1993
John Van Cleve, *Sebastian Brant's "The Ship of Fools" in Critical Perspective: 1800–1991*, Columbia, NC: Camden House, 1993.

Van Egmond 2011
Warren Van Egmond, "Using the Abacus Texts as Sources for Numismatic and Monetary History: Problems and Prospects," *Revue numismatique* 167 (2011): 125–33.

Van Engen 1988
John Van Engen, *Devotio Moderna: Basic Writings*, New York and Mahwah, NJ: Paulist Press, 1988.

Vandenberghe 1984
Stéphane Vandenberghe, *Gruuthusemuseum Bruges: A Review*, Brussels: Die Keure, 1984.

Vanwijnsberghe 2007
Dominique Vanwijnsberghe, *"Moult dons et notables": L'enluminure tournaisienne à l'époque de Robert Campin (1380–1430)*, edited by Jan van der Stock, Corpus of Illuminated Manuscripts 17, Low Country Series 10, Paris, Leuven, and Dudley, MA: Peeters, 2007.

Vescovi 2017
Michele Luigi Vescovi, "An Eschatological Mirror: The Romanesque Portal at Beaulieu-sur-Dordogne," *Gesta* 56, no. 1 (2017): 53–80.

Villon 2013
François Villon, *Poems*, Evanston, IL: Northwestern University Press, 2013.

Viollet-le-Duc 1997
Eugène-Emmanuel Viollet-le-Duc, *Dictionnaire de l'architecture médiévale* [1854–68], introduced by Caroline Mathieu, Paris: Bibliothèque de l'Image, 1997.

Vitullo 2019
Juliann Vitullo, *Negotiating the Art of Fatherhood in Late Medieval and Early Modern Italy*, London: Palgrave Macmillan, 2019.

Vitullo and Wolfthal 2010a
Juliann Vitullo and Diane Wolfthal, "Introduction," in *Money, Morality, and Culture in Late Medieval and Early Modern Europe*, edited by Juliann Vitullo and Diane Wolfthal, Farnham, England, and Burlington, VT: Ashgate, 2010, 1–11.

Vitullo and Wolfthal 2010b
Juliann Vitullo and Diane Wolfthal, "Trading Values: Negotiating Masculinity in Late Medieval and Early Modern Europe," in *Money, Morality, and Culture in Late Medieval and Early Modern Europe*, edited by Juliann Vitullo and Diane Wolfthal, Farnham, England, and Burlington, VT: Ashgate, 2010, 155–96.

Voelkle 1984
William M. Voelkle, *Italian Manuscript Painting, 1300–1500*, New York: The Pierpont Morgan Library, 1984.

Voelkle 2006
William M. Voelkle, "Coins, Mussels, and a Crab in the Hours of Catherine of Cleves," in *Tributes in Honor of James H. Marrow: Studies in Painting and Manuscript Illumination of the Late Middle Ages and Northern Renaissance*, edited by Jeffrey F. Hamburger and Anne S. Korteweg, London: Harvey Miller, 2006, 563–65.

de Voragine 1993
Jacobus de Voragine, *The Golden Legend: Readings on the Saints*, translated by William Granger Ryan, 2 vols., Princeton: Princeton University Press, 1993.

Waddell 1936
Helen Waddell, *The Desert Fathers*, London: Constable, 1936.

Walters 1989
Lori Walters, "A Parisian Manuscript of the *Romance of the Rose*," *Princeton University Library Chronicle* 51, no. 1 (1989): 31–55.

Watt 2011
Melinda Watt, "Renaissance Velvet Textiles," in *Heilbrunn Timeline of Art History*, The Metropolitan Museum of Art, New York, 2011, accessed October 30, 2022, http://www.metmuseum.org/toah/hd/velv/hd_velv.htm.

Welch 2005
Evelyn Welch, *Shopping in the Renaissance: Consumer Cultures in Italy*, New Haven and London: Yale University Press, 2005.

Welscher Gast Digital 2015
"Welscher Gast Digital," 2015, accessed January 20, 2019, https://digi.ub.uni-heidelberg.de/wgd/.

Wenninger 2016
Marcus J. Wenninger, "'als etlich kristen lüt . . . mit dien Juden getantzet hant.' Über die Teilnahme von Christen an jüdischen Festen im Mittelalter," *Aschkenas* 26, no. 1 (2016): 37–67.

Wenzel 1989
Siegfried Wenzel, *"Fasciculus morum": A Fourteenth-Century Preacher's Handbook*, University Park, PA: Pennsylvania State University Press, 1989.

Wenzel and Lechtermann 2002
Horst Wenzel and Christina Lechtermann, eds., *Beweglichkeit der Bilder: Text und Imagination in den illustrierten Handschriften des "Welschen Gastes" von Thomasin von Zerclaere*, Cologne, Weimar, and Vienna: Böhlau Verlag, 2002.

Wieck 1988
Roger S. Wieck, *Time Sanctified: The Book of Hours in Medieval Art and Life*, New York and Baltimore: George Braziller and Walters Art Gallery, 1988.

Wieck 1997
Roger S. Wieck, *Painted Prayers: The Book of Hours in Medieval and Renaissance Art*, New York: George Braziller, 1997.

Wieck 1999
Roger S. Wieck, "The Death Desired: Books of Hours and the Medieval Funeral," in *Death and Dying in the Middle Ages*, edited by Edelgard E. DuBruck and Barbara I. Gusick, New York: Peter Lang, 1999, 431–76.

Wieck 2004
Roger S. Wieck, "Post Poyet," in *Excavating the Medieval Image: Manuscripts, Artists, Audiences: Essays in Honor of Sandra Hindman*, edited by David S. Areford and Nina A. Rowe, Aldershot, England, and Burlington, VT: Ashgate, 2004, 247–63.

Wieck 2007a
Roger S. Wieck, "The Sacred Bleeding Host of Dijon in Books of Hours," in *Quand la peinture était dans les livres: mélanges en l'honneur de François Avril à l'occasion de la remise du titre de Docteur Honoris Causa de la Freie Universität Berlin*, edited by Mara Hofmann and Caroline Zöhl, Turnhout: Brepols, 2007, 393–404.

Wieck 2007b
Roger S. Wieck, "The Sacred Bleeding Host of Dijon in Choir Books and Posters," in *Manuscripten en miniaturen: studies aangeboden aan Anne S. Korteweg bij haar afscheid van de Koninklijke Bibliotheek*, edited by Jos Biemans et al., Zutphen: Walburg Pers, 2007, 385–96.

Wieck 2010
Roger S. Wieck, with a contribution by Cynthia J. Brown, *The Prayer Book of Claude de France: MS. M.1166, The Pierpont Morgan Library*, New York, Lucerne: Quaternio Verlag, 2010.

Wieck 2014
Roger S. Wieck, *Illuminating Faith: The Eucharist in Medieval Life and Art*, New York: The Morgan Library and Museum, 2014.

Wieck 2015–16
Roger S. Wieck, *The Hours of Henry VIII*, Barcelona: M. Moleiro, 2015–16.

Wieck 2016
Roger S. Wieck, "Peindre un miracle: la Sainte Hostie et l'enluminure à Dijon," in *Peindre à Dijon au XVIe siècle*, edited by Frédéric Elsig, Milan: Silvana Editoriale, 2016, 139–53.

Wieck, Voelkle, and Hearne 2000
Roger S. Wieck, William M. Voelkle, and K. Michelle Hearne, *Hours of Henry VIII: A Renaissance Masterpiece by Jean Poyet*, New York: George Braziller and The Morgan Library, 2000.

Wiedl 2015
Birgit Wiedl, "Der Alltag im Geschäft. Aspekte jüdisch-christlichen Zusammenlebens im Spiegel der mittelalterlichen Geschäftsurkunden," in *Tagungsbericht des 26. Österreichischen Historikertages Krems/Stein, 24. bis 28. September 2012*, Veröffentlichungen des Verbandes Österreichischer Historiker und Geschichtsvereine 35; Studien und Forschungen aus dem Niederösterreichischen Institut für Landeskunde, Sonderband, 2015, St. Pölten: NÖ Institut für Landeskunde, 2015, 570–86.

Wijsman 2010
Hanno Wijsman, *Luxury Bound: Illustrated Manuscript Production and Noble and Princely Book Ownership in the Burgundian Netherlands (1400–1550)*, Turnhout: Brepols, 2010.

Wilson 1996
Carolyn Wilson, *Italian Paintings XIV–XVI Centuries in the Museum of Fine Arts, Houston*, Houston: Museum of Fine Arts, 1996.

Wilson and Lancaster Wilson 1984
Adrian Wilson and Joyce Lancaster Wilson, *A Medieval Mirror: "Speculum humanae salvationis," 1324–1500*, Berkeley, Los Angeles, and London: University of California Press, 1984.

Wishart 1900
Alfred Wesley Wishart, *A Short History of Monks and Monasteries*, 1900; repr. Frankfurt am Main: Outlook, 2018.

Witcombe 1998
Christopher L. C. E. Witcombe, "Dürer's Prodigal Son," *Source: Notes in the History of Art* 17, no. 3 (Spring 1998): 7–13.

Wolfthal 1989
Diane Wolfthal, *The Beginnings of Netherlandish Canvas Painting: 1400–1530*, Cambridge: Cambridge University Press, 1989.

Wolfthal 2000
Diane Wolfthal, ed., *Peace and Negotiation: Strategies for Coexistence in the Middle Ages and Renaissance*, Turnhout: Brepols, 2000.

Wolfthal 2004
Diane Wolfthal, *Picturing Yiddish: Gender, Identity, and Memory in Illustrated Yiddish Books of Renaissance Italy*, Brill Series in Jewish Studies 36, Leiden: Brill, 2004.

Wolfthal 2007
Diane Wolfthal, "Florentine Bankers and Flemish Friars: New Light on the Patronage of the Portinari Altarpiece," in *Cultural Exchange between the Netherlands and Italy*, edited by Ingrid Alexander-Skipnes, Turnhout: Brepols, 2007, 1–21.

Wolfthal 2010
Diane Wolfthal, *In and Out of the Marital Bed: Seeing Sex in Renaissance Art*, London: Yale University Press, 2010.

Wolfthal 2016
Diane Wolfthal, "Complicating Medieval Anti-Semitism: The Role of Class in Two Tales of Christian Violence against Jews," *Gesta* 55, no. 1 (2016): 105–27.

Wolfthal 2022
Diane Wolfthal, "Temporary Natural Alterations in Silver-Stained Windows," in *Tributes to Maryan W. Ainsworth. Collaborative Spirit: Essays on Northern European Art, 1350–1650*, edited by Anna Koopstra, Christine Seidel, and Joshua P. Waterman, London and Turnhout: Harvey Miller / Brepols, 2022, 148–63.

Wood 2002
Diana Wood, *Medieval Economic Thought*, Cambridge and New York: Cambridge University Press, 2002.

Wright 2005
Alison Wright, *The Pollaiuolo Brothers: The Arts of Florence and Rome*, New Haven and London: Yale University Press, 2005.

Wüstefeld and Morcos 2015
Wilhelmina C. M. Wüstefeld and Erene Rafik Morcos, *Parchment and Gold: 25 Years of Dr. Jörn Günther Rare Books*, Catalogue 1, Stalden: Dr. Jörn Günther Rare Books, 2015.

Yang 2019
Bin Yang, *Cowrie Shells and Cowrie Money: A Global History*, Oxford: Routledge, 2019.

Yoon 2015
David Yoon, "Art, Craft, Innovation, and Efficiency: Early Medieval Minting Technology," *ANS Magazine* 14, no. 2 (2015): 18–27.

Yoon 2019
David Yoon, "When Is a Kingdom Not a Kingdom?" *ANS Magazine* 18, no. 1 (2019): 6–15.

Young 2015
Spencer E. Young, "Avarice, Emotions, and the Family in Thirteenth-Century Moral Discourse," in *Ordering Emotions in Europe, 1100–1800*, edited by Susan Broomhall, Leiden and Boston: Brill, 2015, 69–84.

Zelizer 1994
Viviana A. Zelizer, *The Social Meaning of Money*, New York: Basic Books, 1994.

Zeydel 1944
Edwin H. Zeydel, *The Ship of Fools by Sebastian Brant*, New York: Dover, 1944.

Zhao et al. 2021
Zhao Hao et al., "Radiocarbon-Dating an Early Minting Site: The Emergence of Standardised Coinage in China," *Antiquity* 95, no. 383 (October 2021): 1161–78, published online August 6, 2021, accessed October 30, 2022, https://doi.org/10.15184/aqy.2021.94.

Zöhl 2004
Caroline Zöhl, *Jean Pichore: Buchmaler, Graphiker und Verleger in Paris um 1500*, Ars Nova 8, Turnhout: Brepols, 2004.

Index of Manuscripts

General Index

Picture Credits

Every effort has been made to trace copyright owners and photographers. The Morgan apologizes for any unintentional omissions and would be pleased to add an acknowledgment in future editions.

INSTITUTIONAL AND COPYRIGHT CREDITS

Image courtesy of Akademische Druck- u. Verlagsanstalt, Graz/ Austria: pp. 25–26 (Figs. 1.1–1.2);

Courtesy of the American Numismatic Society: p. 35 (Fig. 1.10); p. 42 (Fig. 2.1); p. 46 (Figs. 2.4–2.5); pp. 48–49 (Figs. 2.6–2.8); p. 151 (Fig. 6.3); p. 168 (Fig. 6.12); pp. 173–74 (Figs. 6.16–6.17); p. 186 (Fig. 6.26); p. 189 (Figs. 6.30–6.34);

Bourg-en-Bresse – musée du Monastère royal de Brou: p. 149 (Fig. 6.1);

© British Library / GRANGER – All rights reserved: p. 36 (Fig. 1.11); pp. 66–67 (Fig. 3.8);

© The Trustees of the British Museum: pp. 12–13 (Figs. 0.1–0.2); pp. 17–18 (Figs. 0.5–0.6);

Copyright KBR – Manuscripts – MSS. 13076–77: fol. 12v, p. 29 (Fig. 1.6);

The Metropolitan Museum of Art, Bequest of George Blumenthal, 1941, 41.190.442: p. 4, p. 191 (Fig. 6.35); Bequest of George Blumenthal, 1941, 41.190.44: p. 95 (Fig. 4.13); The Cloisters Collection, 1947, 47.101.59: p. 127 (Fig. 5.8); The Cloisters Collection, 1952, 52.121.3: p. 178 (Fig. 6.21); Gift of Coudert Brothers, 1888, 88.3.89: p. 123 (Fig. 5.3); Fletcher Fund, 1919, 19.73.35: p. 207 (Fig. 7.9); The Friedsam Collection, Bequest of Michael Friedsam: 1931, 32.100.36: p. 153 (Fig. 6.5), spine; Rogers Fund, 1923, 23.29: p. 175 (Fig. 6.18);

Image copyright © The Metropolitan Museum of Art. Image source: Art Resource, NY: p. 208 (Fig. 7.10);

Photography courtesy of The Morgan Library & Museum: p. 112 (Fig. 4.26);

© 2023 Museum of Fine Arts, Boston, Charles Amos Cummings Fund, 48.255: p. 74 (Fig. 4.1); Gift of George Cabot Lodge, 20.860: p. 107 (Fig. 4.23);

Museum of Fine Arts, Houston / The Edith A. and Percy S. Straus Collection / Bridgeman Images: p. 133 (Fig. 5.12);

Courtesy of Museo Civico Archeologico, Bologna, Italy: p. 34 (Fig. 1.9);

National Gallery of Art, Washington, Samuel H. Kress Collection, 1952.5.33: pp. 58–59 (Figs. 3.1–3.3); p. 94 (Fig. 4.12); 1939.1.43: p. 121 (Fig. 5.2); 1952.5.20: p. 124 (Fig. 5.4); Rosenwald Collection, 1948.11.128: p. 93 (Fig. 4.11);

Philadelphia Museum of Art, Purchased with the Henry P. McIlhenny Fund in memory of Frances P. McIlhenny, 2003, 2003-89-1: p. 131 (Fig. 5.11);

Prato, Archivio di Stato di Prato, Datini, 1145/1, codice 1403803. Reproduced by permission of the Ministero della cultura. Further reproduction by any means is prohibited: p. 52 (Fig. 2.10);

"Radiocarbon-Dating an Early Minting Site: The Emergence of Standardised Coinage in China," by Hao Zhao, Xiangping Gao, Yuchao Jiang, Yi Lin, Jin Zhu, Sicong Ding, Lijun Deng and Ji Zhang. Published online by Cambridge University Press: August 6, 2021, *Antiquity*, Volume 95, Issue 383, October 2021, https://doi.org/10.15184/aqy.2021.94, p. 1166, Figure 4. Spade coin SP-1 and its reconstruction. The outer mould (bottom left) from pit H2032 is also used to reconstruct the spade coin (photograph by H. Zhao). Copyright © The Author(s), 2021. Published by Cambridge University Press on behalf of Antiquity Publications Ltd., reproduced with permission: p. 16 (Fig. 0.4);

© RMN-Grand Palais / Art Resource, NY: pp. 184–85 (Fig. 6.24 and detail of Fig. 6.24);

Special Collections Research Center, Temple University Libraries, Philadelphia PA: pp. 50–51 (Fig. 2.9);

Archives & Special Collections Library, Vassar College, Poughkeepsie, New York: p. 126 (Fig. 5.6).

PHOTOGRAPHER CREDITS

Janny Chiu: back cover; front cover; p. 2; pp. 9–10; p. 15 (Fig. 0.3); p. 29 (Fig. 1.5); p. 30 (Fig. 1.7); p. 54; p. 60 (Fig. 3.4); pp. 62–65 (Figs. 3.5–3.7); pp. 68–70 (Figs. 3.9–3.11); p. 76 (Fig. 4.2); pp. 78–80 (Figs. 4.3–4.4); p. 83 (Fig. 4.5); pp. 85–86 (Figs. 4.6–4.7); pp. 88–91 (Figs. 4.8–4.10); pp. 96–99 (Figs. 4.14–4.15); p. 102 (Fig. 4.17); p. 106 (Fig. 4.22); pp. 109–10 (Figs. 4.24–4.25); p. 112 (Fig. 4.26); p. 129 (Fig. 5.10); pp. 134–35 (Fig. 5.13); p. 138 (Figs. 5.16–5.18); p. 141 (Figs. 5.19–5.22); pp. 143–44 (Figs. 5.23–5.24); p. 146; p. 156 (Fig. 6.6); pp. 160–61 (Figs. 6.8–6.9); pp. 163–64 (Figs. 6.10a–6.10b); pp. 166–67 (Figs. 6.11a–6.11b); pp. 170–72 (Figs. 6.13–6.15); pp. 176–77 (Figs. 6.19–6.20); p. 188 (Fig. 6.29); p. 194; p. 196 (Fig. 7.1); pp. 198–200 (Figs. 7.2–7.5);

Graham S. Haber: pp. 27–28 (Figs. 1.3–1.4); p. 72; p. 105 (Fig. 4.21); p. 118; p. 125 (Fig. 5.5); p. 159 (Fig. 6.7); p. 181 (Fig. 6.22); p. 187 (Figs. 6.27–6.28); p. 211 (Fig. 7.13);

Schecter Lee: p. 128 (Fig. 5.9);

Hervé Lewandowski: pp. 184–85 (Fig. 6.24 and detail of Fig. 6.24);

© Hugo Maertens: p.149 (Fig. 6.1);

Alan Roche: p. 35 (Fig. 1.10); p. 42 (Fig. 2.1); p. 46 (Figs. 2.4–2.5); pp. 48–49 (Figs. 2.6–2.8); p. 151 (Fig. 6.3); p. 168 (Fig. 6.12); pp. 173–74 (Figs. 6.16–6.17); p. 186 (Fig. 6.26); p. 189 (Figs. 6.30–6.34);

Diane Wolfthal: p. 209 (Fig. 7.11);

H. Zhao: p. 16 (Fig. 0.4).